Be of Good Mind

Be of Good Mind

ESSAYS ON THE COAST SALISH

Edited by Bruce Granville Miller

UBCPress · Vancouver · Toronto

16 15 14 13 12 11 10 09 08 07   5 4 3 2 1

Printed in Canada on ancient-forest-free paper (100% post-consumer recycled) that is processed chlorine- and acid-free, with vegetable-based inks.

Library and Archives Canada Cataloguing in Publication

Be of good mind : essays on the Coast Salish / edited by Bruce Granville Miller.

Includes bibliographical references and index.
ISBN 978-0-7748-1323-5 (bound); 978-0-7748-1324-2 (pbk.)

1. Coast Salish Indians. 2. Coast Salish Indians – History. I. Miller, Bruce Granville, 1951-

E99.S21B42 2007   971.1004'9794   C2007-900495-4

Canadä

UBC Press gratefully acknowledges the financial support for our publishing program of the Government of Canada through the Book Publishing Industry Development Program (BPIDP), and of the Canada Council for the Arts, and the British Columbia Arts Council.

This book has been published with the help of a grant from the Canadian Federation for the Humanities and Social Sciences, through the Aid to Scholarly Publications Programme, using funds provided by the Social Sciences and Humanities Research Council of Canada, and with the help of the K.D. Srivastava Fund.

UBC Press
The University of British Columbia
2029 West Mall
Vancouver, BC V6T 1Z2
604-822-5959 / Fax: 604-822-6083
www.ubcpress.ca

Contents

Illustrations

Acknowledgments

I wish to thank all of the contributors here, people with whom I have had fruitful discussions regarding the world of the Coast Salish peoples. But there are many others beyond this group. Among these are Wayne Suttles himself, who kindly shared materials with me at several points and who once attended a session I organized at the Northwest Anthropology Conference, where my graduate students presented papers about his work. He listened carefully and provided gracious and humble commentary. The students were delighted. Michael Kew, my long-time colleague at UBC, is deeply knowledgeable about the Coast Salish, and I recall with great fondness our many conversations. Doreen Maloney, a distinguished leader of the Upper Skagit Tribe, put me to work for her tribe and shared many insights. As always my thanks to her. It was a great pleasure working with Ken Hansen, the recently deceased Samish tribal leader, on the issue of federal recognition. Vi Hilbert, the world-famous Upper Skagit scholar, storyteller, and elder, remains an inspiration to everyone working in the Coast Salish world, and I thank her for the time she has given me. Elders Floyd and Sherman Williams of Upper Skagit have been wonderful sources of inspiration, support, and information, as have Shubert Hunter, Harlan Sam, Okie and Jean Joe, June Boome, Pearl and Leonard Rodriguez, Pete Dunthorne, and many others at Upper Skagit. Scott Schuyler is of special help, given his many roles for his tribe. My thanks to them all.

Russel Barsh is a tireless scholar and advocate for the resolution of important issues in the Coast Salish world. I thank Al Grove, a legal historian, for the many engaging conversations on contemporary issues and the colonial history of the region. Frank and Mary Malloway of the Stó:lō Nation were my hosts for the many summers I lived in their community and wonderful inspirations to me and my graduate students. I would like to extend my thanks to the many staff members at the Stó:lō Nation headquarters at

Coqualeetza who provided so much help and insight for the UBC ethnographic fieldschool. On that note, my appreciation to my hard-working co-directors of the field school – Charles Menzies, Julie Cruikshank, and Millie Creighton. And thanks to the Stó:lō Nation for hosting the terrific People of the River conferences, which are great gatherings of those interested in the Coast Salish world. Similarly, I thank the Musqueam band for, on a number of occasions, inviting me to speak at "Musqueam 101," a wonderful weekly gathering of community members. The late Vince Stogan kindly agreed to speak with me on several occasions, as has Larry Grant. My thanks to these residents of Musqueam.

There are many others who have gone out of their way to contribute to the understanding of Coast Salish communities, history, and circumstances. These include Pamela Amoss, Mark Ebert, Yvonne Hadja, John Lutz, Ted Maloney, Jay Miller, Gordon Mohs, Pat Moore, Alan Richardson, Pat Shaw, Brian Thom, Nile Thompson, and the late G. Bruce Miller of the Skokomish Tribe – a ceremonial man, artist, and elder of great note. It's been a great pleasure and help to walk the landscape with archaeologists Michael Blake, Dana Lepofsky, Bob Mierendorf of the US National Park Service, and UBC graduate student Kysha Supernant.

Many Coast Salish people have been students in my classes and have contributed to my understanding of their world. Among these are Andy Everson of Comox and Kathy Sparrow, who is of Haida ancestry but is now resident in the Coast Salish territory.

Thanks to Jean Wilson of UBC Press for her help and encouragement. It is always a pleasure to work with Jean. In addition, my thanks go to Ann Macklem, also of UBC Press, for her tremendous labours in masterminding the production of the manuscript. Thanks also to Bill Angelbeck for his help with preparing the manuscript, in addition to his intellectual contributions.

Be of Good Mind

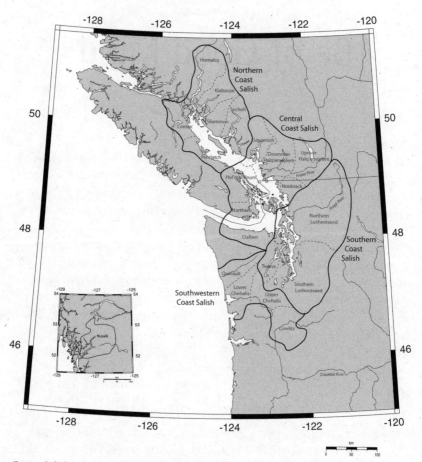

Coast Salish world. *Cartographer: Bill Angelbeck*

Introduction

Bruce Granville Miller

Why a Coast Salish Volume?

The late 1980s and early 1990s was a watershed period in the study of the peoples and communities of western Washington and British Columbia, who, following the name of the language family to which they belong, are known collectively as the Coast Salish.[1] During that period, Wayne Suttles' (1987) *Coast Salish Essays* was published, and in 1990 his edited *Handbook of North American Indians,* volume 7, *Northwest Coast,* appeared in print. As subsequent chapters show, Suttles has been enormously influential, and while he later published additional materials, including a massive grammar of the Musqueam language in 2004, the *Essays* and the *Handbook* are the high-water mark of his approach. Suttles' dissertation work, which he conducted in the 1940s, and his later publications reveal his interest in the anthropological "four-fields" approach (ethnology, linguistics, archaeology, and, with less emphasis, physical anthropology). The preface to his dissertation makes clear how he would go about understanding Coast Salish society:

> In the summer of 1946 when the Anthropology Department of the University of Washington began archaeological work in the San Juan Islands, I spent a few days trying to get what ethnographic information I could from Indians living in and around the islands, information which would be of use to archaeologists. At the time my purpose was merely to determine who occupied the islands in most recent times and to get the location of village and camp sites. But as this work progressed, I came to realize the necessity for getting as full an account as possible of the specific activities that went on at each place. My interest extended first to subsistence and then to the relation of economy to the whole culture of the peoples of the area. (Suttles 1951, i)

His dissertation project led Suttles to pioneer in the emerging field of cultural ecology (described by David Schaepe in Chapter 8), but he retained a broad, holistic frame of reference, and his *Essays* reveals an interest in religion, art, adaptation to contact, and comparative studies of Northwest Coast peoples, among other topics. Of particular interest, though, is his emphasis on regional social networks – on understanding social organization through viewing the Coast Salish world as unified in several senses. "Affinal Ties, Subsistence, and Prestige among the Coast Salish," first delivered as a paper in 1959 and published in 1960, for example, shows the connections between subsistence and prestige economic activities (including potlatching) and the kinship system as well as how Coast Salish people in one region are connected to those elsewhere (Suttles 1960). William Elmendorf, another major scholar in Suttles' cohort, also embraced and developed this theme, particularly in his influential essay "Coast Salish Status Ranking and Intergroup Ties" (Elmendorf 1971). In Chapter 4, Chief Rocky Wilson employs this language of social networks, thus situating his own community within the larger Coast Salish world. Crisca Bierwert does the same thing in Chapter 6, where she discusses webs of kinship.

One could argue that Suttles' work clearly established both the significance of the study of Coast Salish peoples and the relevance of viewing a set of communities under the rubric of "Coast Salish" (although this term did not originate with him) – a topic historian Alexandra Harmon considers in Chapter 1. Previously, the Coast Salish region had suffered as an area of academic interest, not receiving the same attention as did other areas of the Northwest Coast. The Aboriginal occupants of the region were thought to be of less importance than were the Aboriginal occupants of other areas because they had been subject to early and intense assimilationist pressures by the settler populations, which eventually created Seattle, Vancouver, Victoria, Tacoma, and other large communities. For many who worked within a salvage paradigm (which was based on the conviction that Aboriginal life and peoples would soon disappear and that, therefore, any distinctive socio-cultural features should quickly be recorded), the region seemed less than fruitful, although descriptive ethnographic studies were conducted for the Klallam, Snoqualmie, Lummi, Skagit, and others. Typically, these "recipe" books were organized around reporting on a range of topics – curing, kinship, material culture, technology, oral traditions, and so on – rather than around advancing theoretical notions regarding the region. Real, individual people were largely absent, and, in their place, we were presented with a normative culture.

In addition, the Coast Salish world suffered from being regarded as a "receiver area" – an area that received cultural developments that had been created by supposedly "core" Northwest Coast groups such as the Wakashan speakers of the west coast and north end of Vancouver Island and the adjacent BC mainland. Suttles disputed this and theorized ways in which one might understand Coast Salish culture and the presence of dispersed, bilateral kin groups as a development related to local ecology rather than as the absence of a matrilineal clan system (which characterized groups further up the coast). The Coast Salish have commonly been depicted as the victims of raids by the more aggressive, better organized, and (implicitly) more important tribes to the north. In Chapter 9, Bill Angelbeck engages archaeological, ethnohistorical, and other materials to counter such claims and, in so doing, advances a more nuanced view of the Coast Salish. A final point, raised by Harmon (Chapter 1), is that the concept "Coast Salish" may be too narrow. In Chapter 3, for example, Sonny McHalsie reveals the extent to which he and his ancestors maintained important relations beyond the Coast Salish world. Nevertheless, Harmon concludes, and both McHalsie and Rocky Wilson confirm, that affiliations within what we now know as the Coast Salish world were significant.

One could argue that Suttles created an orthodox view of the communities that had long been viewed as comprising a subregion of the larger Northwest Coast culture area. My intention here is not to identify Suttles as acting alone – a number of others of his generation and the one before (e.g., Erna Gunther, Marius Barbeau, Homer Barnett, June Collins, Diamond Jenness, Sally Snyder, Helen Codere, Wilson Duff, Marian Smith, and William Elmendorf) focused specifically on the Coast Salish in at least some of their publications and had much to say on a variety of issues. By his own account, in his student days Suttles was but one among many who were part of a Boasian legacy in the anthropology department at the University of Washington and who made their mark in Coast Salish studies (Suttles 1990, 78). However, by virtue of his longevity and his influence on students, Suttles has arguably had a greater impact on the study of the Coast Salish than has any other scholar of his generation. He also provided much of the flavour of Coast Salish studies through having pioneered small but pivotal concepts. An example is the idea of "advice," a metonymic reference to the set of information regarding kinship, family history, mythology, and so on that is necessary for claimants to upper-class status and that young people would obtain through engaging in spiritual training, listening to stories, and accompanying adults in their daily activities. Advice would, in theory, not be available to lower-class people. The power of this simple idea is that it drew connections between diverse areas of sociocultural activity. In addition, Suttles' continuing influence reflects the great importance of his detailed ethnographies of economic life in contemporary tribal litigation – especially the landmark 1974 case, *United States v. Washington,* better known as the *Boldt* decision, in which Puget Sound tribes regained their treaty rights to half of the salmon catch.[2]

However, just as Suttles' legacy was firmly established, scholarship moved in another direction, as has Northwest Coast scholarship in general, in the period between the 1970s and the present (Mauzé, Harkin, and Kan 2004, xi). The turn of the millennium was yet another watershed in Coast Salish scholarship, with, in quick succession, the sudden appearance of several quite different monographs and edited volumes, including Jay Miller's (1999) *Lushootseed Culture and the Shamanic Odyssey: An Anchored Radiance;* Crisca Bierwert's (1999) *Brushed by Cedar, Living by the River* and her edited volume *Lushootseed Texts* (Bierwert 1996); Brad Asher's (1999) *Beyond the Reservation: Indians, Settlers, and Law in the Washington Territory, 1853-1889;* Alexandra Harmon's (1998) *Indians in the Making: Ethnic Relations and Indian Identities around Puget Sound;* and my own *The Problem of Justice: Tradition and Law in the Coast Salish World* (Miller 2001). These followed shortly after George Guilmet and David Whited's (1989) medical anthropology study of the Puyallup *(Those Who Give More);* Daniel Boxberger's (1989) now classic political economy study of tribal fishing, *To Fish in Common;* and even William Elmendorf's (1993) *Twana Narratives: Native Historical Accounts of a Coast Salish Culture,* a presentation of first-person narrative materials that had been mined for his *The Structure of Twana Culture* (Elmendorf 1960). The Swinomish, together with their research partners, published a powerful and fascinating account of their culture and history – aimed at service providers – entitled *A Gathering of Wisdoms* (Swinomish Tribal Mental Health Project 1991).

These and other works signalled a new era and brought in en masse, and for the first time, real, named Aboriginal people and more detailed and theorized considerations of historical change. The photographs accompanying this chapter (beginning on p. 17) make these points visually and themselves comprise a record of Coast Salish lives and the dramatic changes to their communities. Photo I.1 shows residents of Snauq, a community now encompassed by the Kitsilano neighbourhood of Vancouver, in various sorts of clothing and with distinct responses to the camera. A second photograph, I.2, depicts Upper Skagit people at work running cedar bolts downriver to sawmills sometime around 1900. Photo I.3, taken about 1920, shows current Upper Skagit elder Vi Fernando as a toddler and Jessie Moses, a woman known for her powers of precognition and a powerful influence on current elders. Behind these figures looms sacred Sauk Mountain. The final photograph, I.4, shows Tom Williams in hop fields. He is remembered for bringing the Shaker Church to the Upper Skagit in the early twentieth century.

The Coast Salish peoples in most of the above-named works were shown in relation to other populations, particularly the settlers, rather than in isolation. Largely a stagnant field of study since the 1970s, Coast Salish research had come alive. No longer focused on salvage anthropology, strictly local issues, or assimilation (a genre perhaps best exemplified locally by Lewis' [1970] *Indian Families on the Northwest Coast: The Impact of Change;* and Hawthorn, Belshaw, and Jamieson's [1958] *The Indians of British Columbia: A Study of Contemporary Social Adjustment*), these books reveal the new connections between the larger scholarly fields and work conducted within the Coast Salish realm. The Coast Salish literature can again speak to larger scholarly and real-world issues. There are exceptions to this generalization, of course: significant research in the prior period included Pamela Amoss' (1978) *Coast Salish Spirit Dancing* and Michael Kew's (1970) dissertation concerning contemporary Musqueam. There was also the ethnobiological work of Turner (1975); a festschrift for UBC professor Wilson Duff, edited by Abbott (1981); Aboriginal leader Martin Sampson's (1972) brief study of Skagit history and ethnography; and the early, short writings of Kathleen Mooney (1976). Several others published valuable studies that included, but did not focus on, the Coast Salish, notably Rolf Knight's (1978) seminal work on Aboriginal peoples in the workforce and Paul Tennant's (1990) study of Aboriginal politics in British Columbia.

There has been, to date, no single volume that reflects the array of new topics, new interpretations, and new approaches to the Coast Salish, just as there had been no similar collaborative volume for the Northwest Coast since that edited by Tom McFeat (1966) and prior to the publication of Mauzé, Harkin, and Kan's (2004) *Coming to Shore.* Nor has there been an adequate reflection on how the legacy of early ethnographic studies influences our current scholarly understandings of the Coast Salish. These studies date back to the mid-nineteenth-century work of Horatio Hale (1846), the youthful ethnographer with the US Exploring Expedition of 1838-42; George Gibbs (1877), ethnographer with the US boundary expedition and other government projects; the work of the eccentric and eclectic George Swan (1857); and the work of the "father of American anthropology," Franz Boas (1889); and others. It is equally important to consider the viewpoints of Aboriginal peoples themselves and how Aboriginal peoples have influenced scholarly perspectives. With this in mind, I have pulled together work by contemporary scholars who can comment on a variety of substantive issues, particularly the state of research, and whose work reflects both the influences of the Suttles generation of scholars and new ideas. Some of the contributors are now long-established scholars and others are of a newer generation.

History and Anthropology

Be of Good Mind has other aims as well as those mentioned above. Both the academic and popular literatures have commonly split the Coast Salish world in two, treating those living in Puget Sound and adjacent lands as constituting one world and those in British Columbia as constituting another. This practice fails to conform to the prior Aboriginal reality, before contact with whites and before treaties and borders. While it would be a mistake to argue that earlier scholarship failed to recognize the connections between peoples in what are now two separate nations, political factors have clearly influenced where people have engaged in fieldwork and what they have written about. For the most part, Americans have worked in the United States and Canadians in Canada. I want to make clear that there have been important exceptions to this observation: American Marian Smith, for example, conducted an ethnographic field school at the Seabird Island Reserve in British Columbia in 1945, as Crisca Bierwert points out in Chapter 6. Certainly, Suttles himself taught and researched in both countries and provided anthropological testimony on behalf of tribes on both sides of the international border. However, because much of the work during the period when Suttles got his start was descriptive salvage anthropology, it focused on discrete communities located in one country or the other. Meanwhile, political forces had pushed Aboriginal people to occupy reserves (the Canadian term) and reservations (the American term) whose borders had to remain within those of either Canada or the United States: there was to be no overlapping of federal borders. The Semiahmoo, for example, came to occupy only the Canadian portions of their territories, although they have maintained connections with their Lummi relatives in the United States. US and British/Canadian policy did not allow for recognized groups to have land in both counties (thereby creating a legal question now tentatively being approached in courts in both countries). The creation of reservations and reserves led scholars to study these communities as free-standing political entities. Since the establishment of the international boundary in 1846, differences in Canadian and American contact histories and public policies have created significant differences between historically connected Aboriginal communities. Not surprisingly, regional historians have tended to focus on Aboriginal peoples residing in their region alone. In brief, the connections between communities and individuals across the entire Coast Salish world have not been adequately explored. Several contemporary scholars have explicitly concerned themselves with this problem and have sought to draw out the divergences and parallels. The chapters in this volume continue to address this shortcoming, including that of linguist Brent Galloway (Chapter 7).

I am also interested in pulling together the work of historians, anthropologists, other social scientists, and community intellectuals to create an emergent picture of the Coast Salish realm. As in the case of cross-border studies, it is nothing new for scholars from various disciplines to work together or to mutually influence one another's work. There is a long history of this, but there are now new twists to it. First, professional historians appear to be paying more attention to the developing histories of particular First Nations and American Indian Coast Salish communities and people, although, as Alexandra Harmon points out in Chapter 1, no one has yet produced a synthetic history of the region. Examples of these new histories include the biography of Esther Ross, a profoundly important woman in the twentieth-century history of the Stillaguamish (Ruby and Brown 2001), and Daniel Marshall's (1999) *Those Who Fell from the Sky: A History of the Cowichan Peoples*, a community history. It is probably fair to say that the scholarly production of histories concerning the Coast Salish of Washington State is considerably ahead of those for British Columbia. Most notably, Alexandra Harmon (1998) has written a now widely influential history of the Coast Salish of Puget Sound, *Indians in the Making*. The gap is closing rapidly, however, and exciting new regional histories by Keith Thor Carlson (2003) and others, including John Lutz at the University of Victoria, will continue to dramatically transform our understandings of the area.

There are other reasons why the rapprochement of historians, anthropologists, and community intellectuals is occurring and why it is significant, including the fact that, over the past twenty years, both history and anthropology have changed as disciplines. Americanist anthropology, once driven by functionalist and then assimilationist academic agendas, has moved toward a more thoughtful consideration of the ways in which historical forces act on culture and on local peoples. One might even make this claim regarding anthropologists of the Northwest Coast, most of whom have been heavily influenced by Franz Boas' version of historical particularism. History, for its part, has increasingly embraced minority and social histories. This is evident in new hiring strategies at universities. For example, in 2004-05 my own academic institution, the University of British Columbia (UBC), hired two young scholars whose primary interest is Aboriginal history. While an older generation of historians at UBC has played an important role in the production of Aboriginal history, this was not why they were brought to the university. Together, the two disciplines of history and anthropology, and their Aboriginal collaborators, have created the field of ethnohistory, a discourse that sprang out of the problems associated with providing evidence for the US Court of Claims in the 1940s – a legal enterprise intended to speed up the resolution of land claims and treaty issues facing American tribes.

As Daniel Boxberger points out in Chapter 2, research among the Coast Salish has always been driven by concerns of public policy and litigation. This became evident following the *Boldt* decision, a large-scale legal proceeding in which Barbara Lane and many other formally trained researchers turned their attention to amassing various sorts of materials relating to the issue of treaty-period (i.e., mid-nineteenth-century) life. But academics have long worked for Aboriginal communities on legal matters. Sally Snyder, for example, carried out long-term fieldwork with Samish, Swinomish, Upper Skagit, Sauk-Suiattle, and other communities in the 1940s and 1950s, largely with litigation in mind. Later, she acted on behalf of these communities. As Boxberger describes in Chapter 2, Herbert Taylor of Western Washington University spent much of his career considering issues related to litigation. The intellectual problems presented in treaty, land, and other litigation have pushed scholars to more carefully consider questions of population size, the impact of contact on economic activities, the nature of social relations, the nature of private property, and many other issues. Litigation has also pushed scholars of different disciplines to create detailed and unified interpretations that are intellectually honest, that are in line with all available information (including Aboriginal viewpoints and oral documents), and that might be successful in court.

Most contemporary scholars of the Coast Salish have probably found themselves either producing materials for tribal litigation or testifying in court. Some have found this to be an onerous task and either refuse to participate or do so only once. Many contend that the demands of litigation – report production along with examination and cross-examination – provide greater scrutiny of academic ideas and arguments than does any other venue. The demands of litigation, in brief, have forced a newer, more carefully argued approach to a variety of issues about the Coast Salish area. As Boxberger indicates in Chapter 2, litigation may have profoundly altered the nature of scholarship as it relates to the Coast Salish. I might add that this appears to be largely for the good, in that it has precipitated new discussions and sharpened ideas, and it has also created a real-world forum within which to debate anthropological and historical ideas of very considerable importance. Problems have emerged too, including the ugly spectre of unprepared scholars testifying beyond their competence and/or being unaware of the differences between legal and academic understandings of particular words and concepts (Miller 2004). In addition, scholars have testified against each other in ways that are not always attractive or helpful, and many, including Colin Grier (Chapter 10), remain wary of the relationship between law and scholarship. Academics have been accused of merely being mouthpieces for tribes/bands or for one or another government. Nonetheless, working together on litigation constitutes a third reason why history, anthropology, and Aboriginal forms of knowledge have usefully interpenetrated and why all are represented in *Be of Good Mind*. Boxberger (Chapter 2) cautions, however, that some forms of traditional knowledge are not common property and that they should remain community-controlled resources of the sort articulated by McHalsie (Chapter 3).

In Chapter 4, Rocky Wilson reveals more about the significance of legal engagement. His people, the Hwlitsum, are not yet recognized by the Canadian government, a circumstance that has caused his band to undertake litigation and that focuses his understandings of Coast Salish identity. He points out the participation of his band in Coast Salish social networks, the role of elders in creating internal recognition, and the importance of establishing one's place through honouring one's ancestors. His chapter also reveals the important and still unresolved issue of the existence of Coast Salish communities on both sides of the international border that lack official state recognition. Although this circumstance skews these communities' relationships with recognized tribes and bands, they rightly deserve to be recognized in this volume (see Miller 2003).

While historians are now making a big splash in Coast Salish studies, they are reading ethnographies, and anthropologists are reading histories. Beyond this, however, is the exciting development, at least from my perspective as an anthropologist, of a new generation of historians who have learned directly from community members themselves. This is not news for anthropologists; indeed, Valentine and Darnell (1999) suggest that Americanist anthropology is characterized by Aboriginal people's participating directly in theory making. Now, however, we have the prospect of historians trained in archival methods and informed by world-scale historical questions, who have added to their repertoire the insights of the community and a deep appreciation for Aboriginal epistemologies. This is a powerful combination. For historians, culture is never static, and they have challenged anthropological renderings in which culture appears to be so. Coast Salish culture (or, more aptly, cultures, there is no uniformity in the Coast Salish region) has seemed flat in the hands of anthropologists; the *Handbook* perhaps most thoroughly reflects this approach. While anthropologists have understood that Coast Salish culture changed prehistorically, and while none would argue that life four thousand years ago, during a period of mixed economic activity and before that of the intensification of salmon fisheries, would have been similar to life in 1750, not enough attention has been given to transformations in more recent cultural practice. For example, in Chapter 10 Grier indicates the extent to which archaeologists have uncritically applied ethnographic understandings to archaeological questions. He argues for "side-by-side" research. Critics may quickly dispute my contention and might, for example, point to studies of the rise of the Indian Shaker Church, the transformation of religious practices and concepts in the late nineteenth century, or to Guilmet, Boyd, Whited, and Thompson's (1991) study of the effects of disease on cultural transmission. But even these studies have not adequately dislodged the notion of an ethnographic present. The current dialogue with historians, however, appears to have begun to do this.

Simultaneously, histories appear more relevant and more respectful of community epistemologies and approaches to history. Keith Thor Carlson's work is perhaps most developed in this sense. Now a tenured faculty member at the University of Saskatchewan, Carlson worked for more than a decade as a historian for the Stó:lō Nation. During this period, he attended community spiritual events, listened to community members and leaders of all sorts, puzzled through community politics, and began to form a new idea of how identities had come to be what they are and what an indigenous historiography might be like. This is reflected in Chapter 5 and in previous publications, including the impressive and award-winning *A Stó:lō Coast Salish Historical Atlas* (Carlson 2001). Carlson has taken community oral histories of several sorts seriously and has wedded them to archival and ethnographic accounts. The product, exciting and provocative, is arguably an altogether new hybrid scholarship. Chapter 3, by Stó:lō cultural advisor Sonny McHalsie, shows in detail how he has learned to work with academics such as Carlson and to incorporate and re-analyze materials from previous generations of non-Aboriginal researchers. McHalsie points to the mutual sharing of published and unpublished materials (and suggests that unpublished notes are often more valuable than are the worked-over published materials, a topic taken up by Crisca Bierwert in Chapter 6) and to the importance of mutual participation in spiritual life. For McHalsie, participant observation moves in both directions.

Carlson (Chapter 5) and David Schaepe (Chapter 8) point to another important feature of the post-1990 world and yet another reason to celebrate and encourage the new interdisciplinary scholarship – that is, the ability of communities to employ scholars directly. When I first began to work among Coast Salish communities in the 1970s, they were only tentatively engaging in research and had not fully begun to figure out ways in which they might work with scholars for mutually productive purposes. The Puyallup, for example, had just seized a former tribal tuberculosis treatment centre and were beginning to create a tribal archive. The Stó:lō, too, on the Canadian side, had recently forcibly seized a hospital located in their traditional territories, also formerly devoted to Aboriginal tuberculosis patients, and had begun to develop a research program and archive. Much of the visible and dramatic infrastructure of the communities, including large and attractive tribal centres, gaming and public auditoriums, gymnasiums, shopping malls, and new winter ceremonial longhouses, was not yet present. The implications of the legal victory of the *Boldt* decision were just beginning to become apparent in Puget Sound, and the BC bands were coming alive politically in opposition to the federal government's policy of radical assimilation and termination, which was announced by the Trudeau government's 1969 White Paper.

In the 1970s Vi Hilbert, now an Upper Skagit elder and then a language instructor at the University of Washington, had just begun her own engagement with a group of scholars interested in helping her develop materials about the oral traditions and cultures of the Coast Salish. By the mid-1990s, Hilbert's research group, including both community members and academics Pamela Amoss, Jay Miller, Andie Palmer, Crisca Bierwert, and many others, had produced several volumes and audiotapes. These materials directly reflected Hilbert's own teaching, which she received from her elders, including her aunt Susie Sampson Peter and her father, Charlie Anderson. The publications have had a considerable impact on the work of both those in her group, particularly on Jay Miller's (1999) *Lushootseed Culture and the Shamanic Odyssey,* and those outside, including Carlson. In fact, one might argue that Vi Hilbert has created her own orthodox and spiritually informed view of the Coast Salish peoples and cultures – one that complements Suttles' more academic and ecologically based perspective.

BC bands have entered into their own direct encounter with academics as their governmental infrastructure has developed and their capacity for employing academics has grown. In 1991, for example, the Stó:lō Nation invited anthropologists from UBC to help them with their research. At this point, the nation employed a single academically trained social scientist, the archaeologist Gordon Mohs, and early meetings between Stó:lō staff and UBC professors were held in a small trailer. There were fewer than ten Stó:lō staff at the time of the birth of the UBC graduate ethnographic field school, initially organized by Professor Julie Cruikshank and myself, in

1991. Less than a dozen years later, the Stó:lō staff had grown to well over two hundred, and the nation now employs academics of various sorts, including anthropologists and archaeologists, historians, archivists, GIS specialists, as well as community culture experts. This powerful group came to be known, in jest, as Stó:lō University, reflecting how its members dramatically changed the landscape of scholarship concerning the Coast Salish in Canada, publishing a series of significant books, including the *Atlas* (Carlson 2001) and *You Are Asked to Witness* (Carlson 1996), just as had Vi Hilbert and her research group in the United States. It is because of the groundbreaking work of Gordon Mohs, Keith Thor Carlson, Albert McHalsie, and many others that a disproportionate amount of research about the Coast Salish concerns the Stó:lō communities. *Be of Good Mind* reflects that reality.

Academics on both sides of the border have been called on to produce studies of Aboriginal economic practice to support litigation and to establish Aboriginal rights. In the 1980s, for example, Puget Sound sacred sites were mapped and documented for the purpose of protecting them from intrusive non-tribal economic activities, particularly logging. Later, the relicensing of Puget Power and Seattle City Light under the terms of the US Federal Environmental Regulatory Commission (FERC) called for the production of traditional cultural property (TCP) studies. In Canada, the requirements of documenting tribal practice under the emerging case law of the 1990s have led to the production of traditional use studies (TUS). This sort of work has had the effect of informing academics of the depth of Aboriginal thinking and has created a heightened sensitivity to the cultural landscape. As several of the chapters in this volume reveal, particularly that of Stó:lō leader Sonny McHalsie, understanding the cultural landscape is a critical feature of the new interpretations of the Salish world. And in Chapter 8, Dave Schaepe suggests that contemporary Coast Salish community heritage resource policies constitute significant articulations of identity.

In brief, the scholarship of the contemporary period reflects a new engagement with the Coast Salish people themselves. In many cases, scholars are directly employed by tribes and bands; in other cases, they are under contract to prepare materials for litigation for tribal interests. Scholars are also occasionally employed to provide answers to legal questions posed by non-Aboriginal litigants. The demands of litigation have led to a new look at the landscape and a new vigilance. Within this framework, new questions are being asked and new concepts developed. An interesting example is the effort by Schaepe, Berkey, Stamp, and Halstad (2004) on behalf of the Stó:lō Nation to document Stó:lō practices and beliefs regarding air and water. This is part of the Stó:lō Nation's attempt to protect threatened sacred areas as well as the environment more generally, and it points directly to relevant, but poorly understood, features of Coast Salish identity.

For Coast Salish communities, all of this is occurring during a period of considerable political reawakening and tremendous cultural revival. For example, as recently as twenty years ago winter spirit dancing drew few new participants; today, there are many initiates from a number of Coast Salish communities, and hundreds crowd into longhouses for extended nights of watching and supporting the dancers. These forces, in addition to those internal to academic disciplines worldwide, have drawn together historians, anthropologists, archaeologists, linguists, tribal historians, and culture advisors. There remain issues that are particular to archaeology, and everyone is going to have to continue to rework his or her understandings of Coast Salish studies in light of new archaeological developments.

Archaeology, Anthropology, and History

The archaeology of the Coast Salish cannot be regarded as well-developed in comparison to the archaeology of some other regions of Aboriginal North America. Perhaps because of the rapid urban development in the region following white contact as well as compelling archaeological projects elsewhere, relatively few academic resources have been devoted to this subject. Even departments in large universities in the region, notably the University of Washington, the University of British Columbia, and Simon Fraser University (SFU), have done relatively little to follow the pioneering work of Charles Borden, Roy Carlson, and several others. Over the last decade and a half this has slowly begun to change. UBC established an archaeological field school in the late 1980s, working at several sites along the Fraser River and on the Gulf Islands, and has joined forces with SFU archaeologists to work on several projects. Some of these have the unusual feature of considering the archaeology of the Coast Salish across the international boundary (e.g., the study of the Chittenden Meadows in the Skagit region of both Canada and the United States). Tribes and bands have also come to rely on professional contract firms to obtain archaeological documentation. The resultant "grey" literature has frequently been entered as evidence in the legal record and has enhanced the overall understanding of the archaeology of the region.

Archaeology in the contemporary period is considerably transformed from what it was in earlier times. Now, neither academic nor contract archaeologists can proceed on their own accord in Aboriginal territory; community consent and participation is required, as it is with all forms of ethnographic research. In many cases, Aboriginal communities have created protocols for seeking permission and recording information for community use. In some cases, these protocols have been prepared with the co-operation of archaeologists themselves. In Chapter 8, David Schaepe looks at the participation of professional archaeologists in the conception and creation of the Stó:lō Nation cultural resource management program – including archaeological sites. Arguably, archaeologists of the Coast Salish are among the most responsive to the new environment of scholar-Aboriginal relations and among the most progressive in developing useful and mutually satisfying relationships with Aboriginal peoples in North America.

In many other regions, archaeologists and anthropologists remain much more resistant to incorporating Aboriginal peoples into their thinking and practice. This may reflect the fact that most of these scholars live in the Coast Salish region and that Coast Salish Aboriginal peoples are members of the larger community as well as of the tribe/band. They attend the colleges and universities and participate in academic affairs. Academics teaching courses about Aboriginal peoples see them in great numbers in their classes in the Coast Salish area, and community members themselves teach or give lectures in many of the courses. They push to have their voices and perspectives heard, and they have generously given their time so that scholars may learn from them. This is less true in many other areas, where academics live "away" and the scholarly discourse remains largely distinct from community concerns and voices.

Aboriginal participation, then, includes more than simply issuing or refusing permission to excavate archaeological sites. Community leaders now carefully consider what types of sites, and which sites in particular, need to be studied. There is a new utility to archaeology for Aboriginal communities; archaeological findings can be used to demonstrate continuity of occupation, the range of subsistence activities, and other topics significant in making land claims or, in the case of British Columbia, in supporting bands during the treaty process. Communities, then, have a direct interest in selecting projects that are of utility to them.

Further, communities directly contribute to the interpretation of sites. This is not new, but contemporary archaeologists have built community contributions directly into the initial planning and conceptualizing stage, so that there is constant feedback going on. The long collaboration of tribal expert Sonny McHalsie, historian Keith Thor Carlson, archaeologists Dave Schaepe, Michael Blake, and Dana Lepofsky in Stó:lō territory, and Robert Mierendorf in the adjacent US National Park Service is one such example. Recently, a large-scale, long-term, federally funded "identity" project has been undertaken to examine the movements of Coast Salish people along the Fraser River, the point being to create a historical picture of the migrations, amalgamations, and fissioning that resulted in the contemporary Stó:lō people. Pat Moore has joined several other academics in the project to add linguistic reconstructions to archaeological and historical materials. McHalsie and the elders with whom he has worked have been able to connect features of the landscape to oral records that reveal the significance of the sites. The results of this project are not yet fully in, although McHalsie's chapter in this volume reveals the nature and significance of his contribution.

In Chapter 10, Colin Grier discusses his work in the Gulf Islands and his interest in household archaeology. His previous work (Grier 2003) has helped refine our understanding of how the Coast Salish world (or Salish Sea, in Russel Barsh's terminology) functions as a region by pointing out how island resources relate to riverine occupation. Grier's work also sheds light on ethnographic and ethnohistorical studies of the political organization of the Coast Salish peoples, since the early 1990s an area of lively debate (Tollefson 1987, 1989; Miller and Boxberger 1994; Miller 2001). Notably, his research also requires significant band co-operation with regard to granting permission, identifying sites, thinking through the uses of a site, and establishing a logistical system for his research team. Finally, Grier's work illuminates the operation of temporal corporate groups, an idea that I believe is underplayed in the literature. Here he focuses on difficult issues in the relationship between archaeology and ethnography. He points out that an uncritical imposition of ethnographic conclusions regarding Coast Salish social organization can obstruct the development of an adequate archaeology of the region. He calls for a Coast Salish archaeology that is produced in conjunction with ethnography and, more broadly, with anthropology and that is independent of the ethnographic record. This would produce an archaeology that could contribute to ethnographic understandings and eliminate the teleological quality of Coast Salish studies, which have so strongly emphasized historically known peoples.

These examples of the integration of archaeology, linguistics, history, ethnography, and other disciplines reveal the significance of integrated, multidisciplinary research. Much more remains to be done, and the archaeology of the Coast Salish appears to be about to undergo significant revision. Robert Mierendorf's (1993) work in the US North Cascades shows eighty-five hundred radio carbon years (calibrated 14C years before present) of Aboriginal occupation in the Ross Lake area, and use of high altitude Alpine regions and recent research in Yale Canyon at the X̱elhálh site suggest the development of rock-wall fortifications along the Fraser River and the construction of a "castle-like" stone defensive site protecting a rich storage area (Schaepe 2006). Working out these ideas will require interdisciplinary efforts and will certainly affect our understanding of the Coast Salish peoples.

Who Are the Coast Salish?

Much of the new literature focuses on the critical question, "who are the Coast Salish?" and the related issue, "what are the connections between the contemporary peoples and the historic and prehistoric communities and cultures?" Either directly or indirectly, these questions are reflected in the chapters in *Be of Good Mind,* and they are important for a number of practical and intellectual reasons. First, Coast Salish communities, as I have suggested, are continuing their struggle to clarify and extend their legal footing in both Canada and the United States. The details of this are the topic of another book, but they influence current thinking. For example, in the second phase of the landmark *Boldt* decision, the shellfishing phase, in my own testimony and report I asked: "Who are the successors in interest to the treaty-period people of the Skagit?" This is not an easy question, applied as it is to a people who have long practised exogamous marriage (at least among those of high standing). Coast Salish society has been characterized by kinship ties that stretch over a large area and, in some circumstances, by use-rights to resources in various locales. Today, tribes and bands struggle internally over what constitutes a community and who ought to have membership. For example, over the last decade, various bands have drifted in and out of membership in the Stó:lō Nation, and the Stó:lō Nation and Musqueam band continue to differ over whether or not the latter ought to be regarded as part of the former (the Musqueam argue against this). In the United States and Canada, non-recognized tribes struggle to demonstrate their separateness from established tribes that claim to have incorporated their interests and their people in the nineteenth century.

Anthropologists, for their part, and, more recently, historians, have advanced several competing theories in an attempt to understand the social organization and identifying features of the various Coast Salish peoples. Suttles (1987) emphasizes the importance of the local kin group, which operated within a regional social network and which was based on lineage and the management of resources. Smith (1940) emphasizes mutual identity along watersheds, without formal regional leadership. Jay Miller (1999) points to the importance of spiritual practice and the role of shamanic practitioners in forming regional systems. And Tollefson (1987, 1989) suggests that at least some Puget Salish were organized into chiefdoms. Responses to this work (Miller and Boxberger 1994) argue that colonial processes may have pushed communities into creating more formalized alliances, as commonly occurred with several other Aboriginal regions of Native North America. Yet others (Harmon 1998) emphasize how contact has altered, perhaps distorted, the ways in which Coast Salish peoples

PHOTO I.1 Group near Jericho Charlie's home on Kitsilano Indian Reserve (Snauq): Mary (Yam-schlmoot), Jericho Charlie (Chin-nal-set), William Green, Peelass George, Jimmy Jimmy, and Jack (Tow-hu-quam-kee). *Major Matthews Collection, City of Vancouver Archives, P28N11*

organize their identities. For his part, Carlson (2003) analyzes migrations and social class differences and their basis in cultural patterning in the early historic period.

It seems clear, however, that Coast Salish peoples have long constructed and maintained complex personal social identities that connect them to a variety of other groups. These include immortal beings regarded as ancestral kinfolk, immediate affinal and agnatic relatives, a larger set of more distant relatives, households, and fellow members of "villages" that are sometimes many kilometres in length but that have few structures. There are also patterns of affiliation based on common occupation of water systems; respect for particular regional leaders, use-rights, and resource procurement areas; and the common use of particular languages and dialects. In the contemporary period, the Coast Salish have some sense of common identity with fellow members of this Aboriginal language family, as is indicated by recent efforts to create a Coast Salish political network crossing the international border. To a great extent, though, patterns of identity and affiliations gain importance according to how they are deployed in daily life and, additionally, in times of great upheaval and change. Who the Coast Salish are depends upon the question being asked – a circumstance that has not been sufficiently recognized in the academic literature. It is this flexibility with regard to personal and group patterns of identity that has enabled the Coast Salish to adapt to the devastating problems resulting from contact (Kew and Miller 1999).

Harmon (1998) has rightly observed that, though tribes and bands exist in a form that was determined by the administrative practice of the colonizers, they have nevertheless become the focus of personal and group identity. Washington State tribes are "treaty tribes" in the sense that political and economic rights flow from the language in which treaties encapsulated them in the 1850s. These treaties structure the lives of individual Coast Salish peoples and families. Similarly, as Schaepe points out, the responses of BC bands and tribal councils to the current treaty process and land claims have had a similar impact. However, individuals on both sides of the border also closely identify with kin relations, and these cross tribal/band political boundaries. My own work with contemporary communities suggests to me that the significance of the local kin group, the "corporate group" which is based in the idiom of kinship but that implicitly excludes many potential kinfolk, has not been sufficiently considered. Because my research has largely been concerned with contemporary tribal internal politics, service delivery, and justice systems, my approach to these communities is quite different from that of those engaging in salvage anthropology

PHOTO I.2 Running cedar bolts downriver to sawmills. *Ed Edwards Collection, Upper Skagit Tribe*

and attempting to reconstruct largely dismembered ways of life. My work has shown that contemporary patterns of identity and organization, although not identical with earlier patterns, are powerfully influenced by them. An interesting example of this may be found in the Upper Skagit community in the rapid re-creation of family fishing co-operatives along the Skagit River following the regaining of tribal recognition soon after the *Boldt* decision (Miller 1989a). In Chapter 6, Bierwert points to the significance of extended kin groups as well as to the problems in retaining this sort of social pattern under mid-twentieth-century pressure to assimilate.

My claim is that the Coast Salish continue to form themselves into named corporate groups, known locally simply as "families." Further, many significant issues of contemporary social life might be best approached from an analysis of the ways in which these families interact. What follows is a short sketch of how this approach works and the sorts of questions it might address concerning the core question: who are the Coast Salish? These groups organize many fundamental features of the lives of their members, which is to say that they have corporate functions, including, in many cases, those affecting fishing, ritual life, regular small-scale reciprocity (such as babysitting, care of elders, borrowing cash, the lending of cars). These corporate groups are the entities within which "advice" is shared and taught. Elders gather goods for distribution at ancestral namings held for group members and other important ritual events, and members are initiated during winter dances in the group longhouse (if they have one). Senior members teach or demonstrate important skills, such as basket weaving and storytelling, to junior members. "Magic" is kept private within the group, and group members attempt to restrict access to personal information about health status and other vital issues. In one study (Miller and Pylypa 1995), paraprofessional mental health service providers reported that they were largely unable to provide services to members of outside groups because of the prohibitions against sharing information across family lines. In another case, a tribal basket-making project floundered because elders were unwilling to teach members of other families.

From this viewpoint, tribes and bands can be thought of as being composed of competing families, whose members' loyalties lie more with the families than with the political units that contain them. One political leader reported her efforts to ensure that the families co-operate for the purpose of mutual success (Miller 1989b). Families compete over a variety of internal resources, which are available solely through common membership within the larger tribal/band structure. These resources include seats on tribal/band councils; in both the Canadian and American communities, voting patterns show strong evidence of family loyalties (Miller 1992).

PHOTO I.3 Sauk Mountain, with Jessie Moses
(looking down) and Vi Fernando (child).
Ed Edwards Collection, Upper Skagit Tribe

Further, families compete for available housing, access to health, social, and educational services, influence over community decisions, and tribal/band jobs. In one case in Canada, in recognition of the long-term practice of family leadership within the larger collective, the method of selecting band council members was adjusted to allow for the appointment of family leaders (Kew and Miller 1999). As is the case with many small-scale political systems elsewhere, families unite when necessary to compete with other tribes/bands, particularly regarding fishing allocations.

Unlike the northern matrilineal tribes in the northern Northwest Coast culture region, the Coast Salish have no clan system, with the result that distribution of members to family groups is not clearly channelled.[3] This fact points to the importance of examining individual, household, nuclear family, "family," and even band-level processes of affiliation. Interview data show that many, perhaps most, individuals carefully scrutinize their life chances within the family and the political unit (Miller 1989b, 1992). In many cases, individuals choose to move to a new location, sometimes to a new band or tribe, where, through bilateral kinship, they can claim membership in a different corporate family and where they might have either more resources available to them or a stronger position within the family. An individual's decisions are influenced by her stage of life, the stage in the life cycle of her nuclear family, her household, and the circumstances of the family she wishes to join.

For the most part, families gain members in two ways: birth and recruitment. While members are not necessarily co-resident and may not even live in the same community, they practise regular generalized reciprocity (Mooney 1976), and they depend on one or more leaders who can offer them significant resources. These resources may include spiritual knowledge, "advice," financial assets, control of ancestral names (which may be given to appropriate family members), mastery of local norms of speech making, and various publicly identifiable phenomena associated with high-class status. Other resources may include control of locations for fishing camps, ritual roles, knowledge of the non-Aboriginal bureaucratic world, seats on tribal council, chances at tribal employment, influence in housing policy, and so on. Followers might gain access to these resources through their ties to leaders, but the connections to family leaders vary, and some tribal members are more socially and genealogically distant than are others. Leaders, in turn, offer their resources to family members but may shape their following through strategic allocations. A family, however, always remains a "moral" group rather than an instrumental one (Bailey 1980, 73).

An important feature of the family is its size, and larger families are generally the most successful when it comes to competing with other families within a given polity. In tribal/band elections, for example, adult members can often be counted on to vote for family candidates. And, if a family is large, it is more likely than is a smaller family to have its members holding tribal/band jobs. But because families are not clans, they are not immortal: they follow cycles of birth, growth, and collapse. Families coalesce around able charismatic leaders, but they may splinter following the death of these leaders if there are no suitable candidates to take their place. Family leadership, then, is earned rather than ascribed. Over time, the named families in a community will change, and the presence of a particular surname is no more indicative of the existence of a corporate family group than is the presence of particular Anglo names in a Canadian telephone book.

The approach I suggest here is appropriate for examining contemporary internal political processes, for considering the lives of individuals, and for making sense of much of the confusion in the literature regarding how individuals identify themselves. It also provides insights into how and when

PHOTO I.4 Tom Williams (at left), founder of Upper Skagit Shaker Church, hop picking. *Ed Edwards Collection, Upper Skagit Tribe*

individual members of polities gain access to services, a point medical anthropologist Jen Pylypa and I made regarding medical service delivery (Miller and Pylypa 1995). However, this is not a historical approach per se, although it relies on time depth; rather, it emphasizes the life cycles of individuals and other social units, and it relies on regarding Aboriginal communities from the vantage point of local-level politics. Further, it emphasizes the differences in how tribal/band members are positioned within their own communities, and it points to the importance of the analysis of power in understanding contemporary lives – all of which are issues that have been insufficiently developed in the literature. But this approach must be paired with those developed by historians (and others) to account for the processes of (neo)colonialism as well as with the political economic approaches developed by anthropologists and other social scientists. The latter are represented by Daniel Boxberger in Chapter 6.

The question "Who are the Coast Salish?" must, of course, be answered by community members themselves; the chapters by Sonny McHalsie and Rocky Wilson are part of an attempt to do just this. In Chapter 3, McHalsie discusses the complex and evolving process involved as he learns about his community and how he is connected to the landscape and his ancestors.

He rejects shallow understandings of oral history, which claim that the use of outside sources constitutes a sort of contagion, and he reveals the complex relationship between oral and written materials. Showing how he has engaged scholars and scholarly writing, McHalsie points, as does Bierwert (Chapter 6), to the value of fieldnotes as sources. In particular, he elucidates how the interests of linguists, who are intent on recording, analyzing, and preserving language, may diverge from his own interest in examining the social context within which language is used and of places and names. In Chapter 4 it is clear that Rocky Wilson is also informed by both the narratives of his elders and academic understandings.

Meanwhile, there is a growing debate concerning the role of various academic approaches and how they might help communities represent themselves to the outside world. In Chapter 2, Boxberger observes that, in legal settings, postmodern and poststructural approaches are of little practical value: they don't clearly address legal questions, they appear to lack the authority that courts demand of experts, and they employ a different notion of fact than do the legal systems in both Canada and the United States. They undermine the legitimacy of community self-representations within legal settings because opponents can point to internal disagreement and differing perspectives. For all of these reasons, such approaches simply don't work well in court. He argues that the reality is that legal settings constitute the primary forum for public debate, whether inside or outside the courtroom.

The counter-argument appears to be that communities must make representations to both the outside world and their own members during a period in which community diversity is considerably greater than was the case in previous generations. Coast Salish communities are no longer culturally homogeneous, if they ever were. Now, some members belong to the Shaker Church, others are Seowyn winter dancers, and still others are Pentecostals or Roman Catholics. Many participate in several spiritual and religious traditions, but many do not. Access to wealth and formal education divides communities in new ways. In this argument, pressures to exhibit internal cultural uniformity to the outside world have the potential to silence internal disputes (e.g., with regard to nascent justice systems) (Miller 2001). For this reason, foregrounding the social complexity of communities, as does Bierwert's poststructuralist writing, may be constructive and may potentially allow communities room to manoeuvre in future self-representations. Both positions – the legalistic and the poststructuralist – make important statements, however, and the question of how academics ought to position their research and their contributions remains open.

Conclusion

Wayne Suttles' *Coast Salish Essays* reflects the words and concepts of a life-time of careful, thoughtful, and sometimes inspired work. The result of a long, fruitful collaboration with Aboriginal people and communities, it reflects Suttles' abiding interest in contributing directly to communities while developing his own intellectual program. Sadly, Suttles died in 2005 as *Be of Good Mind* was being prepared. Now it is time for a new collection of essays – one that teases apart the received wisdom, incorporating several voices and addressing a wide range of topics. In this sense, *Be of Good Mind* might be regarded as a sequel to Suttles' *Essays* – a sequel in which ortho-doxy is replaced by heterodoxy and in which anthropology is paired with other disciplines. It is also time for Coast Salish literature to better connect with the broader scholarship regarding Aboriginal peoples, colonization, and globalization as well as to incorporate new forms of scholarly analysis. Once the influence of Boasian-style anthropology diminished in North America, the Northwest Coast culture area was widely thought to have become a scholarly backwater. Until recently this was particularly true with regard to the Coast Salish. The Northwest Coast has entered the broader scholarly imagination primarily with regard to the potlatch and exchange theory. This is most notable in French anthropology, such as Marcel Mauss' (1967) *The Gift* and Lévi-Strauss' (1982) structuralist renderings, some of which relied on examples from Stó:lō communities along the Fraser River. The influence of Northwest Coast art and material culture on European aesthetics has been noted (Clifford 1988). More recently, the work of Sergei Kan (1989), particularly his classic *Symbolic Immortality*, has signalled that the Northwest Coast is again pushing beyond its own borders. The foci of Northwest Coast scholarship – once on myth, art, the potlatch, descent systems, social inequalities, and winter ceremonies (Suttles and Jonaitis 1990) – are now elsewhere.

In the 1970s and early 1980s, at least one major university in the region chose simply to dump anthropology faculty members whose area of re-search was primarily the Coast Salish in favour of those who worked in more exotic and supposedly more intellectually exciting regions of the world, such as Papua New Guinea. But this appears to have been short-sighted and to reflect a lack of concern for the relationship between the local uni-versities and local peoples, along with the old, lingering notion that the Coast Salish lack authenticity and are too assimilated to be of interest. Dur-ing the 1970s and 1980s, little attention was paid to promoting the educa-tion of local Aboriginal people and to attracting them to a university that took their lives and view of the world seriously, never mind to respecting the fact that the universities themselves are built on Aboriginal traditional lands. In the 1970s, insufficient attention was paid to understanding how global trends are experienced or generated locally, and international indigenous concerns were yet to be articulated as a political force and the site of academic interest. These attitudes still persist in the academy and among contract researchers. To some, the Coast Salish world remains of little interest because, as I have been told (as were those many years before me), "There is nothing left to learn. They [members of some particular community] don't know anything now." The assumption is that the culture is preserved in recorded materials and best understood from written sources rather than from members of the communities themselves.

But anthropology has come to understand culture differently since the 1970s, and practitioners of the discipline now view culture as contested, as differently understood even in a single, apparently homogeneous community, and as best represented from several angles of vision. We can now appreciate more fully that culture is as it is lived and practised and that contemporary Coast Salish people *are* the bearers of culture as they know it and act on it. They are not simply lesser versions of their ancestors, even though community members themselves often articulate this viewpoint. Current scholarship recognizes the importance of describing and analyzing the ways in which the state and Aboriginal communities relate today, and the ways in which culture, however it might be thought of and represented, is brought to bear politically. More generally, we can now focus not on how Aboriginal people have been assimilated or exterminated but, rather, on how they have persisted, on how they have created hybrid forms of culture, and on how some forms of cultural practice have been sequestered from outside view. We can understand that some cultural practices have been discarded and others enhanced. We can now work with a broad and interesting range of Aboriginal responses to contact and colonization rather than with the limited vocabulary of assimilation and resistance.

A period is now beginning in which a heightened rapprochement between disciplines can generate exciting new possibilities and in which Aboriginal concepts can play a direct part. There are now much richer answers to the question, "Who are the Coast Salish?" than there were a generation ago, and there is a new literature that enhances our understanding of the humanity of the community through accounts of individual leaders, innovators, and oral traditions. Attention is now being paid to the diversity of communities that were previously seen largely in terms of social classes, or adaptive responses to change, or as simply disappearing into the white world. It is hard to imagine what the issues will be in another twenty-five or fifty years. But the contemporary recognition of diversity allows for the development of insights into the growth of governance and community economic initiatives, as well as into the inequitable distribution of treaty rights to fishing and other resources. In addition, it sets the stage for contemplating what comes next in the Coast Salish world along the Salish Sea. I ask readers to "be of good mind" as they encounter the chapters herein. This is a phrase often heard in longhouse ritual, and, as Sonny McHalsie has said, it refers to the practice of avoiding bad thoughts (which can harm others) and of having faith that the work being undertaken together, in this case by scholars and community members, can continue.

Notes

1   Salishan is a language family comprised of languages and dialects spoken by Aboriginal peoples of British Columbia, Washington State, Montana, Oregon, and Idaho. The language family is divided into Coast Salishan and Interior Salishan (or, commonly, Salish), and there are social and cultural differences between the constituent groups, which often overlap within this division. Today, most but not all of the languages are threatened with extinction. This volume is not intended as a reader on the particular communities either in the United States or in Canada; rather it addresses them as a whole. Within the Coast Salish language grouping in Canada there are fifty current bands, some of which have changed their names in recent years. Most of the Canadian bands have small populations and are organized into tribal councils, umbrella organizations that provide an economy of scale in the provision of services. The membership of these councils varies as bands occasionally withdraw or join. Currently, the Hwlitsum are actively engaged in attempting to gain federal recognition.

There are twenty-four federally recognized Coast Salish tribes in Washington State, and several more are attempting to gain recognition. Among the prominent groups seeking recognition are the Steilacoom, the Duwamish, and the Snohomish. Some of the tribes are organized under the Small Tribes of Western Washington (STOWW), and most operate independently but participate in various intertribal consortia, such as the Northwest Intertribal Court system.

Concerning the question of terminology – communities in Canada are commonly known as "First Nations" and those in the United States are commonly known as "American Indians" or "Native Americans." But terminology is complex and changeable. Many people continue to refer to themselves and others as "Indians"; some community members regard this term as disrespectful and colonialist. The term "Aboriginal people" is sometimes employed as a cover term and "indigenous people" is used to refer to groups worldwide. In practice, all of these terms are used in Coast Salish communities, although "Aboriginal" and "Native" are more commonly used in Canada than they are in the United States.

2   It was anthropologist Barbara Lane, however, who authored the major reports presented for the tribes in this litigation.

3   I do not wish to suggest that the presence of a system of clans fully determines the affiliation of individuals; indeed, research shows that there are many ways in which demographic anomalies can be addressed, people can be reassigned to a new clan, or clan membership can be manipulated.

References

Abbott, Donald N., ed. 1981. *The World Is as Sharp as a Knife: An Anthology in Honour of Wilson Duff.* Victoria: British Columbia Provincial Museum.

Amoss, Pamela. 1978. *Coast Salish Spirit Dancing: The Survival of an Ancestral Religion.* Seattle: University of Washington Press.

Asher, Brad. 1999. *Beyond the Reservation: Indians, Settlers, and the Law in Washington Territory, 1853-1889.* Norman, OK: University of Oklahoma Press.

Bailey, F.G. 1980. *Strategems and Spoils: A Social Anthropology of Politics.* Oxford: Basil Blackwell.

Bierwert, Crisca, ed. 1996. *Lushootseed Texts: An Introduction to Puget Salish Narrative Aesthetics.* Lincoln: University of Nebraska Press.

–. 1999. *Brushed by Cedar, Living by the River: Coast Salish Figures of Power.* Tucson: University of Arizona Press.

Boas, Franz. 1889. The Indians of British Columbia. *Transactions of the Royal Society of Canada for 1888* 6 (2): 45-57.

Boxberger, Daniel L. 1989. *To Fish In Common: The Ethnohistory of Lummi Indian Salmon Fishing.* Lincoln: University of Nebraska Press.

Carlson, Keith Thor, ed. 1996. *You Are Asked to Witness: The Stó:lō in Canada's Pacific Coast History.* Chilliwack: Stó:lō Heritage Trust.

–, ed. 2001. *A Stó:lō Coast Salish Historical Atlas.* Vancouver/Chilliwack: Douglas and McIntyre/Stó:lō Heritage Trust.

–. 2003. The Power of Place, the Problem of Time: A Study of History and Aboriginal Collective Identity. PhD diss., University of British Columbia.

Clifford, James. 1988. *The Predicament of Culture: Twentieth Century Ethnography, Literature and Art.* Cambridge: Harvard University Press.

Elmendorf, William W. 1960. *The Structure of Twana Culture.* Washington State University Research Studies 28 (3), Monographic Supplement 2. Pullman, WA: Washington State University.

–. 1971. Coast Salish Status Ranking and Intergroup Ties. *Southwestern Journal of Anthropology* 27 (4): 353-80.

–. 1993. *Twana Narratives: Native Historical Accounts of a Coast Salish Culture.* Seattle: University of Washington Press.

Gibbs, George. 1877. Tribes of Western Washington and Northwestern Oregon. In *Contributions to North American Ethnology,* ed. John Wesley Powell, 1 (2) 157-361. Washington, DC: US Geographical and Geological Survey of the Rocky Mountain Region.

Grier, Colin. 2003. Dimensions of Regional Interaction in the Prehistoric Gulf of Georgia. In *Emerging from the Mist: Studies in Northwest Coast Culture History,* ed. R.G. Matson, Gary Coupland, and Quentin Mackie, 170-87. Vancouver: UBC Press.

Guilmet, George M., and David L. Whited. 1989. *The People Who Give More: Health and Mental Health among the Contemporary Puyallup Indian Tribal Community.* Denver, CO: National Center, University of Colorado Health Sciences Center, Department of Psychiatry.

Guilmet, George, Robert T. Boyd, David L. Whited, and Nile Thompson. 1991. The Legacy of Introduced Disease: The Southern Coast Salish. *American Indian Culture and Research Journal* 15: 1-32.

Hale, Horatio. 1846. *Ethnography and Philology: United States Exploring Expedition during the Years 1838, 1839, 1840, 1841, 1842.* Vol. 6. Philadelphia: Lea and Blanchard.

Harmon, Alexandra. 1998. *Indians in the Making: Ethnic Relations and Indian Identities around Puget Sound.* Berkeley: University of California Press.

Hawthorn, Harry, C.S. Belshaw, and S.M. Jamieson. 1958. *The Indians of British Columbia: A Study of Contemporary Social Adjustment.* Toronto/Vancouver: University of Toronto Press/University of British Columbia.

Kan, Sergei. 1989. *Symbolic Immortality: The Tlingit Potlatch of the Nineteenth Century.* Washington, DC: Smithsonian Institution.

Kew, J.E. Michael. 1970. Coast Salish Ceremonial Life: Status and Identity in a Modern Village. PhD diss., University of Washington.

Kew, J.E. Michael, and Bruce G. Miller. 1999. Locating Aboriginal Governments in the Political Landscape. In *Seeking Sustainability in the Lower Fraser Basin,* ed. Michael Healey, 47-63. Vancouver: Institute for Resources and the Environment, Westwater Research.

Knight, Rolf. 1978. *Indians at Work: An Informal History of Native Indian Labour in British Columbia, 1858-1930.* Vancouver: New Star Books.

Lévi-Strauss, Claude. 1982. *The Way of the Masks.* Trans. Sylvia Modelski. Vancouver: Douglas and McIntyre.

Lewis, Claudia. 1970. *Indian Families of the Northwest Coast: The Impact of Change.* Chicago: University of Chicago Press.

Marshall, Daniel. 1999. *Those Who Fell from the Sky: A History of the Cowichan Peoples.* Duncan, BC: Cowichan Tribes.

Mauss, Marcel. 1967. *The Gift: Forms and Functions of Exchange in Archaic Societies.* Introduction by E.E. Evans Pritchard. New York: W.W. Norton.

Mauzé, Marie, Michael E. Harkin, and Sergei Kan, eds. 2004. Editors' Introduction. In *Coming to Shore: Northwest Coast Ethnology, Traditions, and Visions,* xi-xxxviii. Lincoln: University of Nebraska Press.

McFeat, Tom, ed. 1966. *Indians of the North Pacific Coast.* Seattle: University of Washington Press.

Mierendorf, Robert R. 1993. *Chert Procurement in the Upper Skagit River Valley of the Northern Cascade Range, Ross Lake National Recreation Area, Washington.* Technical Report NPS/PNRNOCA/CRTR-93-001. Sedro Woolley, WA: North Cascades National Park Service Complex.

Miller, Bruce G. 1989a. After the FAP: Tribal Reorganization after Federal Acknowledgment. *Journal of Ethnic Studies* 17 (2): 89-100.

–. 1989b. The Election of Women to Tribal Office: The Upper Skagit Case. PhD diss., Arizona State University.

–. 1992. Women and Politics: Comparative Evidence from the Northwest Coast. *Ethnology* 31 (4): 367-83.

–. 2001. *The Problem of Justice: Tradition and Law in the Coast Salish World.* Lincoln: University of Nebraska Press.

–. 2003. *Invisible Indigenes: The Politics of Nonrecognition.* Lincoln: University of Nebraska Press.

–. 2004. Rereading the Ethnographic Record: The Problem of Justice in the Coast Salish World. In *Coming to Shore: Northwest Coast Ethnology, Traditions, and Visions,* ed. Marie Mauzé, Michael E. Harkin, and Sergei Kan, 279-304. Lincoln: University of Nebraska Press.

Miller, Bruce G., and Daniel L. Boxberger. 1994. Creating Chiefdoms: The Puget Sound Case. *Ethnohistory* 41 (2): 267-93.

Miller, Bruce G., and Jen Pylypa. 1995. The Dilemma of Mental Health Paraprofessionals at Home. *American Indian and Alaska Native Mental Health: The Journal of the National Center* 6 (2): 13-33.

Miller, Jay. 1999. *Lushootseed Culture and the Shamanic Odyssey: An Anchored Radiance.* Lincoln: University of Nebraska Press.

Mooney, Kathleen. 1976. Social Distance and Exchange: The Coast Salish Case. *Ethnology* 15 (4): 323-46.

Ruby, Robert H., and John A. Brown. 2001. *Esther Ross: Stillaguamish Champion.* Norman: University of Oklahoma Press.

Sampson, Martin J. 1972. *Indians of Skagit County.* Mt. Vernon, WA: Skagit County Historical Society.

Schaepe, David. 2006. Rock Fortifications: Archaeological Insights into Precontact Warfare and Sociopolitical Organization among the Sto:lo of the Lower Fraser River Canyon, B.C. *American Antiquity* 71 (4): 671-705.

Schaepe, David, Marianne Berkey, John Stamp, and Tia Halstad. 2004. Sumas Energy, Inc: Traditional Use Study – Phase Two: Stó:lō Cultural Relations to Air and Water. Stó:lō Nation with Arcas Consulting Archaeologists, Ltd.

Smith, Marian W. 1940. *The Puyallup-Nisqually.* New York: Columbia University Press.

Suttles, Wayne. 1951. Economic Life of the Coast Salish of Haro and Rosario Straits. PhD diss., Department of Anthropology, University of Washington.

–. 1960. Affinal Ties, Subsistence, and Prestige among the Coast Salish. *American Anthropologist* 62 (2): 296-305.

–. 1987. *Coast Salish Essays.* Seattle: University of Washington Press.

–, ed. 1990. *Handbook of North American Indians.* Vol. 7, *Northwest Coast.* Washington: Smithsonian Institution.

–. 2004. *Musqueam Reference Grammar.* Vancouver: UBC Press.

Suttles, Wayne, and Aldona C. Jonaitis. 1990. History of Research in Ethnology. In *Handbook of North American Indians.* Vol. 7, *Northwest Coast,* ed. Wayne Suttles, 73-87. Washington: Smithsonian Institution.

Swan, George. 1857. *The Northwest Coast: Or, Three Years' Residence in Washington Territory.* New York: Harper. Reprint, Seattle: University of Washington Press, 1972.

Swinomish Tribal Mental Health Project. 1991. *A Gathering of Wisdoms.* LaConner, WA: Swinomish Tribal Community.

Tennant, Paul. 1990. *Aboriginal Peoples and Politics: The Indian Land Question.* Vancouver: UBC Press.

Tollefson, Kenneth. 1987. The Snoqualmie: A Puget Sound Chiefdom. *Ethnology* 26 (2): 121-36.

–. 1989. Political Organization of the Duwamish. *Ethnology* 28: 135-50.

Turner, Nancy. 1975. *Food Plants of British Columbia Indians.* Part 1, *Coastal Peoples.* British Columbia Provincial Museum, Handbook 34. Victoria: British Columbia Provincial Museum.

Valentine, Lisa Philips, and Regna Darnell, eds. 1999. *Theorizing the Americanist Tradition.* Toronto: University of Toronto Press.

1
Coast Salish History

Alexandra Harmon

If there is one indispensable element of an ethnic identity, it is a collective history. Other characteristics – race, biological lineage, territorial concentration, language, religion, economic specialization, or unique customs – may set an ethnic group apart, but none is an essential "building block of ethnicity." Every ethnic group, however, relies on depictions of a common past to express and foster the idea that it consists of a single people with a distinct role in historical events. As anthropologist Manning Nash (1989, 5) observes, shared history "gives the sense of shared struggles, shared fate, common purpose, and the implication that personal and group fate are one and the same thing."[1]

By this measure, there does not appear to be a unitary Coast Salish ethnic group. Granted, there are people today who identify themselves in certain contexts as Coast Salish, some of whom have adopted the name to indicate a specific cluster of Aboriginal communities in southwest British Columbia.[2] But the term apparently originated with anthropologists and linguists for the purpose of denoting a more widely distributed set of indigenous North American peoples who spoke or speak related languages.[3] Although portions of the designated population have been the subjects of separate historical accounts, the many individuals and communities who fall within their own or others' definition of Coast Salish do not publicly claim a collective history that embraces them all.

Nevertheless, the notion of a single, inclusive Coast Salish history is not outlandish. On the contrary, anthropologists' concept of a Coast Salish people was inspired not only by linguistic similarities but also by evidence of past and persisting commonalities and connections of other sorts. The concept points to a useful way of framing a history – one that may be superior in some respects to the standard political frameworks. This chapter explains why that is so. Throughout the centuries for which we have written historical records, and probably for much longer, the people in question have associated and identified with each other on several levels, including levels that bridge tribal divisions and current international boundaries. In various combinations, they have shared experiences not only as residents of local communities and constituents of particular tribal organizations but also as members of extended families, as long-time inhabitants of a distinctive geographical region, and as people called "Indians," "Natives," or "Aboriginals."[4] No portrayal of these people is complete without an acknowledgment of the history they have in common.

If you look in conventional places for a general chronicle of Coast Salish experiences over time, you will look in vain. There are no comprehensive historical monographs or textbooks about such a group. Do a keyword search for "Coast Salish" and "history" in an electronic library catalogue, and a very short list of books will appear on the screen.[5] None claims to tell a sweeping story of the Coast Salish past. Drop the term "history," and your next search will yield a longer list that includes *Coast Salish Essays,* a much-cited collection of writings by the anthropologist Wayne Suttles. Most of Suttles' essays are historical in nature; that is, they consider past and changing circumstances and habits of the people he has studied. Not one, however, purports to be an inclusive narrative of Coast Salish history. Suttles does not even define "Coast Salish." He states merely that his essays "are concerned with the Central Coast Salish of southwestern British Columbia and northwestern Washington, the wider Coast Salish region, the whole Northwest Coast of North America, or in one instance, the Interior Salish of the Plateau" (Suttles 1987, xi). The only elaboration on this statement is a map that shows the locations of Aboriginal language groups along a stretch of America's North Pacific coast, but it does not indicate which are Coast Salish languages.

To ascertain what Suttles and other anthropologists mean by "Coast Salish," you might consult the magisterial encyclopaedia he edited, the *Handbook of North American Indians,* volume 7, *Northwest Coast.* There you will not see an explicit definition of "Coast Salish," but you will read that the term designates a family of fourteen languages spoken in the nineteenth century by indigenous peoples who inhabited three contiguous areas outlined on an accompanying map. The delineated areas stretch north from the Columbia River well into southwestern British Columbia. Switch to a current political map of the same territory, however, and you will not find the phrase "Coast Salish" (see Suttles 1990, 11, 14-15).[6]

To locate published histories that encompass people in the *Handbook's* Coast Salish category, you must search by other terms. Since most histories of Indians focus on a modern political jurisdiction, a region, a particular realm of human activity, or a combination of these, the obvious keywords are place names and the word "Indians" or its equivalents. And sure enough, if you consult histories of Indians in a jurisdiction such as British Columbia or a region such as Puget Sound, you will read about Coast Salish Indians, among others, though not always by that name. The ethnologists' Coast Salish are also among the people who get attention in books on law and governance, land policy, missionaries, and economic conditions affecting Indians of British Columbia or Washington State.[7]

On the other hand, to locate published histories that focus exclusively on Indians in the *Handbook*'s Coast Salish category, you need the names of smaller groups – usually identified as tribes or bands – or the names of geographical enclaves. You will not see those names in the *Handbook*'s Table of Contents. Instead, the encyclopaedia describes, in turn, the Aboriginal cultures of peoples it calls the Northern Coast Salish, Central Coast Salish, Southern Coast Salish, and Southwestern Coast Salish. Separate chapters cover Coast Salish experiences during the past two centuries and are also organized geographically, although by districts different from those selected for the chapters on Aboriginal cultures. Tribe or band names are sprinkled throughout these essays. Other possible sources for the names include publications of the Canadian Department of Indian Affairs and the United States Bureau of Indian Affairs or maps that show present Indian reserves and reservations within the historic territories of Coast Salish speakers (Carlson 1997; Hilbert and Bierwert 1980).[8]

At this point, you may protest that "Coast Salish" refers to people who have seldom had a hand in producing textbooks or scholarly histories; therefore, an inventory of such books is not the only or the best test of whether those people see themselves as a group with a common history. The point is a good one. Indian or Native societies have usually and necessarily told their histories in ways that do not depend on access to print media, including song and dance, the spoken word, and visual artistry (see McIlwraith 1996, 42, 62-64). On the other hand, a number of Indians have published their own written histories, especially in recent years. Among them are groups and individuals whose forebears match the *Handbook*'s definition of Coast Salish. Their publications, whether authored by Natives or by non-Natives working under Native direction, show how they wish to depict their history to outsiders as well as to each other. And none is a history *of* the Coast Salish *in toto;* rather, each is the story of a smaller group – a tribe or band. Typically, the term "Coast Salish" does not even appear in the publication (Carlson 1997; Hilbert and Bierwert 1980; Fish and Bedal 2000; Marshall 1999; Peterson 1990; Suquamish Museum 1985; and Sampson 1972).

This survey of historical literature might lead you to suspect that Coast Salish is solely an anthropological category, and one with dubious utility either for historians or for the people assigned to it. If so, you will be in thoughtful company. The Seminole historian Susan A. Miller (1998, 102), for example, knows of many "tribal thinkers" (including herself, apparently) who cannot "accept the grouping of ... tribal peoples by nontribal scholars into large categories according to esoterically perceived relations among their languages." Even anthropologists now profess mistrust of the classifications they inherited from their predecessors because, as Julie Cruikshank (1998, 2) notes, "Ideas about history, about political processes ... sometimes seemed to be missing from early ethnographies [the bases for most such classifications], leaving an impression that small-scale societies could be represented as isolated, self-contained units, colliding and glancing off one another but clearly bounded in a timeless stratum designated 'traditional.'"

Still, students of history would be unwise to repudiate the Coast Salish concept entirely. A close look at the anthropologists' research reveals that their taxonomy is based on significant historical facts. By analyzing the recorded observations of early non-Native visitors and interlopers, probing the memories of Native people, and taking note of customs passed down to Natives' heirs, anthropologists have determined that a region-wide system of intercommunity relations was a fundamental facet of Aboriginal life for Coast Salish speakers. Overlapping kin and social ties linked residents in each winter village directly or indirectly to residents of other villages. Wayne Suttles (1990, 15) summarizes his colleagues' findings as follows: "Networks of intermarriage and cooperation in economic and ceremonial activities among neighboring tribes regardless of language made the whole Coast Salish region a kind of social continuum." Because of such interconnections, which did not disintegrate when foreign trading ships and colonists arrived in the eighteenth and nineteenth centuries, there is reason to hypothesize that so-called Coast Salish peoples do indeed have a shared history.

Ironically, a good way to see the historical utility of the broad Coast Salish classification is to focus on the smallest possible unit of analysis: the individual.[9] Not coincidentally, it is anthropologists who have collected many of the personal stories that reveal and explain the interlinkages of the various Coast Salish groups. Paul Fetzer recorded one such story from a man named George Swanaset. Swanaset's narrative of his life, from birth in 1871 until Fetzer's interview of him in 1951, depicts an Indian society whose geographical scope was determined not by jurisdictional lines but by far-reaching networks of family ties and social relations. A person who identified with that society typically paired loyalty to fellow residents of a particular place with loyalty to relatives and friends in other "tribes" and places. He or she could belong to more than one "community" simultaneously, and the relative importance of those various affiliations changed with time and circumstance.

For George Swanaset, the proper way to begin a life story was to recite his lineage, in geographical as well as social and ethnic terms.[10] Although his "high-born" paternal grandparents "were Langley people," he said, his father bore a name that "was way deep in that Tsawwassen history" because he "was related pretty close to the Tsawwassen." "On my father's side," Swanaset added, "I was related to Samish." On his mother's side, Swanaset had a white in-law and some half-siblings whose father was "a Spaniard." George's maternal grandmother, who was from Cowichan, married a "high-born" man from yet another community. George began life at Sumas Bar, the community his pregnant mother returned to after leaving George's father. A few years later, "Long Johnny came up to Sumas and got her." Long Johnny was from the Nooksack Valley in the United States, a country that Swanaset would ultimately refer to as home.[11]

Over the course of a long life Swanaset resided, visited, and worked in divers places on both sides of the line between British Columbia and Washington. He had an assortment of companions in these peregrinations, most of whom he considered relatives. His travels started early. "When I was just a boy," he told Fetzer,

> George _____ asked Mother if I could go with him to Swinomish and she said alright, so I went with him to Swinomish where they were having _____ – the Samish from Guemes Is. were returning the Swinomish favor. The Lummis were joined with the Samish in this, and so my mother's relatives, Patrick and Louie Geo. came down from Lummi, with a canoe-full of eats. During this time, Louie, who was living on Orcas Is., asked Geo. _____ if he could take me out there with him, so I went and stayed there for 3 years and I got acquainted with the way they went out there.[12]

George attended two residential schools for Indians, one in the Nooksack district and one on Vancouver Island. A Christian like his mother, he participated in Methodist "camp meetings ... at Chilliwack [in Canada] and Ferndale [in Washington], where the whites and Indians would come together for a week." Baseball games, weddings, and funerals also drew people from the various communities that constituted George's world. At his own first wedding, he recalled, "there were people from Sumas, Matsqui, Lummi, and Cultus Lake; and many Nooksack families." He and his bride moved in with a friend on the Washington side of the border, but George "used to go across the line to the Fraser River to gill-net, working for different canneries." During the fall and spring he found employment south of the border, cutting wood for steam engines, steamboats, and shingle mills in Bellingham. Widowed after a few years, George took a second wife from British Columbia; and for that reason, he later worked and lived a while at New Westminster and then at Katzie. When his second wife proved unfaithful, he went back to the Nooksack area.

By Swanaset's account, his Nooksack friends pressed him into a leadership position in their Indian community. "In my early days," he said, "Geo. _____ was regarded as the chief of the whole tribe in all serious matters. The Lyndens were not included in this, because they had homesteaded together." By the early twentieth century, though, "whenever there would be a case involving one of our people in Bellingham, they'd come for either Jim Antone or me." After Antone died in the great flu epidemic of 1918, the people made Swanaset their chief by acclamation at a big tribal meeting. Like groups "all over Puget Sound," who had formed an organization called the Northwestern Federation of American Indians, Nooksack Indians were gearing up to sue the United States government for dispossessing and neglecting them. When federation officers asked the Nooksacks to name someone who could present their case for a bill to authorize suit, a committee chose George "on account of [his] understanding of the old boundaries and ... the nature of the claim." But Swanaset confessed that he was uninformed about the tribe's status under US law until the local government agent said "the Nooksacks weren't treaty Indians."

After the Court of Claims squelched Nooksack hopes for compensation, "there was trouble in the tribe," George said. "Some thought that because I was not an offspring of this tribe I should be turned out. It was about 50-50 but I lost ... My friends ... thought it didn't make any difference who was chief as long as he could carry on with the old customs." George's friends were numerous or influential enough that he subsequently served as a councilman in a reorganized Nooksack tribal government.

Immersing himself in Nooksack affairs did not mean neglecting the affiliations that had always facilitated Swanaset's circulation within a wider social sphere. Far from it. Mingled with accounts of his political activities are reminiscences about visits to, favours from, and other bonding relations with friends and relatives scattered across southwestern British Columbia and western Washington. Those social ties took visible form, affirming George's prestige and intricate lineage, whenever a loved one died. Mourners came to the funerals from all his familiar haunts. Naming the communities represented at a funeral, as he did each time he told Fetzer about a relative's death, was Swanaset's way of declaring membership and claiming distinguished status in a far-flung, heterogeneous community that had time-honoured ways of recognizing its own.

Four interrelated themes run through Swanaset's narrative: his family members' diverse places of origin and residence; his pride in and cultivation of social contacts in myriad locations; his geographical mobility; and his identification as an adult with one local "tribe." Swanaset took pains to name his kin and friends throughout the region around the Puget Sound and the Strait of Georgia. By visiting, travelling to worksites, relocating, hosting visitors, taking two successive wives, arranging the marriages of younger relatives, participating in recreational and political activities, and sponsoring and attending ceremonial gatherings, he periodically confirmed, renewed, and expanded his and his family's social connections. From that perspective, the boundary between Canada and the United States had little or no meaning for George Swanaset. For some purposes, however, he claimed the rights of a US resident and a tribe that looked to the US government for patronage and redress. He saw no contradiction between his international kinship ties or mobility and his allegiance to Indians of the Nooksack Valley. And although he welcomed or accepted relations with non-Indians and embraced aspects of non-Indian culture from Christianity to baseball, he retained a strong sense of belonging to a different society – an Indian society. In fact, telling tribal history and his personal history to non-Indian outsiders, such as lawmakers or Paul Fetzer, served to confirm Swanaset's status as an Indian and Nooksack tribe member. With every individual and group name that he dropped into the conversation, he identified another filament in the net of social ties that defined who he was and where he belonged.

Not once in his narrative, as recorded, did George Swanaset say the words "Coast Salish." Yet, arguably, that phrase is useful shorthand for the principal social context of his life. In all but one of his anecdotes about Indians, the characters appear to fit ethnographers' conception of the Coast Salish. Referring to them as Coast Salish does no greater violence to Swanaset's way of thinking than does calling them Indians of southwestern British Columbia and western Washington or using the names of their different "tribal" communities. Swanaset himself did not name the extensive region he called home, although it was obviously important to his sense of self, and he identified people as often by their place of residence as by the tribal labels then in use.

The themes of George Swanaset's narrative are those that most of his ancestors, descendants, and Indian acquaintances (and their ancestors and descendants) would probably have emphasized if induced to talk about their own lives. Swanaset's account lends animation and colour to a picture that appears in clear outline when we assemble other evidence of Native activities in the region during the past two centuries. Government reports, censuses, recorded reminiscences, and anthropologists' observations show a persistent flow and intermingling of people from and among the many pockets of Indian population around northwestern Washington and southwestern British Columbia.

For example, early in the 1900s, the US Office of Indian Affairs (OIA) made an effort to locate Indians of western Washington who had previously escaped its notice. A special OIA investigator learned and documented not only that Indians regularly married and moved across supposed tribal lines but also that the international border was no barrier to marriages and movement. Along with the information on the great number of Indians who moved among tribal enclaves in Washington, he collected data on dozens of people who had birthplaces, former residences, and relatives in Canada (Bishop and Roblin 1911-19; *Report of the Commissioner of Indian Affairs* 1854-55, 450).

Three decades later, the anthropologist June Collins heard from an elderly Native man about one reason for that cross-border fraternization: ceremonial gatherings. John Fornsby, an octogenarian from the Skagit River district of Washington, told Collins (who referred to him as a Coast Salish Indian) that "Victoria Indians" attended a "potlatch" his father gave during the late 1800s. An aunt brought her Nooksack relatives to the same event. The guest list reflected and facilitated relationships of other types between members of the different communities, which may explain why Fornsby had a grandson who became "chief" of "the Victorias." Many people in the grandson's generation made cross-border connections as well. About the time Collins interviewed Fornsby, another researcher in the Skagit community found that Indians from north and south of the border were periodically converging there for traditional religious ceremonies. As late as the 1970s, when Pamela Amoss studied similar religious practices among the Nooksacks, their ceremonies routinely drew Indians from multiple locales in British Columbia and Washington (Collins 1949, 316, 325; Wike 1941, i, 3; Amoss 1978, 27-28; Suttles 1963, 512-25; Galloway 1990, vii-viii; Nugent 1982, 75, 76; Mooney 1976, 325).

Relying on evidence of this kind, scholars have reached a strong consensus that wide-ranging social connections and multiple or layered group affiliations have characterized Coast Salish speakers and their progeny from precolonial to modern times. A diversity of local customs and circumstances has not kept people from forging chains of kinship between communities.

Individuals have associated and identified not only with nuclear family members, housemates, and village neighbours but also with assorted cousins and other shirt-tail relatives distributed in various coves and valleys kilometres away. Because of the Coast Salish preference for marriage outside the local community and their custom of reckoning lineage bilaterally, the webs of kinship have been extensive, especially among the well-to-do, most of whom have consequently had a choice of family affiliations. "At different times in ... life, depending on the circumstances," June Collins (1979, 244) explains, a person might select "one or another of the many descent lines available." Frequently, choosing a "descent line" has even meant choosing a new place to live. Thanks to exchanges of personnel, some individuals in virtually every local settlement have had relatives and personal experiences in other Indian communities. Along with the relocating people have come folklore and other knowledge, including the songs, dances, and stories that constitute a major part of family histories (see Allen 1976, 163-69; Amoss 1978, 27, 28; Collins 1974, 11, 118).

When we think about the history of people who have linked themselves to each other in this manner, it behooves us to think outside the box, especially the political or jurisdictional box. Why define our subject by such conventional parameters as the boundaries of Canada, the United States, British Columbia, the State of Washington, or specific Indian reserves or reservations when Indians have not defined themselves and their associations solely by those parameters? Political boundaries have provided many a historian with a default focus of study, but they have not limited Native people's range of operations or self-images.

Historians' habit of focusing on Indians in a particular political jurisdiction is a legacy of colonialism. After Britain and the United States agreed to divide the Pacific Northwest between them in 1846, the severed territories and their inhabitants were targets of differing government mandates and subjects of separate government record-keeping. The colonial powers proceeded as though the Aboriginal peoples within their borders could be corralled and grouped in convenient administrative units whose primary building blocks were village populations. Officials and bureaucrats then generated records that lend themselves to compartmentalized histories. But compartmentalized histories belie the fact that Native peoples were not so easily sorted and segregated.

Each colony – the United States and the Canadian province of British Columbia and its predecessors – asserted a legal right to all the land within its purported boundaries. Each tried to isolate Indians on small reserved tracts. In no case, however, did the colonial rulers confine all Indians to those tracts. Like the Nooksacks of George Swanaset's story, many Coast

Salish speakers and their descendants never lived on the reserves. Those who did could usually leave without penalty, even during periods when they were the targets of oppressive government resocialization campaigns. They left, among other reasons, to continue customary subsistence activities or engage in new ones, often in the company of Indians from other settlements. John Fornsby, for example, supervised Indian crews who worked at off-reservation hop ranches. As Fornsby and Swanaset knew, Indians could also leave the nation-state that claimed jurisdiction over them. Uncounted hundreds crossed the international line to visit friends and relatives, earn money, attend school, find mates, establish new homes, or assume new legal identities (Miller 1996-97, 74; Collins 1949, 329).

Colonial officials declared a new order but could not unfailingly enforce their decrees. Years after Skagit headmen signed a treaty promise to restrict their intercourse with people in Canada, John Fornsby saw Indians from Vancouver Island at a Skagit potlatch. Moreover, the potlatch took place at a time when American and Canadian authorities were trying to suppress such "uncivilized" practices. Beyond the reach of reservation officials, Fornsby also participated in other forbidden ceremonies.[13] And George Swanaset's mother evaded Canadian officials' watchful gaze when she joined her new husband in a community of Indians who had declined to live where US government officials expected them to live.

While seemingly subjected to colonial rule, then, people of Native ancestry continued to associate with each other in ways that hinged more on Aboriginal notions of kinship and respect for local customs than on government edicts. Granted, the proclamation of an international dividing line, the authorities' allocation of Natives to specified Indian enclaves, and statutory definitions of "Indian," "band," and "tribe" eventually prompted Natives to recharacterize their local affiliations for some purposes.[14] For instance, by middle age George Swanaset called himself a Nooksack Indian, at least when dealing with agents of the US government. Yet Swanaset's initial reasons for joining his stepfather's "tribe" in Washington State had little or nothing to do with colonial legalities. And he apparently paid no heed to colonial divisions when there were fish to catch in British Columbia. By Aboriginal custom, he could fish where there were people who regarded him as kith or kin.

Even after he became a spokesman for the Nooksack Tribe, Swanaset remained part of a larger Indian community that extended beyond the reach of American law. And why not? Law was a recent, foreign imposition. The United States and Canada, treaties between tribal "chiefs" and colonial sovereigns, written rules and centralized law enforcement, reservations and reserves, racial categories such as Indian and white – all were unknown in Coast Salish territories until a generation before Swanaset's birth. It is hardly surprising that those alien impositions did not promptly replace indigenous ways of ordering the world. Few non-Indians, however, knew the extent or meanings of the social and economic patterns that linked Natives to each other in defiance of categories such as Canadian, American, Nooksack, Tsawwassen, status Indian, or treaty Indian. Moving much of the time on the margins of colonial society and motivated by values and loyalties invisible to officials, Indians often eluded jurisdictional radar.

Over time, most people of Native descent also resisted schemes intended to erase the cultural markers of their "Indianness," detribalize them, and meld them into colonial society. Many have identified as tribe members in spite of laws or racial ideology assigning them to a different category. For example, during the US government's search for unenrolled Washington Indians, a man named William Price presented himself as a Klallam Indian even though his father was Welsh and his mother was a "full blood" from "Bella Colla" or some other "Alaska tribe." Price apparently based his self-identification on his birth in Aboriginal Klallam territory, his residence as an adult at an off-reservation Klallam camp known as Boston, and his Klallam neighbours' confirmation of his history. "I was with the white people ever since I was four years old," he explained to the OIA investigator, "but these Indians in Boston know more about me then I do they all know me" (Bishop and Roblin 1911-19 [spelling error appears in original]).

By carrying on relations with each other according to precolonial custom, the Boston Klallam and other Indians throughout a large contiguous area have experienced a history that does not fit within jurisdictional lines drawn by non-Indians. The family affairs, travels, and intercommunity associations described by George Swanaset are fundamental components of that history, for they have promoted a shared sense of a collective past – a Native past. They have stitched innumerable lives together, one marriage or visit or other thread of kinship at a time, and thus fashioned a patchwork-quilt history that is arguably broad enough to cover most of the people whose ancestors spoke a Coast Salish language. Scattered across the quilt are pieces representing the histories of localized settlements; but attached securely to those pieces and running between them are dozens and dozens of interlaced family histories. In other words, because of their extensive interactions, Indians of northwestern Washington and southwestern British Columbia may have a common history after all. For lack of a better term, we might call it a Coast Salish history.

However, mixed with the evidence of a Coast Salish history is evidence requiring two caveats. Again, George Swanaset's narrative is instructive. First, his narrative contains an anecdote suggesting that ethnographers'

"Coast Salish" category is too narrow to encompass some important, shared Native experiences. During the Great Depression, Swanaset went to the Klamath Indian Reservation in southern Oregon "to see the country." There he "got a job helping spray the timber for bugs" and "saw how they really carried their customs," which seemed the same as his. "I told them the history of our struggles here," he said proudly. In other words, Swanaset did not choose Native associates who fit the Coast Salish classification only; he felt an affinity for additional Native people and perhaps for "Indians" in general (Fetzer n.d., 26-27).

In this respect, too, Swanaset was true to ancestral tradition and representative of many of his peers. Even before colonization, the people who spoke Coast Salish languages did not plant an impassable fence around themselves. Their relations extended in some instances to nearby speakers of unrelated tongues. William Price was not the only Indian from beyond the Coast Salish pale who was integrated into a Coast Salish group. In fact, relations with members of more remote tribes increased after colonization because Coast Salish people encountered them at trading posts, boarding schools, seats of government, and other colonial venues (Harmon 1998, 36-37).[15] By the early twentieth century, Natives in British Columbia as well as Washington State had established multi-tribal organizations that mirrored the white view of them as members of a single race. In succeeding decades, it became commonplace for the descendants of diverse indigenous peoples to think of themselves as Indians and to assume that Indians shared history and traditions distinguishing them from non-Indians (see Nagel 1996, 101, 116-17, 121; Cornell 1988, 126; Tennant 1990, 137-38).

Swanaset's narrative requires a second, more significant caveat to the conclusion that the Coast Salish have a shared history. His story shows that categories narrower than Coast Salish – even or especially the small enclaves and administrative units favoured by colonial authorities – have by no means been irrelevant to Indians' sense of their group membership and traditions. On the contrary, Indians in the Coast Salish region have had unique experiences at local levels, with marked consequences for their identities. In Swanaset's case, the US government's assertion of jurisdiction over Indians and its ways of grouping and dealing with them ultimately influenced him to attribute greater or different significance to his Nooksack affiliation than he might otherwise have done.

By the time he spoke with Paul Fetzer, Swanaset had a reputation as a leader of the Nooksack Tribe. His political career began when people in the community asked him to speak for them in American forums on questions of Nooksack legal status and property rights under US law. The tribe he spoke for was itself a political-administrative entity that had come to life under laws of the United States. Later, Swanaset joined a more formal tribal government, organized as permitted by a US statute of 1934. The new tribal organization encompassed the "Lyndens" that Swanaset mentioned as well as other bands of Indians whose previous relationships with the Nooksacks had been more social than political. If, instead of remaining among the Nooksacks, Swanaset had permanently relocated to either of the communities where he took a wife, he would have owed the conditions of his political life, his property rights, and probably his tribal designation to laws and policies formulated in Canada rather than the United States. He would have lived among people whose experiences under Canadian governance differed in notable ways from the Nooksacks' history.

The Nooksack chapters of Swanaset's story thus reveal a paradox that complicates any attempt to view Coast Salish history in the aggregate. Indians from Coast Salish Aboriginal areas have often acted as though international and tribal boundaries did not matter to them, but those boundaries and their consequences have in some respects mattered a great deal. American jurisdiction resulted in legal institutions that eventually channelled Swanaset's energies and influenced his self-image. Under different political jurisdictions, Indian populations have evolved differently. Laws have determined which people have been counted as Indians in particular circumstances, whether and where those people have had land and political privileges, which government services they have received, and who their associates have been for purposes such as resource use and self-government. New or redefined tribal groups have been the result. As the legal scholar Carole Goldberg-Ambrose notes, law has the power to promote or support "particular forms and scope of community" or a "particular focus of identity" for Indians. It "can create an official vocabulary for the discussion of group life that reinforces certain conceptions of political identity and excludes others" (Goldberg-Ambrose 1994, 1123-24). People of Coast Salish descent – for all their networking, mobility, and creative evasion of government directives – have not been immune to the law's influences on their identity (see Barman 1999).

More specifically and especially, the 1846 division of Coast Salish homelands between the United States and Britain has had practical repercussions that figure prominently in and distinguish the histories of current local communities. On the south side of the border, the US government dealt with indigenous populations from the beginning as though they were landholding nations. During the 1850s, federal agents promised in treaties to compensate named tribes for ceding all but a few specified tracts of land between the Cascade Mountains and the Pacific Ocean above Grays Harbor. North of the international border, however, most colonial officials were unwilling to take the same approach. At first the Crown delegated the supervision of Indian affairs to the Hudson's Bay Company, whose chief officer paid a dozen Aboriginal groups for some land on Vancouver Island and promised in written contracts that the groups would have continued use of their village sites and enclosed fields. A few years later, colonial governors assumed responsibility for dealing with Indians of British Columbia and explicitly eschewed such treaties, contending that the Aboriginal inhabitants had no compensable right to land or resources. Grudgingly and sometimes tardily, they just set aside scattered patches of ground for a few Native families each. These Canadian and American government actions differed significantly in their aims and, thus, in their long-term impacts on affected populations, although neither government achieved all its goals. Whereas the United States purported to create larger tribes by consolidating sundry communities on as few reservations as possible, the dominant policy in southwestern British Columbia was to keep Natives separated in small bands (Harmon 1998, chap. 3; Tennant 1990, chaps. 3 and 4; Harris 2002, chaps. 2-7).

Additional details suggest how the histories of Coast Salish communities diverged because of such dissimilar government policies. When American negotiators convened a treaty conference at Point Elliott in 1855, they thought they were dealing with more than ten named Indian tribes or bands, yet they agreed to reserve only four tracts of land for those groups. Vaguely aware that intermarriage facilitated relations between the supposed tribes, they expected each reservation to house multiple tribes, some of which would relocate. A reservation at the mouth of the Skagit River was supposed to attract not only nearby peoples on Puget Sound known as Samish, Swinomish, and Lower Skagit but also two or three tribes in the Cascade foothills. For Indians on the upper Nooksack River, the closest reservation was on a peninsula downstream, already home to people with whom Nooksack relations were historically edgy. Although the government never herded all Indians onto the reserved lands, its policies did eventually result in several reservation populations composed of two or more previously autonomous bands (Harmon 1998, chaps. 4-6).

Just on the other side of the international frontier, neighbours of the Nooksack contended with authorities who proceeded quite differently. In 1858, under siege by gold seekers rushing to their territory, Indians in the Fraser River Valley extracted a pledge from British Columbia's governor that he would secure their home and fishing sites. Because it was not a formal treaty, this vague promise was the governor's to break or reinterpret. He and his successors claimed the power to decide unilaterally whether and where to establish reserves. Eventually, they reduced the Natives' land base to a string of small tracts administered as separate entities, despite the Fraser River bands' close affiliations (Carlson 1997, 59-82; Harris 2002, 141-44).[16]

Even within US or Canadian jurisdiction, the makeup and histories of Coast Salish groups have varied with differences in the degree and nature of government impact on their lives. For example, after the treaty signed at Point Elliott, both Indians and US officials took diverse tacks in managing Indian-white relations, with divergent consequences for the various Indian populations' cohesiveness and status under law. To those people who did settle on the reservations, federal employees provided assorted services, occasional material aid, and a modicum of protection from resentful non-Indians. But reservation supervisors also insisted on conformity to "civilized" mores and engineered changes in group leadership. Other Native people, including those on the upper Nooksack and Skagit rivers, remained off the reservations, farther from government surveillance but exposed to the machinations of land-hungry and intolerant non-Indian settlers. Federal officials vacillated between neglecting the off-reservation Indians and asserting the power to treat them as government wards. But in the 1930s, when Congress offered most Indians the chance to establish sanctioned tribal governments, administrators declined to apply the new law to several off-reservation groups, apparently because the groups lacked a federally protected land base. Within two or three decades, the Bureau of Indian Affairs had ceased to recognize the landless Indians as tribes, adding significantly to the difficulties those people faced as they tried to maintain enough group cohesion to safeguard common interests (Harmon 1998, chaps. 4, 5, and 6).

In sum, Indians of the so-called Coast Salish region may have a common history, but they also have local group histories so numerous and disparate that a masterful storyteller would struggle to fold them into a coherent, single narrative. This multiplicity and diversity of local histories partly explains why historians have not been able to see the Coast Salish forest for the tribal trees. But the overriding reason for the fragmentation of Coast Salish historical accounts is the allocation of Coast Salish territory between two nation-states. Nation-states have exercised a powerful influence not only on the lives of Indians but also on the vision of historians.

The historian David Thelen (1999, 965) points out that his profession evolved in tandem with modern national governments, "its mission to document and explain the rise, reform, and fall of nation-states." As a consequence, history scholars long overlooked or underrated the significance of many phenomena that span national borders. But recent developments and scholarship – the collapse of powerful states such as the Soviet Union, persuasive historical analyses of nationalism, comparative studies of ethnicity by anthropologists and sociologists – have opened historians' eyes to the "fragile, constructed, imagined" character of nation-states. Thelen is one of many who now want to see more histories with a transnational focus. It is important, he declares, to understand how people, "moving through time and space according to rhythms and relationships of their own, drew from, ignored, constructed, transformed, and defied claims of the nation-state" (ibid.).[17]

Native Americans whose homelands and kin groups were bisected by nation-state boundaries are appropriate subjects for the studies Thelen has in mind.[18] The peoples that ethnographers call the Coast Salish, reconceived as a transnational population with persistent interconnections, would fill the bill. By keeping all the presumed Coast Salish in our field of vision as we follow them through time, we could augment our understanding of the power of nation-states to reshape group identities in general and Indian identities in particular.

Formidable challenges await anyone who tries to do this. Some of the challenges are methodological and practical. Because the story encompasses people in two countries, not to mention several dozen diverse residential communities, the sources of information and events that must be covered are dauntingly plentiful. Defining and naming the subjects of the story is difficult as well. Deciding on a "Coast Salish" framework does not obviate the need to decide more precisely whom to focus on and what to call them. Over more than two hundred years, some Aboriginal groups have disbanded or merged, new groups have formed, existing groups have changed form and nature, and most groups have borne multiple names. Should the story begin with all the Aboriginal Coast Salish and, if so, as defined by whom or using a name or names supplied by whom? Do all descendants of the defined group belong in the story? If not, which ones do belong? To answer the last question, should a researcher identify current groups that claim a historical link to the Aboriginal Coast Salish and work backward? Or does such an approach beg a question that requires investigation?

Equally if not more daunting is the fact that a collective history of the Coast Salish peoples would buck a trend of great import to Indians today – a deepening preoccupation with the histories of specific present-day tribes. Aware that the power to tell their histories is inseparable from the power to determine who they are, Indians are asserting the right – even an exclusive right, in some places – to be their own historians (Miller 1998, 106-7).[19] They are establishing museums and archives, recording oral traditions, commissioning history publications, and conducting public education programs with historical content. And, in virtually every instance, Indians in the Pacific Northwest are choosing to tell – usually with fierce pride – the history of one tribe or band rather than all the tribes or bands in Aboriginal Coast Salish territory.[20]

There are discomfiting ironies in this choice. For one, the impulse to focus on and exalt tribal or reservation histories arises in part because of policies, laws, administrative pigeonholing, and racialized classifications that originated with non-Indians. When colonial regimes made special promises to or provisions for "Indians" and Aboriginal tribes or bands – when they negotiated treaties, established land reserves, or awarded compensatory payments – they made it necessary to identify and define the intended beneficiaries. In many cases since then, people of Native ancestry have related their histories in order to show that they meet government definitions of "Indian," "tribe," or "band" and are therefore entitled to particular resources, eligible for certain services, or exercising an inherent sovereignty. Those objectives have given some of them reason to recast their historic group affiliations (Tennant 1990, 181-84; Harmon 1998, 238-39; Niezen 2003, 242-43; Harkin 1996, 7; Allen 1976, 169).[21]

For instance, during the 1920s, when Indians of western Washington asked Congress for permission to file legal claims stemming from treaty relations, spokesmen for several tribes (including George Swanaset) testified about their history. Legislators would authorize lawsuits only by successors to nineteenth-century tribes and lawsuits seeking monetary compensation for property losses. Understandably, rather than describing the tribes at treaty time as vague, fluid groups and emphasizing the custom of sharing local resources with visiting kin, the Indian witnesses described corporate bodies that had exclusive possession of well-defined domains. A representative of the "Suattle Tribe" insisted that its members, though located on the upper Skagit River, "were not a part of the Skagit Tribe ... were at all times enemies and were at war with the Skagit Tribe on several occasions."[22]

Since the 1970s, federal regulations have encouraged similar depictions of tribal history by western Washington groups who want the Bureau of Indian Affairs to recognize them as tribes named in treaties. Recognition brings economic and legal support for governmental status under US law. To succeed, a petition for recognition must include proof that group members have an unbroken history of association based on common descent, attachment to an ancestral territory, and allegiance to an enduring tribal polity, even though land loss and some federal policies during the past 150 years have worked to scatter the members, divide families, and frustrate meaningful self-government (Harmon 1998, chap. 7 and Epilogue; Castile 1996).

It is ironic, as well, that Indians have often had to rely on the writings and testimony of non-Indians to make a case for their tribes' historical continuity. Those non-Indians usually include anthropologists and government officials whose own cultures and objectives influenced them to describe the tribes as more static, homogeneous, and self-contained than they probably were.[23]

At the same time, both intentionally and unintentionally, non-Indians have made it difficult for Indians to pass down Aboriginal traditions and memories of the distant past. Colonial rulers banned or discouraged "uncivilized" practices such as the ceremonial feasts and give-aways (commonly called potlatches) where guests were enjoined to remember and tell others about the accomplishments, lineages, and relationships that structured the Native world. Government agents put children in schools whose mission was to eradicate Indian culture. Colonists also carried germs and created conditions that caused Native people – especially the learned elders and their potential young pupils – to die in shocking numbers (Boyd 1990; Guilmet et al. 1991, 8). These assaults tore holes in the unwritten pages of most group histories. To fill the voids, Indians have turned at times to non-Indian scholars for information, particularly to ethnographers and anthropologists. The Suquamish Tribe, for example, based its historical museum exhibit in part on elders' reminiscences but also on early twentieth-century ethnographers' reconstructions of Aboriginal culture in the larger central Puget Sound area. Today, anthropologists warn that many such ethnographies reflect the writers' biases, including their concepts of social and political organization, at least as much as they reflect Indian worldviews. Nonetheless, contemporary Indians, hoping to identify their present organizations with robust Aboriginal societies, have embraced some ethnographies as tribal history (Suquamish Museum 1985, biblio.; Cruikshank 1998, 2; Harkin 1996, 1, 3).[24]

For Indians who seek greater respect from outsiders and greater power to manage their own communities, tribal histories can be vital tools. A petition for federal recognition in the United States or a claim to land in British Columbia entails the identification of a current tribe or band with a precolonial society that was discrete and self-governing (Harris 2002, 296-97). When scholars complicate this picture of Indians' history by describing a fluid, supratribal society or arguing that tribal governments evolved in response to postcolonial conditions, they may seem to threaten Indians' quest for power. Consequently, historians and anthropologists who contend that tribal identities have been ambiguous and variable do not always find favour with tribal leaders and history-keepers. As Julie Cruikshank (1998, 162) remarks, scholars began shining a light on the porous and dynamic nature of Native group boundaries "just about the time that indigenous organizations began to recognize the strategic value of using such concepts as 'tradition' and 'boundedness' as a framework to present their claims to collective rights and distinctive identity." The scholars' "emerging preferences for deconstruction may now be viewed as offensive or even as harmful to indigenous people's struggles."[25]

A broad Coast Salish perspective on history may therefore seem of little practical use or even seem dangerous to individual tribes that are struggling for respect and resources. But tribes should not have to deny or apologize for the fact they are composed of people who can claim histories both as tribe members and as Indians belonging to a much larger distinctive group. Indeed, there is reason to rejoice that tribe members have multilayered histories, including a layer of history that is as wide as ethnographers' Coast Salish culture area. When explaining their current tribal associations, members may claim one kind of history, but that does not preclude them from claiming other histories to explain additional group affiliations. Their layered history can be a source of pride. It is the legacy of a sophisticated, far-reaching, and versatile social system that has helped its participants cope with change, giving most of them more than one possible place to belong. The history that links Indians in the present to the world of three hundred years ago, in which most people spoke a Coast Salish language, can be an integral component of a satisfying identity. It is a connection to the considerable power of *inter*connection.

In addition to revealing an important and empowering continuity in Native social traditions, a broad view of Coast Salish history can impart useful lessons about Indians' history in general. It demonstrates that social, racial, and political categories – categories such as kin, Indian, and Nooksack – are not prescribed by nature and are neither universal nor eternal. As they were for George Swanaset, they are the evolving results of childhood learning and later experiences, of comparisons and contrasts among people, of interactions and negotiations in specific historical circumstances, of reactions to shifting power and incentives. Even the most basic assumptions – assumptions about the relationship of identity to birth or residence, for instance – are not universal but vary from person to person, group to group, and historical period to historical period. The governments of nation-states have had considerable power to reshape those assumptions. Accordingly, they have prompted changes in the ways that people of Aboriginal descent have imagined and represented their group relationships. But the powers of nation-states to define or redefine "Indians" and their group identities have also had telling limits. Those powers and their limits are apparent from George Swanaset's life story and, by extension, from the complex, multifaceted history of the Aboriginal people he knew – especially people whom anthropologists call the Coast Salish.

The quests of contemporary Indians for empowering histories are reminiscent of the quests for spirit power that were a central feature of Aboriginal Coast Salish life. Before non-Indians came and Aboriginal religious ideas diversified, virtually all members of respectable families sought power from immortal beings or spirits who wanted human partners. Without help from spirits, they believed, a human lacked the capacity to perform socially useful acts such as healing, acquiring wealth, making canoes, or speaking eloquently. But with power bestowed by spirits, individuals secured respected places in regional society. Like the Indians today who solicit information about their past from elders, young people then depended on elders to teach them how to secure power. In some groups an empowering partnership could even be inherited from an elder (Collins 1979, 247-48, 251). And, like the Indians today who wish to tell their histories publicly, individuals in the past depended on family, friends, and neighbours to help them when the time came to sing their spirit helpers' songs.

Historical heritage now has a role similar to spirit power for many people in British Columbia and Washington State who identify themselves as Indians. Much as their indigenous ancestors expected respect for "having something" from spirit helpers, they hope to be respected for "having" history that links them to those ancestors. Much as families and house groups alluded to their members' powers at ceremonies with multi-community guest lists, organized tribes today claim and enact the histories of their members at public commemorative events, in museums, at annual community festivals, and elsewhere. When Indians tell stories about the talents, wisdom, and accomplishments of Native ancestors, they are expressing pride in and requesting respect for their descent from people who commanded respect during their lifetimes because of the powers the spirits had bestowed upon them.[26] As their ancestors did, they can take pride that the names of those ancestors were known in households and winter villages far and wide. The ancestors could not have imagined some of the names by which people identify themselves today, such as "Indian" and even "Coast Salish," but they would likely have rejoiced that their offspring have names that connect them to a wide array of thriving communities whose members cherish a shared heritage as the original people of their lush coastal homeland.[27]

Notes

1 See also Roosens (1989, 16-17, 160), McIlwraith (1996, 49), and sources cited there. The historian Eric Hobsbawm (2000, 10) writes, "To be a member of any human community is to situate oneself with regard to one's (its) past." To say that members of an ethnic group share or claim to share a history is not to say that those members will not disagree about the facts and meanings of their history. See McIlwraith (1996, 46).

2 E-mail communication, William White, University of Victoria Aboriginal Liaison Office, to Wendy Wickwire, University of Victoria history department, 28 February 2003, distinguishing "Straits Salish" from "Coast Salish" and stating, "I have heard speakers at our own gatherings both traditional and secular sometimes using the term 'Halkomelem Peoples.' If addressing students who happen to come from and of the Saanich/Straits Salish region or from the Coast Salish then we have formally brought forward their respective FN [First Nations] tribal names." See also the University of Victoria Aboriginal Liaison Office website at http://web.uvic.ca/ablo/, where there are links to "Salish" websites, including a site providing instruction in Coast Salish language, also referred to as Holkomelem or Hul'q'umi'num. The site identifies eight "Coast Salish" languages and eight First Nations in "Coast Salish territory" near Victoria.

3 In the *Oxford English Dictionary's* entry for "Salish," the earliest cited use of the term is from an 1831 publication by W.A. Ferris, *Life in [the] Rocky Mountains*, and refers to the language of the so-called Flathead Indians, whom anthropologists identify as Interior Salish. http://dictionary.oed.com/entrance.dtl.

4 Each of the common names for all indigenous Americans is problematic. Each has its advocates and its critics. The currently preferred names in Canada ("Aboriginals" and "First Nations") are different from those preferred in the United States ("Indians" and "Native Americans"). Rather than choose a single term and defend my choice, I use "Indian," "Native," and "Aboriginal" interchangeably and hope that readers will understand that they refer respectfully to negotiated modern social identities and that many of the people so identified use the terms for themselves.

5 I searched the on-line catalogue for the University of Washington libraries.

6 Although the Bella Coola and Tillamook Indians spoke Salish languages, the editors do not count them as "Coast Salish" because their homelands were not contiguous to the territories of the groups so designated.

7 Books in these categories include Fisher (1977); Duff (1964); Harmon (1998); Tennant (1990); Harris (2002); La Violette (1973); Newell (1993); Asher (1999); Christophers (1998); and Knight (1978). The four most popular kinds of history books about Indians have chronicled wars, government policies, non-Indian ideas about Indians, and formulaic histories of particular tribes before their subjugation by non-Indian authorities. See Meyer and Klein (1998, 190).

8 For instance, Tennant (1990, 5-6) draws on Indian and Northern Affairs Canada, "Chiefs and Councillors, BC Region" (July 1988), for a list of tribal groups, including about eight "Coast Salish" groups.

9 Similarly, family narratives are an important basis of Neal McLeod's (2000) argument that members of certain contemporary tribal groups also have a broader Plains Cree history.

10 My source for the summary and quotes that follow is Paul Fetzer (n.d.)

11 Except for Samish and Nooksack, the tribal communities that Swanaset names here were located on the Canadian side of the present international boundary, either along the Fraser River or on the southern end of Vancouver Island.

12 Fetzer (n.d., 4). This is the text as it appears in the original typescript, including the blanks, which represent words or names Fetzer did not transcribe, many of them presumably Indian-language terms.

13 See Collins (1949, 312). The Treaty of Point Elliott, art. 12, provides, "The said tribes and bands further agree not to trade at Vancouver's Island or elsewhere out of the dominions of the United States, nor shall foreign Indians be permitted to reside in their reservations without consent of the superintendent or agent." 12 U.S. Stat. 927. On the anti-potlatch law in Canada, see Cole and Chaikin (1990). The US government prohibited and penalized "uncivilized" practices by Department of Interior regulation rather than by statute (see Prucha 1984, 2:646-49). Efforts to enforce the regulations in western Washington were sporadic and often ineffective (see Harmon 1998, 116-18).

14 In Canada after 1876, a law authorized the Department of Indian Affairs to create tribal or band governments and defined Indians so as to exclude the wives and children of men who were not "registered" Indians (Tennant 1990, 9; Niezen 2003, 32).

15 Indians on the Sauk River, for instance, intermarried with Wenatchee and Chelan people, Plateau Salish speakers from east of the Cascade Mountains (Fish and Bedal 2000, 11, 24). Susan A. Miller (1998, 102) asserts that a "complex network of families and tribes ... has integrated this hemisphere since long before Europeans arrived ... Native scholars should be wary of relinquishing the network in its full complexity as a model for history." But June Collins (1979, 246), writing about the Upper Skagit, emphasizes their preference for marrying into communities where they already had relatives and their reluctance to marry into distant groups, which they perceived as too different and as potentially hostile.

16 In other instances, the Canadian government did lump bands together. See Tennant (1990, 9).

17 See also Porter (2001, 357) and Meyer and Klein (1998, 198). Studies of nationalism and ethnicity include Anderson (1983); Barth (1969); Nash (1989); and Roosens (1989).

18 The number of similarly bisected indigenous peoples is substantial, but historical studies that focus on the consequences of bisection are comparatively scarce. See Adelman and Aron (1999) and Hogue (2002).

19 Some Indians concerned with defending their "traditions" object to the ways that professional historians depict their past "not only as a disciplinary domination, but a colonial domination that is both a reflection of and a constituent part of Europe's colonization and domination of the world" (White 1998, 223).

20 See Suttles (1987, xi). Meyer and Klein (1998, 195) mention the popularity of tribal or reservation histories.

21 Meyer and Klein (1998, 196) note, "The unique status of Native Americans vis-à-vis ... the federal government makes diving into the past a prerequisite for understanding nearly every contentious issue."

22 US House of Representatives, Subcommittee on Indian Affairs, *Indian Tribes of Washington,* 67th Cong., 2d sess., May 24 and June 5, 1922, H-320-7, p. 17.

23 For varying arguments by anthropologists regarding the attribution of political cohesion and structure of Aboriginal "tribes," see Tollefson (1987, 1989); Miller (1989); and Miller and Boxberger (1994).

24 See also Comaroff and Comaroff (1992, 3-5); Meyer and Klein (1998, 186, 194). According to the anthropologist Colin Twedell, a witness in US Indian Claims Commission proceedings regarding the Snohomish Tribe, ethnographers have tended to apply group names to Northwest Indians on the basis of residence rather than on people's actual sense of their group affiliations. See Transcript, Docket 125, Indian Claims Commission, 10-12 August 1953, in Reply Appendix L-2, p. 104, Petition for Acknowledgment of the Snohomish Tribe of Indians, 1988.

25 One well-educated tribe member told me of her fear that *Indians in the Making* (Harmon 1998), which examines changes over time in the structures and status of western Washington tribes, would jeopardize the tribes' powers of self-government.

26 June Collins (1979, 252) asserts that the number of outstanding people featured in Skagit stories about ancestors is "sufficiently large that everyone is descended from at least one." A history published by the Stó:lō Nation, referring to occasions when knowledgeable persons publicly recite stories from Stó:lō oral tradition, states, "Sharing ... stories ... allows the speaker and the audience to share in the communally held experiences, histories, beliefs, and philosophies of the ... people" (Carlson 1997, 195).

27 On names as a "living identity" and a claim to a family history, see Hilbert and Bierwert (1980, 18-19) and Collins (1949, 319, 335).

References

Adelman, Jeremy, and Stephen Aron. 1999. From Borderlands to Borders: Empires, Nation-States, and the Peoples in between in North American History. *American Historical Review* 104 (3): 814-41.

Allen, Edwin J. Jr. 1976. Intergroup Ties and Exogamy among Northern Coast Salish. *Northwest Anthropological Research Notes* 10 (2): 163-69.

Amoss, Pamela. 1978. *Coast Salish Spirit Dancing: The Survival of an Ancestral Religion.* Seattle: University of Washington Press.

Anderson, Benedict. 1983. *Imagined Communities: Reflections on the Origin and Spread of Nationalism.* London: Verso.

Asher, Brad. 1999. *Beyond the Reservation: Indians, Settlers, and the Law in Washington Territory, 1853-89.* Norman: University of Oklahoma Press.

Barman, Jean. 1999. What a Difference a Border Makes: Aboriginal Racial Intermixture in the Pacific Northwest. *Journal of the West* 38 (3): 14-20.

Barth, Fredrik. 1969. *Ethnic Groups and Boundaries.* Boston: Little, Brown.

Bishop, Thomas G., and Charles Roblin, collectors. 1911-19. Applications for Enrollment and Allotment of Washington Indians. National Archives, Seattle Pacific Region, Microfilm 1343.

Boyd, Robert. 1990. Demographic History, 1774-1874. In *Handbook of North American Indians.* Vol. 7, *Northwest Coast,* ed. W. Suttles, 135-48. Washington, DC: Smithsonian Institution.

Carlson, Keith Thor, ed. 1997. *You Are Asked to Witness: The Stó:lō in Canada's Pacific Coast History.* Chilliwack, BC: Stó:lō Heritage Trust.

Castile, George Pierre. 1996. The Commodification of Indian Identity. *American Anthropologist* 98 (4): 743-49.

Christophers, Brett. 1998. *Positioning the Missionary: John Booth Good and the Confluence of Cultures in Nineteenth-Century British Columbia.* Vancouver: UBC Press.

Cole, Douglas, and Ira Chaikin. 1990. *An Iron Hand upon the People: The Law against the Potlatch on the Northwest Coast.* Vancouver: Douglas and McIntyre.

Collins, June M. 1949. John Fornsby: The Personal Document of a Coast Salish Indian. In *Indians of the Urban Northwest,* ed. Marian Smith, 287-341. New York: Columbia University Press.

–. 1974. *Valley of the Spirits: Upper Skagit Indians of Western Washington.* Seattle: University of Washington Press.

–. 1979. Multilineal Descent: A Coast Salish Strategy. In *Currents in Anthropology: Essays in Honor of Sol Tax,* ed. Robert Hinshaw, 243-54. New York: Mouton Publishers.

Comaroff, John, and Jean Comaroff. 1992. *Ethnography and the Historical Imagination.* Boulder: Westview Press.

Cornell, Stephen. 1988. *The Return of the Native: American Indian Political Resurgence.* New York: Oxford University Press.

Cruikshank, Julie. 1998. *The Social Life of Stories: Narrative and Knowledge in the Yukon Territory.* Lincoln/Vancouver: University of Nebraska Press/UBC Press.

Duff, Wilson. 1964. *The Indian History of British Columbia*. Vol. 1, *The Impact of the White Man*. Victoria: Provincial Museum of British Columbia.

Fetzer, Paul. N.d. George Swanaset: Narrative of a Personal Document. Melville Jacobs Collection, University of Washington Manuscripts Accession 1693-71-13, box 112.

Fish, Jean Bedal, and Edith Bedal, with editorial assistance from Astrida R. Blukis Onat. 2000. *Two Voices: A History of the Sauk and Suiattle People and Sauk Country Experiences*. N.p.

Fisher, Robin. 1977. *Contact and Conflict: Indian-European Relations in British Columbia, 1774-1890*. Vancouver: UBC Press.

Galloway, Brent D. 1990. *A Phonology, Morphology, and Classified Word List for the Samish Dialect of Straits Salish*. Canadian Ethnology Service Mercury Series Paper 116. Hull, QC: Canadian Museum of Civilization.

Goldberg-Ambrose, Carole. 1994. Of Native Americans and Tribal Members: The Impact of Law on Indian Group Life. *Law and Society Review* 28 (5): 1123-24.

Guilmet, George M., Robert T. Boyd, David L. Whited, and Nile Thompson. 1991. The Legacy of Introduced Disease: The Southern Coast Salish. *American Indian Culture and Research Journal* 15 (4): 1-32.

Harkin, Michael. 1996. Past Presence: Conceptions of History in Northwest Coast Studies. *Arctic Anthropology* 33 (2): 1-15.

Harmon, Alexandra. 1998. *Indians in the Making: Ethnic Relations and Indian Identities around Puget Sound*. Berkeley and Los Angeles: University of California Press.

Harris, Cole. 2002. *Making Native Space: Colonialism, Resistance, and Reserves in British Columbia*. Vancouver: UBC Press.

Hilbert, Vi (taqws3blu), and Crisca Bierwert. 1980. *Ways of the Lushootseed People: Ceremonies and Traditions of the Northern Puget Sound Indians*. Seattle: United Indians of All Tribes Foundation, Daybreak Star Press.

Hobsbawm, Eric. 2000. *On History*. New York: New Press.

Hogue, Michel. 2002. Disputing the Medicine Line: The Plains Crees and the Canadian-American Border, 1876-1885. *Montana, the Magazine of Western History* 52 (4): 2-17.

Knight, Rolf. 1978. *Indians at Work: An Informal History of Native Indian Labour in British Columbia, 1858-1930*. Vancouver: New Star Books.

La Violette, Forrest E. 1973. *The Struggle for Survival: Indian Cultures and the Protestant Ethic in BC*. Toronto: University of Toronto Press, 1973.

Marshall, Daniel P. 1999. *Those Who Fell from the Sky: A History of the Cowichan People*. Duncan, BC: Cowichan Tribes Cultural and Education Centre.

McIlwraith, Thomas. 1996. The Problem of Imported Culture: The Construction of Contemporary Stó:lo Identity. *American Indian Culture and Research Journal* 20: 41-70.

McLeod, Neal. 2000. Plains Cree Identity: Borderlands, Ambiguous Genealogies and Narrative Irony. *Canadian Journal of Native Studies* 20 (2): 437-54.

Meyer, Melissa L., and Kerwin Lee Klein. 1998. Native American Studies and the End of Ethnohistory. In *Studying Native America: Problems and Prospects*, ed. Russell Thornton, 182-216. Madison: University of Wisconsin Press.

Miller, Bruce. 1989. Centrality and Measures of Regional Structure in Aboriginal Western Washington. *Ethnology* 28: 265-76.

–. 1996-97. The "Really Real" Border and the Divided Salish Community. *BC Studies* 112: 63-79.

Miller, Bruce, and Daniel Boxberger. 1994. Creating Chiefdoms: The Puget Sound Case. *Ethnohistory* 41: 267-93.

Miller, Susan A. 1998. Licensed Trafficking and Ethnogenetic Engineering. In *Natives and Academics: Researching and Writing about American Indians,* ed. Devon A. Mihesuah, 100-10. Lincoln: University of Nebraska Press.

Mooney, Kathleen. 1976. Social Distance and Exchange: The Coast Salish Case. *Ethnology* 15: 323-46.

Nagel, Joane. 1996. *American Indian Ethnic Renewal: Red Power and the Resurgence of Identity and Culture.* New York: Oxford University Press.

Nash, Manning. 1989. *The Cauldron of Ethnicity in the Modern World.* Chicago: University of Chicago Press.

Newell, Dianne. 1993. *Tangled Webs of History: Indians and the Law in Canada's Pacific Coast Fisheries.* Toronto: University of Toronto Press.

Niezen, Ronald. 2003. *The Origins of Indigenism: Human Rights and the Politics of Identity.* Berkeley and Los Angeles: University of California Press.

Nugent, Ann, ed. 1982. *Lummi Elders Speak.* Lynden, WA: Lynden Tribune.

Peterson, Lester. 1990. *The Story of the Sechelt Nation.* Madeira Park, BC: Harbour Publishing for the Sechelt Band.

Porter, Joy. 2001. Imagining Indians: Differing Perspectives on Native American History. In *The State of US History,* ed. Melvyn Stokes, 347-66. Oxford: Berg.

Prucha, Francis Paul. 1984. *The Great Father: The United States Government and the American Indians,* 2 vols. Lincoln: University of Nebraska Press.

Report of the Commissioner of Indian Affairs. 1854-55. Washington, DC: Government Printing Office.

Roosens, Eugeen E. 1989. *Creating Ethnicity: The Process of Ethnogenesis.* Newbury Park: Sage Publications.

Sampson, Martin. 1972. *Indians of Skagit County.* Skagit County Historical Series No. 2. Mt. Vernon, WA: Skagit County Historical Society.

Suquamish Museum. 1985. *The Eyes of Chief Seattle.* Suquamish, WA: Suquamish Museum and Cultural Center.

Suttles, Wayne. 1963. The Persistence of Intervillage Ties among the Coast Salish. *Ethnology* 2 (4): 512-25.

–. 1987. *Coast Salish Essays.* Seattle: University of Washington Press.

–, ed. 1990. *Handbook of North American Indians.* Vol. 7, *Northwest Coast.* Washington, DC: Smithsonian Institution.

Tennant, Paul. 1990. *Aboriginal Peoples and Politics: The Indian Land Question in British Columbia, 1849-1989.* Vancouver: UBC Press.

Thelen, David. 1999. The Nation and Beyond: Transnational Perspectives on United States History. *Journal of American History* 86: 965-75.

Tollefson, Kenneth D. 1987. The Snoqualmie: A Puget Sound Chiefdom. *Ethnology* 26: 121-36.

–. 1989. Political Organization of the Duwamish. *Ethnology* 28: 135-44.

White, Richard. 1998. Using the Past: History and Native American Studies. In *Studying Native America: Problems and Prospects,* ed. Russell Thornton, 217-43. Madison: University of Wisconsin Press.

Wike, Joyce Anabel. 1941. Modern Spirit Dancing of Northern Puget Sound. MA thesis, University of Washington.

2
The Not So Common

Daniel L. Boxberger

The word "common" gets a lot of use in the Coast Salish world. One of the most dominant features of Coast Salish territory is the international boundary that bisects it. As one approaches the border the Peace Arch memorial captures the eye. "Children of a Common Mother" is the saying engraved across the top. The irony is not lost on the Coast Salish people, who refer to the border as the "line," symbolizing the arbitrary nature of a line drawn on a map through their lands by people who had never been there. For the past century the most controversial aspect of Coast Salish life on both sides of the line has been over access to and use of the salmon fishery. In Washington State the 1974 decision in *United States v. Washington* interpreted the treaty phrase "to fish in common" to mean equal access, ushering in a heated controversy (which continues to this day) over treaty allocations of salmon. To begin with, it was the European concept of common property that enabled the penetration of non-Natives into the salmon fishery in both Washington State and British Columbia as the Aboriginal common law was replaced by European common law, which invested regulatory rights in a detached government instead of in a network of kin relations. Inevitably, indigenous rights enter the court system. This is true of the Coast Salish experience in both Canada and the United States. While the legal systems of the two countries vary somewhat, they are both descendants of English common law.

There are many more ways in which the word "common," common enough in itself, could be used to illustrate Coast Salish issues. The word is indicative of the political and economic concerns that have become Coast Salish realities and have engaged anthropology in those realities, which has become a "not so common" experience.

I first entered the Coast Salish world not as an anthropologist; I do not remember whether I even knew then what an anthropologist was. I came as a young college student caught up in the Civil Rights Movement of the

1960s, which, by the 1970s, was being played out in Indian country. Alcatraz was still fresh in everyone's mind, Wounded Knee II was in the news, and the Trail of Broken Treaties was about to commence. In the midst of these nationally publicized events the "fish-ins" of south Puget Sound were locally televised almost daily. In 1971, I was sent to the Lummi Indian Reservation as a VISTA volunteer to develop adult education programs. I had the starry-eyed notion that I was there to "help the Indians," but, as it turned out, they helped me much more than I could ever help them. They taught me a great deal about life, about family, about spirituality, about things that were really important. It was later that I developed an interest in natural resource issues. This came about primarily through my involvement with Lummi adult education, an interest that led to my involvement with the founding of the Lummi College of Fisheries, which is today known as Northwest Indian College. The Lummi College of Fisheries was established on the basis of developing educational programs that were relevant to Native American concerns. It was part of a movement for the creation of Tribally Controlled Community Colleges, which was building nationwide in the 1970s and 1980s. It was through this involvement that my interest in natural resource issues came to fruition, and it was this interest that eventually landed me in a not so "common" position – that of expert witness in courts of law.

For the past few years, I have mostly been trying to understand how this happened. Being an expert witness is not necessarily the most enviable role or the most pleasant experience. As I have come to realize, Native American rights have always been interpreted in the courtroom. I have also come to realize that how we engage research in Native American communities has largely been framed by this legal construct. My questions are these: How does this reality shape the way we do anthropological research? And what does this mean for a contemporary anthropology of the Coast Salish?

A Model of Resource Control
The interpretation of Aboriginal rights in the courtroom is certainly not new. Nor is the court system as a venue for the determination of Aboriginal rights unique to Canada and the United States. As other former colonies of Great Britain, such as Australia and New Zealand, are experiencing, the legacy of colonialism and colonial policy is at the root of contemporary issues of indigenous peoples worldwide. In the last twenty-five years, as anthropology has come to grips with its own legacy of association with colonialism, there has been a great deal of self-reflection and reassessment of the nature of anthropological research. What was considered a viable research strategy in the past is no longer tenable. We can no longer pretend

to do total ethnography or traditional ethnography; nor can we assume that the people who are the subjects of our anthropological research will not have an interest in what has been written about them. In addition to trying to conduct an anthropology that has relevance for the people with whom we work, we are also writing against a century of anthropological legacy that has defined Coast Salish traditions. In fact, the very notion of "tradition" is being reassessed and questioned as a viable construct.

By framing these questions within a political economy of domination and resistance, we see that the relationship of indigenous peoples to the nation-state is a hegemonic one embedded in power and struggle. For the past century or more this relationship has centred on land claims, resource rights, and self-determination. Ultimately, this struggle ends up in the courtroom, where a subordinate people attempt to use the legal construct of the dominant society to achieve some degree of control over Aboriginal rights – sometimes successfully, sometimes not successfully.

Inevitably, this struggle depends upon the flow of traditional knowledge, who controls that knowledge, and who determines what it means (for a recent discussion of this issue see Boxberger 2004). Traditional knowledge, however defined, has generally been treated as though it, too, is "common" property. The Western notion that dissemination of knowledge is an inherent right is under scrutiny in the current age of information. Knowledge is becoming commoditized as we reassess copyright law, infringement, rights of access, and Homeland Security. This is not news in the Coast Salish world, where knowledge has traditionally been seen as property vested in the individual, family, and kin group. While this knowledge was freely shared with anthropologists in the past, that is no longer the norm. This has changed the way we conduct anthropological research. Litigation often requires the presentation of knowledge in a public forum. The necessity of reaffirming rights to traditional resources often requires the relinquishment of rights of control over knowledge in order to achieve the benefits of legal clarification. Thus, I view traditional knowledge as a commodity that may be treated methodologically in the same way as are other resources. It is a commodity that enters the realm of hegemonic power in much the same way as do land, timber, minerals, and salmon.

Of all resources, salmon provide a symbol of the relationship of domination and resistance. In the Coast Salish world, salmon are central to everything it means to be indigenous. In fact, we who work on the Northwest Coast have been accused of "salmonopia"; however, that has a great deal to do with the overwhelming importance salmon play in the economic, political, and ideological realities of First Nations. For the Coast Salish, salmon provide the basis of sustenance, trade, ceremony, and other integral parts of existence. The Fraser River sockeye appear in regular four-year cycles of abundance, providing a mainstay of economic life for many Coast Salish. Sockeye, however, are just one of the species of salmon that are indigenous to the Coast Salish area. Pink salmon ("humpies") appear every odd year. The fat chinook (locally known as "springs") come early in the spring to provide fresh food high in oil content. The sleek coho (silvers) are prime eating when fresh. The lean chum ("dogs") are available late in the fall and into the winter, when they can be taken in abundance to smoke-dry to last indefinitely. Steelhead, while not as numerous as other types of salmon, can, in some streams, provide fresh fish as late as December and as early as February. Salmon are the symbol of the yearly round of existence and, as such, can be used as a symbol of the relationship of the Coast Salish to natural, cultural, and intellectual resources.

Native American resource use can be characterized historically as a process of exclusivity, inclusion, exclusion, and marginal reintegration. While designed from studies of the Pacific Coast salmon fisheries, this characterization is applicable to other resources as well. I would go so far as to say it is universally applicable in the relationship of colonized peoples to colonizing powers. Inevitably, natural resources play the central role in this relationship. I have focused on two variables concerning resource use – control and access – that characterize the participation of Native peoples in the colonial experience. While the specific process will vary from group to group, it always follows a similar pattern. From complete control of the resource before development, Native peoples were gradually integrated into its increasing commoditization. This process can take decades or it can occur within a relatively short period. Eventually, as the commercial aspects of the resource become more capitalized, Native peoples, usually without access to competitive technology or capital, become marginalized. This occurs through a hegemonic process of increasing political control over Native peoples' lives and increasing discrimination in the economic sector. Eventually, Native peoples regain partial access and control through litigation. This final phase of resource use and control has certainly characterized the Coast Salish fisheries in British Columbia and Washington State for the last three decades (Boxberger 1994, 2000). Traditionally, reliance on salmon has been central to Coast Salish culture. Coast Salish people have come to identify themselves as the "salmon people." The cultural history of salmon utilization can therefore be used as a model for other indigenous rights.

Through the early nineteenth century, the Coast Salish were engaged in a well-developed salmon fishery that not only met their needs for subsistence but also provided a surplus for trade and ceremonial feasting. The technology employed represents one of the most sophisticated traditional fisheries in the world. Six different species of salmon were utilized, the most notable being the Fraser River sockeye, which formed the main economic focus for Native peoples throughout the Fraser River system and the adjacent saltwater areas. According to data compiled by Beringer (1982), the centre of salmon-fishing technological sophistication for the entire Northwest Coast was around the mouth of the Fraser River. Hewes' (1973) estimates for Aboriginal consumption rates indicate that this area had among the highest on the Northwest Coast. These estimates were based on Hewes' 1947 doctoral dissertation, portions of which were published in 1973 as a result of fishing rights litigation. The Fraser River sockeye runs were especially important for the Stó:lō along the lower Fraser River and for the Straits Salish groups in the adjacent Gulf Islands and San Juan Islands. The reliance on salmon that characterized Coast Salish culture continues to this day, despite the fact that varying degrees of access have been evident over the past century. It is no coincidence that early non-Native developments in commercial fishing also concentrated on the Fraser River runs and that abundance and accessibility made this an area of special importance.

From exclusive Aboriginal use and control, the process of integrating Native peoples into the commercial salmon fishery was a direct outgrowth of dependence on this resource base. Although the Hudson's Bay Company attempted to market the salmon resource at Fort Langley on the Fraser River as early as the 1820s, it was not until reliable forms of preservation were available that large-scale commercial operations became feasible. The Hudson's Bay Company depended upon the ability of the Coast Salish to produce a surplus for trade in much the same way as they had done when trading among themselves. When new forms of technology were imported in the 1870s, salmon canneries appeared on the Fraser River and Puget Sound, but the industry was off to a slow start until it was discovered that Fraser River sockeye could be taken in abundance. Sockeye are the most desirable species for canning because of their bright red flesh and firm texture. The entrepreneurs who developed the salmon industry in the late nineteenth century found an unlimited supply of sockeye, and lack of regulatory measures meant an unbridled use of the resource. As the Fraser River sockeye migrate through US waters before entering the Fraser River just north of the border, they form the mainstay of the commercial fishing industry of northwest Washington and southwest British Columbia and have long been a point of contention between the two nations, resulting in two international treaties that have allocated the resource between Canadian and US commercial fishers since the 1930s (Boxberger 1988).

Native expertise was essential in the formative years of the commercial salmon industry, and Native people, who possessed the requisite skills as fishers and processors, were strongly encouraged to integrate with it. The earliest commercial operations purchased the majority of their fish from Native fishers, and Native women were employed in the canneries as cutters and packers. Very rapidly, Native people were incorporated into the industry, and their economic lives became a mix of subsistence and seasonal wage labour.

Coinciding with this process of integration, federal policies in both Canada and the United States were directed toward assimilating Native people into the dominant society, which was generally not defined as a fishing society. As the fishery developed, the federal governments rationalized the increasing restriction of Native access to it because the road to assimilation was now thought to be found in reduced reliance on the salmon fishery and increased dependence on agriculture (Boxberger 2000; Harris 2001, 74). Nevertheless, as the industrial development of the fishery accelerated, beginning about 1880 and continuing into the early 1900s, Native people remained a significant force in the industry. In fact, the fishing industry was the "only economic sector in the province in which Indians were well paid and able to maintain a substantial presence" (Tennant 1990, 73). By 1919, the BC fishing industry employed nine thousand people, "the majority of whom were Indians. And more than one-third of all salmon fishermen were Indians" (Pearse 1982, 151). In Washington State a similar process of integration started in the late 1880s and accelerated through the 1890s. By the mid-1890s, the Coast Salish of Washington State were an essential part of the salmon-fishing industry of north Puget Sound, participating as commercial fishers and cannery labour. Utilizing traditional methods of fishing, such as the reef net, and incorporating new gear introduced by the canneries, Native people entered a new role as primary producers in an industry they understood and enjoyed (Boxberger 1988).

During the early 1900s, the decline of Native participation in the fishery began with a process of exclusion that shifted control and access to the non-Native sector. This displacement was caused by the consolidation of the canning industry and the adoption of more capital-intensive fishing technology. In Washington State, by 1935, less than 3.3 percent of the total salmon harvest was attributed to Native fishers. In British Columbia, the rate of attrition of Native fishers was, at first, slower than it was south of the line; however, from 1950 to 1980, the number of Native-owned vessels fell by two-thirds and the number of Native people employed as crew and cannery workers also plummeted.

As is common in issues concerning Aboriginal rights of access and control of natural resources, Native peoples inevitably turn to the legal system to regain any semblance of participation in resource use. Marginal reintegration is typically achieved through litigation – a costly, time-consuming, and risky endeavour. In 1974, the Coast Salish and other Native tribes of western Washington convinced the federal court, in *United States v. Washington*, that the wording of the 1855 treaties guaranteed an allocation of the salmon resource to the treaty tribes. Arguing that the State of Washington had violated treaty rights by refusing to allocate specifically for a Native fishery, the court determined that the treaty phrase "to fish in *common*" meant to share equally, and it set the allocation at 50 percent. Since 1974, the treaty tribes of western Washington have gradually increased their commercial and subsistence harvest to the point where they take the maximum allocation. Also since that time, the treaty tribes and the State of Washington have co-operated to manage the resource in a manner that ensures compliance with the court decision, enabling the reintegration not only of partial access but also of partial control. Further, the ruling has been extended to other natural resources, most notably (in 1992) to shellfish.

In British Columbia the Canadian Constitution Act, 1982 marked an important turning point for Aboriginal rights. Although BC First Nations have a long history of political activism designed to clarify Aboriginal rights to land and resources, their efforts have generally been thwarted by the province (Tennant 1990). Native fishing rights have been tested in the courts on several occasions, including in landmark decisions involving the Coast Salish. In 1984, a member of the Musqueam band was cited for using a net longer than what was allowed by the Fisheries Act. As early as 1868, the Fisheries Act regulated the Native food fishery of British Columbia, and this case was the first to question whether the Native fishery was an existing Aboriginal right (and, thereby, protected by the Constitution) or whether Aboriginal right had been extinguished by the Indian Act. In May 1990, the Supreme Court of Canada ruled in *Sparrow v. The Queen* that the Coast Salish right to fish is an existing right protected by section 35(1) of the Constitution Act. Since *Sparrow* there have been a number of cases attempting to clarify what this means. For example, in August 1996 the Supreme Court of Canada ruled in *Van der Peet*, with regard to the Stó:lō, that selling fish was not an Aboriginal right. Basing its conclusion on a somewhat hazy test, the court determined that selling fish was not "integral" to the culture of the Stó:lō and, therefore, not protected under section 35(1). Anticipating an endless barrage of court cases, the minister of fisheries implemented the nationwide Aboriginal Fisheries Strategy in the 1990s in an attempt to put into place a system of allocation that enabled an Aboriginal fishery that included commercial sales. This program met with little success for Natives and was much resisted by non-Natives. In 2003, commercial sales under the Aboriginal Fisheries Strategy were ended by a lawsuit initiated by non-Native commercial fishers: the court ruled that a "race-based" fishery was unconstitutional (*R. v. Kapp;* overturned by the British Columbia Supreme Court in July 2004, appeal dismissed 8 June 2006). At the same time as the Aboriginal Fisheries Strategy, the British Columbia Treaty Process initiated an attempt by provincial, federal, and First Nations governments to bring treaties to the bands of British Columbia. This, too, has been a dismal failure with regard to clarifying Aboriginal rights. Currently, all indications are that Aboriginal rights in British Columbia will be contested in the courtroom rather than negotiated through treaty or resource allocation schemes.

Natural resource rights have long been at the forefront of Aboriginal rights issues. This model of resource use and control examines the process of the hegemonic relationship between Aboriginal peoples and modern nation-states. It struck me that it might also apply to cultural and intellectual property. Today the use and control of traditional knowledge constitutes the major issue of the anthropology of the Coast Salish. Historical research has analyzed the role of the legal system in effecting transfers of land and resources to colonizing governments and settlers, in legitimizing the political sovereignty of colonial nations, the extraction of natural resources, and the marginalization of Native peoples. This reality has shaped the way in which anthropology has participated in the Coast Salish world. The next step is to try to understand how the shift in research in the Coast Salish world is being shaped by the context of litigation within which it increasingly operates. We must try to understand the role anthropology has played in this process as a participant in the inclusion, exclusion, and marginalization of traditional knowledge and how the context of litigation has shaped the nature of research strategies.

The legal system not only encourages but relies upon traditional knowledge – knowledge that many Native groups would rather not disclose to outsiders. The anthropologist as expert witness has been an active participant in the process of disseminating traditional Aboriginal knowledge. I have chosen five not so "common" examples of Coast Salish research that illustrate this. These experiences are indicative of the trends in research strategies that have been shaped by policy needs and the litigious nature of the Coast Salish world.

Early Ethnography of the Coast Salish

In the beginning there was Boas. We often look at Franz Boas as the father of the anthropology of the North American Indian, especially on the Northwest Coast. However, attempts to describe Coast Salish culture preceded Boas, and these descriptive accounts, produced by non-academic anthropologists, or, perhaps more accurately, amateur ethnologists, continued into the mid-1900s. Indigenous knowledge exists within the framework of kin and community, now as it did in the past. The earliest attempts to tap into this knowledge base were primarily carried out by government officials or missionaries who sought it as a way of achieving the assimilation of Native peoples. These attempts were followed by those of people who might best be termed "curiosity seekers" – local residents and travellers who described "quaint customs" in order to entertain a general audience. Both forms of acquiring Aboriginal knowledge continue today.

In the first category, the Coast Salish were described by George Gibbs (1855, 1877), Myron Eells (1889, 1985), and Thomas Crosby (1907). In the second category, I include Theodore Winthrop (1913), J.A. Costello (1895), Charles Hill-Tout (1900, 1903, 1904a, 1904b), Arthur C. Ballard (1927, 1929, 1935), and Oliver Wells (1987), to mention just a few. From these early attempts, the studies of the Coast Salish have become far too numerous to discuss in detail. Besides, this has already been done, for the most part, in Suttles' (1990) *Handbook of North American Indians,* volume 7, *Northwest Coast,* although this work has its limitations (see Introduction, this volume). Instead, I focus on representative works from several eras and subject them to a content analysis in order to place each within the context of the changing realm of Coast Salish research.

In 1849, George Gibbs came to the Oregon Territory, where he worked in various government jobs, including the Willamette Valley Treaty Commission in 1850 (for biographical information on Gibbs, see Carstensen 1954; Beckham 1969). In 1851, Gibbs travelled south, where he found employment with the treaty commission in northern California. Because of these experiences Gibbs was able to attach himself, as an ethnologist, to the McClellan expedition, which was part of the 1853-55 Northwest railroad surveys. He produced three reports from this expedition, including "Indian Tribes of Washington," which, in 1877, was revised and published as "Tribes of Western Washington and Northwestern Oregon." In 1853, Gibbs met Territorial Governor Isaac I. Stevens at Fort Colville, which started an association that influenced the treaties negotiated in western Washington from 1854 to 1856. In his reports on the railroad surveys, Gibbs outlined recommendations for Indian policy in Washington Territory, some of which were later implemented. His knowledge of Native peoples landed Gibbs a job as secretary to Governor Stevens and the Washington Treaty Commission. Gibbs' charge was to visit the various Indian tribes and to draft a series of treaties for them to sign. In this capacity, he was able to influence policy. For example, Gibbs convinced the treaty commission to create several small reservations rather than one large one, as Stevens had been directed to do by the commissioner of Indian affairs (Records Relating to Treaties 1854).

Gibbs would later serve as head of the territorial militia, and from 1857 to 1862 he would serve on the American Boundary Commission, surveying the forty-ninth parallel, the boundary between Canada and the United States. Part of his responsibility as interpreter and geologist on the boundary commission was to render Coast Salish and other Native place names into English (Boxberger and Schaepe 2001). Gibbs served on the boundary commission in Washington Territory until 1860, and he then worked for two more years in Washington, DC, preparing the reports. He never returned to the Pacific Northwest.

Gibbs produced several works on the ethnology and languages of western Washington and Oregon Indians. The ethnographic works are primarily synopses of what Gibbs learned of tribal distribution and natural resource dependency. Of the twenty manuscripts he produced on Native languages from California to Alaska, three were on Coast Salish (Nisqually, Lummi, and Klallam). His "Tribes of Western Washington and Northwestern Oregon" (1877) was an overview of tribal distribution and general ethnographic information relating to material culture.

The treaties of western Washington were designed to remove the Indians from the path of white settlement, to create reservations, to establish subsistence rights, and to outline a plan for assimilation. Although Gibbs presents his ethnographic overview as a scientific inquiry, his discussion can clearly be seen as a part of the process of colonization. Traditional knowledge is dismissed in a few lines because the Indians "are quick at suspecting some object in regard [sic] their lands" (Gibbs 1877, 223). Instead, Gibbs speculates on recent migrations, especially that of the Klickitat into western Washington and Oregon (Boxberger 1984, 107-10), movements that certainly had relevance for land claims and annuity payments on those lands (as promised in the treaties).

Gibbs' work has been an important resource for anthropological expert witnesses because he "was there" and he identified occupation and location. His publications and his journals are a record of what transpired at treaty time, and they have been mined as an important source in the attempt to identify what the Indians understood the treaties to mean. It is a canon of Indian law that treaties must be construed not according to technical legal meaning but, rather, in the sense they would have been understood by the Indians at the time they were signed (Cohen 1942, 7). Gibbs' facility with Salish languages, his familiarity with the landscape, and his general knowledge of natural resource use and dependency have rendered his work invaluable in litigation. For example, Gibbs overheard two boys conversing at the Chehalis Treaty Council and determined that a tribe previously unknown to whites existed north of the Quinalt and south of the Makah. Briefly listening to the boys speaking Quileute, he could tell that the language was not related to either Salish Quinalt or Nootkan Makah (Gibbs 1877, 172). Nevertheless, Gibbs must be read within the context of his times. "Diminution," "depopulation," and "nearly extinct" were the descriptors he used. The Indians were disappearing, civilization was advancing, and the natural course of events was for whites to take over the country. Gibbs' work is an example of mid-nineteenth-century ethnology, which followed a natural history approach. He made many insightful observations and described the Coast Salish in a manner that gives us a few glimpses into their lives in the 1850s. His work, however, must be read with the knowledge that he was a government official who, as such, had a political agenda. There is very little on spiritual life or any other aspect of expressive culture. Gibbs focused on material culture and localities, both of which were concerns associated with the land that was being transferred to the United States government.

The Boasian Era

Gibbs was followed by numerous researchers. The work of Franz Boas is, of course, legendary on the Northwest Coast. While Boas' work with the Coast Salish was not as prolific as his work with the Kwakwaka'wakw (see, for example, Boas 1891, 1894, 1895), his influence fostered a number of works in the vein of Boasian historical reconstruction and its descendant, the culture element distribution studies inspired by Alfred Kroeber. Students of Boas who worked with the Coast Salish include Edward Sapir (1915, 1939 [Comox]); Hermann Haeberlin (1924, 1930 [Puget Sound Salish); T.T. Waterman (1930, 1973 [Lushootseed]); Erna Gunther (1927 [Klallam]); Thelma Adamson (1934 [Chehalis and Cowlitz]); Marian W. Smith (1940 [Puyallup-Nisqually], 1949 [Stó:lō]); and a colleague of Boas' at Columbia University, Livingston Farrand (1900, 1902 [Quinalt]). Kroeber sent Homer G. Barnett (1938, 1939, 1955 [Coast Salish of British Columbia]) and William W. Elmendorf (1960, 1993 [Twana]) to the

Salish world. As well as being a student of Boas, Waterman was a colleague of Kroeber at the University of California. After the Second World War, the focus of attention on Northwest Coast studies shifted to the west coast.

Boasian anthropology survived at the University of Washington during the late 1940s and early 1950s. Students of that period who worked on the Northwest Coast include Joyce Wike [1945 (Skagit)], June M. Collins [1949, 1974 (Skagit)], Wayne Suttles [1974, 1987 (Straits Salish)], Wilson Duff [1952 (Stó:lō)], Barbara Lane [unpublished manuscripts for numerous Coast Salish court cases], Warren Snyder [1968 (Lushootseed)], Ram Raj Prasad Singh [1966 (Quinault)], Pamela Amoss [1978 (Nooksack)], and Sally Snyder [1975 (Lushootseed)]. Most at some point attempted ethnographic reconstruction in the Boasian tradition. (Suttles and Jonaitis 1990, 78; citations in brackets added)

Most of the anthropologists listed above left the Boasian tradition behind and contributed works in a variety of theoretical discourses. Both Suttles and Duff contributed to Coast Salish anthropology at the University of British Columbia, as did another University of Washington student, J.E. Michael Kew. Earlier Canadian anthropology, however, generally stood outside the Boasian tradition despite the fact that Edward Sapir served as the chief ethnologist of the Division of Anthropology in the Geological Survey of Canada from 1910 to 1925. Two famous Canadian anthropologists who worked for Sapir did research on the Northwest Coast – Marius Barbeau and Diamond Jenness. Both were trained at Oxford under a very different tradition than was Sapir. Neither managed to adapt to American-style anthropology (Hancock 2002, 107-8). Barbeau's west coast ethnography focused on the Tsimshian, while Jenness worked with the Coast Salish in 1935-36 and produced at least three manuscripts, none of which he put into print. "The Saanich (Coast Salish) of Vancouver Island" and "Coast Salish Mythology" remain in manuscript form; *The Faith of a Coast Salish Indian* was prepared for publication by Wayne Suttles in 1955.

It is difficult to select a single work that is most representative of this, the most prolific era of Coast Salish ethnography. The descriptive ethnographies this era produced have been major resources for litigation. Diamond Jenness' work, however, stands out as an intentional contribution to what might be called an applied approach – that is, an approach that was designed to inform policy decisions. An obvious question comes to mind: why did Jenness never publish his Coast Salish research? Jenness was extremely productive. His work on First Nations was immense: he published over one hundred works during his career. *Life of the Copper Eskimo* and *The People of the Twilight* are still considered classic works on the Inuit. His *Indians of Canada* stood as the definitive statement on Canadian ethnography for over fifty years. His five-volume *Eskimo Administration* steered Canadian policy in the North. So, given such a productive career, why did he ignore his Coast Salish work? The answer lies in his motives. Jenness was a civil servant: he was appointed chief of the Anthropological Division of the National Museum in 1925 after Sapir stepped down, a position he held until 1948. Jenness had worked under Sapir, but his approach is more akin to the structural functionalism of Malinowski and Radcliffe-Brown than it is to the historical particularism of Boas. Jenness was especially in tune with Malinowski and Radcliffe-Brown's goal of "applying anthropological knowledge to practical considerations of administration in British colonies" (Hancock 2002, 104; Kulchyski 1993).

Jenness was an outspoken critic of Canadian Indian policy, and he developed a plan for what should be done. Noting that "the more primitive and remote the Indian the more energetic he is and the more self-reliant" (1932, 350), Jenness presented testimony to the Special Joint Committee of the Senate and House of Commons in 1947. His "Plan for Liquidating Canada's Indian Problem within 25 Years" was offered as an approach to assimilation (Kulchyski 1993, 3-6). This plan was attempted twenty-two years later in the infamous White Paper, which introduced a proposal for the assimilation of Canada's Indians and resulted in a nationwide response from First Nations, ultimately causing the Liberal government to back down on its proposal.

This direction of Jenness' work contrasts sharply with that displayed in *The Faith of a Coast Salish Indian*. In his recounting of the belief system of Old Pierre of Katzie, Jenness (1955, 5) notes that "nowhere did he find the religious beliefs of the Indians so well integrated, or their rites so clearly interpreted." Jenness believed that Old Pierre preserved the "true esoteric faith of his forefathers." Old Pierre related "The Katzie Book of Genesis," which outlines the belief in a supreme deity. It has generally been accepted that monotheistic beliefs were introduced via Christian missionaries, an academic argument best described for the Coast Salish by Suttles (1987, 152 ff.). Jenness, however, presented the interpretation that the belief system described by Old Pierre represented an earlier form, and he maintained that he had found a similar belief system among the Salish Bella Coola (Nuxalk) far to the north. He speculated that both represented an older, universal Salish belief system that was supplanted by later systems, such as the Coast Salish X̱á:ls (Transformer) tradition. I was told by Old Pierre's granddaughter that, at the time of Jenness' research, the Creation story was related in Halkomelem and translated for his benefit. This is not evident in Jenness' notes as he did not describe the interview process, but, according to Old Pierre's granddaughter, who was present, this was one of the few times her grandfather related the entire story in one sitting. She further explained that Jenness was able to capture only a small portion of the Katzie Creation story because the translator filtered out certain bits, suggesting that it was even more complex than was the version Jenness recorded.

Despite Jenness' statement that his "task was to study the Indians and the Eskimos of the Dominion of Canada, their history, their manners, their religion, and so on. It was not to investigate their present-day condition or their outlook" (in Kulchyski 1993, 5), he was an advocate for change, as is outlined in his section on the Coast Salish in *Indians of Canada:*

> During the century and a half of their contact with Europeans all these west coast tribes have undergone less intermixture, indeed, but a far greater decline than the tribes of eastern Canada who have been subjected to similar influences for four centuries. For the Europeans who took possession of the Pacific Coast were farther advanced in civilization than the primitive farmers and fur trappers who had settled in the east. Machinery and rapid transportation were ushering in a new age that the Indians could not comprehend and in which they found no place. Their complex social organization, so different from that of any European country, broke down completely. The grades in their society had no significance for the invading whites, and the potlatches that helped to give these grades stability fell under the ban of the law ... The Indians can still provide cheap labour in the fish canneries, but there they compete with more industrious and efficient labourers from China and Japan. The reserves to which they are confined contain fertile tracts of land, but Indians untrained to agriculture cannot rival either Europeans or Chinese in the cultivation of the soil or the marketing of their products. Socially they are outcasts, economically they are inefficient and an encumbrance. Their old world has fallen into ruins, and, helpless in the face of a catastrophe they cannot understand, they vainly seek refuge in its shattered foundations. The end of this century, it seems safe to predict, will see very few survivors. (Jenness 1932, 350)

This observation was written in 1932, before his Coast Salish research, and appears to reflect observations he made elsewhere on the west coast. Jenness' Coast Salish work does not appear to support his assimilationist goals. This could be why, despite the value of his Coast Salish manuscripts, he chose not to pursue their publication. Curiously, through seven subsequent editions, the Coast Salish section in *Indians of Canada* was never modified.

Land Claims and Ethnohistory

Assimilation policies in the 1950s affected the nature of anthropological research in a number of ways. Acculturation studies were in vogue. For the Coast Salish, such works as Marian W. Smith's (1949) *Indians of the Urban Northwest*, Edwin Lemert's (1954) *The Life and Death of an Indian State*, and Claudia Lewis' (1970) *Indian Families of the Northwest Coast* are indicative of this trend. What characterizes this era most, however, is the largely unpublished reports prepared on behalf of US tribes and the US government for the Indian Claims Commission hearings. Initiated by the Indian Claims Commission Act, 1946, which established the Indian Court of Claims, eventually 852 claims were filed and consolidated into 370 dockets. Many cases are still pending, but the Indian Court of Claims was disbanded in 1978 and the standing cases turned over to the US Court of Claims. Several anthropologists contributed to the Indian Claims Commission with Coast Salish research, including Verne Ray, Carroll Riley, Colin Tweddell, William Elmendorf, Wayne Suttles, and June M. Collins. The most prolific, however, was Herbert C. Taylor Jr. He was my advisor while I was a master's student at Western Washington University from 1975 to 1977. Therefore, I was privy to many observations he made on the role of the expert witness that were never put into print. He continued to work on court cases until his death in 1991. In the 1980s, he shifted from working exclusively for the tribes, as he did in the Indian Claims Commission cases, to working mostly for the State of Washington.

Taylor was trained in anthropology at the University of Chicago. When he came to western Washington in 1951, his background was in Rio Grande archaeology. His doctoral dissertation was a seminal work in ethnohistory, exploring the reasons for the demise of the Norse Greenland colonies. When he was approached to work on Indian Claims Commission cases, he had had no ethnographic experience with Indians of the Pacific Northwest. Nevertheless, he would eventually produce reports on several Salish tribes – the Tillamook, Chehalis, and Medicine Creek Tribes (Puyallup, Nisqually, Squaxin, and Muckleshoot) – as well as the Chinook and the Makah. Although these reports were never intended for publication, they appeared unedited, along with hundreds of others, in 1974 in the *Garland American Indian Ethnohistory Series*. Taylor also produced dozens of manuscripts that were never published but are housed in court records. So, although his work on the Coast Salish was prolific, it has not been widely disseminated, for the most part being read only by lawyers and specialists.

The field of ethnohistory in North America had its origins in the Indian Claims Commission hearings. Taylor was at the forefront of this development, publishing document-based articles in early volumes of the journal

Ethnohistory (Taylor 1960, 1962) and adopting historiographic over ethnographic methods. What the multitude of anthropologists – now ethnohistorians – discovered working on the Indian Claims Commission cases was that the courts were interested neither in salvage ethnography nor ethnological theory. Informant interviews were increasingly considered less valid as evidence because of their distance from precontact times. The courts considered theoretical discourse to be speculation. The Indian Claims Commission needed to be informed of the events that had transpired since contact, especially loss of land and resources in the wake of treaties and the creation of reservations, and descriptions of these events had to be supported by documentary evidence. For the courts, documents carry more validity than do oral traditions, and, although early ethnohistorians attempted to combine the two, gradually the reliance on documentary evidence came to predominate.

Taylor's "Anthropological Investigation of the Medicine Creek Tribes" is an example of a work that combines the ethnographic method with documentary evidence. While not exemplary in its application of historiographic or ethnographic methods, the courts found it acceptable. Taylor's insight into the larger context of Coast Salish reality was keen, and he had a presence on the stand. The courts found his presentation of the information convincing, especially because he was able to relate that material to a larger political context. He was fond of saying that the western Washington Indians had to deal with "storms brewed in other men's seas." Realizing that an understanding of Coast Salish history was as much dependent upon national and international events as upon local concerns, he was able to draw this perception into his discussions and appearances on the witness stand but, unfortunately, not into his reports. In transcripts of the court proceedings, Taylor discusses such events as the need for a balance between free and slave states in the Union prior to the Civil War. This explained the slavery provision in the western Washington treaties. The contest of Great Britain and the United States over the northwest, settled only in 1846, was still fresh in 1855 and explained Governor Stevens' directive to break the ascendancy of the Hudson's Bay Company, which led to a provision in the treaties prohibiting trade "at Vancouver's Island or elsewhere out of the dominions of the United States." These insights were not mentioned in the reports; rather, the reports are straightforward presentations of facts, with some "anthropologizing" to make up for the lack of ethnographic material.

In "Anthropological Investigation of the Medicine Creek Tribes," Taylor (1974, 412) advanced the view that ethnographic work among the Coast Salish was no longer fruitful and that documentary evidence was far more reliable: "The modern Puget Sound Indians are almost completely Americanized ... Furthermore the ethnologist naturally tends to rely upon the intelligent native observer, rather than the normal or sub-normal native – it was, however, precisely the intelligent Puget Sound Indian who tended most rapidly to adjust to the American way of life, which meant the shedding of the Indian mores and traditions."

Few today would agree with Taylor's assessment, but it certainly speaks to the approach evident during the era of the Indian Claims Commission. Taylor spent about one hundred days conducting interviews with members of the Puyallup, Nisqually, Squaxin, and Muckleshoot tribes. In all, he interviewed forty individuals, eighteen of whom he considered to be "reliable." In his report he maintained that ethnographic information was less reliable than was documentary evidence because of the distance from the treaty period and because of the inherent bias of his informants, all of whom were aware of the suit in progress and who, therefore, "made fantastic claims of territorial possessions" (Taylor 1974, 460). This echoes Gibbs' concern over the veracity of ethnographic information voiced a century earlier.

Coast Salish research became increasingly focused on historic documentation and less field-based. The attitude that ethnographic work was fruitless pervaded much of the study of Native American cultures at this time, a trend that has only recently come under scrutiny (see Boxberger 2004).

Litigation

Not much went on in Coast Salish research in the 1970s and 1980s. There was a general impression in North American anthropology that the Northwest Coast was an anthropological wasteland. "Boas had already done it all" or "the Indians are all acculturated" were the reasons given for a general lack of interest in this area. The University of British Columbia stood alone as an academic institution interested in Northwest Coast studies during this era. With regard to the Coast Salish, Michael Kew was exemplary. While a few notable works were written during these twenty years (see, for example, Amoss 1978; Kennedy and Bouchard 1983; Tollefson 1987, 1989), most representative Coast Salish ethnographic and ethnohistorical research was carried out on behalf of Native peoples seeking restitution in the courts. Barbara Lane stands out as a "not so common" example of Coast Salish anthropological research. Lane produced dozens, perhaps hundreds, of reports on behalf of Coast Salish and other Native groups. She was a professional expert witness. Her entrée came through her involvement in *United States v. Washington,* the *Boldt* decision, and continued through numerous subproceedings and subsidiary cases relating to the resource rights of western Washington Indians. Subsequently, she presented testimony in British Columbia, Oregon, Alaska, and elsewhere as her expertise as an anthropological expert witness became widely known and respected. Almost all of the research she produced remains in the area of "grey literature," but a few pieces have been published for limited distribution, and a few have been published on the Internet through the Center for World Indigenous Studies in Olympia, Washington.

Barbara Lane received her PhD from the University of Washington in 1953. The title of her dissertation is "A Comparative and Analytic Study of Some Aspects of Northwest Coast Religion." She subsequently spent time at the University of Victoria, where she was mostly interested in Polynesian kinship. In the early 1970s, she began research in preparation for fishing rights litigation, an endeavour that would consume the next twenty-five years. Lane's work primarily focused on the understanding Indians had of the treaties at the time they were negotiated. Her extensive research into the historical record was used to convincingly present interpretations to the court that were widely successful for many tribes. "Background of Treaty Making in Western Washington" (Lane 1977) is just one example of a general discussion of treaty issues. Reports were also prepared on the various tribes and specific issues that came up in numerous subproceedings and other cases.

"Background of Treaty Making in Western Washington" presented an interpretation of the treaty phrase "to fish in common," upon which the fishing rights cases were centred. Giving a brief ethnographic and historic overview emphasizing the importance of salmon, Lane inserts numerous excerpts from contemporary documents that support her contention. Integral to the interpretation of treaty rights in the United States is an understanding of how Indians perceived the treaties at the time of their negotiation. Taking the treaty language apart phrase by phrase, Lane presents her expert opinion of how the language originated and how it would have been interpreted, whether or not the Indians perceived what they were signing, and who the contemporary heirs of succession to the tribes named (and not named) in the treaties would be.

The interpretation of "to fish in common" is one of the most important court actions in the history of Indian law. As *United States v. Washington* made its way through the appeal process and eventually to the Supreme Court of the United States, the interpretation of the phrase was consistent with Lane's opinion of its meaning and today forms the basis of the allocation of salmon in the treaty areas of Washington and Oregon.

Lane contended that the phrase was introduced by George Gibbs, who understood not only the importance of salmon to the Indians but also the disaster that would result if they were removed to one centralized reservation and not allowed to pursue fishing in their usual and accustomed places (Lane 1977, 9). Basing her argument on the official treaty record and on ethnographic evidence, Lane contended that the phrase did not mean that non-Indians would exercise control over Indian fishing; rather, it was her opinion that "at least some of the Indian parties expected to exercise control over 'citizens' fishing at usual and accustomed Indian fishing sites" (14). Relying as much on the non-Indian understanding of Indian fishing at treaty time as on the Indian understanding of the treaty language, Lane presented a persuasive argument that convinced the court that "in common" meant to share equally – thus the court's decision to allocate 50 percent of the salmon harvest to treaty Indian fishers.

> In my view, the most likely Indian interpretation of the "in common" language would be that non-Indians were to be allowed to fish without interfering with continued pursuit of traditional Indian fishing. I think it most likely that the government intended to provide for non-Indian participation in fishing with no thought that this would require any restriction of Indian fishing. (Lane 1977, 15)

Barbara Lane has been widely successful in the role of an expert witness defending Coast Salish rights to natural resources. Subsequent spinoffs from *United States v. Washington* have extended the "in common" language to other fisheries (such as herring and halibut) and other natural resources (such as shellfish and hunting). These extensions have been put into place by the courts and by administrative decisions attempting to avoid further court cases.

Self-Determination

Today the Coast Salish define their traditions largely in reference to salmon. In the wake of fishing rights decisions in both Canada and the United States, the First Salmon Ceremony has been revived. The Coast Salish, who have adopted Western scientific knowledge of salmonid enhancement and management, have combined it with a traditional understanding of the salmon's biological life cycle and its spiritual relationship to Coast Salish people. The Lummi adult education program mentioned above became the Lummi College of Fisheries shortly after the fishing rights case and continues today as part of the more comprehensive Northwest Indian College, a tribally controlled community college based at Lummi, with over two dozen branch campuses around the northwest United States. Most Coast Salish tribes and bands have developed some sort of salmonid enhancement program, such as fish hatcheries. The Coast Salish regained control of the salmon resource at a time when salmon were on the decline. After a century of environmental degradation, industrialization, overfishing, and mismanagement, salmon were becoming increasingly endangered at a time when the Coast Salish were becoming increasingly involved in management and enhancement. They have taken it as their task to reverse this negative trend by resuming the role of guardians of the salmon.

   Guardianship requires the ability to make decisions as a governmental entity. The move to self-governance has been coupled with natural resource and land issues. It was a Coast Salish band, the Sechelt, that was the first in Canada to achieve self-governance in 1986, and it was three Coast Salish tribes – the Quinalt, Jamestown S'Klallam, and Lummi – that were among the first to negotiate pilot self-governance within the United States in 1993. The Sechelt were also among the first to question the direction of modern treaty negotiations in British Columbia by withdrawing from the treaty process and pursuing their claims in court. The primary concern of the Coast Salish of the early 2000s on both sides of the border is over Aboriginal rights and title as it relates to self-determination. A claim to rights requires considerable input from anthropological and historical research. I am involved in this type of research with the Sechelt band as we gather information to support Sechelt claims, but dissemination of this work is years away. Another Coast Salish group, the Stó:lō, have been instrumental in presenting a model to the public that other Native groups across North America will come to emulate. *A Stó:lō Coast Salish Historical Atlas* (Carlson, McHalsie, and Perrier 2001) has brought together historical documentation, oral history, and other research by fourteen scholars, including Stó:lō historians, archaeologists, and anthropologists, in a comprehensive presentation of Stó:lō history and culture. This work is not only comprehensive but also beautifully presented. It clearly outlines the Stó:lō attachment to *S'ólh Téméxw* (our land) and the natural resources it holds. The *Stó:lō Atlas* explains considerable ethnographic data within the context of contemporary Stó:lō life. Much of it details the spiritual life and oral traditions as recorded by Stó:lō and non-Stó:lō ethnographers and interprets these works for contemporary needs. For example, the journey of X̱á:ls (the Transformer) as told by Old Pierre to Diamond Jenness is transferred to a map of *S'ólh Téméxw* along with another story that illustrates X̱á:ls traditions in conjunction with Stó:lō claims to territory (Jenness 2001, 6-7). The Stó:lō have been actively engaged in repatriating intellectual property through the collection of published and unpublished data that is archived in band facilities. Coupled with this is the ongoing collection of new data and new histories that will be used to present an emic view of Stó:lō culture and tradition.

This work and others that are likely to follow received much impetus from the landmark decision in *Delgamuukw v. British Columbia*. In that 1997 decision, the Supreme Court of Canada established that Aboriginal rights exist and that oral history could be used to prove Aboriginal title. This put the onus for clarifying Aboriginal rights on the bands. *A Stó:lō Coast Salish Historical Atlas* was produced by the Stó:lō Nation Aboriginal Rights and Title Department, with the treaty process and the assertion of Aboriginal rights clearly in mind. The decision in *Delgamuukw* did not establish Aboriginal title for the Gitksan or any other First Nation; rather, it established a test for proving Aboriginal title. Known as the *Delgamuukw Test*, it consists of three parts: a band must prove pre-sovereignty occupation (in British Columbia sovereignty was established in 1846); a band must demonstrate continuity from pre-sovereignty occupation until the present day; and, a band must show exclusive possession of the lands that it claims. "Overlapping land claims" is proving to be a thorny issue for BC First Nations, and this is one of the areas where anthropological research is likely to encounter its own internal conflicts.

Once sovereignty is established, a band may attempt to secure rights to compensation for "infringement" of its rights. An infringement "justification test" consists of two parts: the Crown may justify infringement if there is a "compelling and substantive legislative objective" but the Crown must also exercise its fiduciary responsibility. Seemingly contradictory, these two parts of the justification test will take much research time and energy in the years to come. The First Nations of British Columbia have not yet challenged these tests through litigation. Where anthropological research is playing a critical role in collaborative work with Coast Salish bands is in using *Delgamuukw* as a guide for preparing evidence that may eventually be presented in court. Such work involves not merely reviewing the century and a half of work that has preceded it but also gathering new historical, archaeological, and linguistic evidence and oral histories that show continuity and infringement of Aboriginal rights. The type of collaborative work that the *Stó:lō Atlas* presents is an example of the direction Coast Salish anthropological research will take in the years to come. This research will take its cue from the needs of the Coast Salish communities, not the intellectual and theoretical curiosity of the researcher. It is no coincidence that interpretive work (e.g., Miller 1998; Bierwert 1999) is conspicuously absent in works like the *Stó:lō Atlas*. This genre of research, while intellectually interesting, finds little practical application in Coast Salish communities. Perhaps this is because, as Rasmus (2001, 31) has observed, "Bierwert's and J. Miller's works are examples of how anthropologists compete among each other for the authority to speak as/for/about the 'other.' They do this by disenfranchising the knowledge of their colleagues in order to position themselves as truly aware and sensitive to Native peoples and their lifeways." Further,

> The lack of continuity in ideologies between researchers and Native community members results in the open dissemination of the acquired traditional knowledge by the researcher, which in turn leads to the marginalization of a group's intellectual resources. The source community understands the research situation quite differently ... The process of research relies on the extraction of information for analysis and publication. This leads to the marginalization of Native groups from their own histories and traditional knowledge. The publication and deposition of the knowledge in ideologically and geographically remote media and repositories alienates Native groups entirely from the transmission process and is what defines the nature of intellectual hegemony. (Rasmus 2002, 296)

The *Stó:lō Atlas* is an example of a strategy that is directing the course of contemporary Coast Salish research. As Rasmus points out, research agendas should be determined by the needs of First Nations communities, not by the needs of academics. Contemporary Coast Salish anthropologists are working within the context of *Boldt* and *Delgamuukw*, and our entrée into Native communities depends upon the communities' perception that our research has some practical application in respect to land, resources, and self-determination. Not only does our relationship with Coast Salish communities depend upon this perception but our moral and ethical commitments demand it. My hope is that we are witnessing a shift from a politically motivated research agenda directed by the nation-state to a politically motivated research agenda directed by the Fourth World state. Regardless, the legal system will continue to demand that traditional knowledge form the basis of evidence. To what extent are the Coast Salish communities willing to divulge this privileged information?

Conclusion

Early in Coast Salish research, traditional knowledge was incorporated into the realm of academic discourse, with Native consultants engaging in research as willing participants. Repeatedly, early ethnographers comment on consultants who were anxious to record their traditional knowledge before it was lost forever. Through the shift in research strategies, exemplified by the Indian Claims Commission, the Native consultant was marginalized as traditional ethnographies and historical documentation came to carry more weight. In this, the era of self-determination, the Coast Salish are seizing control of their histories through both the reanalysis of existing historical and ethnographic data and the collection of additional oral histories and traditions.

The anthropology of the Coast Salish has been guided by legislative and legal needs from the beginning. The five "not so common" examples discussed – Gibbs, Jenness, Taylor, Lane, and the Stó:lō Rights and Title – are indicative of the needs of the dominant society at the time and reflect how those needs were imposed on the Coast Salish. To deny that this has been the case is to deny the basic methodological premise of anthropological and ethnohistorical research. The *commonality* of anthropological engagement over the last 150 years is indicative of the political and economic concerns that have shaped Coast Salish reality. Anthropology has wrestled with theoretical interpretations that present the colonized as innocent bystanders in the complex world system that subordinates them. Anthropology has also wrestled with its role in that process. Neither the Coast Salish nor any other indigenes have been passive bystanders; rather, they have been active participants in local responses to global processes. Anthropologists have assumed the role of "speaking for" the Coast Salish, making intellectual property a common property. This process is reinforced by the socio-legal necessities of creating economic and political opportunity. Nevertheless, throughout this history there has been a constant undercurrent of Coast Salish traditional knowledge that has persisted in the networks of kin and community. Anthropologists have consistently tried to tap into this knowledge but, inevitably, with a political or personal agenda structuring their research strategy.

I can imagine what conducting Coast Salish ethnography must have been like in the early 1950s, in the 1930s, or the 1890s for that matter. It is easy to look back and see what we would have done differently, the questions we would have asked had we had the chance. Though the important question might be why were the ethnographers doing what they were doing at the time? I recall a letter I received from Erna Gunther stating that she was amazed that I was doing S'Klallam ethnography in the 1970s as she thought she had obtained the last bits of ethnographic data from the S'Klallam in the 1920s. However, she insightfully noted that research strategies change. Every generation of anthropologists laments that it is too late: nevertheless, Coast Salish traditions are alive and well, oral histories thrive, and ethnographic work continues. Most important, I would add, the Coast Salish are taking control of intellectual property as a means of directing the course of an anthropological research agenda that more adequately meets their needs.

References

Adamson, Thelma, 1934. *Folk-Tales of the Coast Salish.* Memoirs of the American Folklore Society, No. 27. New York: G.E. Stechert.

Amoss, Pamela. 1978. *Coast Salish Spirit Dancing: Survival of an Ancestral Religion.* Seattle: University of Washington Press.

Ballard, Arthur C. 1927. Some Tales of the Southern Puget Sound Salish. *University of Washington Publications in Anthropology* 2 (3): 57-81.

–. 1929. Mythology of Southern Puget Sound. *University of Washington Publications in Anthropology* 3 (2): 31-150.

–. 1935. Southern Puget Sound Kinship Terms. *American Anthropologist* 37 (1): 111-16.

Barnett, Homer G. 1938. The Coast Salish of Canada. *American Anthropologist* 40 (1): 118-41.

–. 1939. Culture Element Distributions, IX: Gulf of Georgia Salish. *University of California Anthropological Records* 1 (5): 221-95.

–. 1955. *The Coast Salish of British Columbia.* University of Oregon Monographs, Studies in Anthropology 4. Eugene, OR: University of Oregon Press.

Beckham, Stephen Dow. 1969. George Gibbs, 1815-1873: Historian and Ethnologist. PhD diss., University of California.

Beringer, Patricia Ann. 1982. Northwest Coast Traditional Salmon Fisheries: Systems of Resource Utilization. MA thesis, University of British Columbia.

Bierwert, Crisca. 1999. *Brushed by Cedar, Living by the River: Coast Salish Figures of Power.* Tucson: University of Arizona Press.

Boas, Franz. 1891. The Lku'ngen. In *Second General Report on the Indians of British Columbia,* 563-82. London: British Association for the Advancement of Science.

–. 1894. Indian Tribes of the Lower Fraser River. In *64th Annual Report of the British Association for the Advancement of Science for 1890,* 454-63. London: British Association for the Advancement of Science.

–. 1895. Salishan Texts. *Proceedings of the American Philosophical Society* 34 (147): 31-48.

Boxberger, Daniel L. 1984. The Introduction of Horses to the Southern Puget Sound Salish. In *Western Washington Socio-Economics,* ed. Herbert C. Taylor and Garland F. Grabert, 103-19. Bellingham: Western Washington University.

–. 1988. In and out of the Labor Force: The Lummi Indians and the Development of the Commercial Salmon Fishery of North Puget Sound, 1880-1900. *Ethnohistory* 35 (2): 161-90.

–. 1994. Lightning Boldts and Sparrow Wings: A Comparison of Coast Salish Fishing Rights in British Columbia and Washington State. *Native Studies Review* 9 (1): 1-13.

–. 2000. *To Fish in Common: The Ethnohistory of Lummi Indian Salmon Fishing.* Seattle: University of Washington Press.

–. 2004. Whither the Expert Witness? Anthropology in the Post-*Delgamuukw* Courtroom. In *Coming to Shore: Northwest Coast Ethnology, Traditions and Visions,* ed. Marie Mauzé, Michael Harkin, and Sergei Kan, 323-38. Lincoln: University of Nebraska Press.

Boxberger, Daniel L., and David M. Schaepe. 2001. Stó:lō Mapping and Knowledge of the North Cascades, ca. 1859. In *A Stó:lō Coast Salish Historical Atlas,* ed. Keith Thor Carlson, Albert McHalsie, and Jan Perrier, 124-25. Vancouver: Douglas and McIntyre.

Carlson, Keith Thor, Albert McHalsie, and Jan Perrier, eds. 2001. *A Stó:lō Coast Salish Historical Atlas.* Vancouver: Douglas and McIntyre.

Carstensen, Vernon. 1954. *Pacific Northwest Letters of George Gibbs.* Portland: Oregon Historical Society.

Cohen, Felix. 1942. *Handbook of Federal Indian Law.* Albuquerque: University of New Mexico Press.

Collins, June M. 1949. John Fornsby: The Personal Document of a Coast Salish Indian. In *Indians of the Urban Northwest*. Columbia University Contributions to Anthropology 36, ed. Marian W. Smith, 287-341. New York: Columbia University Press.

–. 1974. *Valley of the Spirits: The Upper Skagit Indians of Western Washington*. Seattle: University of Washington Press.

Costello, J.A. 1895. *The Siwash: Their Life Tales and Legends of Puget Sound and Pacific Northwest*. Seattle: Calvert.

Crosby, Thomas. 1907. *Among the An-Ko-Me-Nums; or Flathead Tribes of Indians of the Pacific Coast*. Toronto: William Briggs.

Duff, Wilson. 1952. *The Upper Stalo Indians of the Fraser Valley, British Columbia*. Anthropology in British Columbia, Memoir No. 1. Victoria: British Columbia Provincial Museum.

Eells, Myron. 1889. The Twana, Chemakum and Klallam Indians of Washington Territory. In *Annual Report of the Smithsonian Institution for the Year 1887*. Washington, DC: Smithsonian Institution.

–. 1985. *The Indians of Puget: The Notebooks of Myron Eells*. Ed. George B. Castille. Seattle: University of Washington Press.

Elmendorf, William W. 1960. *The Structure of Twana Culture*. Washington State University Research Studies 28 (3), Monographic Supplement 2. Pullman, WA: Washington State University Press.

–. 1993. *Twana Narratives: Native Historical Accounts of a Coast Salish Culture*. Seattle: University of Washington Press.

Farrand, Livingston. 1900. Basketry Designs of the Salish Indians. *Memoirs of the American Museum of Natural History* 2 (5): 391-99.

–. 1902. Traditions of the Quinalt Indians. *Memoirs of the American Museum of Natural History* 4 (3): 77-132.

Gibbs, George. 1855. Indian Tribes of the Territory of Washington. In *Report of Explorations and Surveys to Ascertain the Most Practicable Route for a Railroad from the Mississippi River to the Pacific Ocean*. Washington, DC: Thomas H. Ford.

–. 1877. Tribes of Western Washington and Northwestern Oregon. *Contributions to North American Ethnology* 1 (2): 157-361.

Gunther, Erna. 1927. Klallam Ethnography. *University of Washington Publications in Anthropology* 1 (5): 171-314.

Haeberlin, Hermann. 1924. Mythology of Puget Sound. *Journal of American Folklore* 37 (145-46): 371-438.

–. 1930. Indians of Puget Sound. *University of Washington Publications in Anthropology* 4 (1): 1-83. (Originally published as *Ethnographische Notizen über die Indianerstämme de Puget-Sundes,* translated by Erna Gunther.)

Hancock, Robert L.A. 2002. The Potential for a Canadian Anthropology: Diamond Jenness's Arctic Ethnography. MA thesis, University of Victoria. http://www.worldwiderob.ca/rob/pdf/frontmatter.pdf.

Harris, Douglas C. 2001. *Fish, Law, and Colonialism: The Legal Capture of Salmon in British Columbia*. Toronto: University of Toronto Press.

Hewes, Gordon. 1973. Indian Fisheries Productivity in Pre-contact Times in the Pacific Salmon Area. *Northwest Anthropological Research Notes* 7 (2): 133-55.

Hill-Tout, Charles. 1900. Notes on the Sk.qõ'mic of British Columbia, a Branch of the Great Salish Stock of North America. In *70th Report for the British Association for the Advancement of Science for 1900,* 472-549. London: British Association for the Advancement of Science.

–. 1903. Ethnological Studies of the Mainland Halkōmē'lem, a Division of the Salish of British Columbia. In *72nd Report for the British Association for the Advancement of Science for 1902*, 355-449. London: British Association for the Advancement of Science.

–. 1904a. Report on the Sicìatl of British Columbia, a Coast Division of the Salish Stock. *Journal of the Anthropological Institute of Great Britain and Ireland* 34: 20-91.

–. 1904b. Ethnological Report on the StsEélis and Sk·aúlist Tribes of the Halkōmē'lem Division of the Salish of British Columbia. *Journal of the Anthropological Institute of Great Britain and Ireland* 34: 311-76.

Jenness, Diamond. 1932. *The Indians of Canada.* National Museum of Canada, Bulletin 65, Anthropological Series No. 15. Ottawa: National Museum of Canada.

–. 1955. *The Faith of a Coast Salish Indian.* Anthropology in British Columbia, Memoir No. 3. Victoria: British Columbia Provincial Museum.

Kennedy, Dorothy I.D., and Randy Bouchard. 1983. *Sliammon Life, Sliammon Lands.* Vancouver: Talonbooks.

Kulchyski, Peter. 1993. Anthropology in the Service of the State: Diamond Jenness and Canadian Indian Policy. *Journal of Canadian Studies* 28 (2): 21-51.

Lane, Barbara S. 1977. Background of Treaty Making in Western Washington. *American Indian Journal* 3 (4): 2-11. http://www.cwis.org/fwdp/Americas/wwtreaty.txt.

Lemert, Edwin. 1954. The Life and Death of an Indian State. *Human Organization* 13 (3): 23-27.

Lewis, Claudia. 1970. *Indian Families of the Northwest Coast: The Impact of Change.* Chicago: University of Chicago Press.

Miller, Bruce G., and Daniel L. Boxberger. 1994. Creating Chiefdoms: The Puget Sound Case. *Ethnohistory* 41 (2): 267-93.

Miller, Jay. 1998. *Shamanic Odyssey: The Lushootseed Salish Journey to the Land of the Dead.* Menlo Park, CA: Ballena Press.

Pearse, Peter H. 1982. *Turning the Tide: A New Policy for Canada's Pacific Fisheries.* Report of the Commissioner on Pacific Fisheries Policy. Vancouver: Department of Fisheries and Oceans.

Rasmus, S. Michelle. 2001. Repatriating Words: Local Knowledge in a Global Context. MA thesis, Western Washington University.

–. 2002. Repatriating Words: Local Knowledge in a Global Context. *American Indian Quarterly* 26 (2): 286-307.

Records Relating to Treaties. 1854. Record of the Proceedings of the Commission to Hold Treaties with the Indian Tribes in Washington Territory and the Blackfoot Country. Microcopies of Record in the National Archives, Washington, DC, no. 5, roll 26.

Sapir, Edward. 1915. *Noun Reduplication in Comox: A Salish Language of Vancouver Island.* Anthropological Series 6, Memoir No. 63. Ottawa: Geological Survey of Canada.

–. 1939. Songs for a Comox Dancing Mask. *Ethnos* 4 (2): 49-55.

Singh, Ram Raj Prasad. 1966. *Aboriginal Economic System of the Olympic Peninsula Indians, Western Washington.* Sacramento Anthropological Society Papers 4. Sacramento: Sacramento State College.

Smith, Marian W. 1940. *The Puyallup-Nisqually.* Columbia University Contributions to Anthropology 32. New York: Columbia University Press.

–. 1949. *Indians of the Urban Northwest.* Columbia University Contributions to Anthropology 36. New York: Columbia University Press.

Snyder, Sally. 1975. Quest for the Sacred in Northern Puget Sound: An Interpretation of Potlatch. *Ethnology* 14 (2): 149-61.

Snyder, Warren. 1968. *Southern Puget Sound Salish: Texts, Place Names and Dictionary.* Sacramento Anthropological Society Papers 9. Sacramento: Sacramento State College.

Suttles, Wayne. 1974. Economic Life of the Coast Salish of Haro and Rosario Straits. In *Coast Salish and Western Washington Indians*. Vol. 1, 41-570. New York: Garland Publishing.

–. 1987. *Coast Salish Essays*. Seattle: University of Washington Press.

Suttles, Wayne, and Aldona C. Jonaitis. 1990. History of Research in Ethnology. In *Handbook of North American Indians*. Vol. 7, *Northwest Coast,* ed. Wayne Suttles. Washington, DC: Smithsonian Institution.

Taylor, Herbert C. Jr. 1960. The Fort Nisqually Census of 1838-1839. *Ethnohistory* 7 (4): 399-409.

–. 1962. The "Intermittent Fever" Epidemic of the 1830s on the Lower Columbia River. *Ethnohistory* 9 (2): 160-78.

–. 1974. Anthropological Investigation of the Medicine Creek Tribes. In *Coast Salish and Western Washington Indians*. Vol. 4, 401-73. New York: Garland Publishing.

Tennant, Paul. 1990. *Aboriginal Peoples and Politics: The Indian Land Question in British Columbia, 1849-1989*. Vancouver: UBC Press.

Tollefson, Kenneth. 1987. The Snoqualmie: A Puget Sound Chiefdom. *Ethnology* 26: 121-36.

–. 1989. Political Organization of the Duwamish. *Ethnology* 28: 135-50.

Waterman, T.T. 1930. *The Paraphernalia of the Duwamish "Spirit Canoe" Ceremony*. New York: Museum of the American Indian, Heye Foundation, Indian Notes and Monographs, 7 (2): 129-48; (3): 295-312; (4): 535-61.

–. 1973. *Notes on the Ethnology of the Indians of Puget Sound*. Indian Notes and Monographs, Miscellaneous Series No. 59. New York: Museum of the American Indian, Heye Foundation.

Wells, Oliver. 1987. *The Chilliwack and Their Neighbors*. Ed. Ralph Maud, Brent Galloway, and Marie Weeden. Vancouver: Talonbooks.

Wike, Joyce. 1945. Modern Spirit Dancing of Northern Puget Sound. MA thesis, University of Washington.

Winthrop, Theodore. 1913. *The Canoe and Saddle*. Tacoma, WA: John H. Williams.

3

We Have to Take Care of Everything That Belongs to Us

Naxaxalhts'i, Albert (Sonny) McHalsie

I would like to share some of the teachings and acquired knowledge about Halq'eméylem place names and their relationship to various important aspects of Stó:lō culture and history. I have worked at the Stó:lō Nation for the past nineteen years, both directly and collaboratively, researching such topics as Halq'eméylem place names, the mapping of fishing sites, and traditional use studies (historical, anthropological, archaeological, and genealogical). I do my best to recognize the contributions of both Coast Salish literature and oral history to my work. The academic world and the oral history process both share an important common principle: they contribute to knowledge by building upon what is known and remembering that learning is a life-long quest. I would like to share my perspective of our unique Stó:lō culture and history and its importance to the ultimate recognition of Stó:lō Aboriginal rights and title.

It is important that I provide some context on my own background as I believe it has contributed to my personal growth. My father was Nlaka'pamux, also known as the Thompson, and my mother was Stó:lō. My father was from Anderson Creek and my mother was from Chowethel. They both spoke their own languages and were exposed to their own cultures. Over the years, my father was quite involved with our spirituality. He knew what our culture was about. I know that he was kind of critical of things that weren't ours – for instance, the pow-wow. He was always involved with Indian doctors; whenever something was wrong in our family he turned to an Indian doctor. I remember that sort of exposure. His uncle was an Indian doctor, and my father did some Indian doctor work as well. How much training he had in that, I'm not sure. My mother spoke her language. She did a lot of talking in her language with my grandmother when my grandmother was around. But for the most part there wasn't too much exposure to our culture, and I think that was probably because my parents were a product of the residential school system. I think they both thought that it would be better for us not to learn the culture because we were trying to learn Western society's education system. I know that, in the past, some elders said that they didn't want to teach people the traditional ways because they thought that would hold them back. So I kind of think that might have been the mindset that my parents had.

I had limited exposure to our traditional culture when I was younger, but enough to think about the importance of it and to try to understand some of it. I started my work back in 1985 with the Stó:lō and the Alliance of Tribal Councils, recording heritage sites, working place names, and fishing grounds as well as learning a little bit about the different Transformer rocks – all those different things. Prior to that I had no real knowledge of those things. Although, I remember my father once talking about the coyote rock when we were pulling into Lytton one time. I remember him saying, "There's a coyote rock around here." And that kind of stuck in my head. I didn't know what it was all about; it wasn't until later on when I was pulling into that town with our anthropologist, and he mentioned something about the same thing, that I thought, "Wow." I had remembered my dad saying something about a coyote rock at that location as well. I remember my father mentioning that – there's a coyote rock there. My mother never shared too much about our cultural history, although she was probably exposed to it. I mean she knew the language. It wasn't until later on, after she had passed on, that I found out from one of my elders, Selthelmetheqw, a.k.a. Peter Dennis Peters, that my grandfather was quite knowledgeable about place names. One of my personal inspirations for learning was just knowing that my grandfather knew a lot about place names. I remember once interviewing the late Selthelmetheqw, and he said, "Oh Sonny, I wish your grandfather was here right now." He said, "Your grandfather knew way more than ... I did." That was an inspiration to me, just knowing that those place names and that what I was learning about was something that he had known about.

Another inspiration was my grandfather Antoine on my dad's side. He died ten years before I was born. I heard a lot of stories about him being a grizzly bear hunter. I carry one of his names: Naxaxalhts'i. He was the one who was given the name McHalsie, he was the one who, as a young boy, was known as Pa'kups and as he got older he was known as Naxaxalhts'i and then he was known as Mashkest. When he was baptized he was given the name Antoine, and when the Indian agent came to the reserve to record his name he told him that he didn't have a surname and he said he wanted his two adult Indian names – Mashkest and Naxaxalhts'i – so that's when the Indian agent wrote down "McHalsie." So that's the origin of my last name. That's what Annie York told me. Annie York actually told me it was

Naxetsi, but it's only just been the last year now I've found out from my cousin Mamie Henry up in Lytton that it's actually Naxaxalhts'i – I was missing two sounds in there.

My dad told me a lot of different stories about Antoine and the fact that he was a non-drinker, and that's why I'm a non-drinker. I haven't been drinking for over nineteen years now, and prior to that I had quit drinking quite young. When I was twenty years old I quit drinking. That was a big inspiration for me as well. I used to travel through the Fraser Canyon when I drove or caught the school bus from Anderson Creek down to Hope, and I never realized the rich history that was there. I used to sleep on the bus. I took it for granted, looking at all the creeks. And I remember seeing the crosses. I remember seeing the cross at Q'aleliktel, Indian Reserve 20. And I never really thought too much about it, never even asked about it when I think about it now. It wasn't until later on when I started recording place names, I started taking out elders – including Tillie Gutierrez and Al Gutierrez, the late Agnes Kelly, the late Amelia Douglas, the late Rosaleen George – to help me on place names.

S'ólh Téméxw te ikw'elo: This Is Our Land

The linguist Brent Galloway had quite an extensive list of place names, which he documented through working with the elders back in the 1970s. I used his list as something to expand upon, and then worked along with other experts in various fields within our own Aboriginal Rights and Title Department. I worked with our historian, Keith Thor Carlson, and anthropologist Brian Thom. Of course they knew of different anthropologists who did studies here, so we were able to acquire some of those records as well. That includes Wayne Suttles' work with the Q'eyts'i, George Gibbs' 1858 boundary survey notes, Wilson Duff's fieldnotes, Norman Lerman's work with the elders, and Charles Hill-Tout's work. There are even some of the McKenna-McBride Royal Commission interviews, and we were able to take some place names off of that, such as those from Marian Smith's fieldnotes and Oliver Wells' interviews.

I took quite an interest in it and really began to learn what the places mean to the Stó:lō people. And it took quite a few years to try to learn this. One of the other teachings too that the elders tell us is that – and this is an elder who shared this with Stan Greene, one of our local artists – he said that our culture is still there, it's just that it is so strong, it's something that we can't take back all at once. We can take only a little bit of it back at a time. And each time we take a little bit of our culture back it makes us stronger so that we can take back more. And I think about that, and I think about that in an academic sense as well, where, you know, in academia certain ideas, interpretations, and those sort of things, are put forward and are built upon by others. I think those are the same – those two things kind of run parallel to each other. I just kind of look at it differently.

One of the teachings of the elders is that we're always learning; we never quit learning from the day we're born to the day we die. It seems like that was one of the teachings in the past. You're told to do things. You're never told why. You're just told to do it. And that's because that's how we do it! And it isn't until later on that you start putting things together, you start realizing why. So there's a lot of things I've been able to put together like that over the years, in terms of studying the place names, and then at the same time as studying the place names, studying our culture.

In the early 1980s, we were interviewing a number of elders at Coqualeetza. We had a video camera set up, and we had the late Agnes Kelly there and Tillie Gutierrez. That was the time when Tillie Gutierrez shared that one statement with us, and that statement means a lot to me now. It's actually a statement that we include in most of our maps and it's almost like our motto or one of the principles of our Aboriginal Rights and Title Department here at Stó:lō Nation. She said that when she was a little girl she remembered being up in Yale. She said that during the summer when she was fishing up there people would get together – the leaders would get together and start talking about the land question. She said every time they got together before they started their meeting, they all started off with one statement, and that was *"S'ólh Téméxw te ikw'elo. Xolhmet te mekw'stam it kwelat."* And that basically means, "This is our land and we have to take care of everything that belongs to us." I thought that was a pretty neat statement. I knew it was a profound statement about something that was important to us. But I mean, even at that time I knew it meant something, although I didn't quite understand what. Now I have a better idea but, like I said, I'm still learning as well. But I have a better idea of what that means now. And to me now when I look at that statement, that statement *S'ólh Téméxw te ikw'elo* – "this is our land" – that's our statement of our Aboriginal right and title, the statement of our ownership. But then the second part, *Xolhmet te mekw'stam it kwelat* – "We have to take care of everything that belongs to us" – that's our obligation, to take care of what's out there.

What is that "everything"? What is everything to us? Through the place names then, just following various different places, where each place talks about different things that are out there in our land, in our world. *S'ólh Téméxw* means "this is our land" and it also means "our world"; *Téméxw* is the word for "world" or even for "dirt," it's the same word as well. So "land"

– *S'ólh Téméxw te ikw'elo* – "this is our land" or "this is our dirt" or "this is our world." These are the same. That was expressed by Tillie; she said, "this is our land" in the context that she was using at that time. So, what is out there? Through the place names we are able to see all the various uses that our people had for the land – right from the berry-picking spots on the tops of the mountains that had various names. Some examples come from Xoletsa, the frozen lakes up above Yale. I first heard about that from my mom. She talked about going up there to these lakes above Yale as a child, and she said that, you know, back then they weren't supposed to go up there, and she said that she remembered going up there with some of her friends and she said that one of the things they were taught was not to be making a lot of noise when they went to that place – that children weren't really allowed there and they had to be really quiet and respectful. And she said that she and a couple of her friends went up there and they made a bunch of noise and started whistling and hollering. All of a sudden, she said, the mist just kind of appeared on top of the water – and then that's when she took off. I've come across other references that talk about that – I know these don't talk about that particular place – but usually when that mist comes out, then that's supposed to be when the water babies are present in the water. Although none of the elders ever said, "There's water babies up there," they always talk about "there's something up there at Xoletsa." Some elders suggest that it's a *stl'áleqem*, what has been described by Brent Galloway as a "supernatural being."

I think that it might have been *s'ó:lmexw*, or water babies, the little people that live underwater. So Xoletsa is not only a berry-picking place but also a spiritual place. So there's a huge campground up there where many people from Agassiz all the way up to Lytton used to catch a train to Yale and go picking, go picking berries up there. Up in that area there's three different lakes at different levels. There's a lower type of berry that they would gather on their way up to the main camp. They would gather berries there and then they'd move up to the lakes and start picking berries on the lower lake, and then when the berries started ripening at the higher elevations they'd start moving up to the higher lake, the third higher lake. They'd have the camp set up and they'd stay up there for a couple of weeks. At the same time they would be hunting and they would also be eating the little marmots. Lawrence Hope, one of the elders from Yale, said that that was a delicacy to the old people. They always looked forward to going up there and doing that. So there's a lot of – you know there's a lot to learn, just talking about that one place, because you learn about whether or not there's water babies, you learn that it's a place where children weren't allowed.

Ralph George talks about how, as a kid, he remembers there were two trails. The adults had a trail that went right by that lower lake. And he said that when children were there they had another trail that went way around because children had to stay away from that lake. Children were being protected. And so, again, there's another teaching in that there's something about children that they have to stay away from that place, right? He talked about the camps – you know, the different families had their own place to camp. He remembered where his family camped and those sorts of things. There's all kinds of different things when you just talk about that one place, there's so many different aspects of Stó:lō culture and history that you can learn just from that one place. And that's just one of the berry-picking grounds.

Another example of berry-picking grounds is up behind Chowethel at Q'aw. *Q'aw* means "to howl" and that's that dog that was transformed into stone. I just recently learned that that was a place that was attached to the flood story. The only places I was aware of that had to do with the flood story were Popeleho:ys, Mómet'es, Siyeqw, Alwis Ihqeletel, and Kw'ekw'e'i:qw – the Sumas Mountain. Those were all places that had to do with the flood story, and then just last week I was thumbing through the Wilson Duff fieldnotes and I found out that Q'aw and Smimkw, the mountain behind Jones Lake, they're also attached – they also have to do with the flood story, in that they were two mountains that were sticking up above the floodwaters. So now that provides another context for Q'aw – Q'aw is not only this howling dog that was transformed into stone but it is also situated in front of the berry-picking grounds.

I talked to the elders about that place. The late Bill Pat Charlie was talking about how he remembered, when he was a young boy, they used to go and clear the trail: they had a trail that zigzagged up that side of the mountain to the berry-picking grounds behind Q'aw. And he talked about how he and some of his cousins, when they were younger, had to go up and clear the trail and make sure it was clear of any deadfalls, any trees that fell over, anything like that. And halfway up there was a place where there was a camp. This was because, while young people would take three hours or so to climb up there, the elders would take two days. So you can imagine how old they would have been. And so the very old people still went up there even if it took them two days to go picking berries. They would still go up there to pick berries! It would take them one day to get to the first camping ground. Bill said that he and the late Gilbert Ewen and the late Jimmy Peters – all three of them from Chowethel – that it was part of their responsibility to make sure that there was firewood there, and they would have the camp set up so that the elders could camp there. Then, after that, they would camp there and make their way up and just pick berries and spend a couple of weeks up there.

Another thing that Bill mentioned is that Q'aw has to do not only with the flood story but also with <u>X</u>exá:ls (the Transformers), it being one of the places where a dog was transformed into stone. There's also another teaching concerning a place there, where, if they threw rocks over the edge, it was supposed to make it rain during times of drought. I haven't been able to find out the context of that. Bill and his two cousins, Jimmy and Gilbert, went up there and they were throwing rocks over the edge of Q'aw, trying to make it rain. So there's all these different things, these different places – Q'aw doesn't necessarily have to do with the berry-picking ground but it is right in front of it – there's this trail and all these different things that you can talk about for that particular place.

The late Agnes Kelly talked about how they used to go gathering berries up on the ridge behind Lorenzetto Creek – the headwaters of Lorenzetto Creek and the headwaters of Hunter Creek and Jones Lake. She said that her family would start at Skw'átets (or Peters Reserve) and go over that little mountain over to Jones Lake. At Jones Lake they would make their way right back to the very back ridge, and they would follow that ridge that separated those three watersheds and the Chilliwack watershed. They'd follow that ridge and gather berries and then make their way back up through Hunter Creek. Then they would come back home and that would take about two weeks. Not only were they going up there to pick berries, they'd also be picking wild vegetables. So not only would they have the berry baskets there where they were drying the berries but they would also have these strings zigzagging across the camp and over the fires and that, where they'd have different vegetables – root vegetables that they were drying – wild vegetables.

At the same time they would be hunting, so she talked about how they would stop for four days or so just to dry a mountain goat or a deer. Wherever they shot it, that's where they would set up a camp. A few of them would set up a camp there and build this little platform over the fire and smoke the meat, dry the meat. And they would also tan the hide and then they would use it to wrap up the meat once it had been cured. They would take this couple of hundred pounds of meat and dry it so it's a lot lighter. And then they would use the animal's own skin to make the pack, and they would use the tump line and then they would carry it back home. Only a couple of them would stay back and do that. The rest of them would carry on making their way to the berry patch, and, if they got another deer, well, then, some of them would have to set up a camp and dry it or smoke it and then bring it back home.

That was done throughout the whole two weeks that they were up in the berry-picking grounds. At the same time the girls were taught how to make baskets. There were heavy-duty baskets – the coil baskets – but then there were also baskets that they would make with cedar bark. You can make them in an hour or two, and so the girls would be making a lot of those baskets in preparation for the berry-picking trips up the mountain.

Another place is just north of Hope. *Lexwyó:qwem* means "always rotten fish," and it's a name that is found in two locations. So Lexwyó:qwem – "always rotten fish" – is down along the river at what's now known as American Bar. This place is so named because in the fall, after the salmon spawn, the carcasses would end up along the beach there, so that all you can smell is rotten fish. But there's a wind that carries that scent up the mountain, so there's a place up there that Frank Pat talks about as the garden spot. He was saying that when you go up there to pick berries you can smell the rotten fish up there. That's what the late Amelia Douglas was saying as well. And that's why they called that Lexwyó:qwem, because you could smell that rotten fish up there. That's the place where there's a lot of mountain goat. Frank Pat talks about a mountain right up there where the mountain goats have a trail to a steep, rocky area where they seek refuge from the hunter. Even though the hunters could still shoot them with bows and arrows, from their refuge the mountain goat would fall to a place where you wouldn't be able to get them. So they were pretty well safe in that one spot. The race was always to get to that one little spot before the mountain goat.

When you think of those three berry-picking spots there's a lot of culture, a lot of history, that you could learn just talking about those three places. You talk to different elders about each of those places, and each of them has a different experience or a different story. And we can learn from all of them. Those are just three examples; there are a lot of other berry-picking grounds. A number of elders talk about going up to the Coquihalla watershed and taking the train and going up to the different places. Everyone had their own place to go picking berries.

That's one example. There's all these different places to gather berries. And not only that, they are also the hunting grounds as well. And some other places I would find are fishing grounds. Most of them seem to be names that are of villages – I never really heard of any names of actual fishing rocks themselves. But there's usually a village in association with the fishing area. Up in Yale, for example, the most popular one would be

Í:yem, that means "lucky place" or "strong place" and that's according to Tillie Gutierrez and the late Agnes Kelly. The late Amelia Douglas also talked about that place. It got its names because it was a good place to catch lots of salmon. There are a lot of dry racks there as well. Quite a few families from Chowethel, and extended families from up and down between here and Chilliwack, went fishing and had dry racks set up there. And their place is also called Í:yem. Tillie Gutierrez says it was where they used to catch the first salmon for the First Salmon Ceremony. And she says they picked that place because to get down to the fishing rock you had to walk through an arch, and if you're familiar with – there are places where rocks get stuck in the holes and the current just makes these great big holes and pots. There's one of those there, and I guess the river had washed through and so created an arch. They had to go through that arch and lower themselves down the rope to catch the first salmon. And she said that was there right up until the 1940s, and then when they put those fish ladders in there they blasted it trying to flatten the area.

Just from talking about Í:yem, lucky place or strong place, you're learning about the First Salmon Ceremony. So there are all these different things about the First Salmon Ceremony – so what is *that* all about? And so you start talking about the First Salmon Ceremony to people. Or even when you start letting them know about different records that talk about the First Salmon Ceremony, they start finding that there are other ceremonies as well. For example, the Chehalis people have the First Shoots Ceremony. And what is the First Salmon Ceremony about? You start looking into our traditions today. And you start trying to find elements of that First Salmon Ceremony and you realize that it was just about lost! And that it got to the point where only one aspect of the ceremony was being done and that aspect was sharing the salmon. Ten years ago or so, just prior to the revival of the First Salmon Ceremony, a lot of families would still just have people over for the First Salmon Ceremony. They would barbeque their salmon or whatever, and then they would just have a big do and share it with a lot of people. That was the only thing that they would do, and it wasn't until ten years ago or so that we started finding out a little bit more about the First Salmon Ceremony. We heard about how the men were transformed into birds and how they hooked up with Beaver and Rat – some elders say Mouse – but they went down to the ocean where the salmon people are and captured the sockeye baby and brought the sockeye baby up. They threw the diapers in different places, like Coquitlam and Pitt River, the Harrison River, the Chilliwack River. Wherever they threw the diapers, that's where there are a lot of salmon. Then they brought the sockeye baby all the way up to Yale, and the sockeye baby went in the pools up in Yale, and that's why the salmon return each year. And so because of that story, that's why we have the First Salmon Ceremony – or that's one of the reasons why we have the First Salmon Ceremony – and that's because when we have the first salmon we have to return the fish to the water. It's such a sacred thing that we're not allowed to touch it with our hands, the fishers that catch the first salmon are not allowed to touch it with their hands. They used to use their forearms and there were supposed to be certain elders that were supposed to prepare it. They were supposed to have knowledge of prayers, to say prayers to the salmon people, thanking them for the salmon, paying respect for it. The major part of the ceremony was actually sharing; even if you just had one little morsel of the salmon, the important part was making sure that a lot of people shared in that salmon. Then the bones would be saved and returned to the river, and that would involve one of the chiefs, a spiritual person, an elder, and a youth: those four people needed to be involved when that was happening. A prayer was said to the salmon and to the river, and then the bones would be returned to the river.

A major portion of those different traditions was lost, and it's only in the last ten years or so now that more families are doing their own First Salmon Ceremony and actually saving the bones, returning them to the river, and then saying a prayer to the salmon people and to the river. If you go to Í:yem and see the fish ladders there, the elders will tell you there was destruction there. They destroyed the fishing rocks there, so you understand then that this happened all over the place as well, so then you learn about how the CPR and the CNR did great damage to heritage sites, to fishing grounds.

The other thing, too, is that at Í:yem there's the Eayem memorial, there's a monument. It's a memorial to the Stó:lō people: they've got the sign right there. It says, "Eayem Memorial 1938 AD Erected by the Stallo Indians in memory of many hundreds of our forefathers buried here. This is one of six ancient cemeteries within our five mile Native fishing grounds which we inherited from our ancestors. R.I.P." That memorial is set up at the cemetery there at IR 22, also known as Bell Crossing. It was set up by my great-grandfather Dennis S. Peters along with the help of Isaac James, who was his brother-in-law. And they set that up in 1938. I always wondered about its connection to the Great Fraser Midden Cairn, which was erected in the same year. I always wondered if my great-grandfather had seen that one and wanted to do that up there – I don't know. It's something that I've always wondered about because they were both erected in the same year, in 1938. When you look at that memorial what are the key messages? To me, my great-grandfather wanted to make sure that we remember the cemeteries that are up there. He wanted to make sure that we remember the name of the place, the Eayem memorial. It was erected by the Stó:lō, so it is clear that the Stó:lō play an important part there. He wanted to make sure we remember our ancestors – "many hundreds of our forefathers buried here." It is "one of six ancient cemeteries," so that makes you go, "Where are the other five?" The other five would be the one right at Yale, or X̲wox̲welá:lhp; the one at X̲elhálh; the ones at Q'aleliktel, Aseláw, Í:yem; and the one at Lexwts'okwá:m. Those are the six. This is one of those six. These are located "within our five mile Native fishing grounds," so that's the other key message: we are not to forget about our fishing grounds, "which we inherited from our ancestors."

There are a lot of teachings just in the wording of that memorial. It's only last Saturday that we had a memorial for my cousin, the late Herman Peters, or Siya:mia. In preparation for that I wanted to find out a little more about his name because it comes from one of my ancestors. And it's an important name because it's a leader's name. I had known that, over the years; I had seen references to it, but I had never really looked at them. I found out that Siya:mia, the very first Siya:mia, was from Í:yem. That's one thing I've learned as well – that it's really important to have personal connections to places. And I didn't really have a personal connection to Í:yem; it's a place where I don't go fishing. I know my grandfather fished just upriver from Í:yem, where Rita Pete fishes now. My grandfather fished there. And then I know that Dennis S. Peters erected that memorial, our great-grandfather erected that memorial. I often wondered, "Why did he do that?" I looked at the different teachings contained in the memorial itself but, at the same time, wondered what personal connection he had there. I often wondered that, so when I found out that Siya:mia – that's Dennis S. Peters' name as well, I think he was number three, Siya:mia number three. And then the original Siya:mia was right there from Í:yem and actually lived in one of those pit houses there. So I thought, "Wow! So that's the personal connection!" That's probably the personal connection that he had to the place and he wanted to do something. That was his memorial. Not only was he taking care of his own personal connection to the place but he was also taking care of the Stó:lō, remembering our ancestors and the burial grounds and the fishing grounds.

Oral Histories

I think that it is really important to actually have a connection to place. Because you have to look at the oral history and how the oral history is shared: it's called *sx̲wóx̲wiyám*. *Sx̲wóx̲wiyám* are the stories about when X̲exá:ls, the Transformers, travelled to our land to make the world right.

The three bear brothers and the bear sister, who were orphans, were Transformers. They were the children of Red-Headed Woodpecker and Black
Bear. They travelled from the head of Harrison Lake down to the Fraser,
up the river to the sunrise, through the sky to the sunset, and back upriver
again.

You know they did all those different transformations. You know those
sxwóxwiyám stories are important to us. But at the same time, those are
like our stories of creation and it makes these places sacred. But not only
that, we have what we call *sqwelqwel*. *Sqwelqwel* is our own family's true
news, or history. When I talk about different places where my family is
located, that's my *sqwelqwel*. When I talk about Í:yem as a place name –
that's an important place, it's a fishing place, it's a fishing ground. But
when I start talking about Dennis S. Peters setting up that memorial, I
start talking about my grandfather fishing at that one place, and that's my
personal connection to the spot. I think that's a really important part of it.
I think that's what's missing today. I think the only people that have a
really big connection up there is to the fishing grounds. Even when you
look at the cemeteries up there, the cemetery at X̱elhálh, the last person
who was buried there was one of the Frasers back in the 1920s. I don't
think anyone else had been buried up there recently. That's an important
connection that has to happen up there.

Across from Í:yem, though, is a place called Aseláw. The linguist Brent
Galloway wasn't able to get a meaning for it and quite a few elders I asked
weren't able to give a meaning. It wasn't until the late Rosaleen George
and Elizabeth Herrling really started thinking about it. They were saying
the name, *"Aseláw ... Aseláw."* Finally they were able to extract a meaning
out of it, and they said that it had to do with to experience it, to feel it. It
had something to do with that. There's something about that place – you
need to experience it, to feel it. That's the only thing they could get out of
it. They weren't able to provide me with an actual literal translation, but
they said it has something to do with to feel it or to experience it. It's kind
of a neat name. It makes you ask, "What's there? What is it that you have to
feel, what do you have to experience?" When you look at Aseláw, again it's
an important fishing ground right across the river from Í:yem. There's an
old archival photograph of the place, and you can see all the dry racks that
were there. It was made into a reserve – IR 21. It's one of those reserves
that were reduced – the original reserve was supposed to be 43 acres, I
believe, and in the end, after the surveyor for the CNR insisted on a right of
way, they made it smaller, so now it's only 4.1 acres. That's one part of it.
You also find out about the pit houses. There is an important archaeological

site referred to by archaeologists as the Milliken site. Then you ask, "Who's Milliken?" – August, or Auguste, Milliken was from Yale, and he wasn't well respected by our elders because a lot of them considered him to be – let's see if I can find a nice way to put this – an amateur archaeologist. Some might say a pot hunter. He was the one who knew about the site, and he told UBC archaeologist Charles Borden about it. And Borden went up there and made his excavations, along with Roy Carlson and others in 1959-61. Then it became a well-known archaeological site often referred to as the Milliken site (DjRi3). It's over nine thousand years old. There are pit houses there. They went down over twenty feet to find the oldest carbon date. They were able to tie it to fishing through the cherry seeds that they found there. This enabled them to tie it to the fishing that took place there. If you look at the archival photograph you're able to see all the dry racks there. You know the pit houses are there, then there's a cemetery there as well. When I first went there back in 1985 there was a cross there that had a name on it. I recorded the name on it. It was trying to say *Sexyeltel* but it said *Sexyelten*. It wasn't until quite a few years later that I realized who that was. That's my ancestor, my great-great-great-grandfather. His son, Captain Charlie, was originally from there. Captain Charlie's my great-great-grandfather. He was from Aseláw, and he took his first wife from Sq'ewqéyl. His second wife was from Iwówes, or Union Bar, then he finally took a wife from X̲wox̲welá:lhp, or Yale – Mary Anne, after whom Mary Ann Creek in Yale is named. Then he had some children and moved down and took over the place in Ruby Creek. The people there at Spópetes had died from smallpox; there was nobody there. So he moved down there, and because he was down there that's how that reserve became an Indian reserve and became tied to Yale. So that's why the Yale band has that reserve down there – it's because my great-great-grandfather moved down there with his children from Yale.

Captain Charlie's name was S'ex:yel and his father's name was Sexyeltel, so when we were looking at that cross, that was his cross! I put that together a few years later. I had first seen it in 1985, and I knew Captain Charlie was from there. I remember talking to Ralph George, and he said the last time they went up there to try to clean the cemetery was 1967 or 1968. And they brought fence wire up there, and that roll of fence is still laying there. They were going to put a new fence up and they never did do it. So this past summer, the summer of 2004, my sons and I started clearing some of it, but we never quite finished and I tried looking for that cross – you know, nineteen years later – and I couldn't find it. It's got to be there somewhere – it's probably buried. It was one of those iron crosses with a single little name written on it, so it should still be there. It's probably covered in leaves.

Ownership

That's it about Aseláw. As I mentioned, there always has to be a personal connection to the place, so that's my personal connection. I mean the whole story of how I got there raises other issues, other traditions, and other understandings that have to do with ownership of fishing grounds. I mean that could be talked about even at Í:yem as well because I mentioned that my grandfather fished at one of the spots there; I mentioned that my great-great-great-great-grandfather Siya:mia lived right there and had a fishing ground there. But also now at Aseláw, and through Captain Charlie (my great-great-grandfather) and through *his* dad Sexyeltel (my great-great-great-grandfather), I have access to *that* fishing ground. I mentioned earlier as well that my dad was from Boston Bar (Tuckkwiowhum) and my mom was from Chowethel. My mom married my dad and, through the Indian Act, became a member of the Boston Bar band. And so she became registered with the Boston Bar band as Nlaka'pamux. And we have a family fishing ground up there – my grandfather's family dry rack site – we're not allowed to fish there anymore as it is within the closed area. I have a wife down here who is from Shxw'ōwhámél. My older children became registered members of Shxw'ōwhámél, so we were registered Stó:lō. I was fishing up at Boston Bar and I realized, "Geez! When I pass on I'm not going to have a fishing ground for my children. My children need a fishing ground: they need some place where they can fish, where they're not going to have any problems." I was fine because I was a registered Boston Bar band member, so I didn't have any problems. But I knew that they would have problems if they as Stó:lō people – registered Stó:lō people – were going to go up there to fish. I'd met some Nlaka'pamux people out on the river you know, even after I transferred, and they said, "Oh, I don't know why you Stó:lō keep coming up here fishing; you don't need to be up here." I thought about that and I knew I had fishing grounds – had rights to certain fishing grounds in the Yale area. I began to consult with my elders, to inquire where I could fish. I went to see the late Peter Dennis Peters, and he told me about the one spot where Rita Pete fishes; he said that's where my grandfather used to fish and that I had rights to that spot. Rita Pete's mother was my grandfather's first cousin, so Rita is my mom's second cousin, so we are relatives. She was already fishing there. She already had her family there, you know, the dry rack and the cabin, and she was quite comfortable there, so I thought, "Well, I don't know." She already had a lot of her family fishing there. And then, based on the 1905 fishing map, there was a place below Í:yem, actually almost right across from Q'aleliktel, where Dennis S. Peters had a fishing ground. But somebody else was fishing there, one of my cousins from Chowethel. One of the Harris family was fishing there. "Well," I thought, "there's somebody already there, there's only one spot." Rita's got her own family so it's not too likely she's going to share the spot with me as well. I found out that Captain Charlie's spot was across the river and that the last time it was used was 1945 because the dry rack had been buried by a rockslide. The rock bluff there just kind of caved in two weeks after everybody packed up and went down to the hop yards. The rock caved in and buried the whole dry rack. It was never rebuilt, and that's when they moved across the river to Bell Crossing. Of course the freight train was still running, so people were still able to go up there and do *some* fishing.

My uncle Bobby used to go up there and fish, and my cousin Gino remembers going there and fishing. But there was no real long-term fishing – no camp set up. The only way up there was by the weigh freight train, but then it quit running in 1978. After that people didn't really have access to that spot except by boat. No one was up there fishing. But I found out that I had rights to that spot. I talked to Ralph George about it and the late Bill Pat Charlie, and the late Peter Dennis Peters: those were the three elders that I talked to. And all three of them mentioned the different places where I had rights to go fishing. There were already people fishing there, but there was nobody fishing at Aseláw. I knew that Ken Malloway had fished there; however, he prefers to fish from his boat. He likes to set his net and check it from the boat. And I guess the water there was too swift when he tried fishing. He said there was a really good spring hole but he wasn't really fishing there. So there wasn't anyone there. When I asked my elders, I said, "Well, can I go over there and take over that fishing spot?" All three of them agreed. I didn't see them all together – I asked them individually – and they all agreed. I remember the late Peter Dennis saying, "Yeah, by all means! You go there and get using that spot. It should be used. It needs to be taken care of." That was 1993. I went up there. I got myself a Zodiac boat and went up there and started fishing.

The ownership of fishing grounds brings about a whole lot of discussion. I talked to the elders about that. Fishing grounds are family owned, not individually owned. Just like an Indian name – it's owned by the family – the individual that has it doesn't own it. The family gives it to him and the family can take it away. So just like the fishing rock, I remember a controversy about my auntie Rita having the spot where my grandfather fished. And she said that my grand-uncle Oscar, who was my grandfather's brother, had given it to her mother, who was Oscar's first cousin. You know when I talked to the late Peter Dennis Peters about it, because he understands fishing-ground ownership as family ownership, he couldn't comprehend that and neither could I. He said, "How can someone give away something that belongs to the whole family?" He meant how could Oscar give something away that belongs to the whole family, not just to one person. He can't. Ownership of fishing grounds is through family.

But then you wonder, why do people look at ownership as individual then? What happened there? And then I started to understand, well, back in the late 1800s the Fisheries Act was created and all these different laws were made that didn't allow our people to sell fish any more. They said that only saltwater fish could be sold and that it is illegal to sell anything caught in fresh water. So they took away our economy and, not only that, they wanted to start regulating our fishing. So they imposed the fishing permits on our people. What's on the fishing permit? It doesn't talk about the extended family or family ownership. The Department of Fisheries and Oceans didn't take into consideration the fact that we had our own rules and our own regulations about who has access to fishing grounds and who fishes where. We have our own protocols and our own laws. Instead, they imposed a fishing permit that had an individual's name on it. And it said that individual could fish from such and such place to such and such place. So it's almost as though it is wide open: you can fish anywhere in there. According to the government, you can fish anywhere in there. So right away they ignored our own laws and protocols of where to fish. It took the all-encompassing perspective of ownership of fishing grounds – our wide perspective of it – and narrowed it to an individual perspective. So that a lot of our fishers now, up in the canyon, look at their fishing spot as their own. I've heard some of them say, "It's mine and only mine." And, "No one else can fish here, not my brothers, not my sister, not my mom or my dad. This is *my* spot." I couldn't believe it when I heard one of the fishers say that. That's how some of the fishers think. So they have to change that again.

Not all the fishers think like that. You can still go up there and see that wherever there's a dry rack, usually there's a family that owns it there. And the person that's kind of in charge of it, that's what the late Rosaleen George describes as a *Sia:teleq*. The *Sia:teleq* was the person who was appointed by the family to take care of the fishing ground and the access to it, so he was kind of like the co-ordinator of the ground. He wasn't the owner because no individual could own it. But based on his knowledge of the extended family, his knowledge of the various fishing methods, his knowledge of the capacity of the dry rack, his knowledge of the capacity of the camp, of the number of children that extended families had, of the numbers of fishing rocks that were accessible according to the varying levels of the river – with all of that in mind, he was able to co-ordinate. "I'll tell you who can fish now. You should be fishing these rocks now, and this is the number of sticks that you have. And because you have this many children you should be making sure you have this much fish put away." So he kind of co-ordinated all that. From Western society's perspective, somebody who witnessed this would probably assume that he was the owner. But not really, he wasn't really the owner. He was just the person who took care of the site. So looking at some of the contemporary dry rack sites, wherever there's a dry rack and a cabin, I'm quite certain if you talk to the family there, no one is going to claim individual ownership. I'm sure it's a family-owned site, and there may be one of the elders within that site who takes the role of *Sia:teleq*. An example is the Pettis site, Henry Pettis. I don't think he'd claim the site as his: he'd say it's his whole family's, you know. He's probably the one who is looked upon as the *Sia:teleq*. More likely, he has a younger person who's learning to take care of those other duties as well. And look at Grand Chief Archie Charles' camp as well. He has people from Seabird, Chowethel, Ruby Creek, Scowlitz, and perhaps Shxw'ōwhámél. He's got people, all kinds of different extended family members at his camp. And I'm sure that he would not say that he owns it. I'm sure he'd say it's a family-owned site. I'm sure that if you'd ask members of his family and explained to them about the *Sia:teleq*, he'd play that role there. So wherever there's a dry rack – dry rack sites with camps – people still look upon it as a place that's owned by the family.

The other big change involved fishing methods. Historian Keith Thor Carlson talks about this. In the past when people went fishing, their perspective on their fishing ground was based in the land – the fishing rock, the dry rack, camp, and access trail. Back then you had to go down your trail into your camp. You had your dry rack right next to your camp, and then you had to go down to your rock to use your dip net to catch the fish and then bring it up to your dry rack. Every family looked at their sites like that. I'm sure that people who have dry racks still look at their sites like that: their camp is a big element of their fishing ground. The camp and the dry rack play a big part in this. But now, with the use of motor boats, people are using gill nets rather than dip nets. Dip nets were used to fish off the rocks: you fished in the rough waters so the fish couldn't see you when you were dipping them out of the boiling water. Gill nets, however, are used in the eddies, where it doesn't matter whether the fish see you or not. You just set your gill net inside the eddy, either on a pole or, if you're setting it across the bay, on a pulley. Or if it's a big enough bay you can tie to the shore, which is called a shore line, and run your net out and have a big stone anchor or some other kind of anchor to hold it in the eddy. So that changed people's perspective on their fishing grounds. So a lot of the fishers who fish by boats now, I'm sure that if you talk to them about what their fishing ground is, they'll talk about their eddy. Because they don't have a connection to the land part of it, except for wherever they tie their net to the shore. Unless they have a dry rack and a camp, then *that* particular place, you know, they'd have a connection there. But in most of the other places there's no real connection.

So there was a big change in fishing methods, from dip nets to gill nets, and this had an effect on how you perceived your fishing ground. When you look at the 1905 fishing map you can see fishing rocks or fishing grounds that were recorded back then, and you go there now and you take a contemporary map of where people fish, and it makes you wonder. Why isn't anybody fishing where these people were fishing? That's because they were dip netting off a rock and there's no eddy there to set a gill net, so no one fishes there. Or else you look on a 1905 map and you see places where nobody was fishing but people are fishing there today, and it's because, well, there's a nice big eddy there. We didn't use gill nets back then, so nobody fished there. But today people fish there. This creates more problems in terms of fishing-ground ownership because it's almost like a whole new fishery has been created – a whole new boat fishery.

Some fishing grounds may have been taken over by other fishers, like my uncle's spot that he inherited from my great-grandfather (Chief Johnny Ohamil) there at Q'aleliktel. My uncle used to fish there. He used to catch the weigh freight train up, and the weigh freight quit running, so for about seven years he was unable to access his fishing ground. He was finally able to arrange with one of the CNR railroad workers to get a ride up there, and he took my nephew with him. This is in 1984, after not being there since 1978. He got there and someone was fishing there. The protocol is that when the rightful owner gets to the fishing ground, if somebody else's net is there you pull that net out, put it on the shore, leave their fish for them, and then you set your net. You're the rightful owner and you start fishing again. It's still okay for people to fish there. It would be good if they'd contact you and let you know they're going to fish there, but still people are allowed to do that: much of our teaching focuses on sharing. But my uncle got there and somebody was fishing and he was going to pull that person's net out so he could set his net, and that person threatened him with physical violence. He said, "If you touch my net I'll chuck you in the river." So my uncle's a pacifist guy, not a violent fellow. So he didn't pull that guy's net. He tried to set close to it but he couldn't get a good set there so he ended up just leaving, going back home, and he hasn't been up there since. That was twenty years ago.

Now there's the whole big issue out there about ownership of fishing grounds. I first came across it when I was recording fishing grounds. When we started making the forms to record who fished where, we actually included the category "ownership" because we wanted that to be a big part of the forms, that this is who owned the site! But later on we realized that there was so much conflict and controversy over who owned sites, and we as researchers were just not able to say, "This is ... and so and so is the owner." We didn't have the jurisdiction or the authority to say who was the owner, and so our legal advisors had recommended that we just record who the occupants were rather than who the owners were. So you'll notice on some of our fishing forms at the end there we changed the word "ownership" to "occupant" to say who was fishing there. Because one of the questions was "Who fished there before," you began to see that some people did know who was fishing there before. And we'd talk to other people and they'd say, "Oh, so and so was fishing there" and then you'd start finding out whether or not the family that's there has any right to be there.

Sometimes you'll find that families that are connected don't realize that they're connected; that's another thing that was lost – their genealogies. In the past we knew very well who our relatives were, up to our fifth cousins and even beyond that. Because first, second, and third cousins were almost considered to be like brothers and sisters because they shared the same grandparents. And it's the *Sia:teleq* who will know who all our relatives were up and down the river so that we could gain access to different resources. I talked earlier about three important berry-picking grounds, Xoletsa and Lexwyó:qwem and Q'aw. We talked about the berry-picking grounds behind Shxw'ōwhámél there. But I never mentioned the cranberries, like the cranberries down in Vancouver, the New Westminster area: all those places are places our people travelled through our extended family. It's through the extended family, knowing who your extended family is, that you could go down there, and you knew where your family could go picking berries. Qiqa:yt was the name of the south New Westminster/Surrey area. There's a large campground that extended from the Patullo Bridge all the way down to the Alex Fraser Bridge. The late Rosaleen George was saying there's a huge camping area there. She said everybody would camp in that area, sleep there overnight and, during the day, make their way up to the cranberry patches and pick cranberries. They'd stay down there for a couple of weeks doing that, so that's another important part about knowing your extended family because that allows you to get access to different places. Through your extended family you could come down and get eulachon or clams.

You learn the *sqwelqwel* of a particular place, you start learning about your family history, you start learning about the importance of ownership, and you start learning about the different things that had negative effects on our own perspectives of our own laws and our own protocols. I know that there's fishing grounds up in the Fraser Canyon, but then you start moving downriver and start talking about other types of fish. But first, our people went up in the canyon to fish because that was the only place to dry the salmon. If you tried to dry salmon downriver, the dew that forms every night would get on your salmon and just cause them to go mouldy. Whereas you get up in the canyon and the mountainous rock absorbs the heat; it dissipates the heat at night and doesn't allow the dew to form. You don't have to worry about dew forming on the salmon. Plus you have the dry air that blows from the Interior because you're a lot closer to the Interior, so it's a little bit drier. And not only that, you also have the migrating salmon that have just spent the first 160 kilometres in the river, and they lose 11 to 12 percent of their body fat. The higher the fat content, the easier it is for the salmon to spoil. When we dry a sockeye the very thin stomach part of the salmon which is really rich in fat is usually cut out. If it doesn't get cut out, it gets a real strong taste to it after it has dried. That's if it does dry: most of the time the fatty part of the fish doesn't dry because it has too much oil in it. After the salmon lose 11 to 12 percent of their fat, it makes them just ideal for drying. And then you have the weather conditions as well. In addition it's a lot easier to catch the fish in the canyon than it is downriver, especially with dip nets and the *laxyel*, the fishing platforms.

My brother, the late Billy McHalsie, was one of the best fishers I knew. He and one of my cousins, Gilbert Dixon from Boston Bar, used to go dipping all the time. That was one of their favourite pastimes. One time my brother was able to catch 350 sockeye in one hour. Just incredible! In one dip he'd catch six sockeye. When they're running really well it's just a very efficient method of catching them. I think people are just starting to realize the efficiency of that. This past fall, I was up there fishing with my brother Lorn and we wanted to catch springs. Coho were running and also some late sockeye. We said "Yeah, it's awesome – just catch it – look at it." "Oh, it's a coho – let it go." "Oh, it's a spring – we'll keep it." And "Oh, it's too big of a spring – let's let that one go to the spawning grounds." Then when the sockeye was too red – "Oh, let's let that one go to the spawning grounds." So dipping is really an excellent way of selective fishing because you really don't do any harm to the fish, not like with the gill nets. That stresses the fish out a lot. Once they get into your gill net and they sit there too long, that stresses them and then, even if you let them go, their survival rate is really low.

There are all these different things to talk about, just with dipping. You look at the fishing grounds – there are all these different teachings incorporated into that. Like the types of dipping, the structure, the platforms, the types of fish. Concerning the types of fish – in the summer there's just the sockeye and the spring. In the past, everyone dried the spring. But then with the commercial fishing, the older fishing of the chinook salmon or the spring salmon went out of style. So most people dry the sockeye, prefer the sockeye. But you talk to the elders, the elders go, "Hm! I remember my grandparents always drying the spring!" And that's the case with my grandfather as well. He fished across from Scuzzy Creek, up in the canyon. That's an area that is now closed: people aren't allowed to fish in there because it's too close to the Hell's Gate fish ladders. There's a thirteen-kilometre stretch of the river up there where the Nlaka'pamux people aren't allowed to fish anymore. But my grandfather had a dry rack in there, and all he dried was spring salmon. And my cousin Hicks, a.k.a. Edward Philips, was telling me that he remembers my grandfather would dry enough salmon to fill four wagons. They would take the horse and wagon down to get these fish, all these dried fish. And he was saying there were four loads of dried fish, just all spring salmon, that he would bring back home. And he would dry that much because he used to trade with the Okanagan people. The Okanagan people had a horse trail; they used to come over on their horses. And they would bring all types of dried berries and a lot of their buckskin and elk skins. They'd have those gauntlet gloves with all kinds of beadwork or embroidery on them, and then they'd have these elk vests with beadwork and embroidery on them. They'd bring all kinds of different things over, including different types of food and berries, and then they would trade with my grandfather for his spring salmon.

So spring salmon was the important salmon in the past, but not today. Today most people dry the sockeye. In fact, a lot of people like to dry the Stuart sockeye, the very first ones – because they're quite rich and quite tasty. But then, when you start looking at that and say, "Spring and sockeye – why can't you dry coho and why can't you dry the pink and the chum?!" When they start running the weather isn't right any more; there's too much rain up there. In August the blowflies come out. The blowflies lay the maggots on the salmon, and the maggots burrow into the fish and then they spoil it. So a lot of people prefer to have their fish dried by the end of July because at the beginning of August is when the blowflies come out. By the end of August, when the pink salmon and the chum salmon and the coho are running, the drying season's gone, it's over. You can't dry anymore. So *those* types of salmon then became the salmon that were used for smoking. We used more downriver than upriver because most of the salmon spawned in the lower parts of the river. In Chehalis and Chilliwack there were a lot of people who smoked salmon. There was a lot of smoking of the pink and the chum.

If you start looking at those types of salmon and start learning, you then find out that the sturgeon is another important fish. When you start talking about sturgeon you start finding out about more history. For instance, the late Agnes Kelly talked about the importance of the sturgeon to the people from Shxw'ōwhámél. She shared the story about how one of the men from the village, during the time of famine when everyone was hungry, was told by Chichelh Siya:m to go and stand by the edge of the river. He got down to the river and then Chichelh Siya:m – Chichelh Siya:m is the word for the Creator – told him to dive into the river. And so he dove into the river and he was transformed into the male sturgeon. And then, Agnes said, "He was transformed into that male sturgeon so that we could have food in the winter months because the other salmon aren't available in the winter. So we needed something in the winter to keep us fed." She went on to tell the story about how his wife missed him very much, and so Chichelh Siya:m told her to go stand by the water as well. So she went down there and she took some deer meat tied around her wrist. And she was standing on the edge of the river, and then her husband came in the form of a sturgeon and called her. So she dove into the water and she was transformed into the female sturgeon. The elders say the truth of that story is confirmed by the fact that when you cut the head off of a sturgeon, right behind the gills you see that brown piece of meat that almost looks like deer meat. They say that's there because that woman, she had deer meat tied around her wrist when she dove into the water and was transformed into a sturgeon.

Shxwelí

The sturgeon isn't just regarded as food and a resource, it's like an ancestor. There's a connection there, and that connection is known as *shxwelí*. *Shxwelí* is what's referred to as the spirit or the life force, and everything has that spirit and everything's connected through that. I remember when I first saw the word. I first started this job in 1985, and I'd seen the word in the classified word list and I always remember it said: "'Spirit' comma 'life force.'" I never quite understood it. I didn't really know what it was all about. It wasn't until Xa:ytem – the rock down there at Xa:ytem – was first talked about that I began to pay more attention. That's when our elder, the late Aggie Victor, said, "The *shxweli* of those *siya:m*" – those three leaders that were transformed into stone there – "The *shxweli* of those men is still inside the rock." So I didn't – I still don't understand that. What did they mean? The *shxweli*. It's the spirit or life force that's inside that rock. So I went to see the late Rosaleen George and I said, "What is a *shxweli*?" I've never forgotten her answer, and I always tell people because I think it's probably the best way to explain it. She put her hand on her chest and she said, "*Shxweli* is inside us here." And she put her hand in front of her and she said, "*Shxweli* is in your parents." She raised her hand higher and said, "then your grandparents, your great-grandparents, it's in your great-great-grandparents. It's in the rocks, it's in the trees, it's in the grass, it's in the ground. *Shxweli* is everywhere." So I kind of understood that. And I'm still trying to put that together. What ties us? What ties us to the sturgeon? It's the *shxweli*. The sturgeon has a *shxweli*, we have a *shxweli*. So we're connected to that.

Then I remember the story by the late Bertha Peters, Mrs. Dave Peters from Seabird. She's the one who shared the story about Xa:ytem. But she's the one who also shared the story about Xepa:y. She said, "You know that a long time ago there was a very generous man who was always giving and always helping people. And they say that when he passed away he was transformed into the cedar tree. And because he was such a generous man, that's why we get all the different things from the cedar tree." So the trunk of the tree is used for canoes and for the pit houses and the longhouses and the paddles. And all kinds of different utensils are made out of the cedar. And the bark is used for clothing and for diapers and to make rope and twine. And then the roots are used for the baskets – the cedar baskets. And even the cedar boughs themselves are used for spiritual cleansing. In the Interior they use the sage and the sweetgrass for the smudging – well, around here it was the cedar that was used. You know, the burning cedar, the crackling of the cedar is what chased away bad spirits. So in the past they would use that crackling cedar to go into the corners of all the houses to chase away bad spirits that might have been bothering the people. Or else they would use that to smudge people to get rid of the bad spirits. Now today you'll see people using cedar boughs. But in the past the cedar boughs were burned; they were used as a smudge rather than just brushing with the cedar.

We're told that when we go out to use any part of the cedar – and there's certain teachings there as well, as to when you go out and gather the bark, you're allowed to peel bark on only one side of the tree so that the tree continues to live. When you go and you gather the cedar roots, there are four different main roots that come out. There's only one root that we take, and then we leave the other three alone. If you take the other ones you're going to kill the cedar tree. There's all those different teachings that are tied into that as well. But at the same time, we're also taught to say a prayer to Xepa:y, the man. So the *shxweli* of that ancestor is inside each of the trees. So we're not really praying to the tree, we're praying to the *shxweli*, or the spirit, of that ancestor who was transformed into the tree. So again, the tree is not looked upon as just a resource, it's looked upon as one of our ancestors and we need to pay respect to that ancestor so we have, again, the prayer that is said to Xepa:y, thanking him for all the different things that we get. So whenever we go gather bark, cedar boughs, roots – that prayer is said. It's the prayer that is said to Xepa:y. So there's that connection, the *shxweli*.

Look again at the elders saying that the *shxweli* of those three men were inside that rock. Then you've got to wonder, well, what about all the other rocks? So then again you start learning that every single rock where <u>X</u>e<u>x</u>á:ls had travelled through and transformed ancestors into different things, that all of those things has a *shxweli*. And because we have a *shxweli*, we're connected to them. And it's through that *shxweli* that we're connected to them. When you look at Lhílheqey, the mother mountain, and her three daughters, Seyewot, Oyewot, and Xomo:th'iya: they were ancestors who were transformed into those mountains. The *shxweli* of those ancestors are inside those mountains and we're connected to it; we need to take care of

PHOTO 3.1 Serpent Rock, a Transformer site in the Fraser River, north of Hope, BC

that place. You know up and down the valley, wherever one of our ancestors was transformed into a rock – the places – those are special places! You know, that need to be preserved. Because when X̱exá:ls travelled through the land, making the world right, a lot of times not only was there the story about why they were turned into stone but there was also some other teaching involved: there was always some other teaching.

There were a lot of the places where Indian doctors were transformed into stone. Like Alhqa:yem, for instance, at the north end of Strawberry Island, that was an Indian doctor (see Photo 3.1). A woman who challenged X̱exá:ls, like a lot of the Indian doctors who challenged X̱exá:ls, felt that if she were able to defeat X̱exá:ls she would become well known as the person who defeated these strong people who were travelling through the territory. So a lot of them would challenge X̱exá:ls, and they would just end up losing. But because this Indian doctor's power came from the serpent, when she was transformed into stone, that's what she was transformed into – the large serpent Alhqa:yem. *Alhqa:yem* means "the serpent." So when you go there, you see this huge rock there, and you can actually see its coils – three layers of coils – it looks like a snake that's coiled up. You know, that's Alhqa:yem.

There are other places where X̱exá:ls turned the ancestors into stone. Like the hunter Tewit and Talh, his spear, the dog Sqwema:y, and Q'oyits the elk (see Photo 3.2). There's a long story about that as well. That hunter was one of our ancestors, and his *shxwelí* is inside that rock. Anywhere where one of our ancestors is transformed into a mountain, there's that connection that we have, through our *shxwelí,* to that mountain, and we need to take care of it. Some places we may not know the story of the transformation – for instance with Lhílheqey. With Seyewot, Oyewot, Xomo:th'iya, and their dog Sqwema:y, we know there's a story that's shared by Dan Milo about how they were transformed. But there are other places as well that have names and that are more than likely places of transformation, but we don't have specific stories for them. Like the one I can think of, I guess, is St'am'ya, from around Hope. From the downriver area looking up you can see a man lying sideways. You go up to Hope and look down at that same mountain, and you can see a woman lying on the side of the mountain. Downriver you can see the private parts of a man, upriver you can see the private parts of a woman. And *St'am'ya* means, "What are you?" The question is "What are you, man or woman?" Because from one angle it's a man, from the other it's a woman. And that's all we know about it; there's no story that talks about a man or a woman being transformed into that mountain or anything like that. To us there's got to be some kind of a story.

PHOTO 3.2 Tewit the Hunter, a Transformer site located at Hill's Bar in the Fraser River, south of Yale, BC

And then you wonder, "Why isn't there a story?" This is probably the result of a huge smallpox epidemic in 1782, which wiped out at least 66 percent of our people – up to 90 percent of our people. In some cases it wiped out whole villages: every village was affected. Throughout the whole territory every village was affected, so a lot of our culture and history was lost there, and it's slowly rebounding from that. Back when Simon Fraser was going through in 1808, we were still rebounding from the 1782 small-pox epidemic. And then there was supposed to have been another one in 1806, just two years before he came through. His journal talks about the scars of the smallpox epidemic that he saw on the people. Then you start learning why it is that we don't have stories for some of these mountains that have names and that represent certain things. That's a big part of our story: that we lost much of our culture and history through smallpox. If you talk about smallpox, then you think about the government's assimi-lationist policies and the missionaries as well as the residential schools, which forced us to abandon many of our cultural practices.

I was just talking about some of those resource areas. We have that *shxwelí*. We already talked about X̱exá:ls, the Transformers. Any place where X̱exá:ls transformed, that place is important to us. Any of the animals or plants that were transformed, those are important resources to us. Each of the differ-ent villages – I gave the examples of Shxw'ōwhámél and Chowethel for the late Agnes Kelly's story. Tillie tells the same story, and she says that the people in Chowethel have the same story because her grandmother told it to her. Chowethel and Shxw'ōwhámél both have the same ancestor, who was transformed into a sturgeon. Then you move downriver, and then you have the people from Chilliwack with the black bear with the white spot on its chest. And the beaver at Matsqui, and the dog at Kwantlen, and the plant that grows down at Musqueam: you know an ancestor was transformed there. So throughout the territory we have all these different resources that were at one time ancestors who were transformed so we could have those resources. So that establishes a relationship with the resource as well as a spiritual connection to our *shxwelí*, to that ancestor who was transformed. So that brings us back, then, to Tillie Gutierrez's statement: *S'ólh Téméxw te ikw'elo. Xolhmet te mekw'stam it kwelat* – "This is our land and we have to take care of everything that belongs to us." That's why. Those are all the things out there that were transformed, all our resources that we take care of because we are connected to them. We take care of our land because we're connected to the land. That connection to the land is brought about not only through the transformations of <u>Xexá:ls</u> but also through the fact that many of our people – we talked earlier about the Eayem memorial and the cemeteries – and then you start looking at the burial practices of our people. And then you start understanding how important it is for us to become part of where we came from again, like becoming part of the earth. Everything – we're connected to it.

S'ólh Téméxw

Look at the word *S'ólh Téméxw*. The last syllable in *Téméxw* is *méxw* – "to do with like the dirt." What do we call ourselves? We call ourselves Xwélmexw. Not only that, our neighbours, who are considered to be part of the Salish, have that as part of their word to describe themselves – Lillooet-Stl'atl'imx. It's a little bit different; there's an "mph" in the sound. And you have the Nlaka'pamux. And you have the Secwepemc. They all have that little *mexw* sound at the end if their names, just like we call ourselves Xwélmexw. Not only are we Stó:lō, the river people, but we're also Xwélmexw. And so we're connected to the dirt and to the world.

Our burial practices were very important. We had burial mounds and we had tree burials. When I talked about tree burials with the late Rosaleen George and Elizabeth Herrling, they said there was a tree burial across from Frank Malloway's house, across from Yeqwyeqwi:ws. Rosaleen was saying that at that tree burial place, when they used to put the people up in the trees, it was usually the large maple trees that were used. And the branch had to be touching the ground when they put the people in there. The branch had to be touching the ground, that was an important part of it. It had to be connected to the ground. And the one tree burial that was up in Skw'átets, Elizabeth Herrling talked about that. There was a platform that extended across from one maple tree to another.

Researchers do not ordinarily include these kinds of connections in their work. For example, linguist Brent Galloway was talking about how he'd collect the name and the meaning of that name. And that was the full extent of his work. He wasn't interested in any other context that could be provided. For instance, Agnes Kelly – I was talking about how I'd missed out on doing that final day of work with Agnes Kelly – there are probably more specific details I could have gotten out of her. There's one rock with a story of a young maiden who was transformed into stone, and all Brent collected was the name and the meaning of that name, but he never asked, "Why was this young girl transformed into stone?" or anything like that. So there's no adequate context for this story. It's very limited. As for me, I'm interested in those sorts of things. And the other example is amateur ethnographer Oliver Wells. I just get so frustrated reading his transcripts because he was only interested in language. So every single time he writes in his book, "Oh, okay. That's very … that's very nice! I'll come back and talk to you about that." Every time, you know the elder's just going to tell him something, wants to tell him something that's just *so important!* And then Wells cuts him off and says, "What's the word for this?" You know – "what's the word for this" or something. That's all he was collecting – the language. He didn't realize that what these elders were trying to do was to provide him with a context that would enable him to understand – it's not just about the language and the meaning of the words. Oliver Wells contributes a lot to our understanding if you read the transcripts, but it's just so limited. If he had been more interested in those stories and realized their importance, he would have said, "Yeah! Tell me that story!" or "Tell me the story in your language!" or something like that. But quite often, you go through those interviews, and you come to where he says, "Oh. That's a nice story, I'll come back to you." And, of course, he never does. All those stories are lost, and the elders, his informants, were ready to tell them to him. These were important stories that we'd have a lot of use for today, but they're lost.

Another example concerns former UBC anthropologist Wilson Duff. In his fieldnotes he's told a lot about <u>X</u>e<u>x</u>á:ls, the Transformers, and he's told place names that have to do with <u>X</u>e<u>x</u>á:ls. He puts the names, the meanings, in his fieldnotes. He talks about it in there, in the limited context within which he understood it. But if you get his publication – the book – you find that they're all left out! They're not in there. The best source is his notes. For whatever reason he filtered his notes. Like, I don't know whether he just didn't understand the importance or the significance of <u>Xexá:ls</u> and the Transformer stories or what. Everyone has limitations; it all just depends on what they're asking about or what they're trying to understand.

I was talking earlier about our connection to the world, for example, about the roots of words like *Téméxw* and *Xwélmexw* and how they're connected to the earth. How it's important that the trees in which our ancestors were buried had branches that were connected to the ground. There's a sense that I have that when we're buried we go back to the earth. There was a concern about some burial sites that were being washed away up in the Chilliwack River Valley. It seemed like that was okay. It was nature that was doing it, and I talked to Gwen Point about it and that was her feeling too: "Well, they're going back. They're just – the bones are getting washed away and they're going into the water and they're just going back to, you know, where they belong." It wasn't such a big deal. It would be different, I guess, if there was some sort of development that was going in there that caused the bones to be moved somewhere else. That would be totally different from just having nature wash it away. There's that sense of going back to the ground or going back to the earth and of becoming part of the earth again.

There are other examples of what is out there, of the things that we have to take care of. I talked a little bit about some of the places that have taught us things – like the berry-picking grounds – all the teachings associated with them. And some of the hunting areas. I talked a little bit about burial grounds, about fishing. But what are some of the other things that are out there? There are other things that are important.

When I first started this job as tribal cultural advisor, we went to see the elders because, at that time, the CNR was planning on double tracking. They were going to double track the whole length of the railroad track. They were going to put a second track in. And that second track was not only going to affect heritage sites and fishing grounds and habitat but also other places. It was going to affect sacred sites as well. We went to see the elders and asked them, "What is the most sacred site that needs to be protected that's next to the CNR tracks? Within the whole Stó:lō territory?" And at that time the elders said, "The little lake at Iwówes." Because, they said, that's where the *sxwó:yxwey* mask came from. And, as you know, the *sxwó:yxwey* is a very important part of our cultural tradition. It's something that was nearly lost; there was a big revival in the 1980s. I don't think we need to worry too much about losing it anymore. It came pretty close to being lost, I think. This is the late Amelia Douglas' version of the story. She told it in Halkomelem and she also told it in English. It's about this young boy from Iwówes, which means "something that doesn't want to show itself." Iwówes is a village just north of Hope. Brent Galloway wasn't able to get the meaning of the place name, and I took Tillie up there. She and Al were both there, and she kept saying it over and over and then realized, "Oh! Iwówes! It means something that doesn't want to show itself." And so she thought, "Oh! It's the woman!" She just finished telling me about a woman who had been transformed to stone there. There's a woman lying on her tummy. And Amelia and Al said that if you go and roll that woman over on her back, she doesn't like that – she doesn't like to show herself. So after you leave, she rolls herself back over, back on her tummy. So she said, "Iwówes must have something to do with that. It must have something to do with that woman who was transformed into stone. She doesn't want to show herself." She said that when they were little kids they used to call it the "roll-over rock." She said, "The rock is still there." I've never gone looking for it. It should be there in Iwówes.

But the other interesting part of it, too, is that it's a village that's located behind an island. So Iwówes – something that doesn't want to show itself – I think might even have to do with the fact that the village doesn't want to show itself. If you're travelling up the river the village would be hidden by the island known as Lhilheltalets. So it might have something to do with that as well.

There was a young boy from this village of Iwówes. And you see how there's so much to talk about, just at Iwówes. There's that rock. There's the church that's there. You know, if you read some of the missionary records they talk about that village, they actually call it – they have their own way of saying it, but the name of that island was Lhilheltalets. And Lhilheltalets, the origin of *that* name, comes from the water in front of it. When you travel in your canoe, those waves hit the bow of your canoe and then you have the spray. The spray from the bow of your canoe – that's what Lhilheltalets is referring to. There are pit houses there, you can still see the old foundations of the church from there, and there's a dry rack there from the McNeil family from Seabird Island. They fish in that area because their extended family ancestry goes back to that place. Across the river there's a place called Wowes. Like there's Iwówes on this side and then across the river there's Wowes. And I always wondered, what was the connection? I remember Frank Pat talking about a woman who was transformed into stone on the other side of the river, just upriver from Iwówes, along the straight stretch. And he said that you could see her face, you could see her shoulder, you could see her fists – her fists were clenched – and she had them up just above her chest but just below her chin. Not crossed but just up like that. He said you could see her face – her head and shoulders – and see her arms up like that. And every year in high-water time the river would knock her over. And when the water went down he said the elders used to go out there in their canoes with long poles and they'd stand her back up. He said that, after the elders passed away in the 1940s, nobody stood her up, so she hasn't been stood up since. And I remember that! So I was looking at Iwówes, and here's the woman transformed into stone there, lying on her tummy. And then Wowes has another woman who's in the water. And so I wondered, what's the connection, what joins the two? Why is there Iwówes and why is there Wowes? And then, when I took Elder Shirley Julian up there, we talked about that and I had a tour of the area. I told her I didn't know what the connection was, and she said, "Oh! Well, Iwówes and Wowes would be sisters." They're two sisters. One would be the older sister and one would be the younger sister. It's possible that they're sisters and that one was transformed into stone over here and one over there. The fact of the extra sound made one an older sister (Iwówes) and one a younger sister (Wowes). She was saying that's probably the connection: the two might have been sisters.

Sxwó:yxwey

The late Amelia Douglas told me a story about that village where a young boy got sores all over his body. And he was being teased – these sores were very painful – but he was being teased by some of the boys in his village. And they were actually being mean to him, telling him, "Oh, you stink. You should go and kill yourself." So he went to Kawkawa Lake, or Q'awq'ewem, to kill himself. He went to this rock bluff on the north side of Kawkawa Lake. Some elders say that he jumped off, some say that he slipped. But either way, he fell into the water – he drifted down under water and landed on top of the roof of the longhouse of the underwater people. Or the water babies. In our language we call them *s'ó:lmexw*. And they came out and asked him what was the matter, and he said he wanted to kill him-self because of these sores all over his body. Well, the underwater people were able to heal his sores.

When he got there he looked around and he noticed that the under-water people also had sores, and, especially, there was this baby who was constantly crying because it had sores on it as well. And he noticed that wherever they had sores there was spit. People from up top, like us, would spit in the water and it would drift down and lodge on their skin and create those sores. And those underwater people – water babies – couldn't see the spit. But he could see it, so he took a cedar bough and he scraped the spit off, and when he did that he was able to heal all those underwater people.

So Amelia said that he stayed there for about seven years. That is longer than our mourning process. Our mourning process lasts for four years, after which we have our memorial ceremony. That's the end of our mourning process, which means that you let them go. You let them go to the other side, to join our ancestor spirits, they can't hold them back anymore. Because whenever we don't mourn or cry it's like we're holding them back – we need to mourn and cry to let them go.

The boy was gone for over seven years, so as far as his parents were concerned, he was long gone and dead. But one day he announced that he wanted to go back home, and the underwater people were very grateful to him for all he had done to heal them. So they told him that he could have whatever he wanted. And he remembered seeing this basket in the longhouse, and inside he had seen a mask and all the regalia that goes along with it. And he said that that's what he wanted. Because at that time, when he'd first seen it, they told him he couldn't have it. It's very sacred. It has songs and dances. He was told to leave it alone, and he left it alone. So when they told him he could have whatever he wanted, that's what he wanted. So they told him, "Well, you can have it but you can't take it by yourself. You have to have the help of your sister." And so that's why the mask today is owned by the women and danced by the men.

I was taught, since I was a little kid, that I wasn't to spit in the river. I wasn't allowed to spit in the creeks, and I wasn't allowed to spit in lakes. I didn't know why. Remember earlier on I talked about how sometimes we're told to do things but we're not told why, and then later on we find out why. We have to take care of the water babies, and if we spit in the water we're going to make them sick. You know the water babies take care of us and we take care of them. There's always this reciprocation. The young boy was told by those underwater people to go back home and to get his sister to make a basket. While she was making the basket they were getting ready to bring the mask. The night before he went back home his sister had a dream that he was coming home and she told her parents. Her parents got upset with her because, as far as they were concerned, their son was long gone and dead. She said, "No, I think my brother's coming home today." And sure enough, he did show up and he asked her to make the basket. So while she was making the basket the underwater people were trying to figure out how to bring this mask from the lake to that village, to that little lake next to the village. So they asked for the assistance of the animals.

The first animal dug a tunnel and came outside and just around the mountain. You can still see that cave up there on a rock bluff facing toward the river. So that was the first tunnel, and they missed the spot. The second animal was a bird. And the bird dug a tunnel. It came out just around the corner, just upriver of Iwówes. The name *Sqweliqwehiwel* means "many little tunnels." That bird missed the spot as well, so the next one was Beaver. So Beaver dug a hole and came right out at the little lake right next to the village of Iwówes. The underwater people were able to go through that tunnel to bring the mask over. So the brother brought his sister to the little lake and cast her fishing line into the water, and he told her not to be scared of what happens next. When she felt a tug on the line, she lifted it very slowly, and it was one of the water babies who was wearing the mask. It was a small mask, the original mask, because it was a water baby wearing it. It came out and was facing away, and so the first thing you see is this quivering. And if you look at the top of the *sxwó:yxwey* mask you see it has these long – nowadays they use wire but in the old days they used ironweed, so it just quivers. There's wool, tufts of wool tied to it. The mask came out and then it turned toward them. And the late Agnes Kelly says that when that mask turned toward them like that, that moment was called *Swolsi:ya* – like the word for "gift" is *swoles*. And *Swolsi:ya*, that was when the moment when the mask became a gift to our people, as soon as they turned and faced the young boy and the young girl. That's the name that's carried by Al Gutierrez and his grandson – that name Swolsi:ya. So it turned and faced them. And then they taught the young man and his sister all the different songs and dances that go along with it. Songs and dances for birth ceremonies and puberty and namings and weddings and funerals. It's like a cleansing or a blessing to prepare you for the next important phase of your life. Copies of that mask were made and moved downriver. One story talks about how it went down to Welqamex, Greenwood Island. It went down to Kw'ekw'e'i:qw, which is Kilgard, and from Kw'ekw'e'i:qw to Yeqwyeqwi:ws, and from Yeqwyeqwi:ws across to Sq'ewlets, and then down to Xwmethkwiyem. There are all these different versions of how the mask was moved and copies were made. Each time a woman had a child and the child married, another copy would be made. So that's how it made its way downriver.

The *sxwó:yxwey* is an important part of our culture. This was drilled into me by the late Peter Dennis Peters. I remember when my cousin Herman joined the winter dance, and I wanted to know what I could do for him because Herman was like an older brother to me when he lived with us up in Spuzzum. He worked for my dad on the railroad, and he treated me like a younger brother because I didn't have any older brothers. When he joined the winter dance I wanted to know what I could do to help him. I wanted to support him. I knew that he was attending the winter dance quite a bit, quite regularly, and then he announced to his family that he wanted to join. So I went to see his dad, the late Peter Dennis Peters, and asked him about the winter dance. And I was really surprised at what he said, which was, "Well, the winter dance" – he used the word *Syuwel* – "the *Syuwel's*

not really ours. That's something that came from the coast and came up."
He said, "The way they do it came from the coast. In the old days we did
it different. But the way they do it now, that's coast." He said, "But
sxwó:yxwey, that's ours. That came from here, started here and went
downriver." He spoke like a lot of people you hear today, a lot of Stó:lō
people. They don't say the word *sxwó:yxwey* properly. You know, you hear
them say "squie-quay" or "squie-quee" or whatever. But he wouldn't let
me. I would say it the wrong way because I'd heard everybody else saying
it that way! When he was telling me that story he kept making sure – like
every time I had to say it, he'd make me say it three or four times to make
sure I said it right. So he'd stop and he'd go, *"sxwó:yxwey"* (said slowly in a
long, drawn out tone). So I'd have to say it again. And I'd say it and still
not quite get it. So he'd make me say it again. And again, until I finally said
it right. So then he'd carry on talking about it again and then he'd get to a
point where I'd have to say it again. He'd do the same thing with me –
make sure I said it right. So I'm always correcting people now when I hear
them saying it wrong. I tell them the proper way to say it.

That story is the connection for me to that *sxwó:yxwey* because I come
from there. I haven't been able to make a specific genealogical connection
to it other than that I know my great-grandfather, Dennis S. Peters – whom
I talked about earlier, who did the Eayem memorial – he was related to
people at Iwówes, to Chief Bernard there. In fact, he was willed a house at
the village of Iwówes where the mask came from. Tillie and Alan remember that he was willed a house there, and so did Peter Dennis Peters. Peter
Dennis Peters talks about Dennis S. Peters living at Iwówes in a house that
– some old people had passed on and they said that they wanted Dennis S.
Peters to have that house, so he lived there for a while. Tillie and Alan
Gutierrez remember my great-grandfather living there. They said when
they were kids they remember him living in one of the houses there. So
that's the only connection that I have right now but I don't have – I don't
know who willed him that house. That's the connection that we have. I
feel a strong connection to *sxwó:yxwey*, although I'm not able to give a
direct lineage to it. That's what's required now. The families that want to
become involved in *sxwó:yxwey* have to have a direct connection to it.

Sxwó:yxwey is an important part of our culture and it's very well protected. I know in the past there were people who took pictures of *sxwó:yxwey*.
Museums had collected *sxwó:yxwey* masks as well and taken pictures of them.
It's only recently that there is a teaching – and I think it's because of our
overprotection of it – well, maybe not *over*protection. I guess in *some* senses
it might be overprotection, but to protect it we're not allowed to take
photographs of the *sxwó:yxwey*, we're not allowed to record the songs, and

we're not allowed to videotape it. And only certain people are allowed to see it. It's really closely guarded and protected, and you'll notice that, in our publications, we don't have any pictures of *sxwó:yxwey*. Not in any of the three publications that we've done: *You Are Asked to Witness* and *I Am Stó:lō* and then the *Atlas*. The closest one we have is the picture of the little carving representing a *sxwó:yxwey* at the Skowkale longhouse. Even that – even that was a little bit controversial when it came out – whether or not it should be there. But in the end, most people seemed not to mind it there, so now when you want to talk about *sxwó:yxwey*, that's the only picture we can use to talk about it. It's still used today, whenever there are funerals, namings, puberty ceremonies – different things like that. It's a cleansing ceremony.

The other thing, though, I always like to talk about, is how when you look at that story or listen to that story and they talk about the sores on the body, Wilson Duff actually looked at it. But he didn't look at it as a story about smallpox, I mean based on the stories that *he* was told. He said that, based on the genealogy of Mrs. Bob Joe and the origin of the *sxwó:yxwey*, he estimated that the *sxwó:yxwey* must have originated in the 1780s. Now, if you look at 1782, that's when the very first smallpox epidemic happened. None of the elders has ever said that the sores on the young boy were smallpox. But I think it was smallpox. One of our other biggest teachings is that whenever there's something bad, there's always got to be something good. It's kind of a balance, you never really know. An encounter with a *stl'áleqem* could be bad – it could harm you. Or else you could get something good out of it, like the encounter with the water baby. You could learn something or you could die from it! My mother, when she saw little people, she was told by her grandfather, "Next time you see those little people you might die." It could be that tragic. But at the same time, you could also learn something from it.

I keep *that* in mind when I look at the story of the *sxwó:yxwey*. I can imagine if those sores were smallpox, and the huge devastation that that had on our people – nine out of ten people dying – that something good had to come out of it. And when you ask elders today, depending on who you talk to, some elders will say, "Oh, the *sxwó:yxwey* is only a couple hundred years old." Some elders will say, "No, the *sxwó:yxwey* is thousands of years old." And so while you try to disprove or try to prove one of them, you really can't. You can look at the genealogies of some families and say, "Oh, yeah, that must be around 1780." But then what about the other ones who are saying it's thousands of years old? Well, they're partly correct as well because after the smallpox epidemic there were certain teachings

that needed to be retained, and elements of those teachings that were retained were inside the *sxwó:yxwey* story. That's what's made it real, so that
it could be believed and could become a sacred part of our culture and our
tradition. So those old teachings are encompassed in there. To me, that's
why I think that an elder who says it's thousands of years old is right because there are teachings within the story that are probably thousands of
years old. Within this story that's only two hundred years old.

There are other stories about the *sxwó:yxwey*. In the Musqueam story,
their ancestor was Tel Swayel, or Skyborn, because he dropped from the
sky. After he landed the *sxwó:yxwey* dropped at his feet. In Stanley Park at
Lumberman's Arch is the location of an old village called *Sxwó:yxwey*. The
story there is about a man who went to fell a tree to make a canoe, and
when the tree fell into the water it split open and the *sxwó:yxwey* mask came
out. People from Scowlitz and Chehalis talk about their ancestors coming
down from the sky with a *sxwó:yxwey* in their arms as well. Then there's
another story from Burrard that a fisher was seining or dragging with his
hooks in Burrard Inlet and he hooked a mask. You look at all the stories.

The late Rosaleen George told her dad's version of the story – there's a
very similar *sxwó:yxwey* story told at the mouth of the Harrison River, similar to the story told up at Kawkawa Lake, where the *sxwó:yxwey* came out of
the water. She's aware of all these stories. Plus she lived in Musqueam, she
lived in Tsawwassen, she lived in Katzie, and is originally from Chehalis.
She married into Chilliwack. So she's spent a lot of time in the whole Stó:lō
area, and she was quite knowledgeable with the place names. She was instrumental with the documenting of place names because a lot of times she
was able to provide context when all that was collected was the name.

Rosaleen George was especially helpful with the 1858 boundary survey
names; even some of them didn't have their meanings recorded. I'd have
to take the way they were written, their orthography, and try to come up
with the best pronunciation I could. And it was just amazing that Rosaleen
would remember the place! She'd say, "What was that again?!" I'd say it to
her and then she'd say what the proper name is! Just based on my stum-
bling with the proper pronunciation. Then she'd say, "Oh ... I know where
that place is!" And then she'd be able to give some story about it from her
grandparents. She would say, "My grandparents talked about that place.
Where is it?" Then I'd have to look on the map, figure out where it is, and
then she'd say, "Oh, that's where that was! Yeah, my grandparents used to
go do this and go do that over there." She had all this knowledge of the
whole territory just from her experience of living different places and the
fact that she listened – listened to her elders. So I went to see *her* about the

sxwó:yxwey story, and she said, "Well, the *real* story is up there at Kawkawa Lake and Hope." Even though she was aware of all these other stories, and even though she really wanted to make sure that we paid respect to these other stories and recognized that there were other origin stories, she was still able to differentiate between them and to say that the *real* story was up there at Kawkawa Lake. As far as I know today – I think there might be one person at Seabird – but for the most part there aren't any upriver people who are involved with the *sxwó:yxwey*.

Again, the origin of the *sxwó:yxwey* is tied to the water babies. The water babies, or the underwater people, which we call *s'ó:lmexw*, are another important element in the *sxwó:yxwey* story. Just in the places that we find them. There's one up at – they're not only in Sucker's Creek or Kawkawa Creek in Hope – Kawkawa Lake. I've also heard others talk about them at Minto Landing here in Chilliwack, Chilliwack Lake. And Rosaleen had mentioned a place down by Maple Ridge where there are water babies, and then there are supposed to be some down around the Musqueam area as well. The water babies, or *s'ó:lmexw*, are out there in the water. And you have to take care of them by not spitting in the water – that's one of the teachings. There might be other teachings as well. That's the only one I'm aware of right now, though – that we're not allowed to spit in the water because it'll create sores on them. And then they take care of us.

Protocol

The other way we take care of our ancestors occurs when we have our spiritual burnings, each spring and each fall. Families burn food and clothes for our ancestors. Fire is a big part of that, and it's through the fire that the clothes and food are able to reach our ancestors' spirits. There are all kinds of different teachings about that, which I put together after years of being told something and not knowing why and then, years later, finally realizing what it meant. We were told not to use cedar in the fire. When our family started doing the family burnings again and we had been doing it for a couple of years, Peter Dennis Peters would just donate money or something and never really came to the meetings. It was about two years after we were doing the burnings that I remember we had a meeting at his daughter Thelma's house. And he just lived across the street, so he came over. He was really humble and he knew how to teach. He wasn't forcing, wasn't imposing, but he was doing it in a respectful way, and that's the thing that really struck me so much, was how he did that. He didn't come and say, "Okay this is what you guys better do, you'd better do this" or – he didn't do that.

He came over and he said, "Oh, I noticed you guys are doing these burnings." He said, "When you guys first started it I didn't think you were going to stick with it, but it looks like you are so I thought I'd better come over and tell you a little bit of what I know about it." He went on to say, "Well, first of all you have to have it in the morning. So that you always remember that it's always done in the morning." "When I was a young fellow," he said, "It was always in the morning." We were doing it in the afternoon. And there's this flip kind of thing that happens within our family; I think it's lazy people who don't want to get up at four o'clock in the morning to make the fire who want to have it in the afternoon. And they say, "Well, we want our young people there. We can't get our young people there so that's why we want to do it in the afternoon because we want our young people there." To me, it's like they're saying, "Not only are we lazy but we want our kids to be lazy too," so they do it in the afternoon! It has to be in the morning. And then Peter Dennis Peters said, "When you make the fire you can't use cedar in the fire. When the burning ceremony happens all the cedar has to be gone." He said, "If you're going to light the fire and you want to get the fire going with cedar, you light the fire two hours ahead of time to get the fire going and to make sure that all the cedar is gone. And *why*? Because the crackling of the cedar sends the spirits *away*." He said, "You don't want the spirits to be sent away, you want the spirits to come."

Years before I'd heard about little Annie Chapman, who was a good friend of my father's. She used to live with my dad up in Boston Bar, and we used to get bothered by lots of spirits. There used to be people coming up the stairs, and we'd hear babies crying outside, see the breadbox open and close, and the phone lift off the hook and come back down, and hear people walking right through our living room and go into one of the bedrooms. My dad even saw something lift my head up once when I was sleeping on the couch. He said the steps – he heard steps on the stairs – walked right up to the end of the couch and lifted my head and put it back down. There were all kinds of different things that we used to see and hear, so I guess she went – and I didn't see it, my sister was there and saw it. She saw Annie, she went and got some cedar and got the frying pan off the stove and heated the frying pan up. She put the cedar in so that it was crackling and smoking and burning. She took that and went to each corner of each room in the house to chase away the bad spirits. I heard that and didn't understand it: "Okay, I didn't know what that was all about." Then, over the course of the years, I saw all these other workers who would come to our house to try to get rid of bad spirits, and they would take cedar boughs and they would – same thing, they would go to all the corners of the house with the cedar boughs. Or else, when they wanted to take bad spirits off of us, they would brush us off with cedar boughs. When we would leave a cemetery, they would always brush us off with cedar boughs. So I'd seen them doing that. So, again, here's a remnant of what used to be done. Like in the past, those cedar boughs would have been burning, you know, so it was a smudge rather than just a cedar brushing. So when Peter Dennis Peters talked about that, then I was able to put those two things together. "Oh! So that's what Annie was doing. She was chasing away the bad spirits." It was the crackling of the cedar that chased away the bad spirits. When we're having a burning we want the spirits to come, and so we can't have cedar in there.

There are a whole bunch of other protocols as well. Children aren't allowed to be at burnings. Women who are menstruating aren't allowed to prepare food. The way Peter Dennis Peters presented it made it just so much more meaningful. It was just done in such a respectful way – the way an elder would do it. And a respected elder. I mean, it wasn't just being imposed or forced on us or something. You know, just the way he did it, it just meant so much to me. So that's why today when we have our burnings, if I'm involved I do everything I can to make sure it's done in the morning and I do everything I can to make sure there's no cedar in the fire. A few years back we hired – we got this one burner. I won't mention names. We got a burner – we call them *Hihiyeqwels* – to come do some work for us. And he had this other fellow who was a trainee, he was still learning how to conduct a burning. And everybody in Shxw'ōwhámél knew that no cedar was allowed in the fire. Not only did Peter Dennis Peters share that with me, but I talked to Ralph George, one of our elders in Shxw'ōwhámél, and he said the same thing: "Yup, no cedar in the fire and get that fire going early. Yup, in the morning." You know, he confirmed all that, so whenever we do our burning in Shxw'ōwhámél it's always in the morning – get the fire going early. One day, though, we made the mistake of leaving some cedar kindling. We're told that anything that we bring for the fire should all be burned, you shouldn't leave any of it there. So we brought wood, and it's for the burning and it all gets burned. We shouldn't bring too much wood or not enough. We had this cedar kindling there, and we shouldn't have – we should have used it all. It should have all gone in the fire and burned away. We left a couple of handfuls of kindling on the side. Everybody was sitting, the table was set, the food was all prepared and on the table. Just getting with it – the *Hihiyeqwels* were just getting ready. Then all of a sudden the trainee grabbed the cedar kindling and threw it on the fire just minutes before we were going to put the food on it. You should have seen everybody's face. Everybody's jaw dropped. My brother-in-law looked at me as if to ask, "What can we do?" But one of the other teachings is that, when we're at the burning, we have to be of good mind. It's our mind – it's our faith in the work that we're doing that makes the work happen. Right in that moment, we had to remember that.

So we had to be of good mind for the work to continue. We couldn't have any bad thoughts. We couldn't think bad thoughts about that young man who was doing this to us. But I knew I had to say something because after the burning was done we invited the *Hihiyeqwels* over to help share a meal, and we share the same food that we prepared for our ancestors. After the meal, it's a time for people to get up and thank the *Hihiyeqwels,* and if the *Hihiyeqwels* had any messages that's when he shares them with us. That time I really had to share what I'd learned about burning, that whole thing about cedar not being in the fire. The young fellow, he was pretty frustrated because I was pointing the finger at him. I was trying to do it as nicely and as gently as I could. "I just have to tell you," I said, "that this is what Peter Dennis Peters told us, this is what Ralph George tells us, this is what we've been doing for years: we don't put cedar in the fire." I just had to share all these other teachings. And so, in the end, it turned out really well because the *Hihiyeqwels* said, "Well, you know that one of our teachings is that things happen for a reason." And he said that if the trainee hadn't thrown that cedar in the fire I wouldn't have got up and told all these people all these different things that the elders had shared with me. He said, "You probably wouldn't have done that. But because you did it it's almost like the ancestors' spirits might have done that just so that you'd get up and share it." He said, "But now you've told everybody here what you were told." So I felt kind of good about it after that. Again, here's something bad that turns into something good.

Be of Good Mind

I had to learn that, about being of good mind, and just what exactly that meant from historian Keith Thor Carlson. I just shared that last story with him in November 2005, when I ended up going to a conference over in Saskatoon and they were asking questions about the researcher and the community member, how we met, what were the things that you did. And so it forced Keith and me to sit down and talk to each other about, well, how did research happen? Why do we have the relationship that we do? He's spiritual in his way, I'm spiritual in my way. I don't impose my spirituality on him, and he doesn't impose his spirituality on me. We share it. And I remember a few years back, a few years after he came around, he invited me to go to the Roman Catholic Easter mass. Just the way he did it was awesome. He said, "You know, Sonny, you've been sharing your culture with me. You've taken me to the winter dance, you've taken me to *sxwó:yxwey*, and you know, other different things. I've witnessed burnings ... And so I just want to share some of my culture with you!" He said that he's going to Easter mass and he asked if I wanted to go along and watch and to see what they do. And he said he'd explain to me what they did. I said "Sure!" He wasn't trying to Christianize me, he was just sharing. So I went along.

An interesting part of the mass was where they shared, they had the bread and wine and that, and it's actually supposed to transform into the body and blood of Christ. When they were explaining that, Keith said, "Yes, the people that go up, when they participate in that ceremony they have the faith that that is actually happening." You can't see it, like you can't see it happening, but they have the faith that it's happening. He said, "Well, just like you guys, the Stó:lō, when you have your burnings and your food goes into the fire you have the faith that that food is being transformed and is feeding your ancestors and clothing your ancestors. So it's the same thing." So that's when I learned about the importance of faith and that part where, for years, the elders had said, "You've got to be of good mind and have a good heart." I didn't understand what they meant about being of good mind, and that's the faith part of it. We all have to have faith, and its our faith in the work that the *Hihiyeqwels* is helping us with. They always say that, too, like they're not doing the work: they're just our hands and our feet. And they're taking our food, putting – like they're able to do that but it's actually our faith in the work that we're doing that does it. So it took a different perspective, I guess, to help me learn to view some of the things that we're doing, to understand the importance of faith.

We talked about the water babies, and closely associated with them is the *mimestíyexw*. The *mimestíyexw* – and again this kind of goes beyond Stó:lō boundaries and even beyond First Nations boundaries – because a few years back when we go out in the water, there are water babies there. We have to protect those water babies; we can't spit in the water. We have to protect the water – the water is something to me that's sacred, it's got to be protected. And then when we go out into the forest to go picking berries or to go hunting, there's got to be something else up there to protect *us*. And we have to take care of them as well. So the same way I talked earlier about when we have our burnings, we usually set a plate aside for the water babies, a plate of food. It's the same with the *mimestíyexw*, the Little People. When we have our burnings we're supposed to set aside a plate of raw food, of uncooked food. It's just left in raw form and then it's just brought

– it's left. Rather than being burned with the other food it's just left at the edge of the forest. It's left at the edge of the forest to feed the *mimestíyexw*, to take care of the *mimestíyexw*. The *mimestíyexw* are little people who mainly can be seen by younger children. Sometimes they can be deadly, and I mentioned earlier how my mother had seen some *mimestíyexw* when she was a young girl at Ruby Creek. She went up there with her grandfather and her brother, and her grandfather was getting drinking water, filling up the barrels with drinking water, and she and her brother walked up the creek. She heard somebody calling her name. She looked across and there were these little people across the creek, and they were calling her! And she was so intrigued by them that she just about crossed the creek. She said she wanted to cross the creek to go see them and just as she was about to do that she realized that if she tried crossing the creek the water was so swift that she probably would have drowned. She would have drowned in the creek. So she told her grandfather about it, and her grandfather told her, "Well, next time you see those little people there's a good chance that you're going to die."

There's a bad thing about it. But, on the other hand, there's a teaching as well. And the story that I remember the best about it was told by the late Rosaleen George, who was talking about how those *mimestíyexw*, those Little People, bring about good things. In one story she tells how these bones were found. And they had to be reburied. There was a reburial at a place in Sqwa. She said that she'd wake up at night and these Little People would be in her bedroom. They'd just come walking through the walls and just walk up to her and they'd poke her in the side and just grumble. And then they'd leave again. And she had a cousin in Chehalis and a cousin in Musqueam and these Little People were coming and doing the same thing to them – you know, bothering them – and she said there was something wrong. She said it wasn't long after that, when she was talking to her cousins about it, that she found out about these bones. And she realized that these bones were probably the Little People and that they needed to be taken care of. So she made arrangements for them to be buried at Sqwa. And she said after that they never bothered her anymore.

She tells this other story too, about how her grandson was always being mean to his little sister, doing mean things to her and that. And she said that this one day she was at her daughter's place. Her grandson was upstairs, and she was with her daughter and granddaughter downstairs. And she could hear her grandson playing upstairs, and then she could hear him talking to somebody. And she knew he was up there by himself, so she figured it had to be one of these *mimestíyexw* who was up there playing with him. She said that when you see children playing by themselves they're actually playing with the *mimestíyexw*. It seems like they're playing with somebody but there's nobody there. She heard her grandson crying. He came downstairs, and they asked him what was the matter. And he said, "Oh, that little man upstairs told me not to be mean to my little sister anymore." She said there's an example. Of course there's bad things: it could be dangerous to see a *mimestíyexw*, it could cause somebody to die. But, on the other hand, there's still good things as well; there can be teachings too. And that was a teaching that was left with her grandson so that he could no longer be mean to his little sister.

When we go out to the forest to gather berries or to go hunting there are *mimestíyexw* there. As long as we take care of them, they'll take care of us while we're out there. When I'm up there I see them. I know that they're there and I'm sure that there are a lot of other people too. It's understandable that the *mimestíyexw* are an important part of the winter dance and that they're also an important part of the *sxwó:yxwey*. The *sxwó:yxwey* has to do with the masked dances, with the winter dances.

Spirit Power

Another one of our beliefs is that we all have spirit power – even today, even if some of our people don't follow the teachings to go up into the forest at puberty as in the past. In the past, once we reached puberty our grandparents would take us out into the forest to fast, to run, to bathe. There are certain teachings that the boys have to follow, certain teachings that the girls have to follow. The girls would have to do things with their hands so they would have fast hands to make baskets or to pick berries and things like that. And there were certain things that the boys had to do, you know, to become better hunters and better fishers. But the main reason these young people are out in the forest is to try to find their spirit power. What is their spirit power? It would be revealed to them as a vision or something would come to them and that would be their spirit power. That spirit power was something they had to keep to themselves; they weren't allowed to share it with other people. You couldn't tell people what your spirit power was or you'd lose it.

If something special happens to us, we're not allowed to tell it. Just like an encounter with a Sasquatch. That's why a lot of our people don't talk about that because we're taught that something special like that is something that we need to keep to ourselves. So you don't hear a lot of First Nations people sharing their stories about an encounter with a Sasquatch because we're taught that's a special thing, that's not to be talked about. If you talk too much about it, it loses its power. That's something I truly believe because when I do my place names tour and I get to Kawkawa Lake

– because of my own belief and my faith and my connections I have my own experiences that prove that these things are there. For instance, one time I was telling the *sxwó:yxwey* story about the young boy and how he was being teased by other boys who were telling him "Oh, you stink, why don't you go kill yourself?" Just as I was telling that part I connected with his spirit. I felt a connection and I was just sad – just almost – like I almost wasn't able to speak. I had to collect myself before I could carry on telling the story because I got really emotional, because I just connected to his spirit. Another time I was telling the story and I felt like I was losing something, I felt like I was losing something. And so I told the elders about that, and asked, "Should I be telling this story?" I even took family members out there who are connected to the *sxwó:yxwey* and said, "Is it okay if I tell the story?" I said, "This is what I ask – is it okay?" And they said, "Yeah, you have to tell the people what our relationship is because it's to do with the *sxwó:yxwey*, it's important." They said, "The stuff you can't talk about is some of the teachings that they have to follow, like the preparations they make for the dance and all those kinds of things." But I don't know anything about those sorts of things anyway. So I can't talk about it.

I felt like I was losing something. It all depends on the tour group, too. Some groups, I feel really good about it, I just share it. But there are some groups that just make me feel that I'm losing something, like they're taking something away. So I told the elders that, and they said, "Well, you should tell the people that then." I remember that's what Rosaleen said. When I told her, she said, "Well, you should tell them. Tell them that that's how you feel. You know, that you feel that you're losing something when you tell them." So that's what I do, I tell them now. So after I finish telling them the story that's what I tell them. Then I tell them, you know, "Oh, I'm not feeling good today." If I'm not. But I don't tell them that. I just skip around it.

The winter dance is the expression of our spirit power. But it's an expression that's not supposed to be explicit enough so that you can figure it out. That's why a lot of people try guessing. They try to guess. They try to say, "Oh, I think someone's spirit power is this" or "Their dance represents this." In the longhouse it's like "what you have" – that's how they refer to it. You always hear them saying, "*What you have,* you have to take care of that. You've got to keep it to yourself. You're not supposed to tell everybody about what you have." Talking about your spirit power helps you with your life. I think it was one of our elders, Edmond Lorenzetto, talking about that, saying that if you wanted to be a carver you'd get the woodpecker spirit power. If you wanted to be a warrior you'd get the mosquito spirit power. And so it's that spirit power that helps you throughout your life. So whenever you need help or feel you need something, then you can always turn to that spirit power to help you get through your life.

Rosaleen was saying that we've lost that. There are a lot of people who still go through the puberty ceremony, but there are some families that don't do that. And she said, "Even though they don't, they still get a spirit power!" It's the whole ceremony of going out there with your elders and going through that. It's so that it reveals itself to you and tells you what it is. But she said, "That doesn't mean you don't get one!" She said, "You still get one. It's just that you don't know what it is." And she was saying, and Tillie Gutierrez goes on to say, "That's why you're not allowed to point." You know, you go to the longhouse – you're not allowed to point to people. Because when *Xexá:ls* did their work and transformed people into stone, they pointed at them. That's what they did, they pointed at them and then they would be transformed. So, in the same way, some of us have power but we don't know how to control it because we haven't been taught to do that. We haven't gone out with our elders and we haven't had our spirit power exposed to us. And then we haven't been told, "This is how you're supposed to look after it." So people could actually point at somebody and cause them harm without knowing that they were doing it. That's another part – the importance of that spirit power that we're supposed to take care of. So the *mimestíyexw* are an important part of our custom: the *mimestíyexw* are out in the forest. That's why the forest is an important part of our initiation.

Stl'áleqem

The last thing I want to talk about is the *stl'áleqem*. Brent Galloway used to translate this term as "supernatural creatures." But from Western society's perspective, using that term robs it of its meaning because it would fit a lot of things. If you look at Brent's listing in the classified word list, he lists Sasquatch and Thunderbird as *stl'áleqem*. He didn't have to deal with the elders like I did. I went to see Rosaleen and Elizabeth about *stl'áleqem*, and then I got in trouble when I suggested that Sasquatch was *stl'áleqem*. Boy, they both looked at me real sharp and said, "Sasquatch isn't *stl'áleqem!*" And I said, "Oh, it isn't?" "No, it's not a *stl'áleqem*. It's real! It's out there."

The same is true with the Thunderbird. A few years back, somebody called me from one of the universities and asked, "Do you know the Thunderbird – is it a raven or is it an eagle?" So I said, "Oh, I don't know. Ah, let me get back to you on that." I went over to see the elders, and I asked them, "What is the Thunderbird, is it a raven or an eagle?" It took a couple of days and then I got a reply from Shirley Julian, who had talked

with the elders from Stó:lō *Shxwelí,* the language program. She left a message on my phone saying, "The Thunderbird is *shxwexwo:s. Shxwexwo:s* is
not a raven. *Shxwexwo:s* is not an eagle. *Shxwexwo:s* is its *own* bird and it's
real. It's still out there. It's just that the young people don't know it's
there." Click. That was the message! Yeah, so later on we were doing that
study on *stl'áleqem,* and Sasquatch was listed as *stl'áleqem,* "supernatural
creature," and we got in trouble for even suggesting that it was *stl'áleqem.*
So Sasquatch and *shxwexwo:s* are not *stl'áleqem.*

But what *is stl'áleqem? Stl'áleqem* is always associated with water. Some
of the examples are up in Cultus Lake. There's *Hiqw Apel,* the large maggot. In the past, it used to bathe on the edge of the hill by Smith Falls.
People would approach it, and it would roll itself down into the water. I
always wonder about the significance of the story about these two men
from Leq'á:mél who came over. They were training to be *shxwlá:m.* That's
another thing, because where there's a *stl'áleqem* there will be a place where
people who want to become *shxwlá:m,* or Indian doctors, can go train.
That's one of the things I got mixed up on: I thought they got their power
from the *stl'áleqem.* When I suggested that to the elders, again I got into
trouble. They said, "No, *shxwlá:ms* don't get their power from the
stl'áleqem!" I said, "Oh! Well, where do they get their power from?" They
said, "They get their power from *being able to be there.* With the *stl'áleqem.*
Being able to be there and pay respect to the *stl'áleqem,* you know, not
interfering with it but being there. So wherever there's a *stl'áleqem, shxwlá:ms*
would go to train and would interact with the *stl'áleqem,* not get their
power from the *stl'áleqem* but from the fact that they're able to be there
and to co-exist with it. They get their power from that."

I'd heard this story about these two men from Leq'á:mél training to be
Indian doctors. Maybe it was told by Bob Joe. It's in Oliver Wells. The two
men went by canoe to Cultus Lake where that *stl'áleqem* lives. The one
man lowered the other by rope to go see what was down there. He felt a
tug on the rope, so he pulled it up and all that was left of his friend was just
a skeleton. You know, I often wonder, "What's the significance of that?
Like what is that? Why did the *skeleton* come up?!" The story doesn't say
why it came up with the skeleton, the story just ends there. They pulled
him up. There was just the bones. All the flesh was gone. And so it wasn't
until later on that I found out that the *stl'áleqem* was a huge maggot. So
the maggot eats all the flesh off the bones. Right there is where *Hiqw Apel*
is. And so it ate all the flesh off the bones.

That's one *stl'áleqem.* Another *stl'áleqem* is the glowing red eyes that you
see at night. At Chehalis, Chiyó:m, Shxw'ōwhámél. I was talking to someone who had seen it in Chowethel as well. There are probably other places

that I don't know about; these are just instances that I know personally. Lawrence Hope from Yale talks about another one. He says that there's a *stl'áleqem,* an underwater bear, that lives in the little pool next to X̱elhálh, in front of the old village of X̱elhálh. That pool or that eddy there. From there all the way up through Lady Franklin Rapids, right up to Q'aleliktel, to the next set of rapids. That's its territory. The underwater bear lives in that area there. Other ones include the serpent at the top of Devil's Mountain, a large serpent. There's a story about a hunter who went hunting and he sat on a log on top of that mountain, and the log started to move and turned over. It was a large serpent, and he went back and told his people to stay away from that *stl'áleqem.* That's another reason, I see, that the *stl'áleqem* was used. There's a relationship that seems to be established between the local family and their family-owned site and a *stl'áleqem.* A *stl'áleqem* protects their family-owned site. It's a spiritual protection of that site. Other examples of this are found in the story I told of the hunter and Devil's Mountain. I was talking to my uncle, Bobby Peters, who's a hunter. He's a good hunter, and one of the many places he goes hunting is Devil's Mountain. It's a small little mountain just north of Hope there – across the river from Hope. He said you'd be amazed at the number of deer there. He said, "It's such a small mountain but there are lots of deer there. I don't know what it is that brings the deer there." And so when I mentioned the story, "Wow, there's lots of deer there." And so here's this hunter who goes hunting up there, comes back, and tells people, "Watch out for the *stl'áleqem* up there. Stay away from there." So people are told to stay away from there. So only that hunter can go there. Only he can go there to get the deer. Everybody else has to stay away because of the *stl'áleqem.* Then I remembered the other story, too, about – I think this is in Wilson Duff's fieldnotes again. It's a story from Chiyó:m Lake. They say that a woman from Chiyó:m took a husband from Vancouver Island. And this fellow came up and moved up to Chiyó:m. But he wasn't allowed to go to Chiyó:m Lake. Because the family would go up there, and they used to get trout from there, and they would get highbush cranberries and other types of resources that were readily available there. But he wasn't allowed to go there because they said that if he went there he would twist up and die. If you see a *stl'áleqem* you could twist up and die. There's a Halq'emeylem word for that, *xó:lí:s,* which just means "to twist up and die." So here's the *stl'áleqem* again that plays a role, that protects the family's resource: nobody else can come there and see it. Just the family members that the *stl'áleqem* is familiar with are allowed to go there. If anybody else sees it, they'd twist up and die. So you can see that other role that the *stl'áleqem* plays. It kind of protects family-owned sites. But at the same time it's something that's in the water that needs to be feared. When I think about the underwater bear up at Yale there, it's right between those two lower rapids, at the entrance of the canyon. At that first rapid and the second rapid, there's an underwater bear. It's "stay away from there. Don't go up this way." What's beyond that? Awesome fishing grounds where you can go drying salmon. That thing is right there at the entrance to keep people away; no one else is allowed in, and that *stl'áleqem* is going to get you if you go up there. Those things need to be taken care of as well, so wherever there's a site inhabited by *stl'áleqem* it has to be taken care of.

Somebody was asking me an interesting question the other day about *stl'áleqem* – whether, after a site has been developed, a *stl'áleqem* can still be there. We think the spirit of the *stl'áleqem* can still be there and that it should still be protected as though that *stl'áleqem* was there. There are places that I know of, for instance there at Cultus – that marina built right there. It's right in front of that marina where that *Hiqw Apel* used to be. Elizabeth Herrling talks about a huge serpent that used to have a trail, used to actually cross the road there at Seabird, and its right behind Richard Louie's house there, right by the ball field. And she said it used to come out of the slough and go across. Its home was there. I think that she is referring to a *si:lhqey* – the double-headed serpent. So the *si:lhqey*, the double-headed serpent, its home is the whole river system from Hope down to the mouth. Any of the slough channels, the back slough channels, are supposed to be its trails. And that's why the trails kind of meander like that, because they say that's the *si:lhqey* that makes those, makes the trails like that. It makes the slough that shape because that's its trail.

Important things have to be protected. They play different roles, with the Indian doctors, protecting family-owned sites. And overall they're protecting the dry rack areas of the canyon. I know at Sawmill Creek there's supposed to be another one in the first pool. In the very first pool there's these pictographs way up. Tillie Gutierrez said, "I've never seen anyone come out to look for it but at the same time I was worried about *stl'áleqem*." She said there's supposed to be a huge serpent inside that pool. But above the pool were pictographs. She kind of thinks that *stl'áleqem* is protecting those pictographs. She was told this by David Johnny, who was told by his father, Chief Johnny Ohamil, who is my great-grandfather.

Those are basically all the things that I think that are important when you say *S'ólh Téméxw te ikw'elo. Xolhmet te mekw'stam* – "This is our land and we have to take care of everything that belongs to us." This includes anything that has to do with the *sxwóxwiyám. Sqwelqwel*, or *sxwóxwiyám*, meaning the creation stories about *Xexá:ls* and the transformations that they performed with regard to the resources in the mountains and the rocks, and even the rivers – it includes the rivers as well. And then *sqwelqwel* is our own family history about certain places. It concerns where we go to pick berries and where we go fishing. There's a connection that we have to these places through our *sqwelqwel* – a connection with where our spirit powers are, with the *mimestíyexw,* the water babies, the *stl'áleqem,* the origin stories of the *sxwó:yxwey,* and all the different teachings associated with the winter dance. All those different things connect with the *shxwelí.* The *shxwelí* is the thing that connects us to everything. That's what I think needs to be protected, and those are the things that I've learned throughout the years of studying place names and trying to better understand what Stó:lō culture and history is all about. That's my interpretation of what it is. It's important to us, not only, I think – not just because it's our culture and our tradition but also because it's our Aboriginal right and title. It's something that's ours that can't be touched by anyone else. So when we say "Aboriginal right and title" – *S'ólh Téméxw te ikw'elo* – "this is our land" – *Xolhmet te mekw'stam* – "we have to take care of what is ours" – *we* have to take care of it. Because nobody else can. We have to take care of it. It's ours. Those are our *mimestíyexw,* our *stl'áleqem,* our *sxwóxwiyám,* our *sqwelqwel,* our *s'ó:lmexw.* All those things, those are all ours, and we have to take care of them because nobody else can take care of them but us. So to me, that's our Aboriginal right and title.

4

To Honour Our Ancestors We Become Visible Again

Raymond (Rocky) Wilson

Our ancestry is Hul'qumi'num and comes down from the Lamalchi people, a tribe with village sites on the east coast of Vancouver Island and on the lower Fraser River at Hwlitsum, also known as Canoe Pass. Our oral histories tell us that the way of life of the Lamalchi people, the way they survived, was based on what some call a "seasonal cycle," where the people gain their sustenance starting in the spring of the year at the mouth of the Fraser River. In the Lamalchi case, our people would fish for eulachon, spring salmon, and those types of fish as well as pick berries and plants at Hwlitsum and further up the river.

As spring turned into summer, the main sustenance of our people would always be the sockeye salmon. The sockeye salmon was caught and preserved, and our people, because they would catch a lot of salmon for their year-round purposes, would sometimes not return to Lamalchi Bay but would stay year-round on the Fraser River. There were many large village sites all along the banks of the Fraser, a river properly named the "Ka-way-chin" prior to contact with the newcomers. As summer turned to fall and the fishing progressed, the later runs of salmon would come in – the coho salmon and the dog salmon. Some of the people would move back to Lamalchi Bay and finish out the yearly gathering of sustenance in and around their winter village. Our people would also hunt for various animals, including deer and elk. From the late fall until early spring, our people would engage in winter ceremonies, where they would potlatch with their fellow tribes and conduct winter dances and rituals and move around and visit other Coast Salish people. It is important to note that, besides the winter ceremonies and dances, the Coast Salish network would engage in tribal and intertribal marriages. It was customary for the spouses of our people to be chosen by their parents. Marriages were arranged to protect important ownership rights (which were spiritual in essence) and warrior alliances. The linguistic groups consist of Hul'qumi'num (spoken by the Cowichan,

Penelakut, Chemainus, Lyackson, Halalt, Lake Cowichan, and Hwlitsum/ Lamalchi tribes) and Hun'qumi'num (spoken by the Musqueam, Tsawwassen, Coquitlam, Katzie, and Kwantlen tribes). There is also the Upriver Halq'emeylem, spoken by Stó:lō people. There are dialectical differences within these larger linguistic groups. The Island Hul'qumi'num dialect, the Downriver Hun'qumi'num, and the Upriver Halq'emey'lem are similar, but noticeably different in each individual group. All of these groups form part of what is known as the Halkomelem network and, together, make up the Coast Salish peoples.

That is the summary of the way of life of our people prior to the disruption of their lives brought about by the white man. This history has been passed down from generation to generation and was told to me by my father, Andrew John Wilson, who was born in 1899.

As far as our own personal history goes, a story about territory and protocol that has been passed down to me is important with regard to understanding the plight of the Hwlitsum/Lamalchi people. At the time of (and prior to) European contact, there were intertribal wars between the different nations along the coast, including, among others, the Kwakwaka'wakw, Haida, and Yukwilhta. Language was very important in determining who was your friend and who was your enemy. The story says that Lamalchi warriors would approach an enemy canoe and speak to its occupants in the Hul'qumi'num language. If the canoe's occupants did not answer, they would be harshly dealt with and kept from travelling in Hul'qumi'num waters. Our people still had these protocols in place after European contact and even after the colonial regime was set up.

The main turning point in our history came in 1863, when our village at Lamalchi was shelled by a British gunboat called the *Forward*. The incident stemmed from the reported murder of two newcomers, white settlers from Mayne Island, which is part of Lamalchi Hul'qumi'num territory. I would suggest that the newcomers breached First Nations protocol and that that is what led to these killings. Our people, the Lamalchi people, were ostracized for this act of violence: chiefs were hanged and villages vacated because of threats of retaliation on the part of the BC colonial government. Our people suffered from this tragedy, and descendants of our warriors were held in contempt. Since that time the whites have deemed us to be savages and murderers. We, however, view our ancestors as freedom fighters. In our eyes they were protecting their land and resources from being encroached upon by invaders, just as they did in the intertribal wars prior to and during the early stages of European contact.

From a social perspective, the Hwlitsum/Lamalchi intermarried with other Coast Salish peoples. Although there was no clan system among

PHOTO 4.1 Women and children in dugout canoe on the Fraser River.
Major Matthews Collection, City of Vancouver Archives, P137

the Coast Salish peoples, there were arranged marriages within the different tribes throughout the Coast Salish network. For example, my great-great-grandfather Culuxtun (missionary name, Jim Wilson) had maternal ties with the Lummi, and he married a Lummi woman from what is now Washington State. This was before the Treaty of Washington resulted in international boundaries that carved up First Nations territories without our knowledge, never mind our consent. Our connections evolved and developed over time, and we still have a very close connection to the Lummi Nation (my grand-uncle also married a Lummi woman) because they are our family. My grandfather married a woman from Musqueam and my great-grandmother is Musqueam, so we obviously have very close ties with our relatives there. My mother's people are from Katzie, and my great-grandmother is Tuliqviye, Sarah Pierre. Tuliqviye's brother, Xa'xzultun', Peter Pierre, was a famous spiritual leader in the Coast Salish world.

I am saying this to affirm that the Coast Salish network was, and is, very strong. The reality is that, prior to European contact, the Coast Salish people owned all of their territory. The land was given to them by the Creator to have stewardship over. The sense of ownership was different from that held by newcomers, and conflicts with the Canadian government have arisen as a result of these conflicting understandings. The newcomers' notion of fee simple ownership and individual property rights was not present in the the Coast Salish worldview and communities shared some territories. The existence of shared territories has become a problem in treaty negotiations because the government has required that land claims not overlap.

What is important is that we maintain our integrity as Coast Salish people. It is our culture and identity; it is who we are. It is also important that our community be recognized by the Crown so that we can have a voice in the important "rights" issues of our people, from the specific to the generic. We can then consider ourselves made "whole" again. By achieving this end, we will honour our ancestors, knowing that they lived and died for their beliefs.

The Department of Indian Affairs (DIA), in its wisdom, amalgamated the Penelakut and Lamalchi bands shortly after the Indian Act, 1876, was implemented in British Columbia. Epidemics of contagious diseases, mainly smallpox, combined with the aforementioned tragic events surrounding the shelling of Lamalchi Bay (an example of "gunboat diplomacy"), led to the depopulation of our community and probably contributed to the merger of the two tribes. My great-great-grandfather Culuxtun and his brother Culamunthut (missionary name, Charlie Wilson) were important Native spiritual healers, sometimes referred to as Indian doctors. Culamunthut became a subchief, and my great-grandfather Kuts-kana (John Andrew Wilson) became a constable (counsellor) for the newly formed band, representing Lamalchi interests. In 1904, Culamunthut was murdered by a Penelakut man. My grand-uncle's inability, as a spiritual healer, to cope with smallpox and tuberculosis (plus an ever-present land dispute) led to his demise. This family tragedy caused a rift between the recently merged tribes.

In 1884, the cultural genocide of our people was continued with Indian Act amendments that banned, among other things, the potlatch, the spirit dance, and our language. In 1894, the act was amended again, this time to allow for residential/industrial schools for Indian children. Failure to comply with section 137 by refusing or neglecting to send children to these schools resulted in punishment for the parents or guardians. This punishment could consist of a fine and/or imprisonment. My father and his siblings were sent to the Kuper Island Residential School. Our oral histories tell us that the children at these schools were sexually and physically abused. In 1912, there was an incident involving my father's brother. This incident created enough havoc to have our families' children removed from the school. The children were sent to be near the other side of our family, the Lummi, and entered the Tulalip Residential School. When they came back from their stay at Tulalip, which was not a pleasant one, my father and some of his siblings lived on the Musqueam reserve until 1927, when they left because of a dispute (probably over land and maternal rights). The struggle continued for the descendants of the Lamalchi warriors, who were living in a rapidly changing world, where Christianity had displaced the great spiritual healers and where assimilation had displaced the traditional way of life.

In 1927, the Indian Act was amended yet again. This time the iron fist of assimilation would tighten its nasty grip on our people. Indian people were denied their ancestral rights and were now forbidden to hire non-Native legal help to advance their rights. The penalty for assisting Indian people with their rights grievances was a fine and/or prison time, as specified in section 141. In 1951, the Indian Act was amended once more. In the post–Second World War era, human rights were becoming a global concern. The infamous section 141, a large part of the iron fist, was not repealed: it just sort of went away. It would take a number of years to organize a movement that would focus on recognizing our rights from a legal perspective. Our people were dehumanized through the Indian Act, forced to live under horrible social and economic conditions.

My father joined my grandfather, Henry Wilson, and great-grandfather, John Andrew Wilson, who had maintained residence at and around our ancestral village sites at Hwlitsum. Although never deemed "reserve" land, it was our families' home. However, with no legal recourse (due to the strict Indian Act amendments), my father told me that they sort of "melted into the system." Yet, through these troubled times, my father and the rest of the family remained strong leaders and supporters of the Native Brotherhood and its Ladies Auxiliary. This organization was started in 1931 by commercial fishers and continued the ideals of the Allied Tribes of British Columbia, an earlier group that had been devoted to land claims and that, in 1927, had been prohibited by the aforementioned amendments to the Indian Act.

In 1985, after the 1982 repatriation of the Constitution Act, a window of opportunity presented itself through the DIA registration program embodied in Bill C-31. We started to pursue our rights to be registered under section 6 of the new Indian Act and to regain our position in the Coast Salish community. It seemed that this shouldn't be much of a problem and should occur within a very short period of time. We were wrong: it turned out to be a very slow, incremental process. During that time we were a commercial fishing family. We were occupied with our business, with raising our families, and did not have the academic knowledge to pursue the actions that we needed to take. In 1996, after repeated letters had gone back and forth between us and the DIA – protests, appeals, and so on – we decided that we had exhausted every avenue. We decided to file a statement of claim in the courts against the registrar of the DIA. We stated our position very clearly. In the lower court in Victoria, the judge sent a message to the registrar to deal with this matter in a "timely fashion" because it appeared to him that it had gone on for too long. The "timely fashion" never materialized, and more and more letters went back and forth. So back to court we went, and, in 1999, we went to the Supreme Court of British Columbia. The Supreme Court judge decided, after all these years, that the registrar had erred in her decision, and again she was ordered to review the issues and the situation. In April 2000, the registrar, in her wisdom, decided, upon doing her research, that yes, indeed, our ancestral status as Lamalchi/Penelakut/Hwlitsum people did exist. She ruled that we were indeed full members of the Coast Salish community.

At that point there were approximately 225 "status" Lamalchi/Hwlitsum members who were eligible to rejoin the Coast Salish network of communities. Some of the children were not eligible under the provisions of section 6 of the Indian Act, so, counting spouses and children, our membership was in the vicinity of four hundred people. We were still invisible, in a sense, because we didn't have band status or a reserve base. We continued with our mission to honour our ancestors, who, as my father said, were very visible – at one time a large, powerful tribe in the Coast Salish world. Through the disruption of our way of life, the impact of the white man, and early government malfeasance (in the form of failed systems and policies), we were rendered invisible. Our quest now is to become visible again.

We persisted. We applied to the then Indian affairs minister Robert Nault for our band status as Lamalchi/Hwlitsum people. The application was filed on 1 May 2000, and that process is still ongoing. It is indeed a slow-moving process, but since that time we have also applied to the Department of Fisheries and Oceans for the right to fish for food as well as for ceremonial and social purposes. We were denied in 2001, so again, after exhausting every possible avenue, back to the court system we went, this time to the Federal Court of Appeal. Although we didn't actually win the court case, in the year 2003 the Department of Fisheries and Oceans called us into its office. It informed us that it had looked very closely at all of our records and had decided that, yes indeed, in some capacity we were entitled to fish for social, food, and ceremonial purposes. We were given an allocation of five thousand sockeye in 2003, which we successfully caught. Along the way we have worked with the Squamish Nation and have supplied fish for the Penelakut First Nation, our brothers and sisters through history.

In 2003, we held social meetings with the elders of the Hul'qumi'num Treaty Group (HTG). After initial negotiations with the chief negotiator of the HTG, Robert Morales, we met with the elders and chiefs of the communities. They all came into our community, and we provided a salmon feast and a tour of their ancient homelands on the lower Fraser River. On 16 January 2004, we were asked to meet with the elders advisory board, a committee of the HTG. This committee was made up of powerful community elders, ex-chiefs, and ex-counsellors, and I was deeply honoured to be in their presence. The elders unanimously passed a motion to accept us into the HTG. On 5 October 2004, the six chiefs of the HTG, who comprised the board of directors, also unanimously passed a motion to accept us into the HTG.

It is still a complex situation, with the HTG now in Stage Four of the six-stage BC Treaty Process. They are almost set to move into the Agreement in Principle stage. In July 2004, we received a letter from the BC Treaty Commission stating that it would supply us with money through the HTG, which is ultimately responsible for funding. On 25 July 2005, a resolution was passed by the HTG board of directors accepting us into the group, pending completion of the Terms of Union. The big question still to be resolved is whether we come in as an independent seventh member or as part of the Penelakut. We are still working through this sensitive issue. We have been meeting with the BC Treaty Commission for a number of years, and it does agree that we have a right to treaty as ancestral First Nations people. This is another step in a long process.

We fully believe that we are going to attain our place at the treaty table. The bottom line for us is that, in doing this, we will be honouring our ancestors and becoming visible again.

5

Toward an Indigenous Historiography: Events, Migrations, and the Formation of "Post-Contact" Coast Salish Collective Identities

Keith Thor Carlson

Between 1945 and 1965, Robert "Bob" Joe spoke frequently with non-Native interviewers about the origins and history of his tribal community, the Chilliwack. Like most Coast Salish origin stories, Joe's accounts included discussions of heroic ancestors with marvellous powers. But, for Joe, these were not necessarily the most important components of the narratives, let alone the most significant forces in the history of his people's collective identity. From his perspective, what most shaped and gave meaning to contemporary Chilliwack identity was a relatively recent historic migration that resulted in the transformation of his ancestors from high-elevation Nooksack speakers to Fraser Valley–dwelling, Halkomelem-speaking Stó:lō, or "River People."

Though largely overlooked, historical events and large-scale human migrations have played a major role in the process of Coast Salish collective identity formation. An examination of those post-contact migrations associated with tribal ethnogenesis inevitably casts Coast Salish cultural identity and history in a new light. Moreover, such analysis provides historical context for certain contemporary tensions – tensions that exist not only between Coast Salish First Nations and the Canadian state but also among and between variously constituted Coast Salish communities themselves as they struggle to establish viable economies and governing systems within a system of global capitalism and Indian affairs administration.

The following ethnohistorical investigation is not meant to be explicitly political, but it is informed by a contemporary indigenous political discourse that is often heated. Among the Coast Salish people of the lower Fraser River watershed, various conflicts exist over who has the right to regulate and benefit from a limited and rapidly dwindling supply of land and resources. These tensions are typically portrayed in the media as "intertribal" in nature; however, in reality, the expression and composition of the collective units remain largely undefined and debated. At their core,

Social reformation
ethnic reinvention

these disputes engage a fundamental question: where do Aboriginal rights reside and at what level are they operationalized? That is to say, what collective unit holds Aboriginal title and has the right to regulate and benefit from a region's (or location's) natural resources: the band (first nation), the tribe, the nation (super-tribal affiliates), or the smaller extended family groupings? And where, within these groupings, does political authority reside?

At the local level, contemporary indigenous conflicts over land and resources tend to be cast within a historical discourse where invocations of "tradition" imply much more than simple continuity. For example, a group will often assert that its claim to a particular resource is superior to another's because it is more "traditional." Tradition and historical knowledge are invoked to mark authority.[1] Both the validity of the collective group's makeup and the validity of its relationship to resources are substantiated through historical arguments: my band/tribe/nation/family's claim is more legitimate than yours because it is more traditional. History, therefore, is regarded by Salish people as an important arbiter of both identity and political authority.[2]

European contact and colonialism, broadly defined, have been incredibly disruptive forces acting both upon and within Coast Salish society. Together, they have created situations rife with the potential for sociopolitical change. The direction of these changes, and their expressions, however, has seldom been what European observers anticipated. Even within academia, interpretive models and methodologies have obscured as much as they have revealed about the nature of post-contact identity reformations. By alternatively assessing post-contact change in terms of either the benefits of European technology to indigenous cultural expressions or against a balance sheet of demographic decline, the adherents of the "enrichment" thesis and its counterpart the "culture of terror" thesis (a contemporary manifestation of the old "degeneration" thesis) have focused primarily on the impacts of newcomers on Natives and have overlooked the dynamics sparked within indigenous societies. Likewise, structural functionalism and the legacy of ahistorical salvage ethnography are largely responsible for the inordinate attention the process of assimilation has been given in relation to adaptation. Taken together, such factors have largely prevented scholars from looking for significant examples of early contact-era shifts in Coast Salish collective identity and political authority.[3]

Examined here are indigenous histories describing significant change within Coast Salish collective groupings in the first century following the smallpox epidemic of circa 1782. These stories have been largely ignored, despite their centrality to indigenous concepts of the collective self. An analysis of their content and structure demonstrates that the nature of change within Coast Salish collective authority and political identity was driven by indigenous concerns and agendas, even on those occasions when it was precipitated by outside colonial forces. What is more, such analysis contributes to an old academic debate over whether European contact led inevitably to a consolidation or to an atomization of indigenous political authority and collective identity.[4] It is argued here that contact could and did have different results on indigenous identity and authority even within a single cultural group and, what is more, that such changes were not necessarily unidirectional.

In short, this study seeks to historicize the collective identity and affiliations of Coast Salish people by reinjecting indigenous voice and interpretation into a discussion of five separate event-inspired, large-scale migrations and indigenous resettlements. The first involves the origins of the modern central Fraser Valley Chilliwack Tribe. This story is particularly indicative of the role pivotal punctuating forces played in setting in motion the phenomenon of identity reformation. The accounts of this community's arduous migrations from mountainous uplands to the valley lowlands, and its establishment as a genuine Fraser River–oriented collective, illustrate the many complicated social mechanisms a Salish people employed to facilitate a new community's integration into existing social and physical geographies.

The second example discusses the abandonment of settlements at Alámex and analogous tribal clusters along the Fraser River near present-day Agassiz, and the subsequent geographical readjustments to new tribally defined spaces. These stories are indicative of the complex nature of identity politics in the early post-smallpox era, for they document the process through which the participants in these migrations struggled to reconcile tensions that emerged between the pull of their older identities, which were nested in their former homelands, and the need to establish and legitimize their claims to the land and resources of their new territories.

Not all of the movements and collective identity reformations occurred within established tribal systems, however. Stories of class mobility and the establishment of independent, though stigmatized, tribal communities consisting of people who were formerly of the lower and slave classes constitute an important chapter in the history of post-contact Coast Salish identity reformations. Following the first smallpox epidemic in the late eighteenth century, the established elite experienced difficulty regulating the behaviour, as well as the identities, of their former subordinates. Ancient oral accounts illustrate that class tensions have a long history among the Salish that predate European arrival and smallpox. Accounts of the social and political readjustments within Coast Salish society following the first epidemic have provided subsequent generations of Coast Salish people of all classes with precedents to follow as they adjusted to change. In many instances slaves and serfs alike took advantage of the pockets of unoccupied space left between newly reconfigured tribal cores to forge increasingly autonomous collective affiliations of their own. And yet the stigma of lower-class ancestry continues to plague the modern-day descendants of these people.

A third case study is especially useful in revealing that the process of collective identity readjustment was neither swift nor a one-time event. As recently as the late nineteenth century, Coast Salish people seeking to maximize the benefits of a new colonial economy reconstituted their tribal affiliations following a series of migrations designed to allow Fraser Canyon people to gain access to Fraser Valley farmlands. The oral history describing the emergence of the rather loosely defined and somewhat enigmatic Teit, or "upriver," Tribe is particularly useful in demonstrating the extent to which external colonial initiatives assumed a life of their own within Aboriginal society and how the Aboriginal responses were not necessarily what the colonial architects desired or anticipated. Moreover, the emergence of the Teit Tribe represents the first modern expression of a supratribal political identity of a sort that helps explain the forces behind such broad contemporary identities as those associated with the Stó:lō Nation and Stó:lō Tribal Council.

This chapter seeks to elucidate the historical forces that allowed all of these identity networks to become operationalized as such knowledge is essential to understanding the subsequent tensions that appeared between and among variously constituted indigenous collectives as well as those between Coast Salish groupings and different colonial institutions.

The Chilliwack

Robert "Bob" Joe is widely regarded as the foremost mid-twentieth-century Stó:lō tribal historian. His various recorded accounts of the Chilliwack origin story, in particular, stand apart from those shared by other lower Fraser River informants of his generation in terms of their comprehensiveness and detail as well as for the sheer extent of their coverage. Fortunately, Joe was interviewed a number of times over a more than twenty-year period, and so multiple accounts of particular narratives of his are available for review. He co-operated first with the anthropologist Marian Smith in the mid-1940s and then with folklorist Norman Lerman and anthropologist Wilson Duff in 1950. During the 1960s he was repeatedly tape-recorded by his friend and local ethnographer Oliver Wells. As well, during that same decade, he shared aspects of his traditional knowledge with *native voices* →

linguist Jimmy Gene Harris and a number of radio and print journalists. Regardless of what topic his interviewers wanted to discuss, Bob Joe always ensured that they heard the story of the migration of the Chilliwack people from the upper regions of Chilliwack Lake to the Fraser Valley.

Through the story of the development of modern Chilliwack tribal identity, Joe provided the details of Coast Salish social-political structures and functions. Moreover, as with so many other stories concerning Coast Salish collective identity, this one, too, involves a migration facilitated by a historic event (in this case a landslide on the upper reaches of the Chilliwack River) and, implicitly, a coinciding smallpox epidemic along the river's lower courses. Following these events, the narrative documents the reluctant merging of two distinct tribal communities and the emergence of the Chilliwack collective as an accepted member of the Fraser River–oriented community of Stó:lō tribes.

Reflecting the divergence of interests between informant and ethnographers, Bob Joe's accounts of the mountain-to-Fraser-Valley migration have never featured prominently in any of the publications resulting from his interviews. Moreover, the edited accounts of the Chilliwack migration story that have made it to print tend to be somewhat jumbled and confused, a fact more attributable to his interviewers' lack of familiarity with the local geography than to inconsistencies in Joe's narrative.[5] Wilson Duff, for example, in *Upper Stalo,* erroneously assigns the location of the landslide that precipitated the Chilliwack migration to a settlement site referred to as Xéyles, roughly three-quarters of a kilometre upstream from Vedder Crossing. Duff's own fieldnotes, by way of contrast, clearly record the location as "Below Centre Creek,"[6] which is thirty-eight kilometres farther upriver, a site in keeping with the facts as presented in other recordings of Joe's narrative, where the location is given as "just above Slesse Creek,"[7] as well as with Elder Albert Louie's corroborating assertion that Xéyles translates as "side" and not "slide."[8]

As Bob Joe explained, the Chilliwack people formerly lived in a series of settlements along the upper reaches of the Chilliwack River and at Chilliwack Lake. The tribe was led by four brothers, the most prominent and influential being Wileliq, whose ancient origins, as Joe's contemporary Dan Milo related, involved the transformation of a black bear with a white spot on its chest.[9] The Chilliwack settlements were not equal. Wileliq and his influential brothers originally conducted and co-ordinated the tribe's political and social activities from Sxóchaqel, a settlement Joe referred to as the group's "main headquarters" on the north shore of Chilliwack Lake near the river's entrance. (See Map 5.1.) The word "Chilliwack" *(Ts'elxweyéqw)* literally translates as "head," meaning either the headwaters of a river or the head of a person or group of people.[10] One day a young hunter was traversing the series of trails that ran along the ridges of the region's mountains and noticed a crack in the rocks. When he returned to the site sometime later, the crack had grown wider. Fearing that there was "going to be great trouble, or disaster," he warned the people living in the settlement below the fissure that they were in imminent danger of a landslide.[11] However, instead of thanking the hunter, the people "started razzing and laughing at him, saying 'where did you ever hear of a mountain cracking in two?'"[12] The next morning, people living in the neighbouring settlements heard a "rumble." As a result, as Joe explained, "When daylight came, the families that were warned were no more. They were all buried under half of the mountain-slide."[13]

While Joe's narratives do not detail the social and emotional reaction of the remaining Chilliwack people to the tragedy of the slide, it is clear that the avalanche became the pivotal event in their modern collective history. With the slide, Joe asserts, "the main history starts," for it was then that Wileliq and his brothers began moving the Chilliwack Tribe "farther down" the river, embarking on a process of migration and, ultimately, the displacement and slow integration with a number of neighbouring groups.[14] In addition to burying the village near Centre Creek, the landslide also likely temporarily blocked the river's main channels, severing the migration route of salmon trying to reach their spawning grounds near the tribal headquarters a few kilometres upriver on the shores of Chilliwack Lake. Without salmon, and suffering the grief associated with the loss of their kinspeople and the spiritual dangers inherent in living near the site of such massive human tragedy, the Chilliwack could do little else but begin the process of relocation.

According to Joe, after the slide, Wileliq and his brothers moved the tribal "headquarters" twenty-four kilometres downstream from Chilliwack Lake to Iy'oythel, a settlement straddling both sides of the Chilliwack River. Over time, as the population grew, Iy'oythel became crowded, and so the headquarters was again shifted approximately twelve kilometres farther downstream to the open prairie at Xéyles, located a little less than one kilometre upstream of Vedder Crossing. Each time the headquarters moved, the satellite villages followed. By the time Wileliq established himself at Xéyles, other Chilliwack were living in the adjacent settlements around what is now the Soowahlie Indian Reserve. Not too long after their arrival at Xéyles, the brothers decided to move the headquarters again, this time a mere couple of hundred metres farther downstream to Tháthem:als (Lerman and Keller 1976). Joe points to the significance of the move: "At Tháthem:als was born a man who was to become a great leader of the Chilliwacks and to

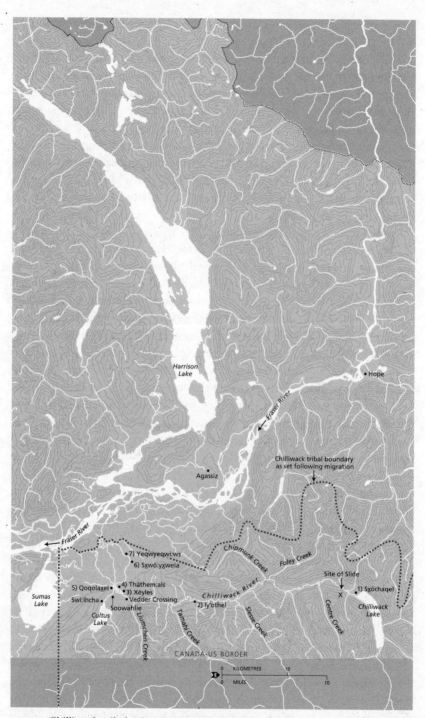

MAP 5.1 Chilliwack tribal migration. *Cartographer: Jan Perrier*

bear the name Wileliq – the fifth man to bear that name since time began" (Duff 1952, 43).[15]

The fifth Wileliq was destined to become a notable leader not only because of his noble bloodline but also because of the remarkable circumstances associated with his birth: Wileliq was a twin, and, what is more, his twin sister was not born until he was a month old. Moreover, Wileliq V's birth occurred at the climax of the era of Chilliwack migration, and he was therefore apparently regarded as special by virtue of his being a product of his antecedents' excursion to a distant location. His birth might best be considered within the context of the Salish spirit quest. Just as prominent individuals ritualistically travel to remote places to acquire spirit helpers, the people of Chilliwack Lake had collectively travelled to Vedder Crossing and acquired a new hereditary leader. Thus, it is not surprising that, under the leadership of Wileliq V, the Chilliwack consolidated their position as a community no longer oriented to the mountainous upper reaches of the Chilliwack River and adjacent Nooksack and Skagit watersheds to the south and east but, rather, to the mighty Fraser River itself. Indeed, until their appearance on the Fraser floodplain, Halkomelem was not even the mother tongue of the Chilliwack people; rather, according to tribal traditions, they spoke a dialect of the Nooksack language called "Kluh Ch ihl ihs ehm."[16]

The arrival of the Chilliwack was a disconcerting development for those already living at and near the junction of the Chilliwack and Fraser rivers. Oral narratives collected in the mid-twentieth century record that, prior to the Chilliwack people's downriver migration, the territory drained by the streams flowing into and out of the body of water now known by the Chinook jargon name of Cultus Lake was occupied by the now "forgotten tribe" of Swí:lhcha people. Like their upstream Chilliwack neighbours, the Swí:lhcha people spoke a dialect of the Nooksack language, reflecting that their social orientation was primarily southward, through the network of trails connecting Cultus Lake to the upper reaches of the north fork of the Nooksack River, and not through what was then the boggy marshland leading from Vedder Crossing to the Fraser River. Another version of the Swí:lhcha people's story, related by Chilliwack elder John Wallace in 1967, explains that the Swí:lhcha were nearly wiped out by smallpox. According to Wallace and others, the settlements at the south end of Cultus Lake and on the flat near Xéyles were completely depopulated by the virus, and the few survivors consolidated themselves in a village at the entrance of Sweltzer (Swí:lhcha) Creek.[17]

The arrival of the Chilliwack people in Swí:lhcha territory did not result in the immediate merging of the remnant population with the new. In 1858, one of the earliest Europeans to visit the area, Lieutenant Charles

Wilson of the British Boundary Commission, described the Swí:lhcha as
still a separate community.[18] A century later, Mrs. Cooper remembered
that, during her childhood in the early twentieth century, though by then
united on the single Indian reserve called Soowahlie, the remnants of the
Swí:lhcha population retained a collective identity that was sustained by
both physical and social isolation from the Chilliwack:

> Those people never associated with the Soowahlie [Chilliwack]. They were Swí:lhcha.
> They were a separate people. There was a line there that they couldn't cross; and
> these people never talked to them ... Not unless they had to. And you couldn't go
> and hunt on their side, and they couldn't hunt on your side ... They kept to them-
> selves and there's very few of them left that belonged there ... See the Band of
> Soowahlie [Chilliwack people] is different from the Swí:lhcha. They were different
> people all together. (Mrs. Cooper in Wells 1987, 106)

So entrenched was the feeling of distinctiveness between the two groups
occupying the single reserve, and so bitter the animosity, that, as recently
as the 1920s, the descendants of the original Swí:lhcha and Chilliwack
communities refused to collect drinking water from the same spring – the
Swí:lhcha of west Soowahlie preferring (or being compelled?) to walk a
considerable distance and take their water from an inferior location rather
than drink from the main Soowahlie source with the Chilliwack people. So
entrenched were the animosities between the two sides that friendly fraternization between members of the younger generation often provoked a
violent physical reaction from adults.[19]

While relations between the recently arrived Chilliwack and the displaced
Swí:lhcha took a long time to harmonize, those between the Chilliwack
and the various Fraser River Stó:lō tribes proper, though initially often
violent, were more quickly rationalized. Albert Louie, an old man in the
1960s, had learned from his elders that the Chilliwack advance to the Fraser
River had not been entirely peaceful. Reportedly, as they edged ever nearer
the Fraser River, the Chilliwack warriors engaged in a series of largely successful conflicts with the Pilalt Tribe over territory and resources considered of central significance to the latter group.[20] *The Fort Langley Journals*
corroborate that, at least during the late 1820s, violent clashes more frequently occurred between the Chilliwack and the older Fraser River (or
Stó:lō) resident communities than between the established Stó:lō themselves (Carlson 2001, 48-49).

This suggests that, during the early Hudson's Bay Company (HBC) fur
trade era, the Chilliwack presence on the Fraser was not yet fully solidified
or accepted by neighbouring communities. Indeed, Chilliwack visitors to

Fort Langley made known to the HBC traders that their homeland was in the upper reaches of a "river that comes in from Mt. Baker" – that is, along the upper Chilliwack River – and an exploration team from Fort Langley that ascended the lower "ten miles" (sixteen kilometres) of the Chilliwack River in the winter of 1828 mentioned seeing cached canoes but no people or settlements (see Maclachlan 1998, entries for December 1828).

Violence, of course, was not the only tool available to the Chilliwack. Wileliq V in particular was especially adept at consolidating both his own personal position and that of his tribe among the Fraser River communities. One of the continuing characteristics of Coast Salish society is that interpersonal relationships operate within a range of possibilities rather than according to a series of fixed rules. Put another way, in a society where authority was not backed by a permanent professional military or judiciary, cultural options existed. These options enabled leaders to choose from among a series of potentially applicable rules, thus enabling them to behave in different legitimate ways. The point was not to pick the correct rule as opposed to an incorrect rule but, rather, to be able to convince others within one's own vaguely defined community or group that the rule one chose to follow and apply was the best and most appropriate for the given circumstance. Historical contact and precedent, of which genealogy was a central component, provided additional legitimacy to any interpretation.

Wileliq V chose as one means of gaining acceptance of his leadership and his community's place on the Fraser floodplain the forging of marriage alliances with some of the more prominent established Fraser River Stó:lō families. On one occasion, an important family from the Katzie Tribe near what is now Maple Ridge invited Wileliq V and his brothers to a young girl's puberty ceremony. During the celebration, the Katzie hosts, impressed with Wileliq, suggested that he "should take" the girl as a wife. Wileliq already had a wife and child waiting for him back at Vedder Crossing, likely a Swí:lhcha woman from an earlier diplomatic marriage, but polygamy was common at the time and so he accepted the offer. What is perhaps more significant is that Wileliq chose to remain at Katzie with his new in-laws until his second wife had a child – a daughter. By living in his newest in-laws' home, Wileliq publicly demonstrated the paramount situational importance of his Katzie connections, and, although he ultimately lost his first wife and child (they eventually grew tired of waiting for him and moved back to the Swí:lhcha settlement at Cultus Lake), his new alliance resulted in his acquiring ownership of certain resource sites within his second wife's family's territory (Bob Joe in Smith 1945, 5:5:10). Wileliq V is undoubtedly one of the "two men from other tribes" Wayne Suttles learned of who "had married Katzie women" and came to be the recognized owners *(sxwsiyá:m)* of valuable sites and "their neighbouring streams, berry bogs, etc." (Suttles and Jenness 1955, 10).

With his regional status much enhanced, Wileliq V eventually returned to Tháthem:als, where he gathered his people and again moved the head-quarters of the Chilliwack Tribe, this time a few hundred metres downriver to a small flat immediately upstream from Vedder Crossing.[21] At this site, he began construction of a remarkable longhouse that was to secure for him immediate recognition and lasting fame. The edifice he built was unique in that it had an inverted gabled roof. Perhaps the best way to visualize the structure is to imagine two classic Coast Salish shed-roofed longhouses butted up back-to-back. The building and the settlement where it stood came to be known as Qoqolaxel, or "Watery Eaves," for running down the centre of the inverted gable was a massive hollowed-log ridgepole designed to catch rainwater like a giant eavestrough. Through an ingenious system of gates and levers, the log could be manipulated during ceremonial occa-sions, causing hundreds of litres of stored water to burst through an or-nately carved opening at the back of the building.[22]

This tremendous structure – which, according to Bob Joe, required a pole over ten fathoms long (roughly 20 metres) to lift the roof planks to allow smoke to escape – became a focal point for central Fraser Valley cer-emonial life. As a reflection of Wileliq's growing stature, the building was constructed through the co-operation and with the assistance of promi-nent families from the neighbouring tribes of Katzie, Kwantlen, Whonnock, Sumas, Matsqui, Leq'á:mél, Pilalt, Chehalis, and Scowlitz.[23] The participa-tion of such a broad spectrum of the region's elite undoubtedly sent a clear message that the Chilliwack Tribe was an established presence in the area.

At some point, Bob Joe explained, not too long before the construction of Qoqolaxel, the Chilliwack River changed its course. Instead of running west after passing through Vedder Crossing and flowing into Sumas Lake, it swung east and then north, running along the base of the mountain and then out to the Fraser River. Branches of this river slowly emerged to the west, and, as a result, the marshy land between Vedder Crossing and the Fraser River rapidly became dryer and suitable for year-long habitation. Onto this land Wileliq V, as an old man, moved the majority of the Chilliwack people to a settlement called Sxwó:yxwela, and there he constructed a sec-ond, less distinctive house, with fewer carvings on the interior house posts. After Wileliq's death his relatives established further settlements at Yeqwyeqwi:ws, Sq'ewqéyl, Athelets, and a few other downriver sites (Bob Joe in Smith 1945, 5:5:12).

Before his death, Wileliq V chose to pass the name and all its invested prestige and power to his grandson[24] (who came to be known in English as

Jack Wealick), though the heir was only a boy of ten to fifteen years at the time.[25] Jack's uncle Siemches, who, as an adult, also acquired the additional ancient name Tixwelatsa, actually exercised leadership until his nephew came of age and had demonstrated his worth and ability.[26] Wileliq V gave Siemches "$20.00, the acceptance of which was [a] sign he'd accept [the] responsibility of leadership." The agreement also included acceptance that the line of leadership would remain with the Wileliq boy's descendants (Bob Joe in Smith 1945, 5:5:10). In 1900, at the age of seventy, Jack died and the Wileliq name appears to have been transferred to his grandson George Wealick. George died at age sixty-one in 1951.[27] In the 1970s, the Wileliq name was transferred to Ken Malloway (born 1953) who has carried it ever since.[28]

This genealogical evidence, coupled with a reference by Bob Joe (Smith 1945, 5:5:101) in which he stated that he knew an old woman who died about 1925 who told him that she remembered seeing the Watery Eaves building still standing when she was a girl, suggests that Wileliq V built the inverted gabled home about 1800. This date is consistent with a Chilliwack migration associated with the smallpox epidemic of 1784. That the HBC expedition of 1828 makes no reference to the structure can be explained if the traders turned back at the rapids approximately three-quarters of a kilometre downriver from the settlement of the inverted gabled home. Corroboration of a circa 1800 date is also provided in the oral history passed to Bob Joe from his elders, who explained to him that Tixwelatsa was the acting chief when the first Europeans arrived in Stó:lō territory. The date Tixwelatsa assumed this role is relatively easy to calculate, given that Jack Wealick was an adolescent at the time. Given Wealick's 1900 death at the age of seventy, Tixwelatsa must have taken over the leadership of the Chilliwack Tribe in the 1820s, just as the HBC was establishing Fort Langley.[29]

Significantly, none of the narratives about the Chilliwack migration makes reference to sudden depopulation other than that associated with the Centre Creek landslide. Possibly, aspects of the story have been neglected, or perhaps the avalanche is meant as a metaphor for smallpox. If, however, the oral tradition is accepted at face value, then, with the exception of the Chilliwack settlement crushed by falling rocks, the majority of that tribe escaped the demographic disaster that so affected their neighbours. Given the relative isolation of Chilliwack Lake vis-à-vis other known habitation sites, and the memories emphasizing the tribe's social insularity (both Hill-Tout and Duff recorded that the Chilliwack were supposed to have been endogamous prior to the migration to Vedder Crossing), it is not unreasonable to assume that perhaps the Chilliwack escaped the first epidemic.

The time of year in which the epidemic reached the lower Fraser River would have affected its ability to spread to relatively isolated communities on the headwaters of tributary river systems like the Chilliwack, given that, at certain times, Coast Salish people spend less time travelling and visiting neighbours. The Chilliwack's resulting numerical superiority, and the fact that they would not have been suffering from the same psychological stress as would smallpox survivors throughout the rest of the lower Fraser River watershed, would undoubtedly have facilitated their migration and territorial expansion.

Bob Joe reports that, during the time of Wileliq VI and VII (circa 1830s and 1840s), the Chilliwack Tribe "split up"; that is, certain families moved to different camps and came to be associated with particular settlements along the lower Chilliwack River and Luckakuk Creek, where the two waterways run through the Fraser Valley floodplain. This physical separation appears to have been accompanied by a degree of socio-political atomization among the Chilliwack Tribe, a process no doubt further accentuated by the colonial government's subsequent efforts to transform each settlement into an autonomous administrative community under the auspices of the British, and then later Canadian, government. According to Joe, this diffusion did not happen all at once; the "scattering had been slow; took years." Meanwhile, under the leadership of Wileliq VI, the tribal headquarters moved a short distance downstream to Yeqwyeqwi:ws.

While this long series of relocations was clearly important to Bob Joe's sense of Chilliwack collective history, perhaps the more important development in terms of significance to the creation of spheres of exclusion and the shaping of collective identity was the establishment of a clearly demarcated and strictly enforced boundary between the Chilliwack and their Stó:lō neighbours from the Pilalt, Scowlitz, Leq'á:mél, and Sumas tribes. It was during Wileliq VI's leadership that "the [tribal] boundary lines were set." As Joe explained, "Before that, lines [which had previously been] only back in mountains now extended to what had been waste land" (Smith 1945, 5:5:5) (see Map 5.1).

The demarcation of these boundary lines represents a significant development in Coast Salish political history. As Wayne Suttles has explained, the standard Coast Salish concept of tribal territories appears to have conceived of jurisdictions not as areas of distinct delineated space but, rather, as an ever-decreasing interest in lands the farther one moved from the core of a tribe's territory. My own research confirms that people from one tribe did not claim exclusive territory; rather, the tribal elites' sense of control of a territory gradually diminished the farther they moved from the tribe's principal settlement and resource sites. Under this system, people from a variety of tribes felt varying degrees of intensity of interest in vast expanses of overlapping territory. Elite polygamous males, for example, felt especially strong proprietary interests over resources near their home settlement, but they retained an active interest in those associated with their wives' parents' territory. This system of recognized shared interest, however, appears to have applied only to Xwélmexw ("people of life" whose lives centred around – but who did not necessarily permanently live along – the Fraser River). Outsiders – different people *(latsumexw)* – who lacked sacred histories linking them to the region, or who had not developed sufficient or appropriate economic and political relationships to allow them access to the same, were simply outside the system.

Fortunately for groups like the Chilliwack, being Xwélmexw was somewhat fluidly defined. In the eyes of the Fraser River–oriented Stó:lō tribes, the Chilliwack had not been Xwélmexw prior to their migration, but they did become so subsequently. Previously, their lives had centred around the upriver transitional zone between the Chilliwack and the Skagit watersheds. Their movement down to the Fraser Valley and into core Xwélmexw, or Stó:lō, space required an adjustment and clarification of their place in the Xwélmexw universe. In practical terms, the migration meant the establishment of formal alliances with the older Fraser River elite as well as the adoption of the Halkomelem language. Once established, the Chilliwack under Wileliq's leadership were keen to consolidate and protect their position along the lower Fraser. To accomplish this, the Chilliwack – or, more likely, the Chilliwack in concert with their new neighbours – carefully defined their territorial boundaries to ensure that they included the lands adjoining the recently diverted Chilliwack River and through to where that water system joined the mighty Fraser. Once it was defined, the Chilliwack fiercely protected their newly consolidated territory. According to oral traditions still circulating, other Stó:lō people caught trespassing in Chilliwack hunting territory were summarily executed.[30]

Thus, through a shrewd combination of violence, strategic marriage alliances, and astute political manoeuvring, all precipitated by a devastating epidemic among their neighbours and a landslide among themselves, the Chilliwack established themselves as the occupants and regulators of a large tract of land and resources stretching from Chilliwack Lake to the Fraser River. Their newly defined tribal territory, as reported by Bob Joe, ultimately included an important communication centre, fishing and salmon-processing sites, and even a profit-generating local HBC fish weir and salmon saltery.

The Abandonment of Alámex

Within Stó:lō history, epic movements loom large not only as a means of forging new collective identities but also as ways of severing existing ones. Not all disputes could be resolved through increased community integration and amalgamation or the definition of strict boundaries. Sometimes, the cultural obligation to reduce conflict and restore balance could be discharged only by community fracture, or what was more commonly referred to in the academic literature as "fission" or diaspora.[31] Such was the case for the families of the Stó:lō Tribe formerly living on the flatlands known as Alámex (the present-day town of Agassiz).

Interviewed by Oliver Wells in the fall of 1964, Chief Harry Edwards of Cheam explained that, within this tribe, a dispute arose over the appropriate placement of a house post within a longhouse. In the early nineteenth century, Coast Salish settlements often consisted of a series of interconnected longhouses, stretching together as a single structure sometimes for hundreds of metres along a river's bank or ocean shoreline. In 1808, Simon Fraser observed one such house in the central Fraser Valley that was 210 metres long and others at Musqueam behind what appears to have been a half-kilometre-long palisade (Lamb 1960, 103, 106). Within these structures, place and space were apportioned according to status, the most prestigious families (or segments of families, given that extended families were not homogeneous by class) occupying the largest and most defensible quarters. Carved house posts depicting family leaders' spirit helpers or the heroic deeds of prominent ancestors anchored certain individuals and families to designated places within the longhouse. Moving a house post was not only a laborious task but it also signalled a change in the status of the family living beneath such monumental carvings. According to Edwards, among the families living at Alámex, "One party was always moving the posts. Well the other party, the other party would move it back again. So they split up, they split up without getting into a fight, you know; they just split up. Part of them went to Ohamil, and the other party moved over to what you call Cheam now. They split up without any quarrel [violence]."[32]

Fourteen years earlier, Wilson Duff recorded from August Jim, a descendant of the people who relocated to Ohamil, a more detailed version of the story of the abandonment of Alámex. His version provides an explanation as to why a certain man's house post might have been unwelcomed within the communal longhouse:

> One day the women and children of Siyita [Sí:yita, a village in Alámex] went to a camp 3 or 4 miles north of the village at the foot of a mountain to dig roots. The

women went out to dig, leaving the children in camp. One woman had left her baby in the care of her small brother. The baby cried and cried despite all the boy's attempts to quieten it, and finally ... [the boy] got angry, made the fire bigger and pushed the baby into the fire. The other children ran to get the mother, but when she returned, baby and cradle had been reduced to ashes.

The unacceptable violence and aggression demonstrated when the boy killed his younger sister only continued to grow as he matured, until ultimately it became more than the settlement's inhabitants could effectively manage and mitigate:

> The boy grew up to become a large strong man, but a troublemaker. Several times, in fits of anger, he killed people, even visitors from salt water. The people of Alámex (Agassiz, the whole area) got tired of him and wouldn't speak to him. Finally, in fear of reprisal raids from down-river, and to get away from this man, they decided to move away.
>
> All of the people from the village of Pilalt [Peló:lhxw, adjacent to Sí:yita] moved across the river to Cheam [Chiyó:m]; the rest moved up-river. Some went to Popkum; the Siyita people, led by Edmond Lorenzetto's great-grandfather, moved upriver to Ohamil; Old Louie's people from Axwetel moved up to Skw'atets. The trouble maker himself moved up-river to Restmore Caves near the mouth of Hunter Creek,[33] and living there alone continued his murderous deeds. (Duff 1952, 42)[34]

(See Map 5.2.) Thus, it came to pass that what had once been a densely populated region of the central Fraser Valley quickly came to be abandoned. The abandonment, however, was not the result of disease or natural disaster but, rather, the concerted efforts of people seeking to both socially and physically distance themselves from a psychopathic member of their community.

While disease may not have caused Alámex's residents to leave the site, sickness may have indirectly facilitated the move. Contemporary oral histories date the abandonment of Alámex at shortly after the HBC established Fort Langley (1827). Three years later, Chief Trader Archibald McDonald conducted an informal census of the Aboriginal population. Analysis of McDonald's report suggests that, in 1830, approximately 1,100 people lived at Alámex (McDonald 1830; Yale 1839).[35] In 1839, a second census compiled by McDonald's successor, James Murray Yale, records that only 427 people were living in the same region. In assessing the ethnographic significance of the HBC records, Wayne Suttles recently concluded that such inconsistencies were indicative of the census' flaws. Given this,

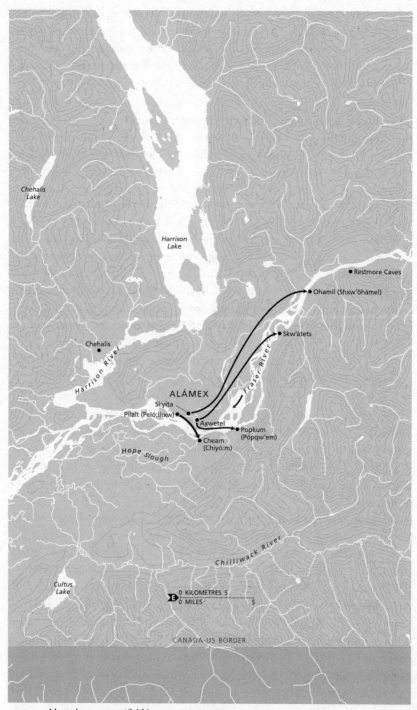

MAP 5.2 Abandonment of Alámex. *Cartographer: Jan Perrier*

he was "strongly inclined not to take McDonald's figures seriously" (Suttles 1998, 258n5). But perhaps Suttles was too hasty in his dismissal. In his accompanying report, McDonald noted his own concerns over the population figures and distribution pattern but assured his superiors that "it is however the fact proved by the repeated examination of the Indians themselves and in particular ... [Sopitchin] who is mostly a resident here, and on whose acct. of the lower Indians we knew to be correct."[36] As no evidence exists for an epidemic in the intervening years, the most likely cause of this large depopulation is migration. It is likely that the abandonment described in the oral histories was well under way by the time Chief Trader James Murray Yale took his census in 1839 and that it was completed shortly thereafter, leaving the settlement sites throughout Alámex empty, or nearly so, by about 1840.

August Jim explained that the people who left the village of Pilalt resettled largely in Cheam near the entrance to the Hope Slough on the Fraser's adjoining southern bank. From there they later dispersed to occupy additional sites along the Hope Slough system leading to the mouth of the Chilliwack River. These people's descendants, still living primarily in the two sites at either end of the Hope Slough, regard themselves as the modern "Pilalt Tribe" and as rightful inheritors of the earlier Alámex occupants' property rights. Those who left the settlements of Sí:yita and Axwetel and relocated to Ohamil and Skw'átets, respectively, had, by the mid-twentieth century, largely transferred their former identity affiliation from the Alámex area to the new region in which they lived. As Duff (1952, 43) learned in 1949, they considered themselves, and were regarded by others, not as Pilalt or Alámex, but as Teit or "upriver" people. These attitudes have proven rather intransigent.[37]

Do the people of Ohamil and Skw'átets, who so clearly acknowledge their migration, feel that they themselves, or at least their ancestors, were interlopers in another's territory? Such does not appear to be the case. Indeed, in addition to recognizing the role of migration in establishing the Ohamil community where it is, the Ohamil people also cite ancient stories of transformation as justifying and explaining how and why they are where they are. In the 1980s, Agnes Kelly explained that it was winter when Xexá:ls, the Transformers, visited the village where the Ohamil people lived. There they found the people starving because it was too difficult to find food in the freezing weather. What made life especially difficult for the people of Ohamil, she explained, was the fact that the salmon and eulachon came into the river only in the spring and summer. In the winter, the Fraser "was empty." Mrs. Kelly's narrative, as remembered by Sonny McHalsie, describes how

Xá:ls the Transformer [the youngest of the *Xexá:ls* siblings] wanted to help the people so he transformed one of the village men into a sturgeon. The man's wife was very lonely without her husband, and so was told to stand by the edge of the river. She carried her lunch – a small piece of deer meat tied in a pouch – on her wrist. As she stood there in the snow, her husband called her to join him. She dove into the ice-cold river. She was suddenly transformed into a sturgeon herself. Because she had lunch tied to her wrist, all sturgeon today have dark tasty meat right behind their gills.[38]

Though the sturgeon transformation story ostensibly refers to the current location of the Ohamil settlement, Franz Boas learned a slightly different version of the story more than one hundred years ago from the chief of Chehalis. According to Chief George, the transformation narrative described events that occurred prior to the people of Alámex's early nineteenth-century migration. Moreover, in this version, although Sí:yita was still located at Alámex, the name was not used to describe a single village; rather, Sí:yita was used to describe the collective tribal grouping of associated settlements. According to Chief George, the primary Sí:yita village was Squha'men, which, significantly, is the Downriver Halkomelem dialect pronunciation of the word "Ohamil," or as it is known in its fuller form, "Shxw'ōhámél." Boas learned that at Squha'men there lived a bear who had been transformed into a man and had assumed the name Autle'n. This man had a daughter who was receiving mysterious erotic nocturnal visits from unknown strangers. News of his daughter's multiple anonymous relationships threatened to bring disgrace on Autle'n's family's good name. After due investigation the father and daughter together discovered to both their shame that one of the visitors was the father's own dog. The second was Sturgeon, who, when confronted, insisted that he had been having relations with the girl for a longer time than had the dog and, that if she were pregnant, surely the child was his:

[The girl's father] remained completely silent but the girl was very much ashamed. When she gave birth to a boy, Sturgeon took him and carried him to the water. He threw him into the river and he was at once transformed into a small sturgeon. Old Sturgeon caught him, killed him and cut him up. Then he served him to the people saying, "Don't throw away any of the bones, but give them all to me." This they did. Then he placed the bones in a bowl and carried them into the water. They came to life immediately and the boy stepped unharmed from the water. He grew up and became the ancestor of the Siyita [Sí:yita] (Boas 1977, 40).

Chief George's narrative goes on to explain that, subsequent to these events, Autle'n eventually ran afoul of the Transformers and was turned into a rock resembling a bear lying on its back. In Boas' time, as today, that rock was still visible on the outskirts of the town of Agassiz. That the Sí:yita people considered the Sturgeon their legitimate ancestor and not Autle'n the Bear, who was forever fixed in a permanent location, is significant. Sturgeon fish were found in abundance throughout all of the lower Fraser River's lower reaches, meaning that the subsequent high-status men carrying the sturgeon name were not restricted to living at a specific place. Just as sturgeon roamed the "River of Rivers" freely, so too could their human relatives and descendants.

The Sí:yita people, led by August Jim's ancestor, were doing nothing exceptional in relocating their settlement. Following the precedent of their Sturgeon ancestor they simply relocated their home to another part of their Stó:lō (River) territory. What might appear to outsiders as discrepancies between the Agnes Kelly version of the story and that provided by Chief George do not appear important to Stó:lō people. For the Ohamil people's collective identity, what matters is not so much the original, or "correct," location of Ohamil but that their ancestor was Sturgeon.

Class Tensions and Tribal Identity

St'éxem

The decision to resolve tension within a collective group by way of community fracture was not unique to the people living at Alámex, nor are narratives explaining how certain people chose, or were forced, to assume new identities as a result of social tensions and through the process of relocation. References to settlement fractures as a result of what were portrayed largely as personality clashes among elite males are found in many standard Coast Salish ethnographies. What have been less well documented and interpreted are the fissions and migrations that occurred as a result of tensions between different social and economic classes among the Coast Salish – as a result of internal indigenous efforts at boundary maintenance – and yet, these form a significant chapter in the story of how many Coast Salish people constructed and discussed their own historical narratives and identity.

Within Coast Salish historical memory, class tension is a common and prominent theme, yet it is one to which scholars have devoted scant attention.[39] Academic analysis of the question of Coast Salish class has revolved

trad
Studies
of class

around three issues: documenting and analyzing the nature of the three-tiered Coast Salish socio-economic structures, differentiating the Coast Salish "class-based" system from the "ranked" strategy of their northern Wakashan neighbours, and, especially, explaining the function of the rhetoric of class within contemporary Coast Salish status maintenance.[40] In addition, some recent archaeological analysis explores the question of the antiquity of Coast Salish class divisions (see Thom 1995; Schaepe 1998). Thus far little effort has gone into appreciating the role of class tension in the unfolding of Coast Salish history and historiographical developments over the past 250 years.

While the subject of slavery is delicate due to the stigma still attached to people of slave ancestry, Coast Salish historical narratives contain many references to slavery and the tension between slaves and free people. Of those circulating among the people of the lower Fraser River watershed, the most detailed involve movements of people signifying changes in status and collective identity. Interestingly, one such story involves the repopulating of a portion of Alámex by slaves after the desertion of the region, as described in the narratives above. This account, and other ones likely referring to somewhat earlier times, explains how certain groups of disadvantaged and exploited people were, through a process of event-facilitated migration, able to begin the process of securing greater personal and collective autonomy and freedom, as well as land and resource rights, while forging new collective identities and acquiring land and resource bases.

The Katzie elder known as "Old Pierre" described to Diamond Jenness how his original Halkomelem namesake, Thelhatsstan ("clothed with power"), performed many wonderful deeds of transformation, improving the world and helping put it in the order it assumes today. An important aspect of this work involved transforming people into forms for which they were most suited – that is, assigning them identities appropriate to their nature. Some of these transformations were targeted at individuals, while others affected groups of people collectively. He transformed his own daughter, for example, into a sturgeon because, despite his admonitions, she spent all of her days playing in the water and at night rested by the shore. Likewise, Thelhatsstan transformed his son, who mourned inconsolably for his sister, into a special white owl-like bird, stating that "Hereafter the man who wishes to capture your sister the sturgeon, shall seek power from you." This bird, Old Pierre explained, was visible only to Thelhatsstan and his descendants. In terms of collective transformations, Pierre explained that some of the people who lived around Thelhatsstan "were so stupid that he made them serfs *(st'éxem)* and divided them into three groups." The first he settled at a site called Hweik on Fox Creek (Reach). (See Map 5.3.) A second group he placed at Xwlálseptan on Silver (Widgeon) Creek, and a third at Kiloelle on the west side of Pitt Lake at its mouth (Jenness 1955, 12). These people were separated both physically and socially from the other Katzie, at least until the late nineteenth century when the combined forces of declining numbers, a shrinking Aboriginal land base, and pressure from Western missionaries and government agents compelled higher-status people to marry people with tainted pasts.

In addition to the three *st'éxem* sites associated with the Katzie, Old Pierre listed other *st'éxem* settlements that also functioned as "tributaries" of other tribes. These included the Coquitlam, who were subjects of the Kwantlen; the village at Loco near Port Moody, which was tributary to the Squamish of North Vancouver; and the settlement of Nanoose on Vancouver Island, whose residents were serfs of the Nanaimo (Jenness 1955, 86). Another of Jenness' consultants from Nanaimo on Vancouver Island added the Sechelt and the Kuper Island settlements to the list of Coast Salish settlements considered *st'éxem* (ibid).

The term *st'éxem,* which Old Pierre used to describe these "stupid" people, is significant, for it is distinct from the Halkomelem word for slaves, *skw'iyéth.*[41] Slaves proper were women or children captured in raids (or purchased thereafter) and their male and female descendants. While many slaves were treated kindly, they and their descendants were nonetheless generally not considered fully human; that is, they were not considered to be Xwélmexw – people of life. Slaves were property in the strictest sense and, as such, could be treated or disposed of as their owner saw fit: exploited, sold, or even killed (Duff 1952, 92-84; Barnett 1955, 136-37, 249-50; Suttles 1990, 465; and Donald 1997, 34, 91, 126-28, 279-84, 295-98). *St'éxem* people, on the other hand, were indeed humans, but humans who suffered from a severe stigma.

The term fluent Halkomelem speakers use for high-status people is *smelá:lh.* They explain that the word translates as "worthy people." When asked what they mean by "worthy" they have explained that worthy people "know their history." Low-class *st'éxem* people, similarly, are considered to have "lost" or "forgotten their history" and, as such, to have become "worthless." The choice of the verbs "lost" and "forgotten" is significant, for they imply a historical process of change: people become *st'éxem* after they have become dissociated from their history. Thus, theirs is a history of losing their history; and, in lacking history, *st'éxem* people had neither claim to descent from prestigious sky-born or transformed First People nor the ability to trace ownership rights or affinal access privileges to productive

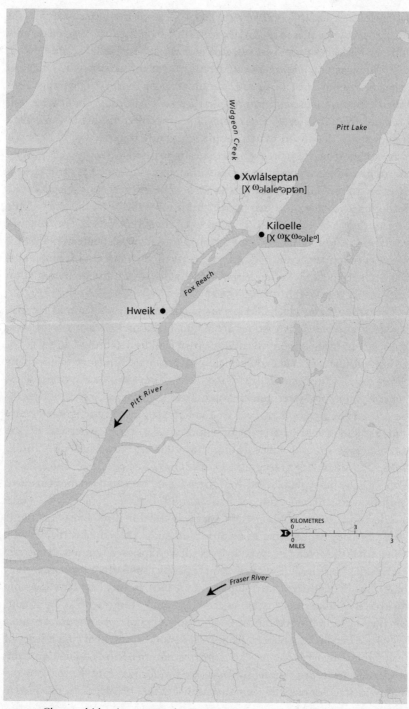

Widgeon Creek

Pitt Lake

● Xwlálseptan
[Xʷəlaleˀəptən]

● Kiloelle
[Xʷᴋʷᵒəlɛˀ]

Fox Reach

Hweik ●

Pitt River

KILOMETRES
0   3
E
0   3
MILES

Fraser River

MAP 5.3 Class and identity among the Katzie. *Cartographer: Jan Perrier*

property sites. In this regard, Old Pierre's use of the term "serfs" to describe *st'éxem* people is rather appropriate for, as Jenness learned, *st'éxem* villages "enjoyed their own communal lives without interference, but the overlord villages could requisition from them supplies of firewood, salmon, deer-meat, or whatever else they required ... Apparently the tributary villages accepted their position and obeyed their overlords without question" (Jenness 1955, 86). *St'éxem* people were, in the strictest sense, "worthless."

Given that the historical narratives of *st'éxem* people always place them in separate settlements, or in separate dwellings within the settlements of high-status people, it is clear that, within Coast Salish society, status and identity have long been intimately and inescapably linked to spaces and places. While Old Pierre explained the permanent status of *st'éxem* communities generally as the work of the Transformers *Xexá:ls*, who at the dawn of time elevated the humble and reduced the haughty to permanent subordination (implying that there is a long history of class segregation and mobility in Salish society), he nonetheless acknowledged distinct developments in the *st'éxem* settlements' histories. As "semi-independent" villages they had their own leaders, healers, and family names; as well, they held their own winter dances, suggesting that the people could at least forge relations with the spirit world distinct from their overlords (Jenness 1955, 86).

Indeed, I believe Jenness' and his contemporaries' interpretations of their Coast Salish consultants' discussions about the dawn-of-time origins for *st'éxem* people are not meant to imply that the particular *st'éxem* communities described in the narratives were all created at the beginning of time but, rather, that *st'éxem* people (as individuals) were considered to have been created at the dawn of time and continued to exist throughout time. Only later, as a result of specific historical events, did *st'éxem* people consolidate, somewhat independently of their masters, into separate settlements to form collective affiliations. Thus, though *st'éxem* communities could not legitimately claim descent from ancient "First People," and were therefore unable to forge links to families with such histories and their associated natural resources, they (as distinct collectives) nonetheless lived historically subsequent to their genesis as separate (though tributary or subordinate) settlement communities. Put another way, while *st'éxem* individuals do not have a history that is culturally recognized as legitimate, *st'éxem* communities do, and those histories appear to be products of relatively recent (post-smallpox) historical events – events that have historical meaning only because they facilitated group migrations, which, in turn, provided people with a historically nested collective identity.

References to these developments are found in numerous indigenous historical narratives. One of Jenness' Nanaimo consultants explained that the above listed *st'éxem* communities emerged "about four generations ago ... [after] an extraordinary severe winter gripped the land and nearly half the population died of starvation." (Jenness 1955, 86). According to this particular narrative, the winter was so devastating that many families were completely wiped out. Among the survivors were many orphaned infants and children who were raised among the surviving adults' own children. But because the survivors were without true parents of their own, and without recognized or acknowledged blood relatives to train them, "people of established families would not marry them."

> They therefore intermarried among themselves, and for protection built small houses close to the big houses that sheltered a number of closely related families, in return for whose protection they assisted in various tasks such as hunting and gathering of berries and firewood. They received the name st'éxem (low people) because they could not marry into established families, yet they were not slaves; they could not be bought and sold, but were as integral a part of the community as the families they served. (Jenness 1955, 86)

St'éxem people were, therefore, creating separate community histories outside of the dominant paradigm of ethnogenesis metanarratives used by the hereditary elite, who justified their status in terms of claims of direct descent from heroic ancestors.

Assuming Jenness' unnamed Nanaimo consultant was at least seventy years old in 1936 (placing his birth around 1860), assuming twenty-five years between generations, and also assuming that the people discussed in the story who lived four generations earlier were in the prime of their lives (their mid-twenties), we can roughly date the devastating winter of starvation to sometime in the late eighteenth century, or to approximately 1785. It is likely, therefore, that the devastating winter that caused the creation of entire communities of *st'éxem* people was associated with the smallpox epidemic of the same era. Even if the devastating winter is not a metaphor for smallpox itself, it is reasonable to assume that the smallpox survivors would have faced a series of harrowing winters as they struggled to cope with the physical and social ramifications of the disease. It is probable, in other words, that smallpox survivors may have faced winter starvation as a result of not being physically, socially, or psychologically capable of gathering and preserving adequate winter food supplies.

Charles Hill-Tout's Kwantlen consultants likewise linked the emergence of the *st'éxem* communities, and especially the Coquitlam settlement (located just upriver of New Westminster), directly to the calamity of a devastating winter. It was during the time when Skwelselem IV was leader of the

Kwantlen (four generations before the siya:m-ship of Chief Casimir, who was chief when Hill-Tout conducted his investigations) that "a severe and prolonged famine ... caused by a great snowstorm of unusual duration ... decimated the tribe." At that time the Coquitlam, who had apparently until then been living in separate houses within the main Kwantlen village at New Westminster, "were sent away ... to the marshy flats opposite, across the river," where they were compelled to fill the marsh with stones and gravel and convert the site into a fishing ground (Hill-Tout 1978, 70).

Franz Boas' consultant Chief George also related the story of the Coquitlam servitude to the Kwantlen in terms of forced movement across the river to prepare fishing grounds and in terms of their subsequent freedom. What is more, he, too, dated this change in *st'éxem* status to roughly the turn of the eighteenth century, saying that the Coquitlam gained their autonomy "five generations ago, when wars were raging on this part of the coast" (Boas 1894, 455). Perhaps most significantly of all, Chief George also explained that the Coquitlam were originally subordinate people because they were descendants of the Kwantlen chief's slaves. From a relatively early and obscure piece of linguistic analysis conducted by Hill-Tout (1978, 33), we learn that the literal meaning of *st'éxem* is "offspring of female slaves sired by their masters." If this is the more accurate description of the Coquitlam people's history, then we can perhaps best understand *st'éxem* peoples' otherwise odd status as neither free-born people of wealth nor slaves as a product of their birth: illegitimate children of high-status men, they were denied the right to claim hereditary prerogatives and privileges through their father due to their mother's slave ancestry. Coast Salish extended families, as a rule, were not homogeneous by class. But *st'éxem* people could neither claim their father's noble birthrights nor gain access to the specialized training of the upper classes, both of which were required to demonstrate good pedigree. As such, they were people without history, for their father's history was *lost* to them and their mother's (as that of girls typically captured in raids as children) *forgotten*.

It appears, therefore, that within immediate precontact Coast Salish society a distinction existed between (1) people who traced slave descent through both the maternal and paternal lines and (2) those who traced descent through slave mothers but noble men. This is significant, for if it is correct it explains, and goes a long way toward historicizing, the class distinctions documented and discussed by Wayne Suttles and Homer Barnett, among others, who identified a three-tiered social structure that was demographically weighted to an upper class but who do not fully explain the rationale behind the lower (non-slave) status of certain people (Suttles 1987, 3-23; Barnett 1955, 239-71).[42] Suttles described the demographic expression of

st'éxem
skw'iyéth

Coast Salish social classes as resembling an inverted pear, with a great number of upper class and a smaller number of lower class and slaves. From Hill-Tout's analysis it appears that the lower-class people, whom my own consultants also identified by the term *st'éxem*, were likely people of mixed slave and master ancestry. They constituted, therefore, a social middle ground: free but simultaneously subordinate and dependent. Perhaps these make up the majority of the 30 percent of Coast Salish people listed as "followers" in James Murray Yale's 1839 Hudson's Bay Company census, a portion no doubt also being full slaves.[43]

What emerges is a picture of long-term precontact class tension resulting from the growth of a lower class of people made up of the children of slave/master unions (and undoubtedly those offspring's own children) being suddenly augmented by the influx of orphans ("history-less" people) from the first smallpox epidemic. Literally overnight, the proportion of history-less, or "worthless," people to free people reached an unprecedented imbalance while the region's smallpox-induced depopulation resulted in fewer people overall to fill the Stó:lō physical universe and, therefore, fewer people to compete for plentiful resources. This created a situation rife with the possibility of social change, for the upper-class leadership was undoubtedly less organized than at any time before, and it was faced with the daunting task of re-establishing a degree of societal stability and normalcy. Under these circumstances *st'éxem* people found themselves with an unprecedented degree of freedom, and yet they were frustrated by the continued stigmatization applied by the population of free people. Therefore, it is reasonable to assume that a solution was reached whereby these *st'éxem* were permitted to move out on their own into separate villages, where they asserted progressively more and more autonomy until, by the mid-nineteenth century (when the British Crown unilaterally assumed for itself fiduciary responsibility for Indian people), they no longer paid formal homage to their former overlords. And the overlords were no longer able or willing to try to assert their control.

Freedom Village

If the late eighteenth century witnessed the social, political, and economic advancement of *st'éxem* people, there is evidence to suggest that, by the mid-nineteenth century, similar opportunities were presenting themselves to the lowest status members of Coast Salish society – the *skw'iyéth*, or slaves.

In 1949, Bob Joe told Wilson Duff a fascinating story of the separation and subsequent migration of slaves from a community on an island near present-day Hope. According to Joe, the island's occupants had accumulated a relatively large number of slaves through raids against various coastal and interior communities.[44] The population of slaves was also continually augmented by births until it became so large that the owners "wouldn't let them live in [their] houses," and they were compelled to build and "live in their own houses on this little island." It would appear that, over time, the "slave village grew, multiplied and mixed," and the owners found it increasingly difficult to compel obedience and servitude from the increasingly autonomous slaves. Rather than try to impose their will through violence, the owners "held a council over it and decided to leave them alone on the island." In fact, the owners determined to abandon their settlement and leave their slaves behind on the island while they "moved across [the river] to our own home." The slaves, now effectively without masters but living within the gaze of their former overlords, decided to migrate themselves. By joining canoes together with planks from the walls of their cedar longhouses, they created catamarans upon which they loaded their possessions, including (according to the version of the story shared by Mrs. and Mr. Edmond Lorenzetto) a copy of the sacred high-status Sxwó:yxwey mask, which they stole from their former owners (Duff 1950, 5:30, 58). As the slaves undertook this historic action, their "owners ... just watched" and sent word to the downriver tribes "not to interfere." The former slaves then permitted the currents of the mighty Fraser River to sweep their makeshift rafts over forty kilometres downstream until they reached the flats at Alámex, immediately downriver from the abandoned villages of Axwetel, Sí:yita, and Peló:lhxw. There they landed and "rebuilt" a home for themselves at a settlement they called Chi'ckim, but which is more commonly referred to by the English name "Freedom Village." And "from there they scattered through relocation and marriage."[45] (See Map 5.4.)

Bob Joe insisted that, subsequent to their migration, the slaves not only became free but they, like the community of st'éxem people known as Coquitlam farther downriver, acquired the status of an independent "tribe." Even more than that of the Coquitlam, however, their territory was very restricted, stretching only a few kilometres "along the bank [of the Fraser River] from Mountain Slough, which skirts the mountain west of Agassiz, to Haha'm, a rock in the river a short distance above Scowlitz" (Duff 1952, 21). Significantly, their territory, carved out of what had formerly been considered the lands of the Steaten (who were wiped out by smallpox) and the Sí:yita (who had migrated both upriver and across the river as described earlier) did not include any of the valuable berry-picking sites in the mountains behind Freedom Village, nor did it include any of the productive marsh lands of Alámex. Its extent, interestingly, much more closely resembled the sort of land base the BC colonial government later assigned as

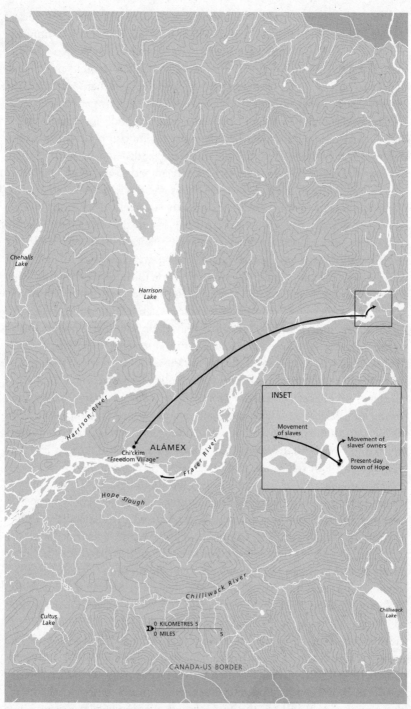

MAP 5.4 Freedom Village. *Cartographer: Jan Perrier*

how does this relate to this administration

reserve lands to all lower Fraser Coast Salish settlement communities: a small tract of land immediately adjacent to a settlement site.

Agriculture and the Creation of the "Teit"

Of all the Stó:lō tribes, the Teit stand out as somewhat of an ethnographic enigma. Wilson Duff was unsure whether the Teit should even be called a tribe, for they appeared to lack some of the fundamental traits associated with that class of collective grouping. Unlike other Stó:lō tribes, whose settlements tended to be clustered in tight geographical proximity, the Teit were scattered along the Fraser River from Popkum all the way to Yale. In addition, Duff reported, and in his eyes, more importantly, the Teit did not have traditions of descent from mythical ancestors and, as such, lacked the strong sense of association with a particular place that characterized other Northwest Coast groups. It was for these reasons, he concluded, that his Teit informants experienced no genuine feeling of internal unity and, therefore, felt free to move about into the territory of neighbouring tribes "with no thought of tribal identity" (Duff 1952, 12, 19-21, 30-37, 40-43, 85-87).

While I question Duff's assertion that the Teit lacked traditions of descent from mythical ancestors (indeed, his own fieldnotes as well as the published reports of both Boas and Hill-Tout reference *sxwóxwiyám* narratives of miraculous First Ancestors from within what is known as the Teit region), he was quite correct in asserting that there is something unique and distinct about Teit tribal identity. The Teit riddle can, however, be answered when one ceases to seek solely geographic and cultural explanations to the exclusion of temporal factors for the causes of the special nature of Teit identity.

It bears restating that the upper reaches of Stó:lō territory, where salmon can be caught and processed with greater speed and ease than anywhere else on the Northwest Coast, have contributed much to the general social cohesion felt by all indigenous people whose lives revolve around the lower Fraser River and its resources. So valuable and important was the salmon fishery that it resulted in a modification of what is generally the standard Coast Salish practice of clustering the largest population centres at the mouths of rivers emptying into salt water or main tributaries. Given that the Fraser River below Yale was generally considered an extension of the open travel routes of the Pacific Ocean (as opposed to the tribally claimed rivers flowing into Puget Sound or the Strait of Georgia), this is perhaps less surprising than it might otherwise be. Nonetheless, the population density of the Fraser Canyon was remarkable.

According to the 1830 HBC census, slightly more than one-third of the total Aboriginal population residing along the lower Fraser River lived in a cluster of settlements along the seven-kilometre stretch of river between Lady Franklin Rock and Sailor Bar Rapids (approximately 2,574 people in the canyon compared to roughly 4,928 along the river's lower reaches).[46] And yet, by 1878, the Department of Indian Affairs listed only 267 Stó:lō living in the Fraser Canyon (Canada, Department of Indian Affairs, 1878), and by 1882 there were a mere 222 (compared to 2,276 living between Yale and the Pacific Ocean) (Carlson 2001, 80). Who were these canyon people, and where did they go? Clearly, something was happening to seriously alter the geographic expression of Stó:lō demographics.

According to Franz Boas' informants, when ascending the Fraser River the last Coast Salish tribe one encountered before reaching Nlaka'pamux territory at Spuzzum was the now all but forgotten Ts'okwám (lit. "skunk cabbage") people. It was from a member of the Ts'okwám Tribe that HBC trader Joseph Mckay acquired a marvellous ornately designed woven goat's-hair blanket in the decade prior to the 1858 gold rush (Orchard 1926).[47] And yet, a generation later, nobody lived permanently in the heart of Ts'okwám territory. The unique canyon geography occupied by the Ts'okwám facilitated not only the economic prestige derived from the salmon fishery but also the ability for effective multi-settlement military defence. As Stó:lō Nation archaeologist David Schaepe has recently documented, each settlement site within the seven-kilometre-long river frontage of Ts'okwám river territory was defended by a massive rock wall (Schaepe 2001, 52). These stone palisades, apparently unique on the Northwest Coast, were more than just extremely effective defensive fortifications: preliminary analysis suggests that they were also connected by a line-of-sight, making the region a truly integrated socio-political unit. Though by eighteenth-century indigenous standards, the Ts'okwám real-estate was among the most coveted in Salish territory, it lacked a feature that Native people had come to consider essential to their survival in the rapidly changing colonial world of the late nineteenth century: flat, irrigable agricultural land.

The fact that the region between present-day Agassiz and Hope was abandoned by the survivors of the late eighteenth-century smallpox epidemic suggests that this stretch of the Fraser, with its relatively small and non-navigable tributary rivers, limited slough and side channel system, and relatively mediocre fishing opportunities, was not especially coveted in pre-smallpox times. That is not to say that this stretch of the Fraser was undesirable, except in strictly relative terms. The archaeological record clearly demonstrates that the area was densely occupied throughout antiquity.

Indeed, the people living there were quite possibly divided into as many as eight small tribal communities, likely similar in scale to the downriver community of Whonnock. If this was the case, the first (in ascending order) was likely clustered around the present-day site of Popkum and around the southern passage between Herrling Island and the mainland. The second would have been centred around a main settlement at the northwest corner of Seabird Island. The third, centred at the mouth of Ruby Creek, might have had satellite hamlets along the upper reaches of both Ruby Creek and Garnet Creek as well as across the Fraser River at the mouth of Jones Creek (although the latter may have been yet another separate tribe). Archaeology sites near the mouths of Silverhope Creek and the Coquihalla River indicate large precontact settlements, and both Emory Creek and American Creek are prime locations for similar finds (David Schaepe, personal communication with Keith Thor Carlson, May 2001). Whatever the makeup of this region's immediate precontact population, oral histories explain that whoever survived the 1782 epidemic probably abandoned the region in favour of taking up residence with relatives living either farther up or down the Fraser River. By the end of the eighteenth century, the region was all but vacant of permanent human occupants.

Thus, while the area between Agassiz and Yale had been partially repopulated by the mid-nineteenth century with emigrants from Alámex, the area above Yale remained the most densely populated in Coast Salish territory. However, as Wilson Duff noted, and as other historians have commented elsewhere, the establishment of Fort Hope and Fort Yale in 1846 "acted like magnets to the Indians, [and] at Fort Yale, which the Indians pronounced Puci'l, a large Indian population gathered, and the canyon villages came to be abandoned in winter" (Duff 1952, 41).[48] The 1858 gold rush and subsequent construction of the Cariboo Wagon Road and Canadian Pacific Railroad accelerated this process, providing canyon fishers with new wage-earning employment and other economic opportunities (see Marshall 1997; Lutz 1992; Carlson and Lutz 1997). Even more important was the government's reserve allocation process, coupled with Western society's general insistence that Native people adopt European-style agricultural pursuits as evidence of their advancement in civilization. These pressures both drove and attracted the canyon people to seek permanent new settlements in the Fraser Valley below.

Within the mid- to late-nineteenth-century Western mind, agriculture and concepts of European civilization were tightly interwoven. Certainly this was the case with those devising and implementing Canadian Indian policy in Ottawa. In 1898, Deputy Superintendent General James A. Smart spelled out clearly the Department of Indian Affairs' position when he specified that the adoption of fixed residency and Western-style agricultural pursuits were prerequisites to taking further steps in the evolutionary process from savage to civilized citizen:

> Increasing acquaintance with Indian affairs can hardly fail to strengthen the conviction that *the initial step towards the civilization of our Indians should be their adoption of agricultural pursuits*, and that if the red man is to take his place and keep pace with the white in other directions, he will be best fitted to do so after a more or less prolonged experience of such deliberate method of providing for his wants. For the transition of nomadic denizens of the forest or prairie, or of such of them as under changed conditions have become vagrant hangers on about the outskirts of settlement, *the first essential is fixity of residence,* and the formation of the idea of a home. Without that neither churches nor schools nor any other educational influence can be established and applied. *Cultivation of the soil necessitates remaining in one spot, and then exerts an educational influence of a general character.* It keeps prominently before the mind the relation of cause and effect, together with the dependence upon a higher power. It teaches moreover the necessity for systematic work at the proper season, for giving attention to detail, and patience in waiting for results. It inculcates furthermore the idea of individual proprietorship, habits of thrift, a due sense of the value of money, and the importance of its investment in useful directions. (Smart 1898, xxi, emphasis added)[49]

Deputy Superintendent Smart's statement illustrates that fixed residency and agricultural pursuits were regarded as essential prerequisites to becoming "civilized." But as historian Sarah Carter (1990) has demonstrated in her examination of the way in which these attitudes were applied to the Aboriginal peoples of the Canadian Prairies, evolutionary models of development could be used to justify holding enterprising Native farmers back from engaging in what was regarded as the more advanced form of profitable commercial agriculture. Popular theories of social evolution demanded that people pass through each evolutionary stage in due course. Adopting fixed residency followed by subsistence farming was equated with proof of Indian people's progress toward being civilized, which, in turn, was seen as essential to surviving in the new world order ushered in by the arrival of European settlers.

As early as the late 1860s, responding to the Western rhetoric and the economic opportunities agriculture provided, many Ts'okwám had taken up private farms near the mouths of creeks between Hope and Yale (Duff 1952, 42) and at the junction of other major tributaries below Hope, especially at the mouth of Ruby Creek across the Fraser from the Alámex migrants at Ohamil. (See Map 5.5.) Five brothers from the canyon settlement of X̱elhálh, whose mother's ancestral ties linked them to Ohamil, relocated there and became neighbours with the recently arrived Alámex group. The majority of the so-called Hope Indians similarly left their settlements near the mouth of the Coquihalla River and adjacent to old Fort Hope to establish themselves on fertile farmland three kilometres down the Fraser at Chowethel.[50]

In 1878 and 1879 all of these sites were designated reserve lands, but the government agent responsible for setting the land aside recognized their physical inadequacy as productive farms for the local Native population: "Between Popkum and above Yale there is scarcely any area of suitable land for Indian reserves. The reserves they have are of thin poor soil easily spoiled by cropping and are really more residential or timber or poor stock runs than anything else, except in patches here and there." The "Yale Indians in particular," he observed, "had no good land [suitable for cultivation] and I had to find them some" (Sproat 1879b).

The replacement land that the agent found was Seabird Island,[51] just upriver from Agassiz. It was allocated not to the residents of a specific settlement, as was the government's usual practice, but collectively "for the Yale Indians Proper and other tribes down to, but not including Cheam" (Sproat 1879b, 19).[52] This is significant in a number of ways. First of all, Seabird Island had not been the site of an Aboriginal settlement since its residents abandoned the village of Sq'ewqéyl near the island's northern tip sometime between 1820 and 1845. Raids by Lillooet people down Harrison Lake and across the portage to Seabird Island had driven them to seek refuge across the Fraser at Skw'átets (Duff 1952, 40). Second, and more important, for the purpose of this study, the government agent learned of Seabird Island from a committee of six prominent Coast Salish chiefs led by the renowned Liquitem of Yale.[53] Finally, and perhaps most important, the reserve was to exclude non-Teit tribal groups, in particular people from Cheam (Cheam being the settlement site just east of Chilliwack where the Peló:lhxw people relocated after the abandonment of the Alámex region).

It is clear that the high-ranking Ts'okwám people considered their future intertwined with the more recently arrived Alámex immigrants at Ohamil, the "Hope Indians," and the Popkum and Skw'átets community. Why Cheam was specifically excluded is not clear. In subsequent years the residents of Cheam played a central role in defending the island from non-Native squatters.[54] Nevertheless, the new Teit Tribe worked consistently as a group to protect its collective interest in Seabird Island from both outside whites and other downriver Coast Salish.[55]

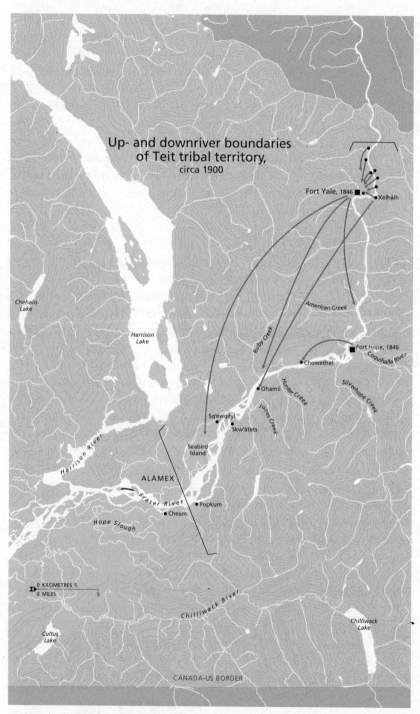

Up- and downriver boundaries
of Teit tribal territory,
circa 1900

Fort Yale, 1846 ■   ● Xelhálh

American Creek

Chehalis
Lake

Harrison
Lake

Ruby Creek

Fort Hope, 1846 ■   Coquihalla River

● Chowethel

Silverhope Creek

● Ohamil   Hunter Creek

Sq'ewqéyl ●   Jones Creek
● Skw'átets

Harrison River

Seabird
Island

ALÁMEX

Fraser River   ● Popkum

Hope Slough   ● Cheam

0 KILOMETRES 5
0 MILES   5

Chilliwack River

Cultus
Lake

Chilliwack
Lake

CANADA-US BORDER

MAP 5.5 Agriculture and defining Teit tribal boundaries. *Cartographer: Jan Perrier*

The migration to Seabird Island of the lower Fraser River's highest-ranking figure, Yale's Chief Liquitem, signalled an important change in regional identity politics. This is because Liquitem and other prominent Ts'okwám personalities who chose to relocate to the Fraser Valley brought with them the sense of tightly knit identity that their ancestors had nurtured in the confined canyon geography and superimposed it on the dispersed and tribally mixed settlements between Yale and Popkum. For these "upriver" Teit people, collective identity became a product of supratribal amalgamation rather than exclusive site-specific mythical genesis. Thus, as the Fraser River tribe whose collective origins are most extensively caught up in post-contact colonial developments, Teit tribal identity has, as Duff observed, often assumed a less well-defined expression than has that of other older tribes.

The migrating Ts'okwám people brought with them a sense of unique canyon identity as well as a certain notion of economic and cultural pride derived from their ownership of the river's richest fishing and salmon-processing sites. Their upriver Canyon identity was superimposed on the various and diverse community identities below. Among the newly merged upper class, which included not only the Ts'okwám elite but also ranking families among the previous generation's Alámex immigrants, a nascent sense of broader collective "upriver" Teit identity emerged that was modelled, it would seem, on other older tribal collectives, but with even greater emphasis on the forces of regional social cohesion that cut across localizing nodes of collective identity. This Teit identity, when conceived within the cumulative context created by the uplands-to-the-valley migration of the formerly more remote Chilliwack ultimately did much to foster the maturation of an even broader sense of Stó:lō collective identity – an identity that encompassed the entire lower Fraser River system. This trend was reinforced by the disruption of status boundaries associated with the increased independence of the various *st'éxem* and slave communities, who likewise took advantage of open spaces created by smallpox-induced depopulation. Thus, although a shared Fraser River Stó:lō identity has been couched in a historical discourse of even older economic and mythic (or metaphysical) historical relationships (McHalsie 2001), in truth it assumed a socially meaningful form largely as a result of specific contact-era historical events. Although Stó:lō communities had been linked through shared regional resource ownership and access protocols and overlapping stories of ancient tribal creation long before European contact, it was the post-smallpox migrations that ultimately tipped the balance and resulted in the broader identity eclipsing the more local ones.

Conclusion: Toward a Coast Salish Historiography

As outsiders, our understanding of Coast Salish collective identity has long been a prisoner of powerful academic and institutional forces. The presentist concerns of an earlier generation of salvage ethnographers and the intellectual legacy of structural functionalism resulted in collective affiliations being interpreted almost exclusively in terms of kinship and lineage, identity being cast as ahistorical and cultural change regarded as unidirectional. Likewise, historians' propensity to view the past through the lens of either the enrichment thesis or its counterpart the degeneration (and "culture of terror") hypothesis fostered the impression that assessments of advances or tragedies in material culture or demographics could alone sufficiently account for the indigenous response to contact pressures. Meanwhile, running parallel to the scholarship were the Canadian government's efforts to craft "band" and "tribal" identities so as to facilitate effective administration and paternal control, all the while reifying popular impressions about how Indian people were traditionally grouped.

Beneath, and before, these externally imposed interpretive models lies a history of collective identity reformation that Salish people have both negotiated and interpreted for themselves. By paying closer attention to the narratives that Salish people emphasize as they explain their history, we are offered glimpses into not only their past but also their indigenous means of processing and interpreting history. We approach, in other words, an indigenous historiography.

Within Coast Salish society, collective identity, like political authority, is situationally constructed. Thus, it has a history. It is neither frozen in time nor a passive passenger on a journey whose trajectory was firmly set by non-Native agents. Each time the deck was shuffled (be it by smallpox depopulation, the introduction of new economic opportunities associated with the fur trade, or government policy designed to facilitate a Western agricultural agenda), Salish people were compelled to relegitimize their collective affiliations. Many, as we know from the extant scholarship, found ways to re-establish existing affiliations. Others, however, seized the opportunity to recast their identity in a new mould. Historical events caused the deck to be reshuffled, and from this state of flux, migration appears to have been the preferred means of facilitating changes in identity. Migrations, and the events that inspired them, provided Salish people with opportunities for adjusting and redesigning social political relations and, through them, collective identity and affiliation. They precipitated amalgamations as well as fractures. They disrupted deeply entrenched class and status structures, providing opportunities for social mobility as well as for the consolidation of political authority. They provide us with insights into the way in which history occurred, was internalized, and subsequently used by Aboriginal peoples. They suggest an event-centred indigenous historiography where identity is fluid, though anchored.

Notes

1 The relationships between tradition and authority are examined in Phillips and Schochet (2004).

2 I discuss the role of tradition and innovation within Coast Salish conflicts over resource ownership in Carlson (forthcoming).

3 Recently, in response to an article arguing the existence of formal precontact Coast Salish chiefdoms, Wayne Suttles, Bruce Miller, Daniel Boxberger, and Keith Thor Carlson, among others, have begun creating a model of Coast Salish identity that recognizes the situational nature of political authority and the historically contingent factors shaping Coast Salish collective identity. This chapter builds directly upon these earlier studies. See Suttles (1989); Miller and Boxberger (1994); and Carlson (2001).

4 Charles Bishop (1974), for example, tackled the question of whether contact had an atomizing effect on Canadian Ojibwa clan structures or whether it caused increased clan solidarity and a new sense of shared collective identity. He concluded that, while there was clear evidence of increased centralization, the inherent biases of both oral and written records could be used to support either position.

5 In addition, audio recordings in the Stó:lō Nation Archives, Stó:lō Nation, Chilliwack, BC (hereafter SNA), reveal that Bob Joe spoke softly and had a deep voice, sometimes making it difficult to understand him.

6 See Duff (1950, 50). I have personally visited the area below Centre Creek and identified the sites of two major landslides. The first involved boulders of more than three metres in diameter, whereas the second was made up of small rocks and talus debris.

7 Lerman (n.d.) recorded Joe as stating that the slide occurred "just above Slesse Creek," which is consistent with the site also being "below Centre Creek" as described in Duff's notes.

8 Albert Louie, interview by Oliver Wells. See Wells (1987, 160). Duff's translation of *Xéyles* as "slide" rather than "side" may have been a simple typographical error. The fact that Wells and subsequent ethnographers, as well as certain Stó:lō people, have accepted the error is indicative of the problems associated with particular ethnographic accounts coming to be accepted as authorities on given subjects.

9 Dan Milo, interview by Oliver Wells, July 1964, compact disc audio copy, SNA.

10 Bob Joe, interview by Imbert Orchard, 2 April 1963, transcripts, CBC Archives, Toronto; copies at SNA. Linguist Jimmy Harris, who conducted research with Dan Milo in the early 1960s, recorded Milo providing a translation of "Chilliwack" as being "back water," referring to the point on a river that was "as far as you can go [in a canoe]." Milo, however, admitted to Harris that he was guessing at the meaning, whereas Bob Joe was confident of his translation. Jimmy Gene Harris, personal communication with Keith Thor Carlson, July 1996.

11 Bob Joe, interview by Lerman, in Lerman (1950-51, 269).

12 Bob Joe, interview by Orchard. See also Dan Milo, interview by Wells, in Wells (1987, 90).

13 Bob Joe, interview by Lerman, in Lerman (1950-51, 269).

14 Bob Joe, interview by Oliver Wells, 8 February 1962, compact disc audio copy, track 2, 4:55, SNA.

15 While Joe describes this Wileliq as the "fifth," five years earlier, when speaking with Marian Smith, he provided an even greater genealogical history in which he explained that the Wileliq born at Tháthem:als was actually the seventh man to bear the name since the beginning of time. Joe himself never referred to any of the Wileliqs by numbers, instead referencing them in relation to one another, as in "the third Wileliq since such and such." In this way the discrepancies in numbers between Smith's and Duff's notes reflect the emphasis assumed by the ethnographer and not that implied by the narrator. See Smith (1945, ms 268).

16 Bob Joe and Billy Sepass both provided Oliver Wells with this as the name of the language spoken by the Chilliwack people prior to their movement downriver and their adoption of the Halkomelem language.

17 John Wallace, interview by Oliver Wells, 3 October 1967, audiotape and transcript, SNA.

18 Wilson refers to them as "Schweltya." See Stanley (1970).

19 Mrs. Cooper, interview by Oliver Wells, 31 March 1968, audiotape copy, SNA.

20 Albert Louie, interview by Oliver Wells, 5 August 1965, audiotape copy and transcript, SNA. See also Wells (1987, 390).

21 Some accounts collected by Wells place the headquarters and principal longhouse right at Vedder Crossing, at the site of the current River Side Café.

22 See Albert Louie, 5 August 1965, audio copy and transcript, SNA. Also, Andy Commodore, personal communications with Keith Thor Carlson, summer 1993.

23 This full list of the tribes who assisted in the building of the inverted gable house is found in Duff (1950, 2:68) and differs from the edited list found in his published material.

24 The various recorded genealogies are confusing on this point. The Halqemeylem word for "grandson" is the same as the word for "grandnephew" (as well as grandfather and grand-uncle). An account of this genealogy collected by Duff records that Wileliq V passed his name on to his grandnephew by his younger brother. Both accounts concur that Jack Wealick became Wileliq VI.

25 Bob Joe in Smith (1945, 5:5:12). Duff's fieldnotes and published accounts contradict what is found in Smith's records. Duff records that Wileliq V had no sons and so passed his name to his nephew, the son of his younger brother. This man, in turn, passed it to his grandson, who was an old man in 1950. I believe Duff was confused. See Duff (1952, 44) and Duff (1950, 1:65).

26 Again, there is some confusion here. Tixwelatsa may have been a different uncle (another brother or possibly even a cousin of Siemches and Wileliq) since the Halkomelem language does not distinguish between such relationships. Additionally, it is important to note that Siemches is the name of one of the original black-bear-with-a-white-spot-on-its-chest brothers who was transformed into a founder of the Chilliwack Tribe at the beginning of time. The name is currently carried by Chief Frank Malloway of Yeqwyeqwi:ws. In a potlatch naming ceremony in the late 1990s, Chief Malloway clarified that the name and all its associated prestige and privileges will eventually be transferred to his nephew Dalton Silver, who will "carry it" so long as he continues to act in a way that brings honour and not shame to the name and his ancestors.

27 Joe explained to Marian Smith that his wife's oldest son by her earlier marriage to Wileliq VI's son carried the Wileliq name in 1951. Wileliq VII was also known as George, who, in addition to being Bob Joe's stepson, was also his cousin. In other words, Mrs. Bob Joe was the great-great-granddaughter (niece?) of Wileliq V's second wife (the Katzie

woman). Wileliq VI was Bob Joe's grandfather's older brother. See Duff (1952, 44). See also Duff (1950, 2:67).

28 In 1992, Bob Joe's grandson, Wesley Sam, told me that his grandfather had quietly and informally transferred the Wileliq name to him. Prior to his death in 1997, Wesley Sam arranged for the name – pronounced "Wi-ley-lug," which Sam explained was the older and more correct Nooksack-style pronunciation of Wileliq – to be transferred to his infant grandson. Sam's family later arranged a naming ceremony, where it was explained that the name was to be "shared" between the grandson and Wesley's own son Bruce.

29 I am grateful to genealogist Alice Marwood, who drew my attention to Jack Wealick's grave marker, and who patiently provided guidance as I struggled to make sense of the complicated Wileliq family tree. I am also grateful to Sonny McHalsie, who spent at least two full days with me as I struggled to plot and understand the information on Wileliq genealogy found in the various oral histories recorded by Oliver Wells, Wilson Duff, and Marian Smith.

30 Patrick Charlie and Robert Joe, in Duff (1950, 4:37). More recently, Ken Malloway (Wileliq) has often told audiences of Natives and non-Natives alike how the Chilliwack formerly killed trespassers.

31 Community fission was not an unusual process in societies with social organization like that of the Coast Salish. Fission, without much historical context, is described in most standard Coast Salish ethnographies. It occurred for a variety of reasons, some as mundane as sanitation or to gain access to new sources of firewood, although both these concerns were typically met by seasonal rounds and the steady supply of wood, which was deposited along the sides of the Fraser River and its tributaries in yearly floods and freshets. One of the most sophisticated discussions of the social tensions and mechanism used to facilitate community fission is found in Sally Snyder's unpublished doctoral dissertation, wherein she describes how new leaders occasionally arose among the Skagit and challenged the existing elite by forging their own settlement community. She also documents how these new communities attempted, often unsuccessfully, to legitimize themselves through the hosting of potlatches and other ceremonial activities. See Snyder (1964).

32 Chief Harry Edwards, interview by Oliver Wells, 8 October 1964, compact disk audio copy and transcript at SNA, 283.

33 These caves were destroyed by the construction of the Trans-Canada Highway in the 1960s.

34 Likewise, Dan Milo, in 1964, provided additional details about the reasons behind the abandonment of Alámex. According to Milo, there were "a lot" of people living there at the time "And the head man of those people ... had a little son, a small little kid, and that kid gets so rough and killed other kids. And he could do nothing [to stop] this little child. He told his friends, 'the only way we can do it is to leave my kid. We'll leave him. We'll move away from here.'" As a result, the headman told the other boys to take his son behind the little mountain in the woods and to abandon him there. According to the story, "He called, and they answered him at different times, then they just played dumb." The boys came back and the rest of the people were "ready to move." "They took off and came way up to Cheam ... They went to Cheam and they began to get that name [the people of] 'Lexwchiya:m' [always strawberries]." See Dan Milo, interview by Oliver Wells, July 1964, SNA.

35 For the 1830 and 1839 census I have combined the Pilalt and Teiton population figures as both tribes dwelled at Alámex. For the 1830 census, McDonald provided figures for "men" only. I have therefore multiplied his totals by 4.4, the ratio of men to other family members found in the 1839 census.

36 McDonald's report is presented in full in Maclachlan (1998, 221).

37 Indicative of this is the reaction of certain people living in Ohamil and Skw'átets to the "Map of Pilalt Territory" produced in 2000 by the Cheam band. This map included as "Pilalt" those upriver lands associated with the Ohamil and Skw'átets settlements. People in these upriver communities did not necessarily interpret the map as a gesture of their shared and common interest in land and resources but, rather, more as a provocative move by the people of Cheam to assert control over "Teit" resources. For some contemporary politicians of the upriver settlements, it was a "wake-up call that all us Teits need to start working together more" (personal communication, May 2001, with a band councillor from Seabird Island who asked not to be identified by name).

38 This is a commonly told story among the people of Ohamil. Sonny McHalsie recorded the version related here in Keith Thor Carlson with Sonny McHalsie (1998).

39 Leland Donald's excellent and provocative *Slavery on the Northwest Coast* is one of the few studies to confront the issue of class tension within Northwest Coast society and history. Unfortunately, due to what he refers to as a lack of sources, his analysis is particularly thin on the Coast Salish. See Donald (1997).

40 For an overview, see Suttles (1990, introduction).

41 Jenness (1955, 86) also noted the distinction between the term for serf communities and the common expression for slaves.

42 Sally Snyder, however, does attempt to provide a more interpretive discussion of the significance of class distinctions within Coast Salish society, and she does this by looking at the symbolic associations between class, property, and gender. See Snyder (1964, esp. 72-100).

43 While 30 percent of the total Coast Salish population are listed as "Followers of all descriptions," only 12 percent of those living along the Fraser River proper are so identified. See Yale (1839, 30-53).

44 In his fieldnotes Duff (1950, 2:56) lists Sechelt, Vancouver Island, and the BC interior as the sites from which the slaves were taken.

45 All preceding quotes relating to the story of Freedom Village were taken from Duff (1950, 2: 56-58), which provided a slightly richer account than the block quote found in Duff (1952, 21).

46 Plottings of place names here differ from those found in Harris (1997). I believe my map more accurately reflects actual Aboriginal settlement sites, but for this all credit goes to Sonny McHalsie and the elders who translated the HBC orthography into proper Halq'emeylem.

47 See William C. Orchard, *A Rare Coast Salish Blanket,* Leaflet of the Museum of the American Indian, Heye Foundation, No 5. (New York: Vreeland Press, 1926).

48 The phenomenon of Native people moving to live nearer European outposts and settlements was repeated numerous times in British North America. See, for example, Ray (1974, esp. chap. 7, 125-36).

49 I am indebted to Amber Kostuchenko for this citation.

50 Oral history records that Governor James Douglas promised Chowethel to the Hope Indians as a reserve (Sonny McHalsie, personal communication with Keith Thor Carlson, June 1993). In 1879, Reserve Commissioner G.M. Sproat reported that the move to Chowethel took place around 1858, which would be consistent with the Douglas story. Chowethel was not officially designated a reserve until 1879.

51 Named after a steamboat that ran aground on the island.

52 I am grateful to Hillary Blair for drawing my attention to this document.

53 See Chief James of Yale, testimony before the 1913-16 Royal Commission, SNA.

54 In 1891, twenty-seven white squatters built rudimentary houses on the Seabird reserve and attempted to have their claims to the land recognized. See A.W. Vowell to

Superintendent General, 19 May 1891, RG 10, reel C-10139, vol. 3795, file 46607-1, Indian Affairs, Library and Archives Canada, Ottawa. See also LAC, F. Passingham to P. McTiernan, 21 February 1891, RG 10, reel C-10139, vol. 3795, file 46607-1.

55 In 1958, the various bands making up the Teit Tribe succeeded in having Seabird Island officially designated as an independent band with its own local chief and council. See the excellent local history of Seabird Island by Blair (1999).

References

Barnett, Homer Garner. 1955. *The Coast Salish of British Columbia*. Eugene: University of Oregon Press.

Bishop, Charles A. 1974. *The Northern Ojibwa and the Fur Trade: An Historical and Ecological Study*. Toronto: Holt, Rinehart and Winston.

Blair, Hillary Kathleen. 1999. Settling Seabird Island: Land, Resources, and Ownership on a British Columbia Indian Reserve. MA thesis, Simon Fraser University.

Boas, Franz. 1894. Indian Tribes of the Lower Fraser River. In *The 64th Report of the British Association for the Advancement of Science for 1890*, 454-63. London: British Association for the Advancement of Science.

–. [1895] 1977. *Indian Myths and Legends from the North Pacific Coast of America*. Trans. Dietrich Bertz. Victoria: BC Indian Language Project.

Canada. N.d. RG 10, Indian Affairs, Library and Archives Canada, Ottawa.

Canada. Department of Indian Affairs. 1878. Indian census of Yale Tribe, 1878. RG 10, vol. 10012A.

Carlson, Keith Thor, ed. 2001. *A Stó:lō Coast Salish Historical Atlas*. Vancouver/Chilliwack: Douglas and McIntyre/Stó:lō Heritage Trust.

–. Forthcoming. Innovation, Tradition, Colonialism, and Aboriginal Fishing Conflicts in the Lower Fraser Canyon. In *Reconstructing Canada's Native Pasts*, ed. Susan Neylan and Ted Binnema. Vancouver: UBC Press.

Carlson, Keith Thor, and John Lutz. 1997. Stó:lō People and the Development of the BC Wage Labour Economy. In *You Are Asked to Witness*, ed. Keith Thor Carlson, 109-24. Chilliwack: Stó:lō Heritage Trust.

Carlson, Keith Thor, with Sonny McHalsie. 1998. *I Am Stó:lō: Katherine Explores Her Heritage*. Chilliwack, BC: Stó:lō Heritage Trust.

Carter, Sarah. 1990. *Lost Harvest: Prairie Indian Reserve Farmers and Government Policy*. Montreal and Kingston: McGill-Queen's University Press.

Donald, Leland. 1997. *Aboriginal Slavery on the Northwest Coast of North America*. Berkeley, CA: University of California Press.

Duff, Wilson. 1950. Fieldnotes. Book 2. Stó:lō Nation Archives, Chilliwack, BC (hereafter SNA).

–. 1952. *The Upper Stalo Indians of the Fraser Valley, British Columbia*. Anthropology in British Columbia, Memoir No. 1. Victoria: British Columbia Provincial Museum.

Harris, Cole. 1997. *The Resettlement of British Columbia: Essays on Colonialism and Geographical Change*. Vancouver: UBC Press.

Hill-Tout, Charles. 1978. Ethnological Studies of the Mainland Halkomelem. In *The Salish People: The Local Contribution of Charles Hill-Tout*. Vol. 3, *The Mainland Halkomelem*, ed. Ralph Maud. Vancouver: Talonbooks.

Jenness, Diamond. 1955. *Faith of a Coast Salish Indian*. Anthropology in British Columbia, Memoir No. 3. Victoria: British Columbia Provincial Museum.

Lamb, W. Kaye. 1960. *Simon Fraser: Letters and Journals, 1806-1808*. Toronto: Macmillan.

Lerman, Norman. 1950-51. Lower Fraser Indian Folktales. SNA.

–. N.d. Lower Fraser Indian Folktales. SNA.

Lerman, Norman H., and Betty Keller. 1976. *Legends of the River People*. Vancouver: November House.

Lutz, John. 1992. After the Fur Trade: The Aboriginal Labouring Class of British Columbia, 1849-1890. *Journal of the Canadian Historical Association* (new series) 2: 69-94.

Maclachlan, Morag, ed. 1998. *The Fort Langley Journals, 1827-30*. Vancouver: UBC Press.

Marshall, Daniel P. 1997. Rickard Revisited: Native "Participation" in the Gold Discoveries of British Columbia. *Native Studies Review* 11 (1): 91-108.

McDonald, Archibald. 1830. *1830 Census*, Fort Langley. Hudson's Bay Company Archives, Winnipeg, Manitoba.

McHalsie, Albert "Sonny." 2001. Halq'emeylem Place Names in Stó:lō Territory. In *A Stó:lō Coast Salish Historical Atlas*, ed. Keith Thor Carlson, 134-53. Vancouver/Chilliwack: Douglas and McIntyre/Stó:lō Heritage Trust.

Miller, Bruce, and Daniel Boxberger. 1994. Creating Chiefdoms: The Puget Sound Case. *Ethnohistory* 41 (2): 67-29.

Orchard, William C. 1926. *A Rare Coast Salish Blanket*. Leaflet of the Museum of the American Indian, Heye Foundation, No. 5. New York: Vreeland Press.

Phillips, Mark Salber, and Gordon Schochet, eds. 2004. *Questions of Tradition*. Toronto: University of Toronto Press.

Ray, Arthur J. 1974 *Indians in the Fur Trade: Their Role as Hunters, Trappers and Middlemen in the Lands Southwest of Hudson's Bay, 1660-1870*. Toronto: University of Toronto Press.

Schaepe, David M. 1998. Recycling Archaeology: Analysis of Material from the 1973 Excavation of an Ancient House at the Maurier Site. MA thesis, Simon Fraser University.

–. 2001. Rockwall Fortifications: Reconstructing a Fraser Canyon Defensive Network. In *A Stó:lō Coast Salish Historical Atlas*, ed. Keith Thor Carlson, 52. Vancouver/Chilliwack: Douglas and McIntyre/Stó:lō Heritage Trust.

Smart, James A. 1898. *Sessional Papers*. Department of Indian Affairs Annual Reports, xxi.

Smith, Marian. 1945. Fieldnotes. Royal Anthropological Institute, London, UK.

Snyder, Sally. 1964. Skagit Society and Its Existential Basis: An Ethnofolkloristic Reconstruction. PhD diss., University of Washington.

Sproat, Gilbert M. 1879a. Indian and Northern Affairs Canada. LTS, vol. 5/1, 5 August (note accompanying map).

–. 1879b. Field Minutes. Indian and Northern Affairs Canada. LTS, vol. 18, 309.

Stanley, George F. 1970. *Mapping the Frontier: Charles Wilson's Diary of the Survey of the 49th Parallel, 1858-1862, While Secretary of the British Boundary Commission*. Toronto: Macmillan.

Stó:lō Nation Archives. N.d. Elders' Oral History Audio Collection. SNA.

Suttles, Wayne. 1987. *Coast Salish Essays*. Vancouver: Talonbooks.

–. 1989. "They Recognize No Superior Chief": The Strait of Juan de Fuca in the 1790s. In *Culturas de la Costa Noroeste de America*, ed. Jose Luis Peset, 251-64. Madrid: Turner.

–, ed. 1990. *Handbook of North American Indians*. Vol. 7, *Northwest Coast*. Washington, DC: Smithsonian Institution.

–. 1998. The Ethnographic Significance of the Fort Langley Journals. In *The Fort Langley Journals, 1827-30*, ed. Morag Maclachlan, 163-210. Vancouver: UBC Press.

Suttles, Wayne, and Diamond Jenness. 1955. *Katzie Ethnographic Notes, and The Faith of a Coast Salish Indian*. Anthropology in British Columbia, Memoir No. 2. Victoria: British Columbia Provincial Museum.

Thom, Brian David. 1995. The Dead and the Living: Burial Mounds and Cairns and the Development of Social Classes in the Gulf of Georgia Region. MA thesis, University of British Columbia.

Wells, Oliver. 1987. *The Chilliwacks and Their Neighbors*. Ed. Ralph Maud and Brent Galloway. Vancouver: Talonbooks.

Yale, James Murray. 1839. *1839 Lower Fraser River Census*. Hudson's Bay Company Archives, Winnipeg, Manitoba.

6
"I Can Lift Her Up ...": Fred Ewen's Narrative Complexity

Crisca Bierwert

How did our elders live? The question permeates contemporary discussions of identity, even those discourses that are vibrant with aesthetics of wikis, blogging, and podcasts. And while identity politics today is largely future-oriented and revels in contestation, in questions of who people "want to be," identity politics in many First Nations communities is also strongly inflected by issues of human rights and resource rights. The question of how elders lived is fraught with implications for those First Nations communities where negotiations of future possibilities require legally defensible knowledge of the past.

In the Stó:lō Nation of southwestern British Columbia, elders' knowledge and archived historical information helps form a charter for treaty rights, commercial fishing rights, economic development opportunities, and access to sacred sites. The House of Elders is integral to the political constitution of the nation, and elders bring richly varied experiences of political history to Stó:lō Nation decision making. Certainly not all elders are or were political activists, but all of those who lived in the twentieth century faced the debilitating effects of colonialism and interacted with agents and institutions of colonial policies. They made history in larger or smaller ways in shared networks of experience, in traditional and innovative practices. As a result of their individual and collective engagements, Stó:lō Nation citizens today are able to continue their advocacy for recognition and for human, territorial, and resource rights.

Native scholars Devon Mihesuah (1998) and Donald Fixico (1998), among others, have called for more complex studies of Native American histories – studies that bring First Nations perspectives to light along with what is typically an outsider's analysis of white-Indian interactions. In fact, the histories of the Pacific Northwest have only recently begun to focus on colonial encounters, making the political and economic contexts of First Nations peoples' experiences in British Columbia more visible. Paul Tennant

(1990) vividly documents colonial processes in the province, and Dianne Newell (1993) has carefully outlined a political history of Pacific Coast fishing that includes rich data on First Nations fishers. Cole Harris (2002) has detailed the making of reserves, providing a closer look at both the policy making of the state's administrators and the activism of First Nations leaders. An even more detailed study of interactions between agents of the state and local First Nations activists informs Douglas Harris' case studies of fishing rights issues (2001). And recent anthropological studies combine archival studies with oral histories to provide further nuanced analysis. Bruce Miller's examination of Coast Salish legal systems focuses on the engagement of traditional ideas with Western legal principles, showing complex variation and negotiation of differences (Miller 2001). Julie Cruikshank (2005) has, most recently, placed epistemological differences regarding the notion of ecology in high relief with her study of how indigenous travellers and residents, explorers, agents of the state, and scientists perceive glaciers. Brian Thom (2005) has situated First Nations elders' accounts of ecology and place within the context of British Columbia Treaty Commission negotiation. My work layers cultural studies of personal, political, and ecological narratives in historicized analysis (Bierwert 1998, 1999).

To complement this increasingly clear historical backdrop, this chapter explores an archive that allows us to study historical transformation from a very localized perspective: that of a sixty-year-old elder, not from today but from 1945. The thoughts of this elder, Fred Ewen, allow us to see the complex perspectives of an elder from a time well before the emergence of the term "First Nations" – a time when the name "Stó:lō" was used only by elders who were speakers of that language.

The accounts that I offer here exist within a larger corpus of texts recorded in the summer of 1945 by several students working with elders on Seabird Island and nearby areas in Stó:lō country. There are many such archives waiting to be revisited. The documentation of Harry Hawthorn and several students, including some First Nations students, in the 1950s provides comparably rich information that also merits study (see Hawthorn, Belshaw, and Jamieson 1958; Hawthorn 1966). Further, the records of Diamond Jenness, Wayne Suttles, and Wilson Duff, all of whom worked with Stó:lō elders in the 1930s and 1940s, contain treasures of cultural commentary that may be recovered through close readings, enabling us to place "salvage" documentation alongside contemporary observations (see Jenness 1955; Suttles 1955, 1987; Duff 1952).

Through such examinations, it is possible to better understand a comment made by Stó:lō historian Sonny McHalsie. In 2001, McHalsie (2001, 32) wrote, "After nearly 150 years of colonial efforts to impose foreign ways of thinking and living, the degree to which traditional ways and concepts of place and family continue to inform Stó:lō identity would no doubt surprise and frustrate the early architects of Canadian Indian assimilation policies."

"Ways and concepts of place and family" are the focus of my analysis of Ewen's commentary, the purpose being to illuminate how Ewen's views wrestled with the social transformations of his time. Ewen's statements show that he was neither a fully "authentic" relic of a past culture nor an agent of steadfast resistance to colonialism. He was not even simply something in between. His views are complex, and they reveal contradictions and transformations in the social fabric of his life. His views show layers of different kinds of social awareness; at times he appears to deny change, at other times he reveals himself to be at odds with change, and at still other times he is comfortable with social transformation. The fact that he is not classifiable is, in my view, what makes his views typical. In any event, his narratives illuminate the social complexity within which he lived and the "ways and concepts" that he helped to shape so that they would be present for McHalsie and other Stó:lō people to experience in the future.

Such complexities suggest that we understand Ewen as a party to "emergent" cultural systems, to use the language of Raymond Williams, who distinguished emergent forms from those that comply with dominant, hegemonic, controlling forms (the colonizing forms) and also from those that are "residual" – that is, those that are like "vestiges," not articulating well with dominant cultural forms. But what is this "emergent" category? And can the term be applied to cultural transformations that are not explicitly political? I return to these questions after a close reading of Ewen's narratives.

Prologue to Ewen's Narratives

In January 2000, I drove a rented car from the Seabird Island Reserve café with a retired anthropologist, Estelle Sillen Fuchs, who had done her first field research on Seabird Island in the summer of 1945 with a Stó:lō elder named Fred Ewen. We were in a caravan that included a pickup and an SUV driven by two of Ewen's grandchildren and carrying several other relatives. We drove toward the centre of the reserve, then turned off the main road, away from the circle of residences and community buildings that comprise the reserve, following the traces of what had once been a dirt road to Ewen's house. We bumped along as far as we could and then walked on to the area that seemed to be where the house had been. The area was overgrown with brush. There was no open clearing left, and we could find no real trace of the house. Nor were there any traces of the fruit trees that had once grown between the main road and the home. But Ewen's kin, and Fuchs also, recognized the place where the house had been from the terrain, from remembering and imagining being there in the past. "This looks about right," one would say and would then be joined by another. They looked not at the ground for the remains of the foundation – for there were none – but out toward the surrounding mountains, toward the river to the east, and toward the levee to our west.

This chapter draws on Fuchs' fieldnotes from that summer, which contain recollections and remarks made by Fred Ewen.[1] The notes are a rich legacy – remembrances of lived history documenting a place that once existed but does so no longer. This "place" is not only a physical place but also an ontological/epistemological place – a place where a particular life and a certain knowledge existed within a precise span of time. Ewen's house, now vanished, stands as a metaphor for his life and knowledge. Like the house, his knowledge, his very specific knowledge, is gone, except for the recollections of his surviving children and grandchildren – and these notes. Thus, these notes are like the landscape surrounding the house: they point toward his knowledge and his life and, consequently, encourage us to see them as landmarks enabling us to situate the life he knew.

The Social Context of the Narratives, 1945

The Ethnographer's Story

In the summer of 1945, Estelle Sillen Fuchs was a graduate student in anthropology at Columbia University. She was also a young war bride,[2] working with other students on a field school project to document the culture of Seabird Island Aboriginals. The field school had been organized by Professor Marian Smith to provide advanced students with practice in applying ethnographic methods as well as to help fill out documentation of Northwest Coast Aboriginal cultures. The project was to inventory all major ethnographic categories, complementing Smith's work among Puget Sound Salish peoples during the previous decade. The intent was to "salvage" cultural information before those who knew of the "old ways" died out.

Colonization had been established relatively late in the Stó:lō area. A trading post was established on the lower Fraser River in 1824, but settlers did not pour in until the gold rush of 1861. Reserves were first surveyed, without treaties in this area, in the 1880s, and boarding schools were established for Aboriginal children. Resource exploitation focused on timber and fish, and land was cleared and drained for agricultural development.

But federal administration did not permeate the lives of First Nations people until the twentieth century. The opportunity to archive information about the "old ways" was great.

Fuchs' interviews with Fred Ewen were structured by her ethnographic motivations. Although her notes include a welter of stories, long descriptions, short informative statements, and lists, and although these are arranged one after the other with no headings, they fall clearly within the categories of mid-twentieth-century anthropology. Place names, potlatches, religious practices, material culture, kinship and marriage rules, more on religious practices, magic, more on kinship, childbearing, taboos, more on material culture, and more potlatches: these are the broad topics in the order in which they were covered. Secondary categories fill out the sections on kinship and religion: acquiring traditional medical knowledge, curing stories, beliefs in ghosts, arranged marriages, polygyny, adultery, illegitimacy, postmortem practices, remembrance, masked dancing, and songs. The repetitions show that Fuchs was determined to acquire information on topics that were key to the ethnography of the day. These secondary categories show us that she was also interested in what was exotic, intriguing, tumultuous – and that Ewen complied with fascinating information and animated stories.[3]

These notes could have been compiled into a rich ethnographic account of "precontact" cultural practices. Once, they could have formed the foundation of an ethnographic "first," which was something that Marian Smith had hoped to accomplish. Today, that discovery potential has been realized by others. The precontact information has ethnographic value in that the general contours of Ewen's account corroborate the information provided by Barnett, Suttles, and Duff at about the same period. Even the sensational material on magic and shamanism conforms to what others described, being comparable with regard to situations involving magic and/or shamanism, to the ways in which storytellers developed intrigue, and to the ways in which details startled and provoked attentive audiences. However, the ethnographic richness of the material is not lessened because, in publication terms, it does not constitute a Coast Salish "first": the particulars are no less fascinating to an outsider, no less informative to Stó:lō people.

Estelle Fuchs' recollection of her exchange with Fred Ewen is that she knew she was "getting" great material and that she was, indeed, eliciting it. Talking with me in 1999, after reviewing her own notes for the first time since 1945, she was struck by the amount of historical detail they contained. She was greatly pleased by the quality of the information, and she was also pleased with herself for having elicited and recorded it. Commenting on the details of a doctoring story, in which Ewen explains that his kin gave an Indian doctor a gold Chinese ring with two cranes carved on it for his services, Fuchs and I had this exchange:

ESF: Well, I think I understand the reason all of this came to me. I won't call it "natural." It was the way I like to look at things myself. Because I believe in histori- cally orienting it. I am quite sure that I prompted to find out this kind of detail. I'm sure I did. I don't think he himself would have just been doing all that. [He com- mented on the ring because] I probably said [inflected] "Did you pay him?"

CB: And he recognized by this point your interest not only in things typical of an older time but also of his own time.

ESF: And my interest in such a detail. The ordinary accounting would just give the specifics of the curing. (personal communication 1998)

Fred Ewen's Story

In the first half of the twentieth century, Stó:lō lifeways were receding; they were not being glorified or revitalized as they would come to be. And the hegemony, the dominance, of white cultures and institutions was not named as such. "Civilization" permeated the landscape, and change was seen in terms of the linear progress of economic "development." For the first dec- ades of the twentieth century, petitions by Native leaders detailed griev- ances concerning land rights, fishing and other resource rights, poverty, education, and religious freedom (Carlson 2001; Ware 1983). However, by 1945, as the Second World War ended, the administration of Aboriginal peoples became routinized, and federal power was very strong. Aboriginal leadership in British Columbia also developed powerful organizations and became influential union leaders in the timber industry. In Stó:lō country, economic development was uneven. Many men were well integrated into the wage economy, and most Stó:lō adults worked picking hops during the summer. Technological "progress" marked the little cities of the Fraser Valley; however, reserves were less developed by this progress. Electricity was available on some reserves but not all. Unfortunately, Fuchs' notes offer only glimpses of economic practices.

In 1945, Seabird Island was a resettlement area for First Nations people. Unlike most of the Stó:lō reserves, Seabird had not been an active perma- nent residence site when it was declared a reserve. Thus, unlike most Stó:lō reserves, Seabird Island became a home for many First Nations people who moved there because it had been made a reserve, with many of them com- ing from nearby Thompson-speaking territory located just upriver from traditionally Stó:lō lands. Ewen often contrasted the Thompson ways of his Seabird neighbours with his own Stó:lō ways, using those specific terms of identity and referring most often to contrasts in spiritual practices and concepts. The practices Ewen described most vividly were those having to do with death, and he said that he teased his Thompson neighbours a lot because of their fear of ghosts.[4]

Sifting through the texts, we can assemble a biography. Ewen's mother, Lucy, came from the Popkum Reserve; her father was from Popkum and her mother was from Musqueam. Her first husband, Ewen's father, was Chinese, and he was killed while blowing up stumps to clear land on their Seabird Island homestead. Lucy remained with her four children on the Popkum Reserve. When Ewen was three years old, he went to live with his older sister, Suzanne, who was married to a Chinese man and lived upriver. When he was five, he moved downriver to the Coqualeetza Residential School in Sardis. He returned home in the summertime, and his mother arranged for her elders to teach him in traditional ways. He retained his native Halkomelem language, learned to speak English in school, and, from a classmate, also learned to speak Chinook jargon. While he was at Coqualeetza, his mother married again, once more choosing a Chinese man.

Ewen left school when he was about fifteen and began logging. For most of his life, he worked as a carpenter. When he was about eighteen, he married Josephine Alec. His wife's mother was Stó:lō and her father was a Chinese man who was a philanderer and who abandoned his family. Josephine and Fred lived at Popkum for a time. After their first daughter was born, Fred built a house for them on the land his father had cleared, across the river on Seabird Island – which had become the Seabird Island Reserve. They had four daughters, and Josephine died shortly after the youngest was born. Fred raised his children at home; they did not go to residential school.

Fred's younger brother, Henry, fought in the First World War, married, and died in an automobile accident. Fred's younger sister, Alice, married a Chinese man and had children, but she became ill and died on what her husband had hoped would be a therapeutic trip to China. Josephine's brother, William, became a friend of Fred, but Willy also died by 1945. Fred's and Josephine's mothers, both named Lucy, lived into old age and helped Fred raise the children.

In 1945, Fred Ewen was probably about sixty years old.[5] His mother had died, but his mother-in-law still lived. His oldest daughters were married, one of them to a member of the Seabird Island Reserve; the youngest daughter, Helen, then twenty-one, was still living with him. He was also raising three of his grandchildren while continuing to live in the house he had built for his family.

Themes in the Narratives

Stó:lō Lands: Layered Maps

In 1945, Frederick Ewen had been living and raising a family on Seabird Island Reserve for forty years. Yet the reserve system was not the map he described to Estelle Fuchs, and it was certainly not the primary map that occupied his understanding. Unlike many Stó:lō people, he was, in a sense, a relocatee because he lived on a reserve that had been created by a colonial administration, and it was not land that was recognized as part of the band he was born into. This had implications for his life, and these permeate his commentaries. In terms of conceptualization, Ewen's references to place fall into three clear categories: (1) Stó:lō organization of land, (2) the reserve system, and (3) individual claims to land. While he did not name these as separate systems, he used different vocabularies and described different attributes for each. While he did not use the word "conflicting" to describe the co-occurrence of these concepts, his descriptions and narratives clearly articulate conflicts. Thus, we can see "from the ground," from an individual's perspective, what scholarly analysis shows us of the colonization of Aboriginal spaces (see Tennant 1990; Harris 2002).

When speaking about the Seabird Island Reserve, Ewen situated places according to their political history. On the first day of his collaboration with Fuchs, Ewen explained that, in contrast to most of the reserves, which were formed around older village sites and political groups, the Seabird Island Reserve was a recent historical entity. He told her that there are old *sqamil* sites on Seabird, depressions from pit houses and sweathouses that people once used, but that the former occupants "never [comprised] a band" (i.e., a political organization). He also plainly stated that his own land, the land upon which he had built his house and which had been his father's, came to be on the reserve as a result of political administration. Fuchs' notes are a bit rough at this point, but Ewen's remarks come through fairly clearly.[6]

> Seabird Island was once called Maria. The steamboat used to come past it, to Yale [where the impassable Fraser Canyon begins]. The top [upriver] end was Seabird Bluff; the slough [at the downriver end], near the present-day church was called Maria Slough. Ewen's father took up a homestead here of 320 acres, but he blew himself up while blowing stumps [to clear land]. Ewen's mother was left to raise the children. They [provincial agents] came with canoes and surveyed the land into a reserve. Ewen's mother didn't know what was happening. The father's land was taken into the reserve.

What is interesting here is that Ewen first describes Seabird Island as a geographic formation, situated in relation to the Fraser River and transportation. The days of the steamboat would have been the days of his grandfather, who, we learn later, developed a good business running settlers' goods upriver in his canoe. Then Ewen tells the political story – how his family lost a homestead. The stories of geography and economy will re-emerge later on; but here, at the start of the interviews, Ewen not only tells the story of his family's loss of land but he also contrasts that political map to geographic and economic maps.

In this summary, we see contrasts and intersections, first between Stó:lō land use and private homesteading, and then between these conceptions of ownership and the colonial construction of Indian reserves. Ironically, Ewen's connection to Seabird Island comes through his father's private homestead and his decision to move onto that land after it was marked by the state as part of the reserve. Later, Ewen explains that this move cost him his affiliation with his natal reserve, the Popkum Reserve, which was his mother's home. Another irony lies in Ewen's father's choice of land. Ewen explains that his father selected the Seabird site in part because – under the old system of land use – he had rights to use it through his Stó:lō wife. Thus, Ewen's father was drawing on two contemporaneous land rights systems: (1) the Stó:lō system (his wife having come from Popkum, he had, as the member of an extended family, rights to the land nearby) and (2) the colonialist system (as a non-Indian immigrant [remember that his father was Chinese] he had the right to homestead). This is a fascinating example of someone attempting to deploy different land-use concepts to justify his claims to ownership.

The undoing of this strategy was also the result of multiple land-use systems, and it came after Ewen's father died. Because the land had "only" a Native widow claimant, colonial surveyors did not recognize it as a private homestead. Thus, the land was incorporated into the new reserve and, as part of the Seabird Island Reserve, made "Indian."

The reason that moving to Seabird Island cost Ewen his formal (administrative) affiliation with Popkum, which he considers himself to be "from," was that he could have band membership (i.e., be legally Indian) only on the reserve where he was living. Ewen also explained that he and his kin effectively lost rights to his grandfather's land at Popkum because no one in his generation remained resident on that reserve. The story of Ewen's land, and of the Seabird Island Reserve, then, illustrates not only the cutting off of Stó:lō land resources but also the cutting off of the Stó:lō right to individual legal ownership of resources in multiple locations as well as their right to have their kinship networks recognized under Canadian law. We hear more about this later.

Ewen's descriptions of Stó:lō territory presents a strikingly different picture from that offered above. In effect, he drew a verbal map of the land from above the Fraser Canyon to the land of the Musqueam, his mother's father's people, now located in downtown Vancouver. Ewen used the term "Stó:lō" to describe his people and their territory, and he defined the boundaries of the Stó:lō geographically, linguistically, and culturally.[7] Fuchs' notes, which plot the Stó:lō territory along the Fraser River, list thirty-five place names in Halkomelem and more in English (filled out in spots with comments on the origin of a name or the mention of a person living there).

Either as part of this telling, or as a response to Fuchs' prompting for basic information, Ewen explained that the traditional kinship system was based on the extended kin group – the *skumliqw* – with descent being on both the mother's and father's side. He gave the names of kinship relationships in Halkomelem and noted that a kin group spanned numerous residence groups, each of which was an extended family in itself.

That Ewen integrates kinship affiliations into the Stó:lō landscape is clear because, in his recitation of Stó:lō territory, he includes numerous references to specific people. He sometimes mentions that these people were originally from another village, indicating that he considers them to be part of an extended group that originated from that place. (Fuchs' notes are not that detailed, but Ewen may have meant either that people formerly lived in a particular village or that their names and ritual privileges, as well as their right to use resources such as fishing camps, came through kin still living there.) What these references make quite clear is that, in his mind, Ewen maintained two different systems of affiliation: (1) the location of residence, which might be a band affiliation under the reserve system, and (2) the location of origin, which situates kin according to the *skumliqw* system.

In sum, the different kinds of attributes that Ewen invoked – geographical formations, ecological notes, political histories, and kinship links – describe different kinds of "places." While these may co-exist as frames of reference, they clash at particular contested sites (e.g., Ewen's home site) and through particular contested identities (e.g., his band affiliation). The web of kinship connections and places of residence in this Stó:lō cognitive map has a geographical "shape" that is both topological and continuous. The sites on this map are contiguous, and the groups occupying them overlap. The reserve locations are bounded and fragmented, like Ewen's description of Seabird Island – and they are also detached from concrete geographical formations, as though these existed only on paper.[8]

Political Formations: "Wouldn't Be Chief for Anything"

When Ewen talks of the political administration of Seabird Island, we see conflicts emerging over time rather than being the layered, co-existent contrasts discussed above. As federal political administration became more and more bureaucratized over the first half of the twentieth century, a generation of school-educated leaders matured. Ewen focuses on the character of Stó:lō political leadership, noting changes in its cultural style over his lifetime and reporting, with political cynicism, the tensions between "traditional" (he calls them "uncivilized") and modern leaders. His accounts, being scattered and anecdotal, are not those of a political insider. And they are punctuated by a gritty humour.

According to Ewen, "Ottawa" established Seabird as a separate reserve with its own political administration, and this action angered the old chiefs. As Ewen told it,

> [There] never was chief on Seabird Island. [There were] seven chiefs from Popkum to Yale in charge of Seabird until Capt. Michele [was selected] Chief of Seabird. Chief Michele's uncle went to Ottawa [and] asked that Chief Michele be in charge of Seabird. Chief Michele made it a separate band. The seven chiefs were furious. [They] had no more say over island.
>
> Some of the old kinds of political affinities endured, however, as the new chief chose his successor in his close extended kin, *skumliqw,* relation.
>
> When Michele died, Chief Michele said for Harry Joseph to take his place. Harry Joseph [is] "uncivilized." [He] is like people 3 generations back ...
>
> Michele [was] a *Skw'átets.* Harry Joseph also [is a *Skw'átets*].

"Skw'átets," the term that Ewen uses to locate Michele and Joseph, is the name of a reserve, now commonly called the Peters Reserve. But Ewen is not referring to band affiliation here: he is referring to the place these two men are from.

Ewen explained more about this close association. They were not close relatives, he said, but Michele had shared his fishing place with Joseph. Michele liked Joseph because he had nursed him through a sickness. When Michele died, Joseph had kept the fishing site, and he cared for Michele's wife until "last year." Thus, the affiliation between the two was deep and personal. In Ewen's overview of the politics of place, he marks their shared place of origin as the primary relationship, a shorthand for the complex connection between the two that developed over time and space, ultimately reaching to Seabird Island.

Thus we see in this story a challenge to the authority of the "old chiefs" who shared control of the territory before it was made into a new reserve. We see how the old kinds of kindred connections spilled over into the newly established position of band chief. Despite the political savvy of Michele's uncle, who travelled to Ottawa to install his nephew, men carrying on something of the old-style way of life occupied the position of chief. And this continued when Michele handed the leadership role to his kinsman and friend Harry Joseph, who was "uncivilized," having been educated in the old ways.

When he talks about the future, Ewen presents an entirely different perspective on tribal government from that depicted above. He said that, in the present, while Harry Joseph was chief, Michele's son-in-law was "next in line" for the chiefship and that younger men were challenging this fact: "The young fellas trying to push the chief off these days. The Indian agent don't allow. The agent doesn't want an educated, civilized man in there. Doesn't want to be bothered by letters all the time." Here, Ewen notes a complicity between the "uncivilized" band leadership and the federal Indian administration. When the leadership is not literate, the Indian agent does not have to be bothered with "letters all the time." A new generation is trying to exercise a leadership that will be able to effectively communicate with federal bureaucrats, and it sounds as though Ewen supports this. This statement provides an interesting contrast with his earlier ones, in which Ewen seems to value the strong personal connections between Chief Michele and Harry Joseph, even though he was cynical about how Chief Michele attained his position. As the colonial administration develops under the direction of federal authorities, we see a new contradiction emerge – that between valuing the *skumliqw* and valuing a band leadership that could effectively engage in written argumentation with the state.

Ewen's political views are not consistently progressive: his cynical stance on tribal politics does not let any chiefs go unscathed. He believed that, in his lifetime, Stó:lō leaders were not effective: "Wouldn't be chief for anything. He gets no salary. People all time say, 'He should be fired,' 'He's no good,' etc." Far from rendering his homeland as a tidy relic of the past, Ewen's political narrative constantly favours forms of authority that replicate those of the federal government. Still, the topological connections between people and places, the conceptualizations that characterize past social organization, continue to provide the framework within which Ewen locates people – at least those of his generation and older. He expresses his affinity for "old-time" leaders even as he reveals their inability to lead a generation that is literate and increasingly knowledgeable about dealing with state laws.

Kinship: Coherence

Ewen's description of *skumliqw* relations reveals conflicted social positions as well as conflicting social systems. In this section, I examine his account of a past form of kinship, which has the kind of coherence that is a classic of the unchanging ethnographic present. This is a retold past – the past of his elders, not his own experience – for the most part, although he applies his knowledge of this past to his life. (In later sections, I explore how this coherence is problematized when Ewen discusses experiences from his own lifetime, including others' transgressive behaviour.) In dealing with the past, Ewen's commentary is rich, regularized, and comfortable, and Fuchs' notes preserve a folksy and humorous style.

Describing a series of overtures to marriage arrangements, for example, Ewen describes the courtship behaviour of a young man: "[If] the girl's parents have no wood in [the] fire, go out & get wood to bring to [the] girl's fire ... If [the] girl's parents don't want you, [they] take the wood & throw it out of [the] *sqamil* ... [Then] keep on." Ewen goes on for several paragraphs narrating the actions of the young man – hauling water, providing fish or game – and describing the disparaging remarks of his prospective in-laws. Industry and persistence might not succeed – but these were necessary. Ewen notes dryly, "Gotta have patience or an Indian [will] never get a wife."

Typically, Ewen's generic ethnographic accounts go on at some length. He describes the key life rituals (a naming ceremony, a marriage, a funeral), reciting what was done to prepare for them, which rituals were involved, what kinds of speeches were given. It is clear that he possessed prized information on the ways of the past.

In most of these accounts, Ewen speaks as though he were living in the past rather than simply recalling it. His account tells what "you" do in certain situations: "Go out and get wood ..., keep on," and so on. When discussing other topics, he does not use the second person; here, he used it to indicate responsibility, even though his immediate audience is a young white woman. He appears to be reporting what was told to him, speaking as an elder might speak to a young man. He is the authority, and he is "in" the past while providing this account. He thus perfectly fulfills the ethnographer's desire for ethnographic authority. But it is also interesting that Ewen's telling here *performs* what is only described in other (published) accounts. It is a re-enactment rather than a description. Fuchs' note taking, in recording Ewen's style of address, preserves a brusqueness, a story re-counted as though "man-to-man," with the elder calling for the young man to quit being a "young buck," to efface his pride. The tone of this telling is wonderfully and unusually authoritative: it is blunt, and it pro-motes a specific kind of masculinity.

Ewen notes that he learned much about the past from his elder, Pierre, who was charged by Ewen's mother with the responsibility of teaching him about traditional ways. Pierre was from Skw'átets, and he was a close rela-tive, although Ewen does not say exactly what the relationship was. Ewen knew him only as an old man. Pierre taught him traditional family legends, including a Grizzly Bear transformer epic that Ewen related, and he taught him about the "old ways" when he was home from residential school in the summer. It may be Pierre's position of authority that Ewen replicates in telling about the old ways.

When Fuchs asked for examples, Ewen provided her with colourful sto-ries. For example, Ewen said that, long ago, a married couple was sup-posed to stay together and that children were brought up very strictly. He described the conventions of polygyny, saying that, when he had enough wealth, a man could practise this in order to help out his first wife. When Fuchs pressed for details on these matters, Ewen gave examples from Pierre's life. With regard to polygyny, he described how Pierre had four wives, which is the exact number Ewen had given when discussing the cultural rules pertaining to this practice.

The following passage illustrates how Ewen would alternate between telling stories and generalizing about cultural practices pertaining to adul-tery. This story must have occurred quite a long time ago (recall that Pierre was an old man when Ewen met him).[9]

Pierre told about [a] husband and wife who always quarrelled. [The] man [was] jealous because [the] woman had been with [an]other man. [The] husband told her, "Maybe you'd ... be happier with [the] other man" and said he wouldn't bother her or [the] other man. "Just go to his fire."

They did go.

The [first] man hunted with the other fellow. Everybody [was] happy.

[Then, the] young fella [who had taken the wife] said, "I got your wife. I did a bad thing." Young fella said, "I'll give you somebody you can stay with. I'll give you my sister."

The man talked to his sister. [The] woman wants to know about the man. After all, the other woman left him.

Then the sister married the other man.

Ewen's generic description follows immediately:

> If the man had children with the 1st wife, the man's father would keep the children. The woman leaves everything behind her, leaves with nothing, never takes even an awl. [She] starts up new again. [In this story,] her new husband's sister will use all the other woman's property after she marries the 1st husband [because his first wife left it in his household].

Then Ewen provides three summations that may be responses to Fuchs' prompting.

> This sort of thing happened very seldom. And there had to be great talks between [the] wife & husband, great talk by [the] old people ...
> If [a] woman just wanted to leave [her] husband and return home, her parents would not accept her. Parents will fetch her right back where she belonged.
> Very little jealousy. Don't get that kind of trouble. Rules is strict & good.
> Nothing like killing another man over a woman.

In the first section Ewen retells a story that Pierre evidently told him. Ewen assumes the storyteller's position, including direct quotes from the "young fella" who took the other man's wife. Then he generalizes about Stó:lō practices. The first coda articulates a broader social rule: there had to be "great talks" before a household could be rearranged. Here, without naming the *skumliqw*, Ewen indicates how the extended kindred would intervene in personal choices. In the third coda, Ewen generalizes an ethos – "very little jealousy," the implication being that the society did not "trouble" itself over marital changes. None of these explanatory materials speaks from the past, as did the story about courtship.

Some of the stories that Ewen told to illustrate cultural practices and cultural rules involved white men who had married Aboriginal women. One example was of a white man whose Aboriginal wife had died. This man followed Stó:lō seclusion practices and did not consider remarriage until the "poison" of her loss had left him. These are newer stories than those that had been told from Pierre's perspective: they are stories from his lifetime, depicting people of his own age. They imply something about gender dynamics, as those marrying in were men, but they also demonstrate how people of other races were woven into Stó:lō life for, as Ewen uses them, they illustrate how the "old ways" were so pervasive that the whites moving in followed these rules.[10]

Another perspective that Ewen provides is an explicit comparison between the "old ways" and present practices – a comparison that may well be an undercurrent in the above passages. For example, "In the old days, a girl couldn't go alone anywhere. Had to have someone with her. Can't talk to girls & boys the way they do now. Have to keep walking – unless parents say so ... If parents say no to marriage, it was *no.*"

Unlike in his commentary about the courtship practices of young men, or his retelling of Pierre's stories, Ewen's sensibilities here are located in the present. He conveys an "old-timer's" moral indictment of "the way they do now." It is possible that Ewen is here talking about a "now" that includes the time when his own daughters were growing up as well as the "now" of 1945. If the intensity of Ewen's comment reflects his experience as the father of daughters, we do not see any evidence of this in the notes. Recall that, by 1945, most of his daughters were grown and married. If Ewen gave personal information here, whether to praise his daughters' past behaviour or to express fatherly exasperation, Fuchs kept that in confidence.

So far, I have referred only to information about the past that Ewen gathered from Pierre (and presumably from more general conversations with others). However, he also credits his mother with teaching him a great deal about past cultural practices. He said that she was the one who urged him to build a house on his father's land after his first daughter was born. She also explained to him about cultural practices involving women's knowledge. For example, Ewen says that she told him how to handle the afterbirth when a child was born. Placing it under a rock in the cold waters of a river would help "cool the womb" and contribute to the spacing of children. As he points out, "She didn't have to teach me. I was a boy. But she did." He attributes the spacing of his own children to his following this practice.

With regard to spiritual matters, his mother was a traditional dancer who would perform in the longhouse. And she also used *siwil* – ritual words – that were capable of exerting a powerful influence over others. Ewen's mother took him to the longhouse, where he first learned her song and those of his grandparents. As a singer, he came to be a principal supporter of longhouse dancers, but he was not an initiated dancer. Ewen told Fuchs lots of stories about *siwil* – unfortunately, there is not enough space to go into that in this chapter – but he said that his mother would not teach him the ritual words or precisely how to use them.

The following story dramatizes the powerful effect of Ewen's mother's knowledge – and the way he was able to draw on this knowledge in his own life. Although this story, about the birth of Ewen's daughter Ethel, focuses on practical knowledge from the old ways, and although its sense of deep connectedness and mutual reliance comes in part from the fact that this is a birth story, Ewen gives the story allegorical power because he talks about the relation of past knowledge to future survival.

> Ethel [was] like a doll, small. I can lift her up to the window and see her entrails, she was so thin ...
>
> Willy had gone to call granny. By the time she came, Ethel was half-hour old. Her skin [was] so thin and fine.
>
> I had a lot of bear oil, and my mother had told me that when a baby is newborn, don't use water if the baby is born before its time. Use bear oil to bathe the premature baby. Before granny got there I rubbed the bear oil all over her and wrapped her in cloth.
>
> By golly, that kid got big.

In sum, and this is not surprising, Ewen presents a coherent diagram of a smooth-running kinship system. The stories emphasize a social philosophy that promotes accord: people "get along." This is what Ewen wants most to communicate; and this is what, it appears, Pierre communicated to him. His perspectives on the past shuttle between illustrative stories and cultural generalizations, statements recollected from the past, descriptions, commentary on the past, and contrasts between past and present. In watching him move from one perspective to the next (as in the passage above), we can see that Ewen is presenting more than a seamless portrait. He is not only tracing the connections among past practices but also setting the discursive stage for identifying contrasts between the past and the present – a stage that Fuchs prompted him to explore more critically, as we see in the next section.

Sensitive Topics: Contradictions

Some complicated contradictions emerge in Ewen's discussions of kinship issues involving sensitive subjects. Ewen's commentaries about illegitimacy reveal conflicting concepts of kinship that are so complex that the past/present contrast is insufficient to express the emergence of new ideas.

The subject of illegitimacy comes up twice, and Fuchs may have pressed for details. In the first instance, Ewen sternly reports that "a girl's own close relatives could kill her if she had an illegitimate baby, and they would kill the baby. The boy would be punished as well." Fuchs must have asked for specifics because the notes show Ewen backpedalling: "Not sure what they did with the child – not sure [the] girl & boy [were] killed [but] knows it was a terrible thing. Deserved great punishment."

The second commentary develops an involuted story about a fourteen-year-old girl who became pregnant. In this story, we see family conflict and the emergence of a clash between the "old ways" (gendered male) and Christian ways (gendered female).

> Father was a young man who was her second cousin – that is, someone she could not marry. There was a "big racket, big fuss." The girl's father, Robert,[11] "was gonna kill the baby. The people said no, 'God forbids.' In older times, [they] did kill [the] baby. Robert said he wouldn't stand for it ... [He] told his dau[ghter] she'd have to get away from this place."

Ewen went on to explain what happened later. The daughter moved to another reserve, where relatives arranged her marriage to a forty-year-old man. The baby's father recognized him as his son. Robert died while his grandson was still a baby. Many years later, the daughter's husband died and she remarried, moving to her new husband's reserve. At that time, her son came to live with her and her new husband, resuming his connection with his mother's kin group and her natal reserve. Eventually (and Ewen notes the irony), the son took the land of his grandfather.

This story is only nominally about the problems of illegitimacy (or, more properly in this case, incest); rather, it is about transformation over time. Robert's emotional reaction is representative of the fury that Ewen said would arise in the event of an illegitimate birth. The consequences for the daughter are severe and the punishment is "great" – as Ewen had said it would be when he spoke in general terms – she would not see her father again. Nor would her father see her or his grandson. Clearly, the story demonstrates something about the old ways by showing how they were subverted. The phrase "God forbids" signals how Christian ideals entered into negotiations over the boundaries of sex and kinship. As Ewen tells the story, Robert is the bearer of the "old ways." The old authority does not simply erode, nor is it simply overruled; rather, a more "merciful" alternative is produced. Or, to situate this story within a hegemonic frame, traditionally dominant ideas about incest and illegitimacy are overcome by a newly dominant Christian discourse. A transitional solution draws on old ideas – the intervention of the *skumliqw* ("the people") to arrange a marriage between a young woman and an old (or older) man (Moses and Langen 2001) – to bolster something new (i.e., keeping the baby). The most interesting twist is that the stigma of illegitimacy is so far removed that the problematic baby eventually takes over his grandfather's land. The once "terrible thing" is not only not redressed but the child in question takes over – in Oedipal fashion – the "kingdom." Ewen presents this as an epic, which it certainly is. Whether it expresses fear of change or simple irony is left to us to imagine.

Siwil and Violence

Just as Fuchs explored historical complexity in her dialogue with Ewen, so we can assume that he tested her openness. The notes record numerous episodes that Ewen presents as being controversial. Many of these involve tragedy or injustice, and they implicate Fuchs' world: the world of institutional authority.

One such story focuses on the power of a Stó:lō clairvoyant and also tells of the death of Ewen's brother-in-law. Ewen's stark statements express different structures of feeling from those we have seen so far. These statements are like cracks through which we can glimpse conflict and violence.

> Fred Ewen's brother in law, William Alec was drowned. A white man probably got him drunk. [He] was drunk and went overboard. Fred Ewen got Louie here. [Louie was a seer, the clairvoyant.] He [Louie] went to Cheam. [He] took a deck of cards, [and he] played a game. Joseph Douglas won twice. Louie said Joseph Douglas would find the drowned man. Joseph did get him. Louie knew Willy Alec would have a flask of whiskey in his pocket.

The story is painful, but Willy's drowning is even more painful because of the circumstances of his death. The sentence "A white man probably got him drunk" stands out here. And Ewen elaborated on this white man in another telling, in which he states, "Found the white man who said he hadn't report this because didn't know where he lived. He went through court martial but got out. Got six months for selling liquor."

Willy's betrayal by a white man in the first story is exacerbated in the second story by the information that he "got out," that selling liquor was of more legal consequence than was causing a death. Both the white man and the justice system are indicted in Fred Ewen's tale.

A second example portrays the city as the source of undoing:

> A fella from Spuzzum had a daughter who didn't ever go anyplace. Once though she went to Vancouver. [She went to] jail. The policemen tried to get her home. [She] kept running back to Vancouver. [The father said to the woman who used *siwil*,] "Maggie, here's $40, get my daughter home." In three days that girl went right home to her father. Maggie stayed right here. The father stayed up near Spuzzum.

Here, a Stó:lō power is again the focus of Ewen's story, but the antagonism is between Vancouver (and whatever resulted in the girl in the story being jailed) and the First Nations people.

The destructiveness of alcoholism permeates Ewen's story of his brother Henry's death.[12] In some ways, Henry Ewen's story is sadder than Willy Alec's, and there is no criminal to blame here. As the story develops, we see the complex of factors that led to Henry's accidental death.

> Henry was a mechanic. He knows a lot. He lived here. He did get a wife. She left him. He drinks. He had been overseas in the 1916 war for 4 years. When he came back again, he spent all his money, every cent ($700 and back pay). He got place in Port Kells above Coquitlam [on the outskirts of the city of Vancouver]. There was [40] acres land from Settlement board, with 20 years to pay. There were cattle and a barn. He lived there and got himself wife from ____. He brought her to Port Kells.
>
> [After his wife had left him,] he took a trip in Westminster. Here he came to 6th street. A hill come down there awful steep. He was smashed with a truck. The car was thrown over the track.
>
> A truck run over his head. That was 8 years ago.[13]

Although Ewen doesn't link his brother's death to drinking, he does link the break-up of his marriage to it. The sense we get of Henry is that he was a despondent veteran alienated from his home and living in a dangerous world. That two of these stories concern the deaths of male relatives is probably not coincidental. Ewen is clearly talking about significant tragedies that occurred in his adult life, and he reports the hazards of the world as he saw it.

In these stories, Ewen places dominant cultural forces in an antagonistic relationship with Stó:lō people. Just as "Ottawa," Indian agents, and Christian ideas are in conflict with Stó:lō people, so are cities, alcoholism, and the legal system.[14] It is a mark of Ewen's even temper that he tells these stories with irony rather than with bitterness.

Opposition in the Family

A conflict of central and immediate concern for Ewen during the summer of 1945 involved disagreements among his kin over property rights. The shifting frames of political power and varied conceptualizations of land and kinship work together as both constraining and liberating forces within the context of Ewen's efforts to create new strategies, to draft emergent cultural forms.

The land in dispute was that which Henry Ewen had held on the Seabird Island Reserve – land that was vacant, having no house on it. (Recall that Henry had built a house on his settlement property in Port Kells.)[15] The conflicts among the kind of land claims discussed above – private property rights, residence location, and claims to reserve lands – complicated disposition of the site.

Ewen talked frankly and with a great deal of frustration about the future of Henry's land. Ewen wanted to control rights to his brother's land, which he said had been his grandfather's land. Indian law (meaning the law of the state) would not let him leave a will designating an heir to his property; land had to be inherited by someone who occupied it. The claim to Henry's land would revert to one of Henry Ewen's wife's relatives, who was willing to occupy it, unless Fred Ewen could arrange an heir. Fred conceived a plan to adopt one of his grandsons who was a Seabird Island band member in order to pass the land along to that child. The irony is that, according to Ewen's account, the band chief went along with his idea but his own son-in-law did not. Here are the notes on his story:

> Last fall [Ewen] asked Janie and Sandy for one of their boys. Gonna give him Henry's place, build a house for them. Told Sandy and Janie they could take things off that land for the child they chose. Fred Ewen talked to the Chief and everything.
>
> Sandy went to see Chief ... [the chief told him this:]
> "Fred Ewen gave his grandchild a piece of land. Wants me to settle Willy and (grant) claim to the timber on that land. If you say you'll build a house for that boy, I'll call a meeting and tell William Andrew [Henry's brother-in-law] to disdain claim."
>
> Sandy said, "No, Fred Ewen can't have my child. I won't put my child in bushland."
>
> So, Willy Andrews took that place and in two months made $1600 from the timber.
>
> Sandy wanted Fred's place. [It's] open ground. But that Henry's land [has] better timber. [They] could use the money from that to have the land cleared.

The loss of the land and the timber money clearly annoyed Ewen, but the social conflict also clearly distressed him. The way he tells the story accentuates his point. He starts as if the issue was primarily a matter of the sentimental value of a modest family claim – then we learn that a bundle of money was lost. What lodges in the midst of the story is Ewen's irritation that his son-in-law rejected his advice.

This behaviour did not align with Ewen's *skumliqw* expectations, which required a son-in-law who served him and the extended family. And Sandy was not the only son-in-law to disappoint. When naming his daughters' husbands, Ewen remarked with regard to a son-in-law from another reserve, "He is a Chief's son. He wouldn't do any work for Fred."

Ewen did acknowledge that he limited his own options in this case. "Why did he have to give the land to a son, rather than a daughter?" The question doesn't appear in the notes, but we can assume either that Fuchs asked it or that it was in Ewen's mind. In his next comments, we see how a male-centred sense of honour kept him from considering giving the land to a daughter: "Can't settle land on a girl; [that's like] honoring another man. Am I gonna give an abler man a gift of land? [I] would leave the land to Audrey or Renee [granddaughters he was raising] but ain't gonna honor my daughter's [husband]."

The father of daughters, Ewen found himself caught between two conflicting sets of patriarchal claims. The old Indian law, the rules of the *skumliqw*, would have given rights to the land – through his daughter's marriage – to her husband and his kin group. But Ewen's son-in-law was not really part of the *skumliqw*. Having no conviction in his son-in-law's loyalty to the wider kin group, and without the effective operation of the old extended kin group *(skumliqw)*, Ewen was caught. He refused to pass the land rights through his daughter to a man who did not fulfill his expectations of what a son-in-law should be.

Even though these former practices no longer ruled how property would be passed along, they did rule how Ewen felt about his options. The problem for him was not only that he had to deal with a new set of laws imposed by the state but also that the contradictions between old and new ideas – and their power – created an impasse. His story about losing control of this parcel of land was generated not only by the limitations of colonial administration but also by the contradictions between two generations and their respective values.

This story provides valuable insight into Ewen's agency with regard to negotiating conceptual systems that were sometimes contradictory. Here we see Fred Ewen working to negotiate land for future generations, being thoughtful and strategic, exercising what agency he could but failing to save the land because he could not give it to "another man." The conflicting value systems may have made it difficult for Ewen to see the obstacles clearly. Rather than critiquing Indian law for the limits it imposed, rather than seeing the limits of his own views on kinship and property, he focused on criticizing his son-in-law for opposing him.

Holding to the *Skumliqw*

Skumliqw relations disappointed Fred Ewen in a number of ways – ways he would joke about but that he pointed out nonetheless. He explained how, in the old days, the *skumliqw* would have provided a man with another wife should his first wife leave him or die. But Ewen's *skumliqw* hadn't helped him in this way. One relative promised him a daughter if Ewen chopped a lot of wood for him, making reference to the work a son-in-law was supposed to do for his bride's family. Ewen chopped the wood but got no wife. The only member of his wife's family available to him was his mother-in-law, he quipped, and she was too old. In addition, Ewen's daughters had made their own arrangements for marriages; he spoke of one daughter "running away" with the man she loved, which is to say that she took up with him without his paying court to her father. In Ewen's day, when a relationship failed and there was a child involved, that child stayed with the mother's family – not with the father's, as it would have done in former times.

Still, Ewen was deeply committed to maintaining his *skumliqw* relations. He often identified individuals as being part of this kin network. Some were specific kin whose relationship could be summed up in a kin term; others were part of the broader kin group, and Ewen would recite their connection. All of those whom he referred to as part of the *skumliqw*, however, were senior, of his own generation or earlier.

One aspect of maintaining kin ties that Ewen did control involved his connection with his daughters and mothers-in-law. He was close to both older women, and he even invited one of his mothers-in-law to stay with him as she became elderly (although she declined because the memory of her daughter was too painful for her). As for his daughters, Ewen particularly, if briefly, noted that he had raised them at home. Although others of his generation had sent their children to residential school, he had kept his girls at home, a decision that involved considerable effort. When they were first attending school, he explained, he took the girls to Cheam – five or six miles away – in a canoe, when he could see no better than he did "now" (he was nearly blind). Later, they went to public school in Agassiz.

Thus, despite the conflicted social position he found himself in, and the changing kinship dynamics within which he lived, Ewen reveals how much he was imbued with the ideas of traditional kinship relationships he had explicated so carefully for Fuchs. The poignancy with which he shared the instructions he had received from his elder, Pierre, and with which he reminisced about the stories of his elders and their crises, was laden with awareness of how personal relationships had been undermined by the boundaries of reserve membership, the changes wrought by the Indian Act (especially in marriage), and the limitations of Aboriginal land rights. All these colonial acts had been superimposed on traditional social relations, changing the rules that kin needed to consider when negotiating their domestic interests – interests that were fractured by laws that broke the foundation upon which the *skumliqw* had been based.

Despite these difficulties, Fred Ewen's commitment to kin relations was something that he communicated to his children and to their children, and it gave them a basis upon which to build new and solid forms of family connections. In the winter of 2000, when Estelle Fuchs and I visited Seabird Island, despite the fact that Ewen's land and his grandfather's land were vacant, the shared affection of the generations who gathered with us demonstrated the success of Fred Ewen's love and will.

Being Half-Breed

The tension between the collapse of the economy and politics around which *skumliqw* relations were formed, and Ewen's efforts to maintain them, must have been exacerbated by factors that he never discussed in this context: his racial background and its implications. He was quite frank about being half-Chinese, and he tells his family story without commenting on this fact. With regard to every aspect of life, he speaks as a person who is fully Stó:lō. He was raised by his mother, a native speaker of Halkomelem, and instructed in the old traditions by an elder: thus, everything about Ewen's upbringing made him Aboriginal. But the presence – and absence – of Chinese relatives also shaped his life in ways that we are able to see thanks to his emphasis on the importance of the *skumliqw*. His father's death left him bereaved, but his father's being Chinese left him without half of the kin relations he would have had had his mother married a Stó:lō man. His mother's marrying yet another Chinese man exacerbated this divide. Both of Ewen's sisters also married Chinese men, again depriving Ewen of possible kin links that marriages to local men would have brought to the family. And the fact that Ewen's wife, Josephine, was half-Chinese meant that she brought only one-half the local kinship links that a Stó:lō woman would have brought. It appears that none of the Chinese men in this extended family brought lasting connections from overseas or lasting resources. Thus, the net effect of this constellation of kin was that Ewen experienced a shortfall in potential social resources, ensuring that, in a time of great change, he would be isolated even more than most.

What about Fishing?

A fascinating silence in these records surrounds the subject of fishing. Ewen spoke about working as a carpenter and at the mills. From other sources, we find that Ewen was a fisher, at least at an earlier time in his life. His name is listed among those receiving Indian fishing permits (Ware 1983), and he did tell Fuchs a little about technologies related to fishing. If he spoke about fishing rights or fishing as a practice, Fuchs did not record it.

This appears to be an area that was too far outside the ethnographer's project for her to pursue in her notes.[16]

Fred Ewen's Narrativity

Born in the 1880s, Fred Ewen began to experience social transformation at a time when most Aboriginal people spoke their native language but when the incursions of colonialism were well under way. He worked to establish his home in Aboriginal country; to look after close relatives; and to cultivate the strengths, abilities, and opportunities available to himself and his kin in a changing world. In 1945, the notes archiving his experience exceed by far what ethnography could grasp at that time. The information he provides spills over conceptual categories that might have defined Stó:lō culture and practice in terms of the past, just as his experiences defy the constraints and fragmentation that the reserve and property system imposed on his kinship relations. It is not only the details that break out of the ethnographic categories, however. The stories that Ewen told reveal unsettling transformations, political conflict, racialized antagonisms, and deep contradictions: these were social ills that, at that time, anthropologists generally sought to contest but often failed to engage in their fieldwork.

Ewen was not a social theorist, not a political activist, not a man given to philosophical thought regarding changing times. He did not reframe or rearticulate the tremendous structural constraints within which he was living. The terms "racism" and "colonialism" would have meant much different things to him in 1945 than they do to us today – distant things – if they meant anything at all. The terms "identity" and "gender" would have been foreign to him. His way was to tell stories, not to coin concepts; to situate his knowledge in terms of lived experience, not to step back from life. Yet, more than once, in going over her notes with me, Fuchs would point to a passage and say, "This was something he wanted to tell me."

And as for Estelle Sillen Fuchs, despite her regrets over not making notes on contemporary life in Stó:lō country in 1945, she listened. She encouraged the richness of Fred Ewen's telling. She paid attention to the social themes that emerged in his stories and also described the residual lifeways that she was charged with documenting.

What may be surprising to us is that the kinds of statements Ewen makes bear such striking resemblance to what people say now. Like many a gruff commentator of today, he was cynical about tribal authorities and suspicious of political conniving, although he tried to work with institutions of power. He made fun of people whose views were different from his own; he appreciated differences in peoples' lifeways; he knew that the allure of urban living, drinking, and sexuality were powerful and not to be trusted, and he knew that there were powers that could counter this.

When he told about past injustice his narratives included punchlines whose irony made people laugh even as they took in the tragic nature of what he was saying. These were the devices that helped him to make sense of the past and to address the future without bitterness. The present and its conflicts were more difficult.

Ewen speaks little in these notes about the future. That is the most troubling part of this work, it seems to me. This man, whose understanding of how to live in the world seemed to have lost ground, seems not to look ahead to the futures of his children and grandchildren. Yet this may reflect the ethnographer's project and the backward-looking gaze she arrived with. It helps us to look back at these notes, then, from our present time. According to what his family members have said, Ewen did, evidently, raise his family with a deep sense of connectedness, despite the contradictory forces with which he struggled. While he was not able to secure the land base he wanted for them, he gave them something to carry through changing times: his profound caring.

Conclusions

The efficacy of today's Stó:lō leaders would doubtless impress Ewen deeply. The issues at hand – treating for land rights compensation and for the right to run a Stó:lō Nation commercial fishery – would likely astound him. But the issues encountered would not be news. The legacy of Ewen's comments helps us to appreciate the historical reach of colonialism and the contradictions continuously faced by First Nations peoples.

What are the emergent cultural forms in Ewen's narratives? We do not, in fact, see the beginnings of a Red Power movement, or a Constitution Express, which led to embedding First Nations representation, women's status, and treaty issues into the Canadian Constitution as well as to the legislative and judicial recognition of injustices caused by policy and law. The beginnings of these things were there in Ewen's time, but he was on the margins. Nonetheless, we do see in his accounts the social and structural conflicts that gave rise to these political movements.

Most obviously, we can see the absences that are marked in his telling: the *lack* of effective political authority and the *lack* of justice speak clearly of the need for new forms. Also clear, albeit a bit less obvious, are the contrasts in conceptions of place established by (1) the federal administration and the reserve system and (2) the Stó:lō conception of contiguous land. That the "cutoffs" of Stó:lō land were unaddressed is implicit in Ewen's detailing of the social world that linked the fragmented reserves. We can see, with hindsight, the eventual emergence of the federally recognized

Stó:lō Nation as a politically viable unit. And this unit originates, of course, in the "old ways," in the residual culture. However, the Stó:lō Nation more or less brings together the separate reserves, and, crucially, it draws its strength from the kinship linkages that span these reserves. Thus, these contemporary, cross-reserve Stó:lō connections are new, emergent social forms that are replacing the connections that once linked people from old village sites – the connections that Ewen described in 1945. And these new connections have quite different relationships to resources than did the old ones as the landscape and resource base have changed so much. But these emergent social forms could not have been predicted from the structure of reserves alone. The one-house-one-affiliation reserve and band structure might have precluded cross-reserve collaborations had the reserves not been made so small and the Stó:lō people's prior patterns of interactions not been so extensive.

Most difficult to discern in Ewen's accounts are the emergent social forms that derive from the structural conflicts that were most problematic to him – those he had with his kin. Gendered relationships were complicated and shifting. Fred Ewen, respected as he was, did not lead his family as a patriarch – or with the power his mother seemed to exercise.[17] He clearly held ideas of kinship solidarity that were simply not reinforced by the marriage practices in his and other families. And he held ideas about women's access to land rights that were limiting. His experiences and his discomfitures hint at a future that he would not see – one in which federal law would unravel some of the patriarchal strictures imposed upon First Nations women under Canadian law. First Nations women who had married "out" and had lost their natal band affiliation regained it; if they had married non-Aboriginals and so lost their Indian status, they regained that. And with the restoration of women's status came the implicit acknowledgment of their political power and their autonomy. This was something that the *skumliqw* system (at least in Ewen's view) had not anticipated. Thus, this "restoration" of women's power may not be a restoration to an old way of being a Stó:lō woman but, rather, to a new way that subsumes the old.[18]

Finally, the case of the contested property points to an emergent social form that did develop in Ewen's time (if not completely successfully, at least for him): the band leadership as a mediator of kinship relations and a negotiator of how resources are distributed among band members. This is another social form that Ewen did not remark on precisely but that may be seen in his stories. No longer did the *skumliqw* gather, no longer did all kin involved have "great talks." The chief took an active role and exercised authority that was vested in one person. This central responsibility for an Aboriginal chief seems to have been a new kind of authority in Stó:lō country (although it was well tried throughout the British Empire). Although Ewen shows this authority to us, he does not comment on it, perhaps because he saw the tribal authorities as being so generally ineffectual. But this new lodging place of power, although it would take a long time to develop, seems to have had its roots in the adjudicating role that *skumliqw* gatherings once played.

In 1945, Fred Ewen was asked to be an expert on the past – the information for which anthropologists were so eager at that time – but he gave much more. He was a good teacher then, and, thanks to Fuchs' fieldnotes, is a good teacher now. With his assistance we can discern conflicts between kinship affiliation and political organization that provided the driving force behind the Stó:lo‾ people's involvement in the political movements of the late twentieth century. Contradictory ideas about place and kin meant that social discontent was experienced by those who were not otherwise involved in politics and land rights struggles – those (like Ewen) who were settled and comfortable and employed. With good intentions, with humour, with intensity, and sometimes with irritation, Fred Ewen's complex and contradictory narratives show us how personal knowledge and experiences are imbricated in the powerful and contesting social forces of a historical moment, and that such narratives – especially with hindsight – help us see the friction points from which emergent cultural systems may arise.

Acknowledgments
This chapter was made possible, in part, through funding from the Fulbright-Hayes Doctoral Dissertation Research Abroad Program and from the Wenner Gren Foundation.

Notes
1 All of the notes and narratives referred to and quoted in this chapter come from Smith (n.d.), which archives Fuchs' fieldnotes.
2 I contacted Estelle Fuchs in 1998 and sent her the notes. She had not seen them since the end of the field school. We met during 1999 to work on typed transcripts, and we travelled together to Seabird Island in February 2000. Her husband, who was on the European front, returned safely from the Second World War. In the fall of 1945, Fuchs held her first faculty appointment. Her later research focused on the anthropology of education and included research in West Africa, US urban areas, and in Navajo country.
3 Fuchs told me that, in retrospect, she regretted never having made notes on the tremendous richness of contemporary life in 1945. She was still a graduate student at that time, and this was her first field experience. For the rest of her academic life, she would work on contemporary cultural issues, balancing theoretical and applied anthropology, making major innovations in the ethnography of education.
4 Ewen told several tales of his Thompson neighbours being terrified of ghosts and ghost stories. Stó:lō people could be frightened by encounters with ghosts but were equipped with ritual practitioners to "handle" their concerns.

5 Frederick Ewen's death certificate says he was seventy-five when he died in 1960 in Mission, British Columbia.

6 Fuchs' notes on the first day are bare fragments. I repeat the information here as it is stated in the notes, although I fill out the sentences, add words in brackets, and slightly rearrange them.

7 Unfortunately, it is not possible, within the scope of this chapter, to review Ewen's cultural comparison between the Stó:lō and other First Nations peoples.

8 Harris (2002, 275) calls the reserve the "point of attachment" between First Nations people and their territory. This phrase nicely suggests the fact that the reserves were tiny bits of the social and geographic landscapes of which First Nations people experienced themselves as a part. As Brian Thom (2005, 35) puts it, "One does not need a surveyor's plan in hand to know where family or community property boundaries are in Coast Salish cultures: one needs a good understanding of genealogy, toponomy, mythic history and the 'sign posts' of continued use."

9 This is one subject on which Ewen's commentaries vary from those of other elders interviewed that summer. Other elders described violent treatment of women who committed adultery – but at the hands of husbands known to be especially violent and possessive.

10 Fred Ewen's mother's husbands were, of course, other potential examples, although there is nothing in the notes about them beyond what I have already included.

11 This name is changed.

12 We can only imagine that a close relationship existed between these brothers. Fred and Henry were probably about five years apart in age. Ewen tells no stories about growing up together, and Henry doesn't figure in any illustrative anecdotes. On his 1916 notice of induction into the army, Henry listed Frederick Ewen as his next of kin.

13 British Columbia Vital Statistics lists Henry Ewen as being thirty-eight years old at the time of his death in New Westminster in 1928.

14 Ewen's references to residential school, though frank about the isolation and abuse of authority, were matter-of-fact in comparison to these stories.

15 An Indian had to give up his Indian status, Ewen explained, to purchase private property. He gave the example of an Indian man who was "half Frenchman was adopted over in Cheam [reserve] later took up the white man's side to take up land." Ewen's father's and mother's history with land was another extended case.

16 That summer, Fuchs attended a cemetery clearing, where she had the opportunity to eat some freshly caught and roasted salmon. She also visited a fish camp up in the Fraser Canyon with other students.

17 Ewen's stories of his mother's actions complicate the representations of women's power – and of gendered relations – beyond what could be discussed here. These are worthy of further study.

18 It is very possible that Ewen's views of the "old ways" were also inflected by colonial ideas that his elders communicated to him and that were reinforced by the gendered structures of power in the political and economic contexts in which Ewen lived.

References

Bierwert, Crisca. 1998. Remembering Chief Seattle: Reversing Cultural Studies of a Vanishing American. *American Indian Quarterly* 22 (3): 280-304.

–. 1999. *Brushed by Cedar, Living by the River: Coast Salish Figures of Power.* Tucson: University of Arizona Press.

Carlson, Keith T., ed. 2001. *A Stó:lō Coast Salish Historical Atlas.* Seattle: University of Washington Press.

Cruikshank, Julie. 2005. *Do Glaciers Listen? Local Knowledge, Colonial Encounters, and Social Imagination.* Vancouver: UBC Press.

Duff, Wilson. 1952. *The Upper Stalo Indians of the Fraser Valley.* Anthropology in British Columbia, Memoir No. 1. Victoria: British Columbia Provincial Museum.

Fixico, Donald. 1998. Ethics and Responsibilities in Writing American Indian History. In *Natives and Academics: Researching and Writing about American Indians,* ed. Devon A. Mihesuah, 84-99. Lincoln: University of Nebraska Press.

Harris, Cole. 2002. *Making Native Space: Colonialism, Resistance, and Reserves in British Columbia.* Vancouver: UBC Press.

Harris, Douglas. 2001. *Fish, Law, and Colonialism: The Legal Capture of Salmon in British Columbia.* Toronto: University of Toronto Press.

Hawthorn, H.B., ed. 1966. *A Survey of the Contemporary Indians of Canada: A Report on Economic, Political, Educational Needs and Policies.* Ottawa: Department of Indian Affairs.

Hawthorn, H.B., with C.S. Belshaw and S.M. Jamieson. 1958. *The Indians of British Columbia: A Study of Contemporary Social Adjustment.* Toronto/Vancouver: University of Toronto Press/University of British Columbia.

Jenness, Diamond. 1955. *The Faith of a Coast Salish Indian.* Ed. Wilson Duff. Victoria: British Columbia Provincial Museum.

McHalsie, Albert (Sonny). 2001. Origins and Movement. In *A Stó:lō Coast Salish Historical Atlas,* ed. Keith T. Carlson, 32-33. Seattle: University of Washington Press.

Mihesuah, Devon, ed. 1998. *Natives and Academics: Researching and Writing about American Indians.* Lincoln: University of Nebraska Press.

Miller, Bruce. 2001. *The Problem of Justice: Tradition and Law in the Coast Salish World.* Lincoln: University of Nebraska Press.

Moses, Marya, and Toby C.S. Langen. 2001. Reading Martha Lamont's Crow Story Today. In *Native American Oral Traditions: Collaboration and Tradition,* ed. Larry Evers and Barre Toelken, 92-129. Logan, UT: Utah State University Press.

Newell, Dianne. 1993. *Tangled Webs of History: Indians and the Law in Canada's Pacific Coast Fisheries.* Toronto: University of Toronto Press.

Smith, Marian W. N.d. Collected Papers. Royal Anthropological Institute, London, file 268, box 2.

Suttles, Wayne. 1955. *Katzie Ethnographic Notes.* Ed. Wilson Duff. Victoria: British Columbia Provincial Museum.

–. 1987. *Coast Salish Essays.* Seattle/Vancouver: University of Washington Press/Talonbooks.

Tennant, Paul. 1990. *Aboriginal Peoples and Politics: The Indian Land Question in British Columbia, 1849-1989.* Vancouver: UBC Press.

Thom, Brian. 2005. Coast Salish Senses of Place: Dwelling, Meaning, Power, Property and Territory in the Coast Salish World. PhD diss., McGill University.

Ware, Reuben M. 1983. *Five Issues, Five Battlegrounds: An Introduction to the History of Indian Fishing in British Columbia 1850-1930.* Sardis, BC: Coqualeetza Training Centre for the Stó:lō Nation.

7
Language Revival Programs of the Nooksack Tribe and the Stó:lō Nation

Brent Galloway

A comparison of the language revival programs of the Nooksack Tribe in northwest Washington and the Stó:lō Nation in the lower Fraser River Valley, British Columbia – programs that are working in different countries to preserve and revive the same Aboriginal language – shows two very different approaches. These approaches are conditioned by social and cultural differences, linguistic differences, political differences, personal differences, and national differences as well as by the many similarities and close, collaborative kinship relationships that have always existed between the two groups. The programs are exciting and show some evidence of success with regard to both language preservation and language revival.

The languages shared across the border are Upriver Halkomelem (hereafter, Halq'eméylem) and Nooksack (hereafter, Lhéchelesem). (Halq'eméylem is pronounced much like "Hal, come mail 'em," but the "q'" is pronounced further back than a "k" and is glottalized [hælq'əméyləm]; Lhéchelesem begins with a sound made like a voiceless blown "l" and the e's are pronounced much like the "u" in English "much" [ɬʌ́čələsəm].) Both are derived from village names central in their respective territories – Halq'eméylem from Leq'á:mél, now called Nicomen (Galloway 1993b) and Lhéchelesem from Lhechálos, a village abandoned in the 1850s and now in Lynden, Washington (Galloway and Richardson 1983). Both languages are members of the Central Salish group of the Coast Salish branch of the Salishan language family. Lhéchelesem and Halq'eméylem are the language names, but the people call themselves Nooksack ([nʊxʷsǽʔæq] Nuxwsá7aq "always bracken fern root," or "bracken fern root people") and Stó:lō ([stálo] "river"), respectively.

Currently (2007), there are about four elders who are fluent first-language speakers of Upriver Halq'eméylem and about twenty moderately fluent middle-aged second-language speakers of the language. The last first-language speaker of Lhéchelesem died in 1977 and the last partial speaker died in the 1990s, but there is one partial speaker who began learning the language in about 2000 and continues to add to his fluency (more about him below).

The language, tribal, and village names given above are written in the practical orthographies of both languages. Both language names have the verbalizing suffix "em," which makes the names also mean "speak the language of (Leq'á:mél or Lhechálows)." Lhéchelesem was the primary and original language of the Nooksack Tribe and was spoken from Mount Baker to the edge of Bellingham, Washington; in a village on the south end of Cultus Lake, British Columbia; and in small portions of the Matsqui area in British Columbia (Galloway 1985). Halq'eméylem was spoken from eight kilometres above Yale, British Columbia, down to just above Matsqui; Downriver Halkomelem was spoken from Matsqui to Vancouver; and Island Halkomelem was spoken between Malahat and Nanoose on Vancouver Island.

About three hundred years ago, men of the Nooksack Tribe started getting wives from the Chilliwack area, and these women spoke Halq'eméylem (Galloway 1985). This practice slowly increased until there was a large number of wives and children who spoke both languages. Due to prohibitions against marrying relations, there were also intermarriages with speakers of other neighbouring languages, such as Lummi (a dialect of Northern Straits Salish) and Skagit (a dialect of Lushootseed), but not as many as there were with Halq'eméylem speakers. The number of Lhéchelesem speakers gradually started to decline. In the 1950s, there was only a small number of fluent speakers of Lhéchelesem, including George Swanaset (d. 1960) and Sindick Jimmy. Fortunately, they worked with several linguists (Suttles, Fetzer, Amoss, Efrat, Thompson, and Galloway), leaving fieldnotes (for example, Amoss 1955-56, 1969-70), papers (for example, Fetzer 1951) and numerous tapes of Lhéchelesem (see References). In 1977, the last fluent speaker, Sindick Jimmy, died, but Galloway and Richardson (1983) did some further work with partial speakers Louisa George and Esther Fidele. Those few members of the Nooksack Tribe who still speak an Aboriginal language speak Halq'eméylem (a handful) or Skagit or Lummi (less than a handful). English is universal on both sides of the border. So far, linguistic publications on Lhéchelesem include Amoss (1961), Galloway (1983, 1985, 1992, 1993a, 1996, 1997), and Galloway and Richardson (1983). There are also comparative word lists, which contain Lhéchelesem words (Boas and Haeberlin 1927; Haeberlin [Thompson] 1974; Galloway 1988a; Kuipers 2002; and perhaps others).

Halq'eméylem has been more studied by linguists than has Lhéchelesem: Boas (1890), Hill-Tout (1902, 1904), Elmendorf and Suttles (1960), Harris

(1960), Oliver and Casey Wells (1965), Galloway (1970-present), and Burton, Wiltschko, and Urbanczyk from the 1990s to the present. The first full grammar of the language was provided by Galloway (1977) and updated by Galloway (1993b). A pedagogical version of this was published by Coqualeetza as Galloway (1980) and included a 2,300-word list and many illustrations of cultural artifacts and photos of elders. A comprehensive dictionary by Galloway will be completed in 2007, and computer copies of the English-to-Halq'eméylem portion have been available to the Stó:lō Nation and Nooksack Tribe since about 2000; copies of the Halq'eméylem-to-English portion have been available since late 2004.

The Canadian Halq'eméylem Language Revival Efforts: A Brief History

Halq'eméylem language revival efforts began with the work of Oliver Wells and Casey Wells (1965); lessons taught by Richie Malloway and Alec James (circa 1969); the Skulkayn Heritage Project (1972), which began an elders group that still meets; the Nooksack Tribe's Halq'eméylem Workshop (1974-82); and the Coqualeetza Education Training Centre (1975-present), which created the first Halq'eméylem Language Department and program and introduced the official Stó:lō Orthography and lessons developed by Galloway in 1974-75. Accounts of that program can be found in Galloway (1975, 1976a, 1976b, 1979, 1980, and, especially, 1988b). Coqualeetza and the Stó:lō Nation worked separately from 1995 until about 2001, when they reconciled; Coqualeetza continues its teaching, and the Stó:lō Nation has continued a successful program called the Stó:lō Shxwelí, which began in 1995. Gardner (2002) offers an excellent, in-depth study of the Halq'eméylem revival effort in Canada.

Linguist Jimmy Gene Harris' initial work with the language inspired amateur anthropologists Oliver Wells and his brother Casey Wells to also begin recording interviews with elders; Casey developed an orthography – the Practical Phonetic System (PPS) – and, with Oliver, transcribed a good deal of the Halq'eméylem on the recorded tapes. Oliver published a word list, a map of place names, and much cultural information; he also documented and helped elders and their families revive Salish weaving with the use of Native dyes and looms. He died prematurely in 1971 but left fifty tapes, which have been transcribed, and much of the additional information has been published posthumously (see Wells 1987). Richie Malloway and Alec James, two fluent elders, set up classes to teach Halq'eméylem using PPS. Unfortunately, while PPS is systematic and fully capable of capturing all the complex sounds of the language, the Wells brothers were not able to use it accurately enough to enable Malloway and James to succeed in applying it to their language revival efforts.

In 1972, members of the Scowkale Reserve (then spelled "Skulkayn") got funding to tape record interviews with elders and started the first Elders Group, which was based on fluency in Halq'eméylem. They made many hours of tapes and worked mainly on language preservation. I had been working with an elder on a nearby reserve and met the Elders Group in 1972, at which time I found that Randy Bouchard had given two of the elders some training in his orthography. I made a few revisions for the Upriver dialects to allow the orthography to capture the three phonemic tones and to avoid some underlined characters.

In the summer of 1974, I began working with the Nooksack Tribe using this orthography, and I applied to the Coqualeetza Education Training Centre in British Columbia to start a language revival program with them. I moved to Chilliwack from California in January 1975, and we started devising lessons, doing research at the weekly meetings of the Elders Group, and working with a full-time elder (who was also my assistant). After a few months, with the staff of the Coqualeetza Education Training Centre, we began field testing the lessons at Scowlitz, Seabird Island, Tzeachten, and Katz reserves as well as in Sardis. The work continued until 1980. At that point, in three Halkomelem teacher training courses at Fraser Valley College, I had trained ten speakers (mostly elders) in the writing system, lesson development, and classroom teaching. Chief Dan George spoke at the graduation ceremony of our first class. One of the graduates was also trained to replace me as head of the Halq'eméylem Language Department, so I trained myself out of a job.

I continued working with the Halq'eméylem Workshop of the Nooksack Tribe between 1975 and 1982. When I left the area most of the graduates of the teacher-training courses were teaching the language on different reserves (Scowlitz, Chehalis, Seabird Island, Katz, Tzeachten, Cheam, Sumas, etc.). One, Nancy Phillips, had been teaching in a reserve school in Chehalis, British Columbia, using an unsystematic orthography developed by the principal; she quickly adopted the Stó:lō Orthography and continued teaching the language until she died many years later. The Stó:lō Sítel Committee took over working with the Elders Group on cultural curricula. These curricula were developed in collaboration with the local public school districts and were accepted and used in the public school system, where they continue to be taught.

Another graduate, Elizabeth Phillips, was the youngest totally fluent Halq'eméylem speaker, and she has now taught several generations of younger speakers, both at Coqualeetza and through the Stó:lō Nation. Another, Edna Bobb, taught the language at Seabird Island until she died in the late 1990s; she had worked with me to transcribe all the Halq'eméylem

in the fifty Oliver Wells tapes. Another graduate, Tillie Guttierez, continues to teach at Katz Reserve. Roy Point, a graduate who, with his sons
Steven and Mark Point, was instrumental in the Skulkayn Heritage Project,
continued teaching informally until he died in 2000. One of my young
students in the staff classes, Peter Lindley, studied the language further
with Elizabeth Phillips and became reasonably fluent. He taught extensively in reserve classes, schools, and pre-schools and continues to teach
today.

Several years after I moved away, Coqualeetza started a Halq'eméylem
immersion course. This was an ambitious course and got some good results; however, it led to some disagreements between the Stó:lō Nation
and Coqualeetza and so was discontinued. The Stó:lō Nation started its
own Halq'eméylem program, called the Stó:lō Shxwelí ("the Stó:lō way"),
and Shirley Norris, a Cowichan speaker who moved to the Chilliwack area
and learned the Upriver dialect and the orthography, proved to be an enthusiastic and dynamic teacher trainer. With the assistance of a number of
courses run through Secwepemc Cultural Education Society (SCES) in
collaboration with Simon Fraser University, over a dozen young and middle-aged Stó:lō people were trained as Halq'eméylem teachers. Crucial in
this effort, besides Shirley Norris, were elders Elizabeth Herrling, Rosaleen
George, and (later) Elizabeth Phillips as well as linguists Strang Burton,
Martina Wiltschko, and Sue Urbanczyk. I taught the third and fifth semes-
ter Halq'eméylem classes. The dozen or so students became close friends
and formed an excellent network among themselves and their teachers.
They began actively teaching what they had learned on all levels: they did
that at home to children and grandchildren, at pre-schools, in reserve classes
and reserve schools, and in public schools. These activities were partly organized through the Stó:lō Shxwelí and partly through the students' own
contacts. They spoke Halq'eméylem whenever they socialized as well as at
home to their families. About eight completed all their courses and got
certificates in First Nations languages in a relatively new provincial program. They had two graduations in 2000, one at SCES in Kamloops and a
later one, in the fall, at the Scowkale Reserve. I spoke at the second one,
where I confessed that I had never been sure the language would survive
long into the twenty-first century but that, for the first time, thanks to this
crop of vigorous younger speakers, I felt that it would. Elizabeth Phillips
gave a speech in Halq'eméylem. Curricula include CDs of spoken and sung
Halq'eméylem, lessons, and interactive games that Strang Burton developed with the help of elders. The graduates continue to be creative, developing new flashcards, language master cards, printed lessons, classroom
games, and so on.

Since then, Shirley Norris left the Stó:lō Shxwelí offices and went to work to help teach Halq'eméylem at Seabird Island. But Strang Burton and his colleagues continued working with Elizabeth Phillips, Elizabeth Herrling, and Rosaleen George, taping and developing curricula. In fact, they developed several volumes of a textbook on Halq'eméylem for a language immersion course in an attempt to give some younger students a high level of fluency. It was first proposed that this immersion course would run for six months or so, but, thanks to advice from Jimmy Gene Harris (who had just retired from teaching ESL with the Ford Foundation in Thailand), a three-year Halq'eméylem immersion course was begun in Sardis. This class was completed in 2004, its purpose being to produce the most fluent young speakers yet. A number of the graduates have begun teaching Halq'eméylem. Meanwhile, the students with certificates continue teaching the language on various levels. In 2001, one of them, Catalina Renteria, became the developer and head of the Nooksack Tribe's new language program.

The Nooksack Tribe's Language Revival Programs

The first Nooksack Tribe language revival effort of which I am aware was the Halkomélem Workshop. It began in 1973 and was instigated by Nat Dickinson. In early 1974, Nat phoned me in California and asked if I could come up to help with the Halkomelem Workshop since he had gone as far as he could without being able to write the language systematically. The workshop comprised a marvellous group of elders who were fluent in Halq'eméylem (and each was also fluent in either Lhéchelesem, Skagit, or Lushootseed) as well as some younger family members wanting to learn. I joined them for the summer of 1974, developed and used the first version of the Stó:lō Orthography, and transcribed Halq'eméylem and Lhéchelesem for them. I also shared words and phrases and grammatical knowledge that I had learned from my studies with Stó:lō elders, which I had begun in 1970. One Halq'eméylem speaker from this group is still alive, but Sindick Jimmy, the only fluent Lhéchelesem speaker, as well as Louisa George and Esther Fidele, the last two partial speakers of Lhéchelesem, have all died. Sindick and Louisa were both Halq'eméylem and Skagit speakers. Sindick had been approached several times to teach Lhéchelesem, but he saw no hope for it; however, fortunately, he worked with Amoss, Efrat, Thompson, and myself on Lhéchelesem, enabling us to record many words, sentences, and stories.

I continued weekly meetings with the Nooksack Tribe's Halkomelem Workshop until 1982. In January 1975, I returned to Sardis to set up the Halq'eméylem Language Program and Language Department for the

Cóqualeetza Education Training Centre, which I ran until 1980. In 1982, I moved to Vancouver. The Halkomelem Workshop continued to meet as an elders group to share meals, but it no longer worked on the language (although some members continued to use the meetings as occasions to speak Halq'eméylem). The group also continued to meet with the Canadian Coqualeetza Elders Group several times a year (at Christmas and at the annual summer Elders Gatherings held in a different location in British Columbia each year).

Some elders tried their hand at teaching in pre-school or early school classes; however, because they lacked classroom management skills, this endeavour did not last long. It wasn't until 2001, when, thanks to Phillip Narte's application, the Nooksack Tribe got a three-year grant from the Administration for Native Americans (ANA) for language revitalization that it was able to again start working on Halq'eméylem revival. The tribe hired Catalina Renteria, one of my students from the third- and fifth-level Halq'eméylem classes (which were partly immersion) – Linguistics 332-3 and 432-3 in the Simon Fraser University catalogue – and one of eight or nine who completed SFU's Certificate of Indian Languages in Halq'eméylem in 2001. She was not able to apply for the position of co-ordinator of the language program until six months into the grant, when the first round of shortlisted applicants was disqualified (one due to lack of fluency; one did not come to scheduled interviews). She then had to continue working at her old job as head of human resources for the Nooksack Tribe for several months until a replacement could be found. In spite of this, she achieved the goals of the grant, hired some excellent staff members, and developed an outstanding program. I have assisted her periodically, as has Dr. Mercedes Hinkson, formerly of SCES in Kamloops, where she set up the last three levels of the Indian Language Certificate Program and got me involved (she has since moved to Bellingham, where she continued to work with the Northwest Indian College).

One of the hallmarks of this language program is the production use of digital video materials. At the very beginning, Catalina contacted Dr. Robert Balas, then of Western Washington University (WWU) in Bellingham. He had developed a highly successful interactive digital video program, La Taupe ("the mole"), to teach French at WWU and was willing to work with Catalina to adapt it to Halq'eméylem curricula. I met with them, saw a demonstration, and, at their request, was taped on digital video pronouncing the 2,300-word Classified Word List (Galloway 1980) as well as an introduction to the alphabet and sounds of Halq'eméylem, along with a few dialogues with Catalina. The Classified Word List and Grammatical Sketch

(Galloway 1980) has served as a pedagogical grammar and dictionary for about twenty years, and it is now available on video and may be used as a mini-dictionary.

La Taupe works on Macintosh computers, and Catalina hired one of Balas' students, Marcus Goodson, as well as Balas himself to aid in putting the tape into the system as a prototype. The English and Halq'eméylem are typed in and linked with digital footage and audio captured from the digital recording. As a result, students can type in English to get Halq'eméylem (or the reverse) and can gain access to the video of the speaker pronouncing the words or phrases. The student can also record his/her pronunciation on the computer and compare it with the speaker's pronunciation. Balas found that students using La Taupe require less contact hours with teachers and do better in pronunciation and written tests than do those who do not use the system. He also found that students can take exams in the same way (the exams can be graded at the computer by the instructor). An additional feature of the program is that it allows students to work at their own speed, select what they want to practice, and enjoy the computer technology.

When Catalina approached me to record my full Halq'eméylem dictionary, I suggested that she ask Elizabeth Phillips to do it. She was busy teaching the Halq'eméylem course in Chilliwack, so we had to arrange a two-week period when we could work with her. We estimated it would take two weeks to do the recording (eight hours per day) based on the time it took to record the 2,300 words on the Classified Word List. I flew in from Regina and we started recording; however, Elizabeth, who had made cassette recordings of my English-to-Halq'eméylem portion of the dictionary on her own, had recorded the cassettes using a very slow, careful pronunciation (which students often requested for reference) rather than a natural speed. Also, since my dictionary has pronunciations from about fifty different speakers with whom I've worked, there were a number of pronunciations with which Elizabeth was not familiar. So after recording the first twenty pages of the 660-page English-to-Halq'eméylem dictionary, we stopped, and, at Elizabeth's request, we began recording over again with me reading the various dialect forms at a normal conversational speed and with her pronouncing only those words with which she was familiar. Thus, we have corrections on some words, Tait subdialect pronunciations for all of them (many of which I had not recorded before), and subdialect pronunciations that were now recorded in both a male and a female voice. The only problem is that we need to edit out the repetitions as Halq'eméylem words or phrases are repeated each time they have more than one meaning.

We didn't realize this at the start of the filming; the pronunciations need to be captured only once and then linked to the appropriate Halq'eméylem orthographic spelling, which is typed in. We hope to arrange this in the near future, but meanwhile we will be transferring the videos to CDs.

Catalina and Marcus have designed curricula for several levels of initial classes in Halq'eméylem, and Catalina has now field tested these in evening credit classes at Northwest Indian College. She and Marcus have designed conversational dialogues, and these have been recorded on digital video with combinations of speakers: Elizabeth Phillips and me, Elizabeth and Catalina, Catalina and various top students, and Catalina and Marcus (who has also learned some Halq'eméylem). Catalina has made video recordings of final exams and has incorporated the work of those students who did perfect or near perfect work into the curriculum materials (with their permission, of course). So far, students have been enthusiastic about using La Taupe and the curricula.

In addition to these materials, the grant required the tribe to pass ordinances for cultural and language preservation and repatriation as well as to work out links for credit with local colleges (in this case, Northwest Indian College). These tasks have been accomplished. In May 2002, I was invited to a ceremony to acknowledge the presentation of two hundred hours of Halq'eméylem CDs and one hundred hours of Lhéchelesem CDs. A Social Sciences and Humanities Research Council grant had permitted me and a research assistant, Sonja van Eijk, to make these CDs, from original and copied cassettes and reel tapes, for the Nooksack Tribe. That project took two years and involved copying all of the Skulkayn Heritage Project tapes as well as all of the Oliver Wells tapes and the tapes I had made of elders in Halq'eméylem onto four sets comprising three hundred hours of CDs. I keep one set, and the Stó:lō Nation has two sets – one for archival purposes and one that can be checked out of the Stó:lō Nation archives. Two-thirds of a set, which was all we could copy until the grant ran out, was given to the Nooksack Tribe. The grant also allowed us to make two sets of CDs from the extant Lhéchelesem tapes as well as one set of CDs from the extant tapes of the Samish language (which I made with the last two Samish speakers). The Samish Tribe also paid for a copy, as did Dr. Henry Davis (a UBC professor of linguistics who received a grant for this purpose), so that UBC could have a set. Several of Henry's grad students have worked since 2001 with the last speaker of Samish (one of the speakers I worked with has passed away but the monolingual speaker is still alive). I arranged for Sonja van Eijk, who had done most of the work digitizing and making the CDs, to fly to the presentation with me to be honoured for her work. She suggested I look up some Lhéchelesem words we might say and write them down for her, along with some Halq'eméylem words she might use, if required. I did a search of the data entered on the grants for a Lhéchelesem dictionary and found four or five sentences and a number of words that would be appropriate to utter at public ceremonies. I printed them out and taught her some. Before the presentation ceremony, Catalina, Marcus, Sonja, and I met with George Adams, who would be doing the ceremonial work. He was very interested in the Lhéchelesem words and sentences, and I had made a copy for him and others as well. Besides being fluent in Lummi and partially fluent in Halq'eméylem, he knows many Lhéchelesem place names and a number of words, and he can read the orthography quite well since it differs only in a few letters from the Halq'eméylem orthography. We went through and practised some of the Lhéchelesem sentences and words. I had invited all the remaining linguists who had made the recordings to come to the ceremony (Barbara Efrat, Pamela Amoss, Laurence and Terry Thompson, and Allan Richardson, who had taped place names with the last partial speakers when we visited and photographed all the sites years before). The whole Nooksack Tribe was invited to the outdoor ceremony and salmon barbecue. About 150 people came, as did Pamela Amoss (who made the first recordings of Lhéchelesem when she taped George Swanaset and Sindick Jimmy in 1956) and Allan Richardson (who has worked on the ethnohistory of Nooksack place names since the 1980s). Pamela, Allan, Sonja, and I stood and had blankets given to us as songs were sung and several speakers and witnesses were called. George Adams gave an excellent speech explaining the work being done at the ceremony, and he also gave a short speech in flawless Lhéchelesem – the first time that language had been spoken in public in nearly thirty years. He also said that this was the beginning of the return of Lhéchelesem, which can now once again be spoken by its people. And in this he has proven correct.

We had collectively figured that, after several years of Halq'eméylem lessons, some of our students would be able to try their hands at Lhéchelesem as the orthographies required are nearly identical and as there are also a number of grammatical, syntactic, and lexical similarities. We had not counted on the talents of George Adams. He signed on to the language program and began transcribing the Lhéchelesem CDs in the Nooksack orthography. He has been working with and trying to think in the language ever since. His answering machine message is 90 percent Lhéchelesem and 10 percent English. He has written a dozen e-mails to me in Lhéchelesem, many without English translation, and I reciprocate in kind. As we tried more complex sentences, we added a translation line. His Lhéchelesem is nearly flawless.

Thanks to a small internal grant from the Social Sciences and Humanities Research Council of Canada, George, Catalina, and I collaborated for a year to discover the syntax of Lhéchelesem through working on several long stories told by Sindick Jimmy to Pamela Amoss in 1956. We completed the parsing, interlinear translations, and syntactic analysis of both (the second is on how to become an Indian doctor and is over one hundred lines in length). We gave two joint papers at the 2004 International Conference on Salishan and Neighbouring Languages in North Vancouver (Galloway, Adams, and Renteria 2004a, 2004b), and both George and Catalina gave speeches in Lhéchelesem when they presented the papers. We are able to joke and have short conversations in the language now, and George has left phone messages on my answering machine that are all in Lhéchelesem (firsts for the language). We presented the second story at the next Salish conference and I intend to write a grammatical sketch of Nooksack. We intend to apply for a grant to support more collaborations and the proofing of the computer files so that they may be integrated into a draft Lhéchelesem dictionary. The next several years will also see a draft grammar of Nooksack/Lhéchelesem come to fruition. In the summer of 2006, Richardson and I finished a final draft of a book-length manuscript on Nooksack place names, using the photos and slides we took thirty years ago. And George has just started to design Lhéchelesem lessons. We intend to work together with Catalina Renteria to put together a CD set for classes, and George has already begun teaching a small informal class. Both George and Catalina are trained in linguistics and are experienced teachers of Indian languages (Lummi and Halkomelem, respectively).

A final positive development is the successful work of the First Peoples' Language and Culture Committee of Washington State. This group, comprised of elders, educators, and representatives from most of the twenty-nine tribal groups in the state, has been at work for five years or so. By the end of 2002, working collaboratively with the State Board of Education, they had succeeded in developing an ordinance – WAC 180-78A-700 – that would establish procedures for the tribes to train their own language and culture teachers, that would recognize each tribe's right to do this, and that would certify and ceremonially validate any such teachers once the tribe felt that they were qualified to begin teaching the language and culture in the public school system. The ordinance would establish that, once qualified by a tribe and once having shown proof of having been trained in recognizing symptoms of child abuse, these teachers would become certified through this process, which takes place between each tribal government and the state government. The teachers would then be eligible to teach in any public school and would be paid in accordance with regular teacher salary scales. The ordinance does not provide the money to do this, but tribes have usually been able to obtain funding for those Indian language/culture teachers who have regular teaching credentials (e.g., a master's of education, etc.).

Catalina has been active in the First Peoples' Language and Culture Committee of Washington State and invited eleven people representing Nooksack to come to a public hearing in Olympia, WA, in 2003 and the press conference that followed. I was invited, along with ten Nooksack tribal members, including elders; a tribal council member and her brother (who had written the language grant) and sister (who was involved in another grant for cultural and linguistic repatriation); George Adams; and Marcus Goodson (who would take digital video footage). There was a meeting the night before to plan the presentation, at which time it was revealed that the board, while very favourable toward the ordinance, had concerns about whether the Congress' recently passed No Child Shall Be Left Behind Act superseded the Native American Languages Legislation of the 1980s. It also wondered whether this most recent legislation would require more stringent qualifications for Indian language/culture teachers and whether it might be a roadblock that could delay, or even prevent, passage of the ordinance. Supporters on the Board of Education had said that if it voted that a delay was necessary in order to provide time to understand the new legislation, then passage of the ordinance might have to be rescheduled until March or so of 2003.

At the hearing the next day – Wednesday, 15 January 2003 – there was a morning meeting next to the hearing room in Olympia, the state capital, which allowed for last-minute news, the assembling of tribal supporters, and some Native religious preparations. We were then invited to join the audience in the hearing room, and there were about 150 supporters from many tribes, mostly tribal language teachers, elders, a few linguists, and local school district members.

After an opening song and a very effective presentation of the program and of the need to support a new generation of speakers and teachers, several speakers argued that, since the teaching of language and culture to the next generation will decide whether those languages and cultures survive or die, no one would be more concerned with competent training and fluency than the main stakeholders – the tribes themselves. Who is better qualified to ensure the accuracy of Aboriginal teaching than the elders and tribal members on education committees? At the end of the speeches, it was explained by our delegation that it was a part of Nooksack culture to have closing songs and to give small gifts to thank people for listening and witnessing. Then, as the final songs were sung, necklaces and a few other gifts were given to the board members. These people spoke very positively and said they looked forward to their scheduled vote in two days, at which time they intended to pass the ordinance.

There was a press conference after the hearing, and our group talked mainly with a reporter from the *Bellingham Herald*. The evening of the hearing, the First Peoples' Language and Culture Committee had arranged for a feast and potlatch at the longhouse of the Skokomish Tribe near Shelton, Washington. Catalina and I had delivered salmon from the Nooksack Tribe the day before, and a number of the tribes had contributed to help out. We arrived several hours before the ceremony to ensure that the fires would be lit in the longhouse to warm it sufficiently for the elders and others. There had been a spirit dance in the longhouse the night before, so the fires from that had kept it warm in the morning after the spirit dance was over. Members of the Skokomish Tribe were cooking all over the tribal complex. A reporter from the *Seattle Post-Intelligencer* was present, having been given permission to observe and write about potlatch preparations.

The house posts of the longhouse were decorated with boughs, and long tables were set out on the dirt floor. As people arrived they sat in groups in the bleachers. When it got close to 7:00 p.m., people were shown where to sit, with elders and those being honoured sitting at all the tables and others being served in the bleachers. Songs and prayers were offered, and everyone was invited to start eating. The quantity and variety of food was incredible: fresh oysters, butter clams, whole crabs, breaded geoduck clams, geoduck soup, fresh shrimp, sockeye salmon (both fresh and smoked), elk, venison, Labrador tea, potatoes, salads, breads and biscuits, desserts. Throughout the meal, songs (including exciting *lahal*, or gambling, songs) and dances were performed by various tribes.

After the meal, the master of ceremonies, who had been announcing the performing groups and supervising, invited certain people to speak about the ordinance and the positive support given by the Board of Education. The entire board was present, and a number of them made some very eloquent and supportive speeches. The governor of the state had been invited but sent a representative in his place. The message read from the governor congratulated the tribes and the board on a successful and important collaboration and supported the passage of the ordinance.

The final part of the evening included the potlatch, which consisted of each tribe calling out elders and a few others they wished to honour for their work in language preservation and revitalization efforts. First, about four elders were called up as witnesses and were seated in a row facing the centre of the longhouse (after it had been cleared of tables). Then each elder called came out and sat in chairs on blankets that had been blessed and spread on the floor. Each was given a blanket that was draped over his/her shoulder. The elders from the Nooksack Tribe were called, including two of Sindick Jimmy's daughters, Catalina's mother (a Halq'eméylem speaker), George Adams, Phillip Narte (who wrote the successful language project grant application) and his sister, Adelina Singson (who had just finished her work on the repatriation grant), and me (for my work on the language). Each tribe had one or two speakers who talked about the people seated on the blankets and explained what each had done.

After that, there was more singing and gifts were passed out to all participants. All had been strongly urged to take home whatever food was left on the table and were given plastic bags in which to carry home feast leftovers (called *smeq'óth* in Halq'eméylem from the root *meq'*, "satiated with food, full from eating"). After a few more speeches and a closing song, everyone was thanked and left, with hands being shaken all round.

The next day, the First Peoples' Language and Culture Committee had a meeting from 10:00 a.m. to 2:00 p.m. to work out a general template for how the training and validation of teachers would be conducted. In the end, the guidelines approved were very general, though Catalina Renteria and George Adams presented the detailed plan designed by the Nooksacks and the Makah, and others also passed out some specific plans. Finally, it was thought best to keep the template generic and to include only those elements that all the tribes and the Board of Education required.

On Friday morning, many tribal members and supporters stayed for the actual vote. There were about seventy-five people in the audience, some camcorders, and so on, and, and after a few supportive words, the vote was taken. It was eight to zero in support of the ordinance and passed unanimously. The Indian representatives cheered, sang a thank you song, and left. Several reporters were present in the hall afterward, and several of the groups talked with them, including our group of Nooksacks.

The significance of this ordinance and the preceding and following work by both the Board of Education and the First Peoples' Language and Culture Committee cannot be overemphasized. A supportive partnership and collaboration was forged that I believe will be very important to the survival of the Indian languages of Washington State. I learned, toward the end of the week, that something similar had been done in the State of Oregon. I am unaware of any similar initiatives in British Columbia, but there have been many gatherings of First Nations language and culture teachers from all over the province, and there has been significant federal and provincial support of efforts to preserve and revive these languages and cultures. In the following section, I compare and contrast British Columbia's and Washington's efforts to revive Halq'eméylem.

Similarities and Differences in Language Efforts, Cultures, Politics, and Nations

With regard to preserving and revitalizing Halq'eméylem, the fact that the same orthography is used on both sides of the border facilitates exchange of curricula in all media. A certain amount of this has been done and, as time permits, continues to be done. The Stó:lō efforts have had the advantage of sustained support, a larger population, and more available elders than are found in Washington. On the other hand, much travel is required to pick up the members of the Elders Group, which has been the backbone of the Stó:lō effort. With regard to the Nooksack Tribe, while the elders were helpful during the Halq'eméylem Workshop era, they did no sustained work on the language for fifteen or sixteen years afterward, and no one was employed to run a language program. However, thanks to innovative technology and extensive training with the Stó:lō, Catalina Renteria was able to jumpstart the first grant-funded program since the 1970s. In both countries language revitalization efforts began with the design and the field testing of lessons. In the Nooksack case, credit for students was possible due to the presence of the Northwest Indian College and the terms of the ANA grant. At the start, no such advantages existed for the Stó:lō at Coqualeetza. However, thanks to the SCES/SFU collaboration, the students in the certificate program between 1996 and 2001 were able to get credit (and I believe some students were able to get credit before that). The students in my Halq'eméylem teacher-training courses in the 1970s were all elders or adults and were not seeking credit from Fraser Valley College (though that probably could have been arranged); however, their graduation was validated by ceremonies, as were those of the later Stó:lō graduates and as will those of graduates in Washington. In both countries, tapes and CDs are resources that can enable students to learn transcription, new vocabulary, and stories; and in both countries these resources are being increasingly used. Galloway and Wolfson (1993) also discuss some language revitalization options for Canada. As the last first-language Halq'eméylem speakers die, tapes and CDs will become the best resources for continued study and attainment of fluency, as they are now for those wishing to learn Lhéchelesem. Fluent linguists can help, but they seldom have the vast vocabulary of the elders and often rely on written transcriptions that they have gathered from elders in order to supplement the tapes and CDs. The opportunities to develop networks of student learners as cohorts who can be mentored by elders, linguists, and CDs are the same for both the Stó:lō and the Nooksack; however, because of the sustained effort among the Stó:lō, more of these have been developed in British Columbia than in Washington.

There are a number of cultural similarities between the Stó:lō and the Nooksack. They share winter spirit dancing, ceremonial rules, gatherings, canoe races, meals for elders, and many relationship ties. In fact, there are a fair number of people who are card-carrying members of both the Stó:lō Nation and the Nooksack Tribe. The fishing technology is similar for each group, the differences being due to different runs of fish. Wind-drying of salmon is common in the Fraser Canyon, whereas the Nooksack rely more on sea fishing and other types of seafood. Some of the unfortunate things shared between the Stó:lō and the Nooksack include problems with alcohol and drugs, a loss of cultural and linguistic identity among the young, and some substandard housing. However, language and culture programs help combat the second of these and sometimes even the first. And, with the Stó:lō, progress is being made in housing on a reserve-by-reserve basis. As for the Nooksack, they have considerable funds gained from a successful casino run by the tribe, and an effort is being made to use profits to benefit the whole tribe, to purchase more land, to build housing, and to provide programs for youth. Both the Stó:lō and the Nooksack have strong fishery programs, which are Indian-run in Washington but are subject to federal control/interference in Canada. Due to competition for time and funding, many of these factors affect the implementation and progress of language and culture revitalization. From the start, among the Stó:lō there were more people working on language revitalization than there were among the Nooksack, and, due to sustained efforts over the years, this number has doubled, tripled, and quadrupled. Such effort is new among the Nooksack, and it will grow only if sustained funding is available to hire staff and to maintain them at decent salary levels. This was the case for a while, but when the ANA grant for revitalizing Halkomelem expired at the end of 2003, the future became uncertain. Since then, the Nooksack Tribe has provided funding for two positions that involve working with the education co-ordinator but that are under tribal council supervision. If new grants are not found, this effort could founder.

There are numerous political differences between the Nooksack and the Stó:lō, though they share elected councils. The Stó:lō have numerous small reserves, each having an elected chief and council and being free to pass federal support funds to the Stó:lō Nation language revitalization efforts or to run its own. Seabird Island and Chehalis run their own. Most of the rest use the Stó:lō Shxweli. The Nooksack did not sign a treaty with the federal government in the 1850s and 1860s, so they did not get a reservation; rather, they were given or sold land as individuals and were expected to homestead. They were somewhat fragmented but had get-togethers with the whole tribe (i.e., Nooksack Days) and had hereditary chiefs and elected councils into the 1940s. Around this time, they purchased some land and applied to have it set aside as tribal, or reserve, land. They applied for federal recognition and eventually received it. The small stand of land near Nugent's Corners enabled them to build a tribal centre. This was the situation when I worked with them in the 1970s. They gradually enlarged their tribal staff and received grants to help them do this. The funds that they received from the casino they built in the early 1990s enabled them to expand tribal services to tribe members and (recently) to buy land outright or to use the casino as collateral for loans to buy land. They have gradually acquired parcels of land for housing (several of these were acquired before the casino), for new offices, for tribal police, and for other economic and social developments. Their political system has changed so that chairs of the tribal council are elected, but rival political factions cause instability, as do occasional management problems regarding the casino and grant administration. Nevertheless, on the whole, the Nooksack are making impressive progress and are ready for an expanding language revitalization process.

There are also differences between the Nooksack and the Stó:lō due to state/provincial differences and those between Canada and the United States. My impression is that, regarding the language revitalization program, grants in the United States require more legalistic and political hoop-jumping than do those in Canada. At least it seems that the staff involved in the actual language revitalization program for the Nooksack have had to establish tribal ordinances, work with the State Board of Education, and work with Northwest Indian College to fulfill the goals of the grant, whereas the staff of the Stó:lō Halq'eméylem revitalization program do not have to do much of this sort of thing and are thus able to spend more time working with different grade levels in local educational institutions both on- and off-reserve. It may be that these hurdles have already been cleared and/or that they were taken care of by upper-level grant writers and administrators. In any case, it is to be hoped that such stability will come to the Nooksack programs as well.

A Look to the Future

The future of Halq'eméylem and Lhéchelesem is still precarious, but there is now considerable cause for hope that Halq'eméylem will survive as a new generation of speakers continues to learn to transcribe and tell stories and to acquire vocabulary from the last first-speakers as well as from the CDs and videos of the elders. This is true on both sides of the border, but the Nooksack program is more precarious than is the Stó:lō program because stable funding is not yet guaranteed. However, the tribal council, the tribe, and the Department of Education are all supportive of the language program staff; it is hoped that this combination will lead to the continuation of stable funding. The ordinance passed in 2003 will allow the Nooksack to accredit their own language and culture teachers and to train the members of a new generation so that they can work with the remaining elders to save the language and culture. The First Peoples' Language and Culture Committee has continued to actively support the training and accreditation of Indian language and culture teachers in Washington, and several tribes have teachers who have been so accredited. The Nooksack Tribe has several teachers who need only a few more courses before they can become accredited by the tribe.

Most linguists who work on Amerindian languages currently believe that language revival is a difficult process but that it is entirely possible for most languages if the following eight conditions exist: (1) adequate tape or digital recordings of the language; (2) a linguistic and/or good pedagogical grammar and dictionary; (3) dedicated teachers and students; (4) sustained adequate funding for teachers and students; (5) sustained adequate teaching time (not one hour per week but at least one hour per day, preferably with language immersion); (6) lack of life-threatening conditions such as war or famine; (7) simultaneous cultural revival programs; and (8) the political support of the tribal government as well as state/provincial and federal governments. Over the last thirty years I have seen a number of successful programs that have the preceding eight assets, but gains can be wiped out and languages lost if efforts are not sustained and new students (especially younger ones) are not successfully acquired at least every few years. It is not clear whether a critical mass of students and teachers is required, although, unless the student is a linguist and/or fluent in a related language, it is probable that at least one teacher, elder, or linguist is required.

Amerindianists are divided as to whether language resurrection is possible, but my feeling is that an increasing number of us believe that, while it is very difficult, it is possible if conditions one through eight are met (see above). What is resurrected will be more complete if the students continue learning from documented sources and adding to their vocabulary and grammatical knowledge. And it will be more successful if there is a peer group working together to learn the language – a peer group that will stay in touch and make an effort to actively use the language and teach it to their families.

Just as good political and social relationships can positively affect linguistic and cultural revival, so linguistic and cultural revival can positively affect political and social relationships. Sometimes this results in reintroducing the language and useful cultural practices at tribal meetings and ceremonies, with regard to the tribal management of resources, and in relations with non-Indian politicians and governments. Just as language and culture provide distinctive and successful patterns of thought, so they help spark tribal and personal identities and successful coping mechanisms. The revival of spirit dancing, which started being practised in the open in the 1960s, is a good example of this (Amoss 1978). During that same period efforts at cultural and linguistic revival worked hand in hand to help thousands of Amerindian/First Nations peoples to reproduce and transform their identities in exciting and productive ways.

The future of Lhéchelesem is brighter than it has been in twenty-five years because there is now an experienced language teacher who can read, spell, and speak Lhéchelesem and who wants to begin the effort of reviving it. There are enough recorded materials to do this, and it has been done for a few of the world's languages in the twentieth century, such as Hebrew, one Australian Aboriginal language, and a number of California Indian languages. Work on the latter is being conducted at the University of California Breath of Life Workshops, one of which I attended in June 2002. I heard songs sung and speeches and short stories told in languages that had been extinct for up to 250 years. The Breath of Life Workshops, run by Dr. Leanne Hinton, team up prospective language learners with linguist mentors who show them how to gain access to old recordings on tapes and wax cylinders as well as how to read the transcriptions of their ancestral languages made by Spanish missionaries and early and modern linguists. They form networks to support each other, and, once the annual summer workshops are over, the library collections that house the materials provide graduates with various materials. Linguist mentors who graduate and move away can either return for the summer, keep in contact, or be replaced by new graduate students in linguistics. It is true that none of these efforts will result in someone attaining the fluency of the last speakers to be fully in control of most of the vocabulary of their language, but functional literacy and fluency is possible. All of us, even elders, continue learning throughout our lifetimes, and this is especially true with regard to language and culture.

References

Amoss, Pamela T. 1955-56, 1969-70. Nooksack Language Fieldnotes and Tapes. Seattle: University of Washington. Copy in Galloway's collection, Regina, Saskatchewan.
–. 1961. Nuksack Phonemics. MA thesis, University of Washington.
–. 1978. *Coast Salish Spirit Dancing: The Survival of an Ancestral Religion.* Seattle: University of Washington Press.

Boas, Franz. 1890. Fieldnotes on (Upriver) Halkomelem, Scowlitz Dialect. American Philosophical Society, Philadelphia.

Boas, Franz, and Hermann Haeberlin. 1927. Sound Shifts in Salishan Dialects. *International Journal of American Linguistics* 4: 117-36.

Burton, Strang. 2000. Introduction to Spoken Halq'eméylem. Stó:lo Shxwelí Language Program, Chilliwack, British Columbia.

Burton, Strang, and Henry Davis. 1996. Stative Aspect and Possession in Salish. *International Conference on Salish and Neighbouring Languages* (Vancouver) 31: 13-22.

Efrat, Barbara S. 1970-72, 1974. Nooksack Language Field Notes and Tapes. Copy in Galloway's collection, Regina, Saskatchewan.

Elmendorf, William W., and Wayne Suttles. 1960. Pattern and Change in Halkomelem Salish Dialects. *Anthropological Linguistics* 2 (7): 1-32.

Fetzer, Paul S. 1950-51. Nooksack Language Field Notes and Files. In Galloway's collection, Regina, Saskatchewan.

–. 1951. Nooksack Enculturation: A Preliminary Consideration. Term paper, Department of Anthropology, University of Washington, Seattle.

Galloway, Brent. 1971. Some Similarities between Semology and Phonology, with Illustrations from Chilliwack Halkomelem. Paper presented at the 6th International Conference on Salishan Languages (ICSL), 16-18 August, Victoria, British Columbia. (All ICSL papers after 1973, except late papers, are printed in a collection of working papers distributed in advance to the participants.)

–. 1973. Practical Phonetic System (PPS), Part 3. Manuscript. (Written for Casey Wells in order to give IPA equivalents and articulatory explanations for his PPS, in which all Halkomelem words from Oliver Wells' and Casey Wells' fieldwork and writings are published.)

–. 1975. Two Lessons in Time in Upriver Halkomelem. Paper presented at the 10th International Conference on Salishan Languages, 14-16 August, Ellensburg, Washington. Also found in special issue, *Lektos* 1 (1975): 56-66.

–. 1976a. The First Upper Stalo Calendar, 1976-77. Illustrations by Sonny Wilson and Vaughn Jones. Coqualeetza Education Training Centre, Sardis, BC.

–. 1976b. Lessons in Upper Stalo Halkomelem (twenty-nine lessons). Coqualeetza Education Training Centre, Sardis, BC.

–. 1977. *A Grammar of Chilliwack Halkomelem*. PhD diss., University of California. Ann Arbor, MI: University Microfilms International (#77-31364, 2 vols.).

–. 1979. Models for Training Native Language Instructors. In *Conference Report,* "Wawa Kunamokst Nesika," British Columbia Native Language Instructors Conference, 25-27 March, Richmond, BC. Victoria, BC: Office of Indian Education, Ministry of Education, Science and Technology.

–. 1980. The Structure of Upriver Halq'emeylem: A Grammatical Sketch and Classified Word List for Upriver Halq'emeylem. Coqualeetza Education Training Centre, Sardis, BC.

–. 1983. A Look at Nooksack Phonology. In *Working Papers of the 18th International Conference on Salishan Languages,* compiled by Eugene Hunn and Bill Seaburg, 80-132. Seattle: University of Washington.

–. 1985. The Original Territory of the Nooksack Language. *International Journal of American Linguistics* 51 (4): 416-18.

–. 1988a. Some Proto-Central Salish Sound Correspondences. In *In Honor of Mary Haas, from the Haas Festival Conference on Native American Linguistics,* ed. William Shipley, 293-343. Berlin: Mouton de Gruyter.

–. 1988b. The Upriver Halkomelem Language Program at Coqualeetza. *Human Organization* 47 (4): 291-97.

–. 1992. Computerized Dictionaries of Upriver Halkomelem and Nooksack and 3-D Semantics and the Halkomelem Dictionary. In *Amerindia: Revue d'Ethnolinguistique Amérindienne* 7: 47-82.

–. 1993a. Nooksack Reduplication. In *American Indian Linguistics and Ethnography in Honor of Laurence C. Thompson*. Occasional Papers in Linguistics No. 10, ed. Anthony Mattina and Timothy Montler, 93-112. Missoula: University of Montana Press.

–. 1993b. *Publications in Linguistics*. Vol. 96, *A Grammar of Upriver Halkomelem*. Berkeley: University of California Press.

–. 1996. A Look At Some Nooksack Stories. Paper presented at the 35th Conference on American Indian Languages, 95th American Anthropological Association Annual Meeting, San Francisco, California.

–. 1997. Nooksack Pronouns, Transitivity, and Control. In *Papers for the 32nd International Conference on Salish and Neighboring Languages*, compiled by Timothy Montler, 197-243. Denton: University of North Texas.

–. 2001. Language Preservation and Revival: Passing the Torch for Upriver Halkomelem. Keynote address at the 36th International Conference on Salishan and Neighbouring Languages, Chilliwack, BC.

–. 2002a. Language Preservation and Revival: Passing the Torches for Upriver Halkomelem. Paper presented at the Annual Meetings of the Society for the Study of the Indigenous Languages of the Americas, Linguistic Society of America, San Francisco.

–. 2002b. Translations into Halq'eméylem of Dialogues Designed by Marcus Goodson for the Nooksack Tribe's Halq'eméylem Lessons. Levels 1 and 2 (complete). Manuscript at Nooksack Tribe (Deming, Washington) and in Galloway's collection.

–. 2004. Dictionary of Upriver Halkomelem. Halq'eméylem-to-English and English to Halq'eméylem portions (in preparation, 1,670 pp.). Copy at Stó:lō Nation, Sardis, BC, and in Galloway's collection, Regina, Saskatchewan.

–. Forthcoming. Metaphors as Cognitive Models in Halkomelem Color Adjectives. In *The Anthropology of Color: Interdisciplinary Multilevel Modelling*, ed. Robert MacLaury, Galina Paramei, and Don Dedrick. Amsterdam: John Benjamins Publishing.

Galloway, Brent, and Allan Richardson. 1983. Nooksack Place Names: An Ethnohistorical and Linguistic Approach. In *Working Papers of the 18th International Conference on Salishan Languages*, compiled by Eugene Hunn and Bill Seaburg, 133-96. Seattle: University of Washington.

Galloway, Brent, George Adams, and Catalina Renteria. 2004a. Bringing Back the Nooksack Language from the Dead. *University of British Columbia Working Papers in Linguistics* 14: 141-48.

–. 2004b. What a Nooksack Story Can Tell Us about Morphology and Syntax. *University of British Columbia Working Papers in Linguistics* 14: 149-65.

Galloway, Brent, and Steve Wolfson. 1993. Education in Aboriginal Languages: Goals and Solutions for Canada. Discussion Paper 6, National Round Table on Education, 6-8 July, Royal Commission on Aboriginal Peoples, Ottawa.

Gardner, Ethel. 2002. Tset Hikwstexw te Sqwélteltset: We Hold Our Language High – Stó:lo Halq'eméylem Renewal. PhD diss., Simon Fraser University.

Harris, Jimmy Gene. 1960. The Phonology of Chilliwack Halkomelem. MA thesis, University of Washington, Seattle.

Hill-Tout, Charles. 1902. Ethnological Studies of the Mainland Halkōmē'lEm, a Division of the Salish of British Columbia. In *Report on the Ethnological Survey of Canada*. London: British Association for the Advancement of Science.

–. 1904. *Ethnological Report on the StsEélis and Sk·aúlits Tribes.* London: Harrison and Sons.
Kuipers, Aert. 2002. *Salish Etymological Dictionary.* Occasional Papers in Linguistics 16. Missoula: University of Montana Press.
Thompson, Laurence C. 1967, 1969, 1970. Nooksack Language Field Notes and Tapes. Originals at University of Washington Library, Seattle, WA; copy in Galloway's collection, Regina, Saskatchewan.
Thompson, M. Terry, ed. 1974. Hermann Haeberlin's Distribution of the Salish Substantival (Lexical) Suffixes. *Anthropological Linguistics* 16: 219-350.
Urbanczyk, Suzzanne. 2000a. Upriver Halq'eméylem Continuatives, Formal and Functional Arrangement (draft).
–. 2000b. Upriver Halq'eméylem Continuative Stems: A Working Paper. June 15 (draft).
Wells, Oliver, and Casey Wells. 1965. A Vocabulary of Native Words in the Halkomelem Language. Sardis, BC.
–. 1987. *The Chilliwacks and Their Neighbors: The Oliver Wells Interviews.* Ed. Ralph Maud, Brent Galloway, and Marie Weeden. Vancouver: Talonbooks.
Wiltschko, Martina. 1998a. On the Internal and External Syntax of Independent Pronouns in Halq'eméylem. *International Conference on Salishan Languages* 33: 428-47.
–. 1998b. Halq'eméylem Possessives. *International Conference on Salishan Languages* 33: 448-72.
–. 2000a. Sentential Negation in Upriver Halkomelem (and What It Tells Us about the Structure of the Clause). *University of British Columbia Working Papers in Linguistics* 3: 227-48.
–. 2000b. Is Halkomelem Split Ergative? *University of British Columbia Working Papers in Linguistics* 3: 249-68.
–. 2001. Passive in Halkomelem and Squamish Salish. *University of British Columbia Working Papers in Linguistics* 6: 319-45.

8

Stó:lō Identity and the Cultural Landscape of S'ólh Téméxw

David M. Schaepe

> Among those filing writs [seeking judicial declarations affirming
> Aboriginal rights and title] are those bands the provincial govern-
> ment has been touting as examples of how well treaty talks are going
> in its campaign to persuade voters it can bring certainty to the
> province's resource landscape ... However, when it approves logging
> of sites about which aboriginal people express concern ... it does
> more than reveal a contempt for the process, it sends a troubling
> message to those engaged in negotiations. If First Nations can't
> trust the government to act properly where a few hectares of trees
> are at issue, why should it trust it to respect the treaty process where
> the stakes are far higher – survival itself in the eyes of many aborigi-
> nal leaders? – Stephen Hume (*Vancouver Sun,* 13 December 2003)

At the heart of Aboriginal peoples' contemporary political relations with
the "colonial" government in British Columbia are issues of identity, governance, and cultural survival. The British Columbia Treaty Process, established in 1992, involves both provincial and federal levels of government
and provides a forum within which Aboriginal peoples are currently negotiating issues of land claims and self-governance. Within this process
Aboriginal peoples in British Columbia are working to situate themselves
and their respective identities within the political, judicial, and resource
landscapes currently dominated by colonial authorities.

Canada's federal 1969 "White Paper" provides a starting point for this
discussion. A detailed review of the political and geographic history of
Aboriginal relations in Canada and British Columbia is beyond the scope
of this chapter and can be found in the works of scholars such as Paul
Tennant (1990) and Cole Harris (1997, 2002). I present, rather, a general
overview of reactions associated with the release of the White Paper, with a

focus on the Aboriginal population of the Fraser Valley area. The tabling of Canada's White Paper in 1969 – proposing the elimination of "Indian" status – prompted a nationwide resurgence in Aboriginal peoples' activity in defining and asserting themselves at broader levels of collective identity and governance. This is exemplified by the subsequent formation of the Union of BC Indian Chiefs and the National Indian Brotherhood, precursor of the Assembly of First Nations (Pennier 2002, 8). This attempt by the Canadian government to dissolve the federal Indian Act was viewed by Aboriginal communities as an attempt to dissolve their identities and to reconstitute them as part of a community unified and integrated into the Canadian national fabric and governance system. Aboriginal objection to the White Paper was overwhelming throughout Canada.

In British Columbia, as a political and geographic landscape largely without treaties, Aboriginal peoples loudly objected to the prospect of being unilaterally integrated into the broader Canadian society, a proposed act that threatened the survival of Aboriginal identity at a root level. Losing "Indian" status under federal law without gaining provisions for self-governance equalled losing recognition and forced enfranchisement. Objection to this prospect continues today in the assertion of Aboriginal self-governance – the effort by Aboriginal peoples to replace the constraints of the Indian Act and its associated colonial paternalism while maintaining their unique identities.

The ensuing and enduring process of Aboriginal assertions of self-governance within Canada and British Columbia is witnessed historically by the use of anthropological terms referencing expanding expressions of collective identity. Under the Indian Act, the colonial government situated Aboriginal people within the context of Indian "bands" on Indian "reserves" as the most basic, and smallest, unit of collective community structure and geography. Since 1969, Aboriginal communities in British Columbia, and more broadly, have begun identifying and reformulating themselves using anthropological terms signifying larger frames of political reference, such as "tribes" and "nations." For example, in 1975, the self-proclaimed "Stó:lō Tribes" of the lower Fraser watershed drafted and adopted the *Stó:lō Declaration* – a ringing statement of Aboriginal title and rights to all land and resources within their collective tribal territories (Pennier 2002, 2). In 1993, under the collective cultural banner "Stó:lō," a nation was formed that united nineteen Indian Act bands associated with numerous tribes of the Fraser Valley. The Stó:lō Nation – constituting an Aboriginal government and service delivery provider – formed in part for the purpose of engaging the BC Treaty Process, and by 2004 it had become one of the largest Aboriginal organizations in Canada. This shift from "band" to "tribal" to "national" political formation broke the restrictive mould of Indian Act–determined Aboriginal identity and constituted a decisive move toward self-determination and governance.

Coincident with this "outbreak" in Aboriginal identity building was an "outbreak" in the Aboriginal assertion of political and legal jurisdictions over land and resources beyond the imposed geographic constraints of Indian Act reserves. Aboriginal tribes and nations began more forcefully expressing and asserting traditional rights and title to "territories" stretching beyond reserve boundaries. Territorial boundaries evolved as transitions between band-, tribe-, and nation-based forms of identity were negotiated. People and place were obviously linked in this struggle for recognition. Yet, in this pushing "outward," tensions developed internally within many newly formed Aboriginal tribes and nations – entities asserting self-governance while simultaneously subject to the band-level governance and organizational structure of the federal Indian Act. Tensions developed in the relationships between the identities of Aboriginal individuals, communities, and organizations as clearly bounded and narrowly defined by the "closed" system of the federal Indian Act, on one hand, and those identities currently negotiated and formulated within the comparatively vast and volatile "open" arena of Aboriginal rights and title, on the other.

Recent history has witnessed tensions increase as expressions of Aboriginal identities and lands increase in scale – not only externally in relation to colonial authorities but also, at times, within and between Aboriginal organizations and communities. Tensions associated with identity building and asserting self-governance both arise from and generate questions concerning the nature of "traditional" Aboriginal identities, intercommunity relations, relations with land and resources, and governance structures. How was governance traditionally structured and at what level(s) did it exist? How were land and resources controlled and accessed in the past? How did communities interact with one another – politically, economically, or otherwise? What forms of authorities existed within and between communities? What does "traditional" mean as a reference point for culture, and can it be validly applied as a factor in assessing cultural legitimacy? How was identity formed and maintained, and at what level(s) of inclusion or exclusion? Such questions, while generated within the contemporary context of Aboriginal assertions of self-government, rights, and title, have a ring of historical familiarity within the field of anthropology.

While anthropologists have addressed questions of identity and social structure for decades, Aboriginal communities are only more recently attempting to address such questions through their own means, within their own frames of reference, based on their own needs, and for their own ends (as deemed relevant by and for themselves). This is not so say or to imply that such questions, if addressed through Aboriginal research, are in any way segregated from the realm of anthropological research. On the contrary, as a non-Native archaeologist-anthropologist employed by an Aboriginal organization (the Stó:lō Nation) actively researching such questions, I do not recognize a divide but, rather, a continuum between "anthropological" and "Aboriginal" research. As an extension of the field, the acquisition of an anthropological "tool-kit" and the increasing participation and practise of anthropology by Aboriginal peoples and organizations, represents a fundamental shift in the foundation of anthropological practice – from being a subject "other" to a subject "self." I suggest that the paradigm shift(s) potentially attainable in an anthropology situated within Aboriginal practice and perspectives is comparable in degree to the shift in expressions of self-governance and self-determination witnessed in the breakout from colonial paternalism experienced within the realm of Aboriginal land claims, rights, and title.

I focus this discussion of Aboriginal self-determination and identity building on the Halkomelem-speaking, Central Coast Salish people of the lower Fraser River watershed in southwestern British Columbia – the Stó:lō ("People of the River"). The Stó:lō Nation is comprised of a subset of people who mostly speak Halq'eméylem, a language family dialect associated with the upriver portion of the lower Fraser River watershed. As defined for the BC Treaty Process, the Stó:lō Nation asserts a traditional territory equivalent to the lower Fraser River watershed, stretching along the Fraser River from the Gulf of Georgia to the lower Fraser Canyon. I situate this discussion within a historical review of anthropological perspectives on Aboriginal identities among the Coast Salish of the Puget Sound and Gulf of Georgia regions. I emphasize anthropological linkages between landscape and identity as a common ground upon which to locate the following case study. The Stó:lō Nation case study exemplifies one instance by which the Stó:lō have, in part, undertaken anthropological research with the intent of occupying the field of heritage resource management within their territory. This case exemplifies one way in which the Stó:lō Nation has expressed Stó:lō cultural identity at a "national" level of collective identity through the mapping of a Stó:lō cultural landscape.

This self-generated view of Stó:lō identity as embedded in a cultural landscape derives from the Stó:lō Nation's heritage policy and heritage management plan. The timing, motivation, and purpose of the Stó:lō Nation's development of its heritage policy and management plan articulate with a historical process of Coast Salish peoples' assertion of Aboriginal rights and title. This contemporary effort in self-definition and determination counterposes an enduring period of significant cultural disruption and loss, resulting from contact with smallpox in the 1780s (Harris 1997) and continuing today in political-economic relations with figures of colonial authority.

Anthropological Perspectives on Landscape and Coast Salish Identity (circa 1880-1980): Culture History and Culture Ecology

Coast Salish peoples of the Puget Sound and Gulf of Georgia regions of the southern Northwest Coast (Suttles 1990b, 10) have been historically subject to ethnographic description, definition, and analysis as a cultural "other." This is not a particularly noteworthy statement, though it is important with regard to setting an anthropological backdrop to the topic of this chapter – the emergence of a local, emic, anthropological perspective within which Aboriginal people define their identity as cultural "selves" in contrast to being portrayed as cultural "others." My brief historical review focuses on the relationship between the landscape and the definition of Aboriginal identity as a cultural other in a number of major anthropological works pertaining to the Coast Salish. This review recognizes the nature of historical change in anthropological theory and practice as commonplace and is not meant as a deconstruction of my predecessors, whose significant work shaped the field as it exists today. Rather, this review provides a comparative background against which to project the following "Stó:lō cultural landscape" case study.

A historical review of ethnographic work among the Coast Salish (Suttles and Jonaitis 1990), while demonstrating changing disciplinary paradigms and practices throughout the twentieth century, reveals a persistent focus on issues of Aboriginal identity and links to landscape. Landscape, while perhaps not often explicitly stated as such, plays a significant role in many of the anthropological discussions, debates, and angles of analysis carried on over the decades since Franz Boas entrenched the discipline in the region in the late nineteenth century.

Boas first began working among the Stó:lō of the Fraser Valley in the late 1800s, bringing with him a strong interest in the relationship between culture and nature (e.g., 1887, 1894, 1895). As discussed by Thomas Thornton (1997, 209-11), Boas combined notably humanist and geographic perspectives in his collection and study of Aboriginal place names and narratives. Of these areas of research, Thornton states, "Place names are a particularly interesting aspect of culture because they intersect three fundamental domains of cultural analysis: language, thought, and the environment ... Place names tell us something not only about the structure and content of the physical environment itself but also how people perceive, conceptualize, classify, and utilize that environment" (209). Though his stay in this region of the Northwest Coast was relatively brief, a number of Boas' students took up longer-term interests with the Coast Salish. His students, however, carried with them a different perspective with respect to the question of nature-culture relations. Boas' emphasis on cognition and perception (i.e., topology over topography), while maintained elsewhere in the works of Sapir and others, appears to have been largely lost in the approach to landscape applied by the early practitioners of Coast Salish anthropology. Truly Boasian humanist anthropology was not to resurface in the Coast Salish area for another three-quarters of a century.

Anthropologists including Charles Hill-Tout (1903), Marian Smith (1940), Erna Gunther (1973), Robert Elmendorf (1971, 1993), and Wayne Suttles (1960, 1964, 1968a, 1968b, 1984, 1990a) maintained Boas' interest in the relation between the land, resources, and Coast Salish cultures, though from a radically different perspective that neatly separated physical geography and human perception – topography over topology, space over place (Ortiz 1969; Basso 1996; Zedeno 2000; Bender 2002). Understandings of landscape in the works of these prominent anthropologists generally represent strong "culture historical" and "culture ecological" positions. The paradigm underlying the works of these researchers situates people and culture within a frame of reference largely determined by the environment and associated landscape of *material* resources. Attention among the proponents of the ecology-dominated landscape of nature-culture relations focused on the ways in which the "natural"/physical attributes of the landscape acted as the most significant factors affecting human socio-economic structure and cultural development (e.g., Suttles 1984). Physical geography, particularly the notion of the "watershed," was central to this perspective. I focus this discussion on the exemplary and influential works of Marian Smith and Wayne Suttles, which clearly demonstrate this perspective.

Marian Smith (1940) epitomizes the development and use of a topographic watershed/drainage model in describing the Puyallup and Nisqually of the southern Puget Sound. In the first chapter, entitled "The People: Their Contact and Organization," she describes the topographic and environmental characteristics of the area as "one great watershed" (1). Of the relationship between the local geography and people, she states,

In such a country the rivers not only furnished the all-important salmon but also formed the continuous lanes of communication ... The Indians of this region were supremely conscious of the nature of the country in which they lived. They were completely aware of its character as a great water shed. From the geographical concept of the drainage system they derived their major concept of social unity.

> Thus, peoples living near a single drainage system were considered to be knit to-
> gether by that fact if by no other ... Lacking the paraphernalia of political organiza-
> tion, the tie which they recognized as most binding, as most closely paralleling
> what we know as political allegiance, was based upon this geography of the drain-
> age system. (2-4)

Within each primary drainage system were situated what Smith refers to as
"(2) its smaller component the *village drainage;* (3) the *village,* which may
include this latter small drainage ... ; (4) the *village site* ... (5) *village group*
... (6) *house group* ... and (7) *family group*" (Smith 1940, 7). Per Smith's
understanding, as indicative of her frame of reference, the complete social
structure, political organization, and identity of the southern Coast Salish
were mapped out in reference to the physical, topographic landscape on
which they lived and within which they were apparently confined as cultural isolates – inmates of the land. In a contemporary light, one might
describe the Coast Salish relationship with their environment, as envisioned
by Smith, as equivalent to living within a colonial landscape, a closed system – one that constrains movement, economy, identity, and all aspects of
cultural life to the smallest level possible within imposed and unyielding
boundaries.

The mid-twentieth-century works of anthropologist Wayne Suttles may
be more literally defined as culture-ecological than the work of his predecessors, including Smith. His interests are a great deal more process-
oriented, while yet maintaining some flavour of Smith's culture-historical
objective of reconstructing traditional Aboriginal culture prior to colonial
contact. A significant shift seen in Suttles' work involves the opening of
watershed/drainage models to interaction models and social networks while
yet maintaining them as "Models of *Historic* Social Systems" (Suttles 1987,
1, emphasis added). The social processes recognized and described by Suttles
particularly (but see also Elmendorf 1971) significantly altered and advanced the anthropological understanding of the Coast Salish. However,
social processes, while recognized as important, were viewed as being active only within environmentally set parameters and constraints – such as
those dictated by measures of relative resource abundance along the Northwest Coast. This approach is consistent with culture-ecological and
energetics principles advanced by Julian Steward (1955) and Leslie White
(1943). People and social processes are described in relation, again, to the
resource landscape and are defined in relation to resources such as fish,
plants, and animals and their areal distribution, level of abundance, seasonal availability, degree of access, and applicable extractive and preserva-
tive technologies.

The titles of many of Suttles' works, presented here due to their eloquence and precision, reveal this frame of reference – "Affinal Ties, Subsistence, and Prestige among the Coast Salish" (1960), "Variation in Habitat and Culture on the Northwest Coast" (1968a), "Coping with Abundance: Subsistence on the Northwest Coast" (1968b), "Productivity and Its Constraints – A Coast Salish Case" (1984). Statements such as the one that follows speak to the emphasis during this period on a landscape of material resources: "If spatial and temporal variation in resources gets any consideration, it is in relation to technology and seasonal movement. The extent of these variations and their implications for social organization however, are rarely considered. It is my position that the social organization and ceremonialism of the Coast Salish ... is intelligible only in light of these variations" (Suttles 1987, 36). The resource landscape thus maintains its central role as a factor that exerts great influence on, while remaining cognitively apart from, culture. Aboriginal identity is, again, understood as a passive derivative of the resource landscape that shapes human economy, society, and cultural expression.

This brief review provides a few examples of how environmentally based socio-economic models of interaction, expressed as either closed watershed-based systems or intercommunity social networks (Suttles 1960, 1968a, 1968b), emphasized the importance of landscape from an ecological view that was essentially devoid of cultural conception or ideation. Underlying this position is the assumption of a common and universally neutral set of variables within resource landscape measurable in a universal and neutral language of geomorphology or biology. I use "neutral" to mean unbiased or uninfluenced by variable forms of cognition.

A sockeye salmon, a western red cedar, or a viewscape of Cascadian mountain peaks are similarly understood from this anthropological perspective as "a-cultural" material resources and physical geography, for Coast Salish and non–Coast Salish alike. These elements of the landscape are thus treated as constants that exhibit local variation in composition. As constants, though, the elements of the resource landscape, while factoring into a great deal of variation between Northwest Coast Aboriginal cultures, *cannot be directly tied to identity.* Differences in cultural identity are not due to differing understandings of the elements of the landscape but, rather, to (1) the way in which those elements happen to be physically assembled in any particular place, (2) the type of technology available to extract the set of available resources, and (3) the economic process by which resources are extracted, produced, distributed, consumed, and reproduced. Identity arises out of these three primary forms of interaction between people and the environment as associated with technological and economic interaction.

Technological and economic forms of interaction are founded upon, yet are conceptually and cognitively separate from, the landscape. This anthropological framework dominated the depiction of Coast Salish cultures and identities throughout the first three-quarters of the twentieth century.

Anthropological Perspectives on Landscape and Coast Salish Identity (circa 1980-2000): Postmodernism and Political Economy

Coast Salish anthropology experienced a paradigmatic shift in the 1980s, when it moved back toward Boasian humanism. Anthropologists working in this area continued to regard landscape as a significant factor affecting Coast Salish culture and identity, although in a way vastly different from the culture-historical or culture-ecological perspectives described above. This emerging perspective recognized cultural ideation, meaning, and power within the landscape. The essence of this paradigm shift is the assumption that the relationship between nature and culture is not simply hierarchical (based on a resource landscape) but, rather, is characterized by an interpenetration that links and fuses elements of nature and culture: the landscape and people. "Topography" is not replaced by "topology" but, rather, is contextualized within a topological frame of reference. In this frame of reference, nature and culture are no longer easily separable; they no longer relate as strata in a techno-economic/techno-environmentally stacked formation of basal, structural, and superstructural components.

Crisca Bierwert (1986) established a central support in the development of this alternative anthropological perspective of Coast Salish landscape with her semiotic analysis of Stó:lō culture. Following on Sally Snyder's (1964) earlier groundbreaking work *Skagit Society and Its Existential Basis: An Ethnofolkloristic Reconstruction* and, I suspect, influenced by structuralism and works of Lévi-Strauss such as *The Savage Mind* (1966) that hit the anthropological community in the 1960s, Bierwert boldly moved this discussion beyond the realm of resources and situated meaning within the landscape. Strikingly, a multiplicity of meanings rather than any singular meaning is attained in the negotiation of cultural space, time, power, and cognition relative to place. As simply articulated, "Salish people see power as being within a place, not inscribed upon it" (Bierwert 1999, 39). This is an important statement and is particularly relevant to my following discussion of the use of the preposition "of" instead of "in" or "on" in describing Stó:lō relations with landscape. Bierwert brings the discussion of place and landscape into the realm of ideation, worldview, and political economy. Subsequent works on the Coast Salish by Daniel Boxberger (1989), Alexandra Harmon (1998), Jay Miller (1999), Bruce Miller (1998, 2001,

2003), and Keith Thor Carlson (2001, 2003) all recognize the importance of place and resources in the formation of indigenous identity(ies) relative to social organization embedded in religious pretence and practice, the negotiation of traditional systems of law, and the historical formation of collective identity, respectively. The resurgence of interest in place names was also expressed farther afield – in both indigenous and academic communities – in influential pieces by Keith Basso (1996) and Thomas Thornton (1997).

Bruce Miller, like Bierwert, situates landscape within a political-economic framework – within "the play of power in present-day [Coast Salish] communities" (2001, 35). He articulates and positions landscape – of ideas, culture, and the sacred – within an understanding of tradition removed from "now-dated debates concerning whether tradition is best regarded as imagined, constructed, invented, or transmitted intact from the past" (ibid.). While recognizing cultural continuity and links to the past, the discussion of nature-culture relations relocates itself within a contemporary context that focuses on contemporary issues and cultural processes:

> [Regarding the] use of the term "tradition," [Mauzé defines] "a metaphor for identity ... [that] encompasses and illustrates a past, a present and a future. It is not only the memory of the past frozen in time that re-emerges; it is also a reference necessary for elaborating a version of the contemporary world, which is the 'space' where traditional and modern social life occur side by side. *Tradition is primarily a political instrument for regulating both internal and external relations.*" (Mauzé quoted in Miller 2001, 35, emphasis Miller's)

Rejecting the modern Coast Salish world as postcolonial, Miller (2001, 42-43) asserts that the contemporary Coast Salish, within a common context of political and economic inequality, are defining for themselves identities as part of their common attempt to assert both internal and external "meaning" and "control" in their "relations with the state." Miller links this effort to a process of "internal dialogue and dispute within the larger Coast Salish society" reacting to a nation-state that is perceived, in part, as emphasizing "membership within geographical boundaries, rather than landscapes of meaning" (44).

Within a political-economy context, I borrow a term from Sally Snyder in suggesting that landscape – discussed from here on as "cultural landscape" – forms a significant "fissure point" (Snyder 1964) between Coast Salish society and the dominant colonial government. Snyder uses this term to describe points of conflict within Skagit society that arise from sets of relations that are approached from differing positions, sets of values, and perspectives. Fissures differ from ordinary points of conflict, which are common to all societies, in that existing process(es) are inadequate for effectively achieving conflict resolution. For example, in the relationship between people who are members of the same household yet of differing social classes, conflict might arise with regard to the allotment of goods from a potlatch or the positioning of families within a longhouse. Each party validates its position in the relationship with its own set of values and principles, yet schisms remain due to the inadequacy of available conflict resolution processes to bridge the divide between values, social standing, gender, or degree of power. Unresolved disconnects remain as points of contention and conflict within a field of societal fissure points. Such fissures maintain the potential to trigger significant socio-political disruption, powered by lingering conflicts extending to the core of cultural identity, albeit at varying scales of impact (e.g., household, extended family, tribal, or supratribal). I suggest that there are two basic options with regard to resolving fissures: (1) the creation of new means of mitigating conflicts and (2) the decay and collapse of one (or perhaps both) of the entities involved in the conflict. Both options are evolutionary in the sense that they involve instigating change that will affect societal health. And both have the power to reform social identity.

As I recast it, landscape manifests itself as a theatre of potential fissure points in the interplay between Aboriginal and colonial political-economic actors and relations. As this relationship progresses within forums dedicated to land claims and Aboriginal rights and title, and as Aboriginal identities reconstitute themselves to include territories and jurisdictions beyond those bounded by federal reserves, fissure points arise on the contested landscape. And they arise within this relationship not simply due to conflicts over resource use, allocation, and jurisdiction but also due to a basic divergence between two types of value systems, principles, and meanings attributed to the landscape. This sentiment is nicely articulated within a recent case study of the Upper Skagit Tribe's legal battle with Skagit County (Washington) over the proposed quarrying of a Lushootseed sacred site: "the court must accept premises which are neither shared by the judges' own cultures or the legal sub-culture and thereby stand outside of their values and experiences. US and Canadian judges and judicial bodies face the dilemma of 'reckoning culture,' or assigning values to conflicting representations about a site" (Miller 1999, 83). The Upper Skagit lost their case and their sacred site to the cultural reckoning of resource extraction and economic expansion. In losing this site, the Upper Skagit lost an irreplaceable piece of their culture and, ultimately, themselves.

Fissure points in the landscape link directly to issues of identity and, returning to Stephen Hume's (2003) words, "survival itself in the eyes of many aboriginal leaders." Cast in the light of Snyder's notion of fissure points, the concept of landscape provides an outlet for locating points of conflict, identifying fundamental cultural differences, and defining the need for conflict resolution in Aboriginal-colonial relations. Landscape also provides the same outlet for defining fissure points within the constituency of Aboriginal organizations along national, tribal, band, and/or family levels of identity and authority.

One additional point relates to this discussion. The paradigmatic shift experienced over the last quarter century in the anthropological understanding of Coast Salish identity and cultural landscape is being shadowed by a shift in the traditional relationship between anthropologists and Aboriginal people, the latter having once been categorically distanced as "subject others" (Adams 1981, 384). The case study I present below provides an example of one Aboriginal organization's self-identification through directed anthropological research (in the area of heritage resource management) and the assertion of Aboriginal rights and title.

Case Study Preface: The Relationship between Aboriginal Resource Management Practices, Justice Systems, and Identity

Before launching into my case study of the Stó:lō Nation, I should explain the relationship between Aboriginal resource management practices, justice and dispute resolution systems, and identity. Bruce Miller (2001) identifies ties between these three topics in his discussion of three contemporary Coast Salish justice systems. Per Miller's description, the Upper Skagit justice program emerges as a soundly structured and highly functional system. Notably, the Upper Skagit justice system emerged in response to their acquisition of jurisdiction over a portion of the salmon fishery as a result of the 1976 *Boldt* decision.

Regarding the relationship between Aboriginal resource management practices and justice systems, I suggest that the *Boldt* decision brought to the Upper Skagit a clearly defined need to develop fisheries policy and management plans that were rooted in the acquisition of jurisdiction over fisheries resources. I also suggest that the sudden acquisition of this legal authority brought with it the need for regulatory policing and dispute resolution processes, in addition to fisheries research and a resource management framework, within a working justice system. Disputes arising within the defined frame of reference of the Upper Skagit's salmon fishery would be relatively neatly identifiable as systemic fissure points – points of conflict between fishers and resource managers. Conflict resolution mechanisms could be developed within the legal system as fissures arose and cases needed to be addressed. Conflicts arising out of the occupation of the fisheries management field, I propose, provided a practical theatre for the creation of a comprehensive Upper Skagit justice system. This proposal is supported in statements made by at least one Upper Skagit tribal administrator (Miller 2001, 4).

The justice systems established by the Upper Skagit both built upon and defined elements of their cultural identity with respect to fisheries resources. The policies, protocols, and judicial process developed by the Upper Skagit served to separate them from the external influence of the American federal government while also defining the internal relationship between Upper Skagit individuals in terms of entitlements, roles, and responsibilities. In essence, the definition of Upper Skagit identity derives, in part, from the definition of their relationship to salmon, according to their system of beliefs, values, and jurisdiction. These observations describe a Coast Salish organization assuming, within a post-treaty context, legal jurisdiction over a set of resources. The parallel case that I present involves an Aboriginal organization – the Stó:lō Nation – asserting Aboriginal rights and title within a pre-treaty political-economic environment dominated by colonial authority.

The Stó:lō Nation Case: The Stó:lō Heritage Policy and Heritage Resource Management Plan as Assertions of Stó:lō Identity

At its zenith in 2004, the Stó:lō Nation was comprised of nineteen bands of numerous tribal affiliations, forged of many interconnected families (McHalsie 2001a, 32-33) sharing a common culture and connectedness to the Fraser River as "Stó:lō" – People of the River (McHalsie 2001b, 2001c; Schaepe 2001). Population estimates range between six thousand and eight thousand registered members of Stó:lō bands. The Stó:lō Nation asserts a traditional territory (what the Stó:lō call *S'ólh Téméxw* – "Our World") of approximately 1.2 million hectares in the lower Fraser River watershed in southwestern British Columbia (Map 8.1), portions of which are shared with surrounding Coast and Interior Salish First Nations. Stó:lō territory occupies a unique position relative to that of most other First Nations in British Columbia in that it includes Vancouver, the province's major urban centre, and a proximity to the rapid urbanization that is taking place throughout the Lower Mainland and the Fraser Valley. The pace and extent of urbanization experienced by the Stó:lō is a significant cause of concern regarding, among other things, the preservation of Stó:lō heritage sites

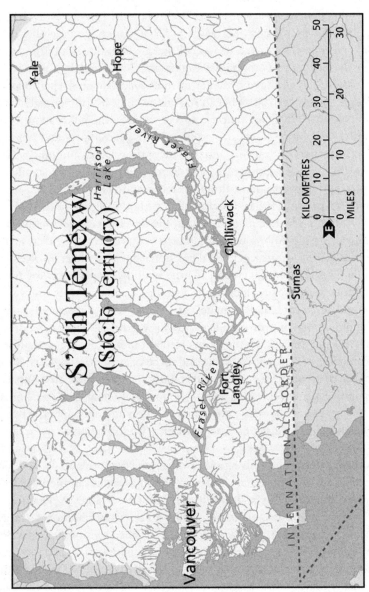

MAP 8.1 S'ólh Téméxw. Stó:lō traditional territory. *Based on a map by Jan Perrier*

and resources. In relation to resource management, the effort of defining Stó:lō heritage sites is not a new one. Stó:lō Nation staff have engaged in this endeavour at various times over the last decade, having produced the nation's first heritage policy in 1995 (Stó:lō Nation 1995; see Mohs 1994).

In 1999, Albert "Sonny" McHalsie (a Stó:lō community member from the Shxw'ōwhámél First Nation and cultural advisor/director of the Stó:lō Nation Department of Aboriginal Rights and Title) and I (a non-Stó:lō archaeologist and resource manager in the Stó:lō Nation Department of Aboriginal Rights and Title) began reworking the existing heritage policy (Stó:lō Nation 1995). Our objectives were to make the policy more comprehensive and more practical in application by developers and heritage resource managers both within and outside of the Stó:lō communities. The need to do this was motivated by five factors: (1) increasingly significant threats to and impacts upon cultural practices and heritage sites as a result of rapidly expanding urban development within S'ólh Téméxw; (2) the Stó:lō Nation's growing involvement in the development referral process through increasing Aboriginal consultation requirements (handled in the Rights and Title Department); (3) the nation's growing direct involvement in heritage resource management; (4) the nation's preparations for treaty negotiations with the provincial and federal governments over issues such as "language, culture, and heritage" as well as "land-use planning"; and (5) the limitations of provincial legislation (i.e., the BC Heritage Conservation Act) and the lack of federal involvement in recognizing, and affording protection to, heritage sites (beyond those of an archaeological nature) in the face of urban development and resource-extraction-related impacts. Comparatively, archaeological sites – the material remains of past human activity – represent the only point of connection and agreement between provincial/federal legislation and what the Stó:lō recognize as heritage sites.

Recent incidences of destruction or disturbance of provincially and federally unrecognized sites that the Stó:lō regard as significant heritage sites (e.g., the disturbance of a landscape feature known as Mómet'es [Pemberton 1999]), let alone the loss of places in which to carry out traditional cultural practices (Schaepe et al. 2004), punctuated the need to more fully develop and more forcefully assert the Stó:lō position on heritage identification and protection. An integral aspect of revising the heritage policy involved defining the typology of the heritage sites recognized by the Stó:lō. The basis for defining Stó:lō heritage site types derived largely from extensive interviews and discussions, conducted by McHalsie and Schaepe betwçen 1999 and 2003, with Stó:lō elders involved in the nation's Halq'eméylem Language Program and the House of Elders. The practical experience gained through "occupying the field" of heritage resource management under the ad hoc implementation of a developmental set of policies provided insight into addressing problems experienced in the field.

Adopted by the Stó:lō Nation House of Chiefs in March 2003, then representing seventeen bands, the Stó:lō Heritage Policy Manual (Stó:lō Nation 2003a, 10-12) recognizes and defines a wide range of heritage sites within S'ólh Téméxw, as partially summarized below:

- *Sxwóxwiyám* sites: Sites, objects, and/or features (material and non-material) of that period of the distant past "when the world was out of balance" accounting for Stó:lō origins, including:
  - *Iyoqthet* (transformation) sites: Features of the landscape created by the "Transformers" *Xexá:ls,* or any other agent(s) of the "Creator" Chichelh Siya:m
- *Xá:Xa* sites: Powerful and spiritually potent "taboo" places of the land-scape (both material and non-material in nature), including:
  - Questing places: Places where people, particularly *shxwlá:m* (Indian doctors), go in quest of interacting with the spiritual or *Xá:xa* realm(s) and acquiring spiritual power
  - *Stl'áleqem* sites: Places in the landscape associated with the location ("habitat") of spiritually potent beings known as *"stl'áleqem"*
  - Spirited places: Places in the landscape inhabited by spiritually potent beings other than *stl'áleqem* (such as *s'ó:lmexw* – "water babies"; *mimestíyexw* – "Little People")
  - *Sxwó:xwey* sites: Places in the landscape associated with origin(s) of the *Sxwó:xwey* mask, regalia, song, dance, and ceremonial
- Ceremonial regalia sites: Sites on the landscape where ceremonial regalia is or was stored or put away, and which may be spiritually potent.
- Material culture objects and sites: The material remains of past human activity (i.e., archaeological sites)
- Traditional activities and/or sites: Activities carried out in the past or present, the nature of which are regarded as Stó:lō and which have been transmitted from generation to generation; as well as those places in the landscape where Stó:lō cultural activities are or were carried out ...
- Halq'eméylem place names: Places in the landscape with recognized Halq'eméylem place names.

A more complete definition of these sites exceeds the space limitations of this chapter. Other sections of the policy manual recognizing and treating such things as language and intellectual properties are not included in this discussion.

The first Stó:lō Heritage Policy (Stó:lō Nation 1995) presented a motherhood statement stipulating protection of recognized Stó:lō heritage sites through "respectful treatment." Revising the policy required first fully defining and reclassifying these sites, then determining what "respectful treatment" meant from a Stó:lō perspective. McHalsie and I undertook the process of codifying Stó:lō cultural teachings, practices, and perspectives in order to provide principles that would function as a foundation for Stó:lō policy and law. In brief, we looked to Stó:lō elders, cultural practitioners, and community members from numerous Stó:lō bands, including some of those that were not members of the Stó:lō Nation's governmental organization. Again, we derived input from "dialogue sessions" conducted with the members of the Stó:lō Nation House of Elders, some of whom were fluent Halq'eméylem speakers. We compiled anecdotal accounts of Stó:lō community members' interactions with various heritage sites and objects (e.g., ceremonial regalia and human remains) (see McKay 2000). From these accounts and dialogues, we noted actions and recorded statements that became principles for what, in general, constitutes "respect." Some examples include "Don't ruin/waste/destroy everything; just take what you need," "know your history," "remember the future generations," and "take care of everything our great grandparents taught/showed us" (Stó:lō Nation 2003a, 5-7). By merging "action" and "philosophy," we derived policy statements that linked overarching principles with specific elements of heritage management. In refining this process, we developed specific guidelines and were able to recommend management measures for the "respectful treatment" of Stó:lō heritage within S'ólh Téméxw on a site-type-by-site-type basis (Stó:lō Nation 2003a, 14).

Coupled with this framework of definitions, principles, policy statements, and management measures was an inventory of sites and places recognized within the policy manual. A manifestation of the heritage policy – depicted as a cultural landscape – derives from the projection of inventoried Stó:lō heritage sites on the land base of S'ólh Téméxw. Applying geographic information system (GIS) mapping technology, Stó:lō heritage site inventories accumulated as type-specific databases that can be plotted in space and mapped as individual or composite images. The latest development in the assertion of a Stó:lō heritage management paradigm, then, is the Stó:lō Nation's creation of the Stó:lō Heritage Resource Management Plan (Stó:lō Nation 2003b), which is based on the amalgamation of the policy with the mapped representation of Stó:lo⁻ heritage sites and places constituting their cultural landscape. Mapping the Stó:lō cultural landscape, implicit in the heritage policy, is thus explicitly actualized in the management plan presented, in part, in Map 8.2. This formulation and expression of Stó:lō

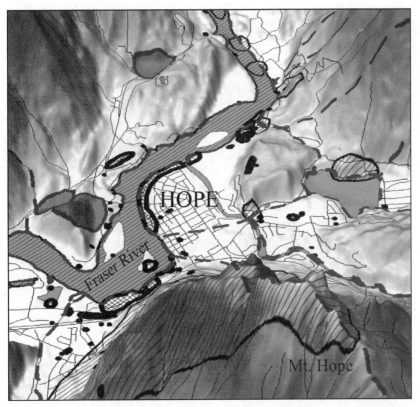

MAP 8.2 Hope area detail of Stó:lō Nation's Stó:lō Heritage Resource Management Plan (2003) – a GIS-based rendering of the Stó:lō cultural landscape depicting locations of Transformer sites, archaeological sites, *stl'áleqem* sites, trails, and place names. *Based on a map by Leanna Rhodes*

identity is unique to the "rights and title" climate currently affecting this community. Using the management plan in relation to development proposals (such as logging plans) permits the identification, not only conceptually but actually, of areas of discord – that is, fissure points – between Stó:lō cultural values, provincial and federal management requirements, and third-party land-use practices. Projecting the plan as a GIS overlay upon any compatible GIS development plans permits the crystallization in space of fissure points resulting from the assertion of competing cultural landscapes and land-use practices (i.e., the "province's resource landscape" [Hume 2003]).

The provincial resource landscape is fundamentally different from the Stó:lō cultural landscape with regard to its connection to "nature" and the environment. Unlike in the Stó:lō perspective voiced by Bierwert (1999,

PHOTO 8.1 Chief Dalton Silver of Sumas First Nation at Lightning Rock (at left), a cultural landscape feature threatened by a contested road construction project on Sumas Mountain, Abbotsford, 2005

PHOTO 8.2 A logging operation in the Chilliwack River Valley, with Slesse Peak ("the Fang") in the background, 2005

39), "power" in the province's perspective is situated in the transformation of resources into wealth within the commercial marketplace rather than located in places of the landscape itself. The Stó:lō fundamentally maintain that not only are all "natural" things alive and animated by a life force *(shxwelí)* but also that, in many cases, they are *ancestral;* that is, they are linked to the contemporary community through the transformative acts of Xexá:ls, the Transformers (see McHalsie, Schaepe, and Carlson 2001). "We drink the water; it's alive. We breathe the air; it's alive too" (Orchard 1983, 5). As noted in the definitions of Xá:Xa sites, power resides in the landscape "and their perception of its (Nature's) laws is to endow every object and agency in their environment with conscious power and being" (Hill-Tout 1903, 10). As Bierwert makes abundantly clear, the value of such power and the meaning(s) of such places, perhaps lodged in a red cedar or a mineral outcrop, cannot be compared with or reduced to the single frame of reference that supports the sale of commodities in a market economy.

It is common knowledge among many cultural practitioners within the Stó:lō community that resources and people are inextricably intermixed and interrelated within the cultural landscape of S'ólh Téméxw, so much so as to be integral to the maintenance of core elements of Stó:lō cultural practices, identity, health, and well-being (Schaepe et al. 2004). Though hardly sufficient to connote the strength of this bond, it is the connective preposition "of" – as found in the translation of the term "Stó:lō" – rather than "in" or "on" that best describes this form of the nature-culture relation. This form of interconnectedness supports the portrayal of the Stó:lō as a *religio-political-economic* society (see Schaepe 2002), "religio" being used in the sense of its literal meaning as the root of the word "religion" – to "link back to" one's ancestors, here found in the resources and surrounding landscape. Stó:lō worldview and cultural practice, including the negotiation of power, are inextricably linked to a timeless spiritual-cultural landscape affecting and "in"-fecting all action, philosophy, tradition, economy, politics, identity, and engagement of contemporary struggles for recognition and self-governance.

I suggest that, in contrast to the Stó:lō position, the colonial government's relation with the land and resources is best characterized as a government *on* the land. The main difference between the colonial and Stó:lō landscape paradigms is what Boas alluded to long ago, Smith overlooked, Bierwert and her postmodern counterparts pronounce, and Aboriginal scholars like Albert McHalsie punctuate as the respective difference between inhabiting an arbitrary "space" and being part of an inhabited "place." Fissure points develop from, and serve to highlight, incompatible though not irreconcilable expressions of colonial versus indigenous identity and relations with the landscape.

Conflict resolution comes, potentially, through the implementation of the management measures defined in the Stó:lō management policy. The new-found ability to clarify points of contention provides a new-found ability to create effective and mutually agreeable conflict resolution processes that foster greater certainty with regard to both the provincial resource landscape and the Stó:lō cultural landscape. Adverse effects on Stó:lō heritage sites, in unfortunate cases where effective conflict resolution procedures are not or cannot be negotiated, are seen by the Stó:lō as eroding aspects of their traditional culture and identity as People *of* the River. Without the benefit of a legal anchor (like the *Boldt* decision), implementing Stó:lō-based management measures beyond Indian reserve boundaries requires political will and places the reconciliation ball fully in the court of the dominant political economy, if not the courts themselves.

Bandying for power and administrative authority over things such as the heritage policy and management plan occurs multidirectionally, both beyond and within Stó:lō communities. Externally, the historically increasing centralization of First Nations political bodies such as the Union of BC Indian Chiefs and the First Nations Summit situates the colonial government as a unifying force for many First Nations who are seeking to gain recognition and increased self-governance. Internally, factionalism persists as Aboriginal people struggle to resituate themselves within an increasing, albeit yet limited, mainstream political and economic visibility. The multiplicity of First Nations political identities that can be variously negotiated and operationalized within a range of structures between "family" and "nation" reflects the multiplicity of meanings ascribed *on* the landscape, as described by Bierwert (1986, 1999). While political organization remains flexible and plastic, as demonstrated by the historic trajectory of the Stó:lō Nation, I suggest that the broad-based cultural roots of Stó:lō collective identity are firmly set within the cultural landscape. The constantly contested balance of power – fluidly forming and reforming – fluctuates as a dynamic system radiating outward from this solid and stable base. The stability in this unstable system lies within the interactive web made up of transcendent and deeply rooted places of the cultural landscape. Like the interwoven fabric in a trampoline surface, the cultural landscape supports the sometimes cohesive, sometimes divisive, yet always shifting mass of individuals vying for authority at all levels of society. Maintenance of this elementary cultural fabric is essential to the survival of Stó:lō identity and cultural practices.

Conclusion

In conclusion, I suggest that the Stó:lō Nation's recent focus on heritage resource policy development and management planning, motivated by a need to address fissure points between itself and the federal and provincial (i.e., colonialist) governments, provides a focused outlet through which Stó:lō identity may be formulated and expressed. The development and implementation of the Stó:lō Nation's *Stó:lō Heritage Policy Manual* (Stó:lō Nation 2003a) and *Stó:lō Heritage Resource Management Plan* (Stó:lō Nation 2003b) highlights elementary paradigmatic differences between Stó:lō and colonial understandings of landscape in the context of anthropological discussions of place versus space (e.g., Zedeno 2000). The outcome of this process asserts Stó:lō identity, which is expressed via the management plan as a Stó:lō cultural landscape.

The Stó:lō broadly identify themselves as the People of the River – not the People *by* the River or the People *near* the River but the People *of* the River. In so doing, they situate themselves in relation to nature as part of the landscape – particularly identifying themselves with the Fraser River. The Stó:lō, as People of the River, are connected to the river in a way that is more substantial than that implied by mere geographic proximity and riverine resource use. The same may be said of their relationship with the cultural landscape of S'ólh Téméxw, in which the river is the central feature of an interconnected cultural system. Such interconnectedness with the landscape necessitates, I suggest, acknowledging the Stó:lō as a traditional religio-political-economic society.

Competition with the colonial government over resource-related rights and title manifests itself in Aboriginal peoples developing resource-specific inventories, policies, and management plans founded on *their* cultural appreciation and understanding of resources and resource use. The Stó:lō Nation's development of a heritage policy and a management plan exemplifies this process. Implementation of both the policy and the plan is currently being carried out as an aspect of negotiations within the uncertain field of Aboriginal-colonial power relations.

The Stó:lō Nation's efforts to preserve Stó:lō heritage resources, as a microcosm of the broader political economic theatre, exemplifies processes engaged in by all Coast Salish and Aboriginal peoples who are actively defining and asserting aspects of their identity as they negotiate positions of jurisdiction and power within a colonialist political-economic realm. Changes in the perception and description of the relationship between nature and culture, the environment and people, are affecting the terminology used to situate people as existing *on, in,* or *of* the landscape. This way of reconfiguring and reckoning the landscape incorporates and reshapes prior anthropological constructs, such as Smith's (1940) watershed model of social organization among the Puyallup and Nisqually, and it builds on a continuously developing postmodern paradigm that brings Stó:lō emic representation to the anthropological table. Practically, maintenance of the places constituting the connective tissues of the cultural landscape is crucial to supporting the fundamental foundation of Stó:lō collective identity and cultural practices, within which intracommunity relations form and reform themselves, and without which what is at stake, as Stephen Hume (2003) points out, is "survival itself."

Acknowledgments

I wish to gratefully acknowledge and thank Dr. Bruce Miller for sharing his overall insight into the Coast Salish world and graciously providing me with the opportunity to participate in this volume. I also wish to thank my co-worker and companion Albert "Sonny" McHalsie for his profound influence as a teacher of Stó:lō culture and for personifying cultural respect. I must thank the members of the Stó:lō Nation and the Stó:lō community who supported and contributed to the work presented in this chapter, particularly Grand Chief Clarence Pennier; the members of the Stó:lō Nation House of Elders, including Joe Aleck and Shirley Julian; and the members of the Stó:lō Nation House of Chiefs. Leeanna Rhodes, Stó:lō Nation GIS technician, graciously produced the maps included in this chapter. I accept responsibility for the content of this chapter and for any inaccuracies therein.

References

Adams, John. 1981. Recent Ethnology of the Northwest Coast. *Annual Review of Anthropology* 10: 361-92.
Ashmore, Wendy, and A. Bernard Knapp, eds. 1999. *Archaeologies of Landscape: Contemporary Perspectives.* Oxford: Blackwell Press.
Basso, Keith. 1996. *Wisdom Sits in Places: Landscape and Language among the Western Apache.* Albuquerque: University of Albuquerque Press.
Bender, Barbara. 2002. Time and Landscape. *Current Anthropology* 43: 103-12.
Bierwert, Crisca. 1986. Tracery in the Mistlines: Semiotic Readings of Stó:lō Culture. PhD diss., University of Washington.
–. 1999. *Brushed by Cedar, Living by the River: Coast Salish Figures of Power.* Tucson: University of Arizona Press.
Boas, Franz. 1887. Notes on the Ethnology of British Columbia. *Proceedings of the American Philosophical Society* 24 (126): 321-28.
–. 1894. The Indian Tribes of the Lower Fraser River. In *64th Report of the British Association for the Advancement of Science for 1890,* 454-63. London: British Association for the Advancement of Science.
–. 1895. *Indianische Sagen von der Nordpacifischen Kuste Americas.* Berlin: A. Asher.
Boxberger, Daniel. 1989. *To Fish in Common: The Ethnohistory of Lummi Indian Salmon Fishing.* Lincoln: University of Nebraska Press.
Carlson, Keith T. 2001. Expressions of Collective Identity. In *A Stó:lō Coast Salish Historical Atlas,* ed. K.T. Carlson, 24-29. Vancouver/Chilliwack/Seattle: Douglas and McIntyre/Stó:lō Heritage Trust/University of Washington Press.

–. 2003. The Power of Place, the Problem of Time: A Study of History and Aboriginal Collective Identity. PhD diss., University of British Columbia.

Elmendorf, William. 1971. Coast Salish Status, Ranking, and Intergroup Ties. *Southwestern Journal of Anthropology* 27 (4): 353-80.

–. 1993. *Twana Narratives: Native Historical Accounts of a Coast Salish Culture.* Seattle/ Vancouver: University of Washington Press/UBC Press.

Gunther, Erna. 1973. *Ethnobotany of Western Washington: The Knowledge and Use of Indigenous Plants by Native Americans.* Seattle: University of Washington Press.

Harmon, Alexandra. 1998. *Indians in the Making: Ethnic Relations and Indian Identities around Puget Sound.* Berkeley: University of California Press.

Harris, Cole. 1997. *The Resettlement of British Columbia: Essays on Colonialism and Geographic Change.* Vancouver: UBC Press.

–. 2002. *Making Native Space: Colonialism, Resistance, and Reserves in British Columbia.* Vancouver: UBC Press.

Hill-Tout, Charles. 1903. Ethnological Studies of the Mainland Halkomelem, a Division of the Salish of British Columbia. In *72nd Report of the British Association for the Advancement of Science for 1902,* 355-449. London: British Association for the Advancement of Science.

Hume, Stephen. 2003. Writs Fly as First Nations Doubt Liberals' Good Faith. *Vancouver Sun,* 13 December, C5.

Knapp, A. Bernard, and Wendy Ashmore. 1999. Archaeological Landscapes: Constructed, Conceptualized, Ideational. In *Archaeologies of Landscape: Contemporary Perspectives,* ed. W. Ashmore and A.B. Knapp, 1-32. Oxford: Blackwell Press.

Lévi-Strauss, Claude. 1966. *The Savage Mind.* Chicago: University of Chicago Press.

Mauzé, Marie. 1997. *Past Is Present: Some Use of Tradition in Native Society.* Lanham, MD: University Press of America.

McHalsie, Albert (Sonny). 2001a. Intergenerational Ties and Movements: Family as a Basis of Nation. In *A Stó:lō Coast Salish Historical Atlas,* ed. K.T. Carlson, 32-33. Vancouver/Chilliwack/Seattle: Douglas and McIntyre/Stó:lō Heritage Trust/University of Washington Press.

–. 2001b. Stl'áleqem Sites: Spiritually Potent Places in S'ólh Téméxw. In *A Stó:lō Coast Salish Historical Atlas,* ed. K.T. Carlson, 8-9. Vancouver/Chilliwack/Seattle: Douglas and McIntyre/Stó:lō Heritage Trust/University of Washington Press.

–. 2001c. Halq'eméylem Place Names in Stó:lō Territory. In *A Stó:lō Coast Salish Historical Atlas,* ed. K.T. Carlson, 134-53. Vancouver/Chilliwack/Seattle: Douglas and McIntyre/Stó:lō Heritage Trust/University of Washington Press.

McHalsie, Albert (Sonny), David Schaepe, and Keith Thor Carlson. 2001. Making the World Right through Transformations. In *A Stó:lō Coast Salish Historical Atlas,* ed. K.T. Carlson, 6-8. Vancouver/Chilliwack/Seattle: Douglas and McIntyre/Stó:lō Heritage Trust/University of Washington Press.

McKay, Kathy. 2000. Reburial: Ideas for Stó:lō Policy and Protocol. Paper, University of Victoria-Stó:lō Nation Ethnohistory Field School, Stó:lō Nation Archives, Chilliwack, BC.

Miller, Bruce. 1998. Culture as Cultural Defense: An American Indian Sacred Site in Court. *American Indian Quarterly* 22 (1-2): 83-97.

–. 2001. *The Problem of Justice: Tradition and Law in the Coast Salish World.* Lincoln: University of Nebraska Press.

–. 2003. An Historical Perspective on First Nations Land Claims and Land Claims Research in Canada and British Columbia. Keynote address at the National Land Claims Research Conference, sponsored by the Union of BC Indian Chiefs, Vancouver, BC.

Miller, Jay. 1999. *Lushootseed Culture and the Shamanistic Odyssey: An Anchored Radiance*. Lincoln: University of Nebraska Press.

Mohs, Gordon. 1994. Stó:lō Sacred Ground. In *Sacred Sites, Sacred Places*, ed. D.L. Carmichael, J. Jubert, B. Reeves, and A. Schanche, 184-208. New York: Routledge Press.

Orchard, Imbert. 1983. *Floodland and Forest: Memories of the Chilliwack Valley*. Victoria: Provincial Archives of British Columbia.

Ortiz, Alphonso. 1969. *The Tewa World: Space, Time, Being and Becoming in a Pueblo Society*. Chicago: University of Chicago Press.

Pemberton, Kim. 1999. Stó:lō Upset as CN Blasts Symbolic Rock. *Vancouver Sun*, 9 August, A1.

Pennier, Clarence. 2002. Stó:lō History. Manuscript, Stó:lō Nation Archives, Chilliwack, BC.

Schaepe, David. 2001. The Land and the People: Glaciation to Contact. In *A Stó:lō Coast Salish Historical Atlas*, ed. K.T. Carlson, 12-19. Vancouver/Chilliwack/Seattle: Douglas and McIntyre/Stó:lō Heritage Trust/University of Washington Press.

–. 2002. Cultural Significance, Cognitive Ecology, and High Elevation Archaeology in the North Cascades – with a View to Mount Cheam. Paper presented at the 56th Annual Northwest Anthropological Conference, Bellingham, Washington.

Schaepe, David, Marianne Berkey, John Stamp, and Tia Halstad. 2004. Sumas Energy 2, Inc. Traditional Use Study – Phase II: Stó:lō Cultural Relations to Air and Water. Report, Stó:lō Nation Archives, Chilliwack, BC.

Smith, Marian W. 1940. *The Puyallup-Nisqually*. Columbia University Contributions to Anthropology, Vol. 32. New York: AMS Press.

Snyder, Sally. 1964. Skagit Society and Its Existential Basis: An Ethnofolkloristic Reconstruction. PhD diss., University of Washington, Seattle.

Steward, Julian. 1955. *Theory of Cultural Change: The Methodology of Multilinear Evolution*. Urbana: University of Illinois Press.

Stó:lō Nation. 1995. Stó:lō Heritage Policy. Document, Stó:lō Nation Archives, Chilliwack, BC.

–. 2003a. Stó:lō Heritage Policy Manual. Document, Stó:lō Nation Archives, Chilliwack, BC.

–. 2003b. Stó:lō Heritage Resource Management Plan. Database on file, GIS office, Treaty and Research Department, Stó:lō Nation, Chilliwack, BC.

Suttles, Wayne. 1960. Affinal Ties, Subsistence, and Prestige among the Coast Salish. *American Anthropologist* 62: 296-305.

–. 1964. Space and Time, Wind and Tide: Some Halkomelem Modes of Classification. Paper presented at the 17th Northwest Anthropological Conference, Pullman, Washington.

–. 1968a. Variation in Habitat and Culture on the Northwest Coast. In *Man in Adaptation: The Cultural Present*, ed. Yehudi A. Cohen, 93-106. Chicago: Aldine Press.

–. 1968b. Coping with Abundance: Subsistence on the Northwest Coast. In *Man the Hunter*, ed. Richard B. Lee, 56-68. New York: Aldine Press.

–. 1984. Productivity and Its Constraints: A Coast Salish Case. In *Indian Art Traditions of the Northwest Coast*, ed. Roy Carlson. Burnaby, BC: Archaeology Press.

–. 1987. *Coast Salish Essays*. Seattle: University of Washington Press.

–. 1990a. Central Coast Salish. In *Handbook of North American Indians*. Vol. 7, *Northwest Coast*, ed. W. Suttles, 453-75. Washington, DC: Smithsonian Institution.

–, ed. 1990b. *Handbook of North American Indians*. Vol. 7, *Northwest Coast*. Washington, DC: Smithsonian Institution.

Suttles, Wayne, and Aldona Jonaitis. 1990. History of Research in Ethnography. In *Handbook of North American Indians*. Vol. 7, *Northwest Coast*, ed. W. Suttles, 73-87. Washington, DC: Smithsonian Institution.

Tennant, Paul. 1990. *Aboriginal Peoples and Politics: The Indian Land Question in British Columbia, 1849-1989*. Vancouver: UBC Press.

Thornton, Thomas. 1997. Anthropological Studies of Native American Place Naming. *American Indian Quarterly* 21 (2): 209-28.

White, Leslie. 1943. Energy and the Evolution of Culture. *American Anthropologist* 43: 335-56.

Zedeno, Maria. 2000. On What People Make of Places: A Behavioral Cartography. In *Social Theory in Archaeology*, ed. Michael B. Schiffer, 97-111. Salt Lake City: University of Utah Press.

9

Conceptions of Coast Salish Warfare, or Coast Salish Pacifism Reconsidered: Archaeology, Ethnohistory, and Ethnography

Bill Angelbeck

> *Friday 13th.* Nothing alarming transpired during [the] night, but as
> Soon as our Indian neighbours [the Quaitlines (Kwantlen)] had time
> to assemble, the advance of the enemy was given out as admitting of
> no doubt; & that their Scouts of the night discerned the force to be
> 30 [up to 50] canoes at least – They made every thing Secure them-
> selves, & only a few resolute fellows Kept peeping at a distance So as
> to have one glance at the enemy – before an actual retreat to the
> woods Should be Commenced: when, to their great ease of mind,
> four or five Small Canoes of the Whoomes Tribe [Squamish] hove in
> Sight round the first point below, which put an end of their Yewkelta
> [Lekwiltok] terror for the present. It is impossible to describe their
> Continual alarm at the very name of this formidable foe: and can
> only proceed from the little mercy they have to expect from those
> atrocious villains when any of them unfortunately fall into their hands
> – Although those here abouts are themselves pretty numerous and
> ought to be able to make a good Stand before Strangers Coming
> upon them, yet on this occasion they Seem to put their greatest faith
> in the protection of the Six White men in the Fort – However in Case
> Something may be pending over us, we keep them all alike at a
> distance. – Archibald McDonald, March 1829, *The Fort Langley
> Journals* (1998)

For the lives of Northwest Coast peoples, warfare was a common occur-
rence throughout their prehistory and history. Images of warfare feature
prominently in contemporary conceptions of Northwest Coast cultures;
however, these mostly regard the northern groups, such as the Haida,
Tlingit, or Kwakwaka'wakw. The Coast Salish are often portrayed not as
warriors but, rather, as victims, subject to the preying of northern raiders –

namely, the infamous Lekwiltok, or the southern Kwakwaka'wakw, as noted in McDonald's journal entry excerpted above. In this chapter, I discuss these conceptions and posit that current conceptions about the nature of Coast Salish warfare result mostly from a late historic peek into Coast Salish life, a window of fascinating historic detail but one that is fogged by the substantial changes that had occurred in the decades prior to historic documentation, particularly regarding the differing effects of disease and the disparity in access to firearms. Moreover, such views ignore substantial archaeological and ethnographic evidence regarding warfare among the Coast Salish.

For this discussion, I integrate the evidence from archaeology, ethnohistory, and ethnography in an attempt to provide a coherent conception of the Coast Salish and their relationship to warfare. Due to the rich literature in ethnography, archaeologists have always sought to include its insights into their interpretation of material remains. Anthropologists such as Boas and Mauss have made the Northwest Coast a signature area of anthropological discussion as well as having provided a sizable bank of oral traditions for rendering indigenous perspectives. The ethnohistoric literature is also a valuable resource, partly because contact in this area occurred more recently than elsewhere on the continent. However, the archaeologist's use of ethnography and ethnohistory can often be relegated to background information rather than being integral to the interpretative process. In an analysis of conceptions of Coast Salish warfare, the incorporation of all three disciplinary sources provides a way to situate the topic from various vantage points. In so doing, some information will be supportive, some will not, but the point is to provide checks and balances in order, ultimately, to provide a broader context than we now have.

Conceptions of Warfare on the Northwest Coast

When the term "warriors" occurs in the literature of the Northwest Coast, it is often in reference to the groups of the north coast. For example, a volume by Lillard (1984) entitled *Warriors of the North Pacific* is mostly concerned with the Tsimshian and Tlingit. Another volume, entitled *In the Wake of the War Canoe*, concerns the exploits of the Haida as recorded in the journals of William Henr y Collison in the late nineteenth century (Collison and Lillard 1981). Even when Edward Curtis decided to make his early film about Northwest Coast culture, released in 1914, it showcased warfare, was entitled *Land of the War Canoes* (after it dropped its original title *Land of the Headhunters*), and concerned the Kwakwaka'wakw.

Even anthropological treatments of Northwest Coast warfare favour the northern groups, whether it's the exploits of the great Tsimshian warrior chiefs, such as Sebassa (Mitchell 1981a) or Nekt (MacDonald 1984), or models of forced redistributive exchange (Ferguson 1983) and slave-raiding (Mitchell 1984). For Codere (1950), the warlike nature of the Kwakwaka'wakw was such that the potlatch was thoroughly imbued with the metaphors of war. Indeed, she argued that it could be seen as a substitute for war, the idea being that the Kwakwaka'wakw had to do something to satiate their hunger for war after it was denied to them after contact.

For the southern Coast Salish, however, warfare is often described in alternative terms. For instance, Suttles and Lane (1990, 495) discussed Coast Salish warfare as "largely defensive." Bierwert (1999, 15-18) comments upon this subject, noting that anthropologists have treated the Coast Salish as "raided people rather than raiding people," and she places this within a long tradition of anthropologists marginalizing the Coast Salish in favour of the northerners and their vivid art. She argues that this preference was nourished by the broad base of literature established by Boas.

Undoubtedly, the above tradition extends to the archaeological treatment of the Coast Salish as well, at least regarding the subject of warfare. By and large, this results more from the fact that more archaeological work has been conducted on warfare-related sites in the north than in the south. The major analyses of Northwest Coast warfare indicate this phenomenon. For instance, Maschner (1997) presents a thought-provoking discussion of "the evolution of warfare on the Northwest Coast," providing insight into the multifaceted causes of regional warfare; however, the majority of his material concerns the north coast.

In another major overview and analysis of Northwest Coast warfare, Coupland (1989) presents equal coverage of the north and south coasts and places warfare within the context of the development of social inequality. Interestingly, he argues that, in the north, warfare is tied (or is parallel) to the development of inequality or ranked society, whereas in the south, warfare did not become important until after the emergence of social inequality (205). In the Coast Salish region, this would be after the Marpole Period (500 BC to AD 400/1000), a period not thought to be greatly associated with warfare (Burley 1980, 65-66). Coupland (1989, 212) argues that Coast Salish warfare was "mainly defensive": "the Coast Salish were drawn into warfare some time after Marpole by the constantly expanding northern warfare complex. This would explain the essentially defensive posture of Coast Salish war."

Schaepe (2006) found warfare to be underrepresented in the anthropological literature for the region overall, but especially so for the south coast. He argues that this passive representation reflects a "lingering colonial and anthropological misrepresentation of Coast Salish peoples as passively 'fighting with food' rather than weapons."

For some of the Interior Salish and plateau region, similar charges of pacifism have been made, particularly by Ray (1933, 1939), who argues that they had been peaceful for centuries: "Warfare is virtually unknown to them and has been since time immemorial" (1939, 35). Several researchers (Suttles 1987; Chatters 1989; Cannon 1992) have countered Ray's arguments. Here, I attempt to counter similar conceptions, beginning with Coast Salish prehistory.

Archaeological Evidence
One problem with analyzing warfare on the Northwest Coast is that most accounts are influenced by historic accounts, which may or may not be representative of how things were practised before contact. This is a problem that has affected every treatment of indigenous warfare worldwide. Ferguson and Whitehead (1992) stressed that all descriptions of indigenous warfare are postcontact accounts, many of which do not fully address the colonial impact upon Aboriginal traditions. Essentially for this reason, Lambert (2002, 208-9) notes that, because its field of inquiry extends far before the time of Western European contact, archaeological evidence gives us an "unparalleled capacity" to understand the extent of warfare. Similarly, for the Northwest Coast, Schaepe (2006) argues that archaeology can help bridge the "contact barrier." For this discussion, I focus on two main types of archaeological evidence: defensive settlements and burial analyses.

Defensive Sites
Defensive settlements are found throughout the Northwest Coast and comprise the primary evidence for conflict, particularly for the Late Period (AD 900 to contact) (Coupland 1989; Moss and Erlandson 1992; Maschner 1997; Maschner and Reedy-Maschner 1998). They indicate that warfare had increased to such a degree that it was deemed necessary to construct defensive fortifications. The major study of defensive sites comes from Moss and Erlandson (1992), who analyzed such sites in traditional Tlingit areas of southeast Alaska. In their chronology, which included thirty radiocarbon dates, the construction of defensive sites began between AD 400 and AD 700, and they begin to proliferate around AD 900 to AD 1400. On the Northwest Coast, the archaeological study of defensive sites began in the 1960s (de Laguna 1960; Bryan 1963; Mitchell 1968). Recent work on the subject has focused mainly on the northern Northwest Coast. In the

Aleutian Islands of Alaska, Maschner and Reedy-Maschner (1998) determined, from available radiocarbon dates, that warfare was endemic from AD 300 to AD 1100 (see also Maschner 1997, 1996). Other important excavations have been conducted in Tsimshian territory in and around Prince Rupert (MacDonald 1989), in the Kwakwaka'wakw territory of Queen Charlotte Strait (Mitchell 1981b), and in the Nuu-chah-nulth region of the west coast of Vancouver Island (McMillan 1999).

In the Coast Salish region, however, such surveys and excavations have been limited. Fortified sites were noted in early histories, but Harlan Smith was the first archaeologist to make some observations about these settlements, recording the locations of certain defensive sites in the early 1900s (Smith 1934, 1907; Smith and Fowke 1901). Decades later, Bryan (1963) provided an overview of twenty-two semicircular trench embankments, mainly in Puget Sound.

In the Gulf of Georgia, there was a type of fortification that was unique to the Coast Salish region: the trench embankment. Its name refers to its archaeological form: its primary remains consist of massive trench and mound features constructed along otherwise unprotected fronts. Natural defences – cliffs, ravines, rocky shores – form the barriers for the remainder of the perimeter. Many traditions maintain that a palisade of cedar planks was placed upon the inside of the trench, providing additional height to the fort walls (Keddie 1996; Buxton 1969). According to some traditional accounts, a line of hidden stakes obscured by brush was located at the base of the trench to provide further obstacles to attackers (Buxton 1969; Bryan 1963; Suttles 1951).

Mitchell (1968) carried out excavations on two trench-embankment sites in the 1960s. Rebecca Spit, located in the northern Gulf Islands, contains a semicircular trench embankment that also features three or four house platforms. Towner Bay, Mitchell's other excavation, is located on a promontory on the Saanich Peninsula on lower Vancouver Island. He was able to uncover the palisade's postholes, which had been erected parallel to the trench embankment. Mitchell contends that these sites were occupied quite recently, sometime around 1600 to 1750, although he provides no radiocarbon dates.

One of Mitchell's crew members continued to pursue a study of trench-embankment sites. Buxton (1969) brought together information on fifty-eight "earthwork" sites and initiated limited excavations on two of them. The first one, Site DeRt 41, is located on a peninsula on Pender Island and consists of a double trench embankment with a shallow midden. She cross-sectioned one trench feature and acquired a small sample of artifacts and faunal materials, though she did not acquire a radiocarbon date. In the end, she concludes, surprisingly, that these were not defensive sites but, rather, trenches built for fish-drying racks. This despite the fact that these were often located in naturally defensible and otherwise inconvenient locations.

In the Victoria area, from Cowichan Head to the north and Metchosin to the west, Keddie (1984, 1996) recorded the presence of nineteen defensive sites. Many have thought these to be historic Spanish forts and to postdate European colonization, in spite of their appearance in numerous historic accounts (from 1774 to the 1860s). Keddie was able to get radiocarbon dates for three sites (Lime Bay, Finlayson Point, and Macaulay Point), which indicated that they were much older than Mitchell had thought, ranging from 460 BP to 1160 BP. Like Bryan (1963), Keddie (1984) argues that there is a relation between burial cairns and defensive sites, and he remarks that the presence of both types of earthworks close together would have suited the "wealthier" individuals (i.e., those who mobilized others to construct them).

Some recent work has revealed the presence of defensive sites in the Fraser Canyon. Schaepe (2006, 2001, 2000) reports that these five sites consist of rock-wall fortifications and that they are the only known examples of such constructions in the Northwest Coast region. Each is located along narrow and rough portions of the river and is close to known settlements. Most are high lookout points on bluffs that would have a line-of-sight trained on other settlements and fortifications. For this reason, Schaepe posits that, among the villages located along the canyon, there was a co-operative network of defensive stations whose point was to stem raids coming upriver.

There are a number of other defensive sites in the Coast Salish region. Some are yet to be documented, and many known sites may not have been analyzed for defensive features or qualities. Map 9.1 shows the defensive sites in the Coast Salish region and is derived from a perusal of the archaeological literature and the site records at the Archaeology Branch of British Columbia. Although radiocarbon dates are few, and come primarily from Keddie's pioneering work in the Victoria region, the number of defensive sites known in the region is substantial.

Defensive sites signify that raiding and warfare were prominent and recurring facts of life. These violent events were damaging and common enough to warrant the construction of fortified walls and trench embankments, and they did affect choice of settlements (Maschner 1996). Blake (1985, 97-99) argues that, archaeologically, warfare would have its most noticeable effects upon a society's settlement system, noting that regular raids would cause settlements to shift to a "defensive posture." More than indicating warfare in the archaeological record, defensive sites indicate how

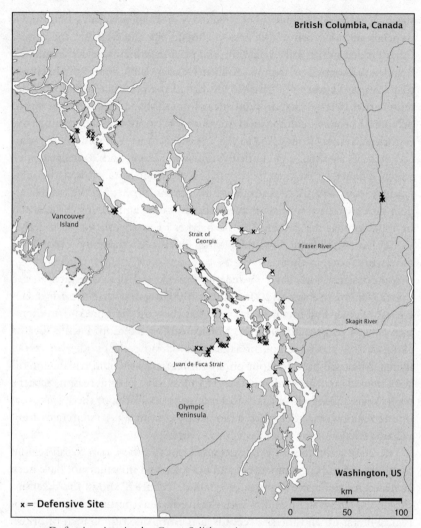

MAP 9.1 Defensive sites in the Coast Salish region

the inhabitants reacted to such threats. Instead of dispersing, they built fortifications and barricaded themselves, attempting to hold their ground. These defensive practices indicate people's intention to protect not only the lives and stores of the group but also their territory. The fact that, as Bryan (1963) and Keddie (1984) note, burial mounds were built close together may indicate the degree of honour accorded to those who died defending their homeland.

The number of radiocarbon dates from the north coast may be greater than the number in the south (though this is a reflection of past research practices as the actual number of defensive sites appears to be distributed throughout the Northwest Coast, including the Coast Salish region). In fact, the distinctive styles of the trench-embankment and the rock-wall fortifications appear to be unique to the Coast Salish. And any argument that these are somehow "passive" in that they were built as a reaction to raids seriously ignores their active element: these sites testify to the active defence of territory in the Coast Salish region just as they do in the north coast region.

Burial Analyses

Evidence for warfare can be seen inscribed in the bones of Northwest Coast people that bear parry fractures on forearms and skull fractures – the marks of lethal trauma that are unlikely to come from accidents (Cybulski 1992, 1999). At the Boardwalk site in Prince Rupert, a "warrior's cache" was discovered, containing a decorated whalebone club, a killer whale jawbone club, a basalt dagger, and so on buried with an apparent trophy skull (MacDonald 1983, 11; MacDonald and Cybulski 2001, 8-9). Such caches are rare, however, whereas researchers have encountered numerous burials that exhibit marks of violence. Cybulski (1990, 1992, 1994, 1999) has conducted the most significant studies of warfare, and his analysis of the Greenville burial ground along the Nass River in northern British Columbia – a case study that he situates within the wider context of the Northwest Coast region – is of particular interest.

One striking discrepancy that Cybulski found was the difference in the amount of violent trauma between northern and southern burials. In the north, 26 percent (n = 288) of the burials revealed such trauma, whereas in the Gulf of Georgia, only 6 percent (n = 311) of burials did so – a significant difference by any measure. From this, Cybulski (1992, 157-58) concludes that there is a marked difference in degree of warfare between the two regions. However, most of the data from the Gulf of Georgia concerned burials from the Locarno Beach/Marpole periods (n = 293, 94 percent; Cybulski 1994) – a time that, as noted above, is not thought to be associated with significant warfare (Burley 1980; Coupland 1989). For the Gulf of Georgia, it is the Late Period that is associated with the onset of warfare, as is indicated by the presence of defensive sites. Only nineteen burials dated to that period, primarily because mortuary customs had switched from below-ground to above-ground graves, as Cybulski (1992, 1994, 77) and others (Burley and Knüsel 1989; Thom 1995) describe. Therefore, the paucity of data for the Late Period in the Gulf of Georgia (as well as other areas) precludes offering a simplistic generalization regarding regional differences from earlier periods. Indeed, from the available Late

Period burials, Cybulski (1994, 76-77) found an increase in interpersonal violence province-wide, rising to 27.6 percent (*n* = 58), the highest point in prehistory (although that percentage is not broken down by region, presumably due to sample sizes). This rise and peak in interpersonal violence does appear to parallel the development of defensive sites, both on the north coast and on the south coast.

Ethnohistory

> *Wednesday 11th.* The weather very Sultry – The men at work Squaring, Sawing, and Clearing ground – The Yeukeltas have been paying another visit to the Musquiams a few days ago – Killed Six men and took away 30 women and Children – This is the first report; it may not turn out So bad – Trade a Sturgeon and bark.
>
> *Thursday 12th.* Weather the same. The heat would be very oppressive without the regular Sea Breeze – The Musquiams who were visited by the Yeukeltas are run[n]ing away up the river. They lost 3 men, 30 women & Children. One Yeukeltas was killed – The Country her[e]abouts is in [a] Continual State of fear by their powerful and Blood thirsty enemies from the Gulf of Georgia and Johnston's Straits.
>
> – James McMillan, June 1828

A large number of current conceptions of Coast Salish warfare may be due to the accounts found in *The Fort Langley Journals* (Maclachlan 1998). In these writings, James McMillan ([1828] 1998, 57), quoted above, notes a "Continual State of fear" regarding the Yeukeltas, or Lekwiltok. A few months before, on 19 March 1828, he wrote, "This warfare keeps Indians of this vicinity in Such Continual alarm, that they Can[n]ot turn their attention to any thing but the care of their family and that they do but poorly." At the beginning of this chapter, I provided an entry from the 1829 journals of Archibald McDonald (1998). McDonald's language is nearly identical to McMillan's: "It is impossible to describe their Continual alarm at the very name of this formidable foe [the Lekwiltok]." Later, McDonald ([1828] 1998, 111) talks about "dreadful terror" and a "general horror at the present of the Yewkaltas by all the Indians we have to do with."

These accounts, certainly, record the fear of a "formidable foe." No doubt the attacks were not simply opportunistic raids for booty and slaves as it is documented that, in historic times, territory in the northern Gulf Islands was taken by the Lekwiltok, who were engaged in a southern expansion (Taylor and Duff 1956). However, these historic accounts do occur long after the effects of contact had altered these societies. By "the effects of contact," I refer primarily to the introduction of firearms and to the devastating impact of disease.

Firearms

Fear of a well-armed enemy is warranted. Prior to contact, the weapons of war – stone and wooden clubs, spears, stone knives, bows and arrows – would have been equally available to all groups. Hence, the importance of the element of surprise in Northwest Coast tactics, with raids occurring during the night and early morning. John Jewitt ([1803-05] 1987) became familiar with this pattern during his years of captivity on the west coast. Such tactics continued, with even more devastating effect, after the introduction of firearms.

Throughout the world, the effect of technology on war has been recorded again and again: the Hittites had the advantage of the war-chariot in Western Asia; the Comanches had the horse on the Plains; the United States had the hydrogen bomb during the Second World War; and so on. In North America, Worcester and Schilz (1984, 103) emphasize that the introduction of firearms "drastically altered relationships between rival tribes" throughout the continent, causing migrations, annihilations, and fierce contests for control of access to the fur trade, which meant access to firearms. These arms were ostensibly supplied to facilitate hunters so as to better ensure the success of the fur trade.

What was true in other parts of the world was also true on the Northwest Coast: the onset of firearms had drastic effects. However, these arms were not evenly distributed throughout the region. To the detriment of the Coast Salish, the Lekwiltok had ready access to firearms decades before they did. Essentially, firearms began to be traded as soon as the fur trade was initiated. For instance, by 1792 "everyone at Nootka was reported to have muskets" (Cole and Darling 1990, 120). Firearms were traded far beyond their original point of entry and were already present among the Kwakwaka'wakw when Archibald Menzies first encountered them in 1792 (Cole and Darling 1990, 120-21; Gunther 1972, 99). However, guns were not as available in regions to the south. Cole and Darling (1990, 121) note that "very few firearms were seen among Indians of the Juan de Fuca Strait and the Strait of Georgia in 1825, and as late as 1838 a census of Puget Sound groups showed the highest incidence of gun ownership (among the Nisqually) to be only 10 percent (Scouler 1905, 201; Taylor 1974, 425)."

Several researchers have noted this inequity. For instance, Mitchell (1990, 358) remarks that "differential access to firearms tipped the scale" in favour of the Lekwiltok, allowing them to gain territory in the northern Gulf of Georgia. Decades before, Taylor and Duff (1956, 64) proposed that the Lekwiltok expansion received its "initial impetus from the circumstance that the Kwakiutl-speaking people obtained firearms before the coast Salish of eastern Vancouver Island did so."

Curtis (1913, 20) records an account of just such a scenario:

> One of the earliest wars of which the old men now tell began when a party of the Lekwiltok attacked a Clallam village on Whidbey [I]sland. The islanders, about to celebrate a wedding, were expecting the arrival of friends from other Clallam settlements, and seeing the canoes of the Lekwiltok coming ashore, they hurried down to meet their supposed visitors, never dreaming that an enemy would approach by day. The northerners, armed with guns, of which the Clallam as yet had none, quickly opened fire, killing many and dispersing the rest in the woods, and then pillaged the houses.

Curtis (1913, 21) later recounted that a counter-attack was mounted upon the Lekwiltok but that "the guns of the northerners were too much for them, and they turned and fled." Also, according to Collins (1950, 337), "the role played by the introduction of the gun should not be minimized in this new emphasis on warfare," with heavily armed northern tribes attacking Upper Skagit and neighbouring tribes who were "still using bows and arrows."

Some historians, however, counter that firearms were not that important. Fisher (1977, 16-17), for instance, points out the limitations of the smooth-bore musket, noting that it is "notoriously unreliable and inaccurate," susceptible to misfiring in the damp settings of the Northwest Coast. He argues that the "Indian bow was probably superior" (16). While it is certainly true that the firearms of the contact period do not hold muster when compared to later rifles, it is probably overreaching to suggest, as does Fisher (17), that "initially, muskets probably made little difference to indigenous people who already had projectile weapons."[1] In any case, he seems to contradict himself when, later, he talks about how men at forts would engage in displaying the "destructive capabilities of muskets or cannon" to local Native groups (39). And, despite the damp climate, it is clear that fur traders did not adopt the bow and arrow. Interestingly, Fisher does not seem to allow that Northwest Coast groups, like the traders, would be able to quickly figure out how best to use firearms in various climates and settings.

Furthermore, Fisher's argument does not account for the great interest in trading for firearms – an interest that was there since first contact. For instance, the Tlingit "virtually all had guns" by 1800, and spears and arrows were "almost wholly out of use" among them by 1805 (Cole and Darling 1990, 121). Moreover, Fisher's explanation does not account for why the traders at Fort Langley withheld such arms from Coast Salish groups because they wanted to sell them for hunting purposes. One of McDonald's journal entries, provided at length below, gives some insight into the multiple tensions surrounding firearms. This entry was recorded after another brutal Lekwiltok attack:

> *Friday 24th* [April 1829] Last night Scheenuck the Sandish Chief, &
> this morning Joe the Cawaitchin Chief arrived both from Vancouver's
> Island with about 70 Skins between them large & Small, with the
> usual great proportion of land Otters ... The Cowaitchens [sic] have
> determined on a vigourous resistance or even on an attack [upon the
> Lekwiltok] in their turn when able to Seize a fair Opportunity – for
> this purpose Joe now Came across with Furs to buy for himself a
> gun and 300 rounds of ammunition for distribution among his
> followers that are already armed – So much amm. to one man in this
> part of the world & in times like the present may Seem imprudent;
> and must Seem Still more So when I remark that heretofore the
> article were entirely withheld from them: but keeping our own
> immediate hunters and Traders in this defenceless State, will I
> presume appear equally impolitic – What is more the natives of
> Vancouver's Island and all along the Coast Can have no difficulty in
> obtaining elsewhere for their Skins ten times the quantity of amm.
> we give, if totally refused them here: & how varied Soever may be
> opinion on the impropriety of giving arms & amm. in Trade, I am
> myself Convinced that an Indian refused this reasonable demand
> according to his notion of things, is not likely to be the first to
> repeat the visit – Indeed from the general horror at present of the
> Yewkaltas by all the Indians we have to do with, I think the more we
> promote the ruin of that detestable tribe, the more effectually we
> secure the good faith of those nearer home, & convince them of the
> acquisition they have gained by the Establishment. In Short, tis my
> firm belief that even the *Complete annihilation* of this truly bar-
> barous banditti would be no loss to the human race.
>
> – Archibald McDonald (1998, 111-12)

In this entry, McDonald reveals that the Fort Langley traders debated whether to sell arms to Coast Salish groups so that they could protect themselves. More than that, he notes that other groups closer to the outer coast could trade for "ten times" the amount of ammunition for their skins than they will offer: a startling equation of imbalance becomes apparent. This excerpt from the journals reveals numerous issues important to this discussion. First, the Cowichan ("Cawiatchin") were seeking muskets and ammunition in order to "Seize a *fair* Opportunity"; second, McDonald revealed that "heretofore the article [firearms] were entirely withheld from them"; third, the traders perceived the Coast Salish to be in a "defenceless State"; and last, McDonald viewed these concerns in terms of the further-ance of the fort, of ensuring that it would continuously have people with whom to trade. His concern was that not selling arms and ammunition to the local Aboriginal people would just drive them elsewhere. The entry reveals that firearms were a significant concern. Though the muskets may have had limitations, they still brought an advantage to those groups that had them.

Disease

Besides technological advantage, another critical factor for success in war-fare is simply having greater numbers than does your opposition. While accurate numbers are difficult to acquire for both the Lekwiltok and the Coast Salish at this time, it is known that substantial changes in population had occurred due to smallpox. As Harris (1994) determines, the Gulf of Georgia experienced a devastating epidemic in the winter of 1781-82. The disease apparently originated in the Columbia River area and spread up-ward through Puget Sound and into the Gulf of Georgia. The extent of smallpox spread along the watercourses, flowing westward nearly to the tip of Washington's Olympic Peninsula, eastward halfway up the Fraser Can-yon, and northward to Comox territory at Cape Mudge and the northern Gulf Islands. In other words, its extent took in the boundaries of the Coast Salish sphere of interaction.

Harris (1994, 609-23) presents census data from the Hudson's Bay Company for the 1830s. He found that population numbers were signifi-cantly greater for the areas beyond the range of the disease, particularly in the upper reaches of the Fraser River and in the Fort Rupert area of north-ern Vancouver Island (Map 9.2). The numbers for the Fraser Valley were substantially less. He argues that "it does seem that this section of the Fraser River once supported far more people than are indicated in the cen-sus of 1830 or than white settlers and ethnographers have supposed" (609). The depopulations likely "created vacuums" that allowed surrounding

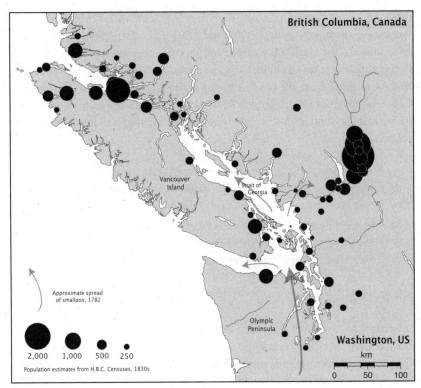

MAP 9.2 Approximate spread of smallpox in 1782 and population estimates in the 1830s

people to migrate. In all likelihood, this was attractive to the Lekwiltok, who were outside the range of the epidemic. Harris (1994, 615) cites the journals of Governor Simpson, who was travelling in Johnstone Strait and who noted that the Kwakwaka'wakw "had been exempted from the smallpox."[2]

Either of these factors – firearms or disease – would be enough to tilt the balance in favour of one group over another, but both occurring in combination makes for nearly insurmountable odds. Coincidentally (or perhaps not), Codere (1950, 98) characterizes Kwakwaka'wakw warfare as "waged on the outnumbered and the unsuspecting, on victims rather than enemies." According to her, in the decades following contact, the Coast Salish clearly played the role of victim.

Ethnography

Ethnographic accounts of the Coast Salish contain numerous instances of warfare and raiding – certainly enough to shed doubt on any notion that these peoples were pacifists or that they engaged in merely reactionary defensive postures. The Spanish of the 1791 Eliza Expedition, which produced one of the earliest historic accounts of the region, remarked that the Coast Salish in the Strait of Georgia appeared "more warlike" than did Wakashan groups on the coast (cited in Suttles 1989, 258). In fact, several Coast Salish groups were known for their bellicose nature. In the late nineteenth century, Boas (1889, 324) recorded that the Nanaimo were quite prone to warfare:

> Formerly the Snanaimuq [Nanaimo] were a very warlike tribe. Their warriors were thoroughly trained. They were not allowed to eat while on the war-path. Before setting out on such an expedition they painted their faces red and black. When near a village they intended to attack, the party divided; one-half hid in the woods behind the village, while the others watched in their canoes. When the latter gave a sign, both parties attacked the village. When successful, the men were killed, the women and children carried off as slaves. The heads of the slain were cut off, taken home, and planted on poles in front of the houses.

Further to the south, on the Olympic Peninsula, the Klallam were also known for being "very fierce warriors, respected and feared for their prowess by the [Puget] Sound tribes and the people of southern Vancouver Island" (Gunther 1927, 266). Curtis (1913, 19) writes that the Klallam were "the most powerful and warlike of all the Salish tribes on the coast of Washington." He notes that "by far the greater part of Klallam traditional history concerned the raids and counter-raids in which they were continually embroiled" (20). In fact, Carlson (2001) has determined that the Klallam made a minimum of seven raids up the Fraser River just during the years recorded in *The Fort Langley Journals* (1827 to 1830).

The Cowichan were also known for repeated forays into the Fraser Valley for slaves and booty. Barnett (1955, 267) notes that the Cowichan had been known to be "actively vicious and warlike." On this point, Suttles (1998, 202) thought that they might have been maintaining an aggressive tone in order to preserve their access to fishing camps on the Fraser River.

Besides whole tribes that were considered to be warlike, professional warriors were common to most Coast Salish peoples. Among the Straits Salish, Suttles (1951, 321-24) discusses the presence of "professional warriors" in nearly every village. Most accounts concern the mid- to late nineteenth century, when there would perhaps be a few warriors resident in any given village – for example, four warriors were known to reside in Lummi and Skokomish villages (Suttles 1951, 323-24; Elmendorf 1960, 467). Among the Twana, warriors "acted as organizers of resistance to foreign raiders" (Elmendorf 1960, 467). Among the Puyallup-Nisqually, Smith (1940, 156) notes that warriors were consulted about impending attacks upon a village and were even put in charge of defending it (though only for the duration of combat).

In order to become a warrior, one needed to put forth great efforts. Barnett (1955, 267) maintains that there were regional differences in warrior practices. For instance, among the Sechelt, being a warrior involved intensive training: the life of a warrior was a "professional one and ran in families. A northern father tried to inculcate the desire to fight in at least one of his sons." Among the Central and Southern Coast Salish, being a warrior required the cultivation of spirit powers. Among the Twana, these powers were known as *sca'laq*, or "bad powers" (Elmendorf 1960, 467). These spirit powers included the yellow jacket (Barnett 1955, 267), thunder power (Gunther 1927), a "lightning whale" (Elmendorf 1993, 141-43), and the south wind (Collins 1974, 115) – animals or forces of nature that had fearful characteristics. Collins (1974, 118, 168-69) notes that, unlike most spirit powers, which were available only during the winter, a warrior's spirit power was available year-round, just as was a shaman's. Warrior powers were difficult to obtain and required extended efforts, again, just as did the powers of the healer (Suttles 1951, 323). During the winter ceremonials, warriors would display their spirit powers, often in spectacular manner, "cutting their own flesh and drinking their own blood at spirit dances" (Elmendorf 1960, 467). Frank Allen, one of Elmendorf's Twana informants, said that the spirit power protected warriors; hence, they had no need for armour (Coast Salish warriors were often known to fight naked, as opposed to northern warriors, who were heavily armoured): "That's no good. People who use that [armour] are no real war men. Warrior doesn't care if he dies or lives! Disgrace for a man to fight with any protection but his power. Skokomish, Klallam have got big heart, don't need that kind of stuff!" (472).

On the other hand, these dangerous spirit powers are what gave warriors an ambivalent status in Coast Salish society. For the Upper Skagit, Collins (1974, 114) remarks that the characteristics of a successful warrior – "a hot temper, an indifference to personal risk, willingness to inflict physical injury" – were at odds with what the Coast Salish considered to be an ideal temperament: a stoic or measured demeanour that was not prone toward injuring others. Similarly, a Stó:lō elder commented that, traditionally, warriors were separated from society because of "the belief that you are not supposed to kill anything" (Angelbeck 2003, 78). The skills of warriors often made then expert hunters, whose expeditions would keep them away for extended periods.

Ethnographers note that Coast Salish warriors were not simply defensive but, rather, often took the offensive. Barnett (1955, 268) maintains that one common cause for attacks was the grief experienced over the death of a child or close relative: "The psychology was oddly logical. Reasoning that it was unfair for him to suffer so acutely while others were without grief, the bereaved person encouraged a murdering and plundering expedition to relieve his suffering by imposing it on others." Also, offensive attacks occurred in retaliation for attacks suffered in one's village or in an ally's village.

Many ethnographers acquired accounts of major retaliations upon the Lekwiltok by an alliance of Coast Salish tribes – some successful, some not. In a narrative acquired by Collins (1974, 117), John Fornsby recounts a retaliatory raid upon the Lekwiltok by a great warrior named Old Snatlem. In his telling, the Salish attack the Lekwiltok village despite the fact that the Lekwiltok had guns and they did not:

> Old Snatlem killed about ten men that time. He was a powerful young man. He caught the people who were staying in one house. He was singing *tubcádad* [warrior power]. He killed about ten people. Old Snatlem packed the heads – ten of them – packed them out. It took him a long time to come out. They thought he had got killed, but he came out, carrying ten heads – men's heads and women's heads. Some of the *yúk'wta* were hiding in the woods. He cut off ten heads and tied them together. He just brought out the heads to show to the people; then he threw them away. He used to be mean, but he was a good man when he was not mean. The *yúk'wta* shot the people and killed quite a few Lower Skagit and Snohomish. Those folks down there had guns. The people from here had all arrows and bows. Those fellows he killed were right on the island here, when the *yúk'wta* killed some Lower Skagit.

Boas (1889, 324-25) records one account that tells of how the Sechelt and the Nanaimo came together to avenge a deadly attack by the Lekwiltok:

> They sent out jointly, and met the Lekwiltok at Qu'sam (Salmon River). In the ensuing struggle the Si'ciatl and Snanaimuq were victorious, but many of their warriors were killed. They brought home many heads of their enemies. The friends of the Snanaimuq, however, were sad when they heard of the death of so many of their friends, and they resolved to take revenge ... Another battle was fought at Qu'sam, in which the Lekwiltok were utterly defeated, and in which many slaves were captured.

Thus, the Nanaimo and Sechelt punished the Lekwiltok for the losses they suffered in achieving a victory. Of course, those two Salishan successes led to even greater retaliations by the Lekwiltok and their allies. A series of successful Lekwiltok attacks followed in the Gulf of Georgia and Puget Sound. Eventually, this led to an alliance between several Coast Salish tribes, who defeated the Lekwiltok in a battle at Maple Bay, near Cowichan Gap, a few years before 1850 (Curtis 1913, 35). The alliance included Cowichan, Klallam, and Puget Sound tribes, among others. According to one account provided by Curtis (33-35), the alliance met on Kuper Island and then encountered the Lekwiltok on the open water of Maple Bay prior to their ascent of the Cowichan River, where they intended to sack Salish villages. The Suquamish warrior Kitsap played a dominant role, and it was said that his spirit power aided not only himself but also others in his canoe:

> Kitsap puts up a black flag, that means he wants to fight. And Kitsap shouts, "Go after them now!" Kitsap is in the bow now and big lice come out of his head and crawl all over everyone in the canoe. And Kitsap turns around and says to the people in his canoe, "Don't scatter my ammunition now, just let my ammunition alone. That's from my power now, just let them crawl on you!"
>
> And before that fight began Kitsap had told all his party, all the Sound Indians, to use their spears and try to split the [Lekwiltok] canoes like he was doing now. And they did that, all the Puget Sound war men stabbing the [Lekwiltok] canoes and splitting lots of them. When a canoe would split, those [Lekwiltok] would stop shooting and try to save themselves and the Sound people would shoot them down or club them in the water ...
>
> They said the [Lekwiltok] never made any noise when they were fighting, but the Sound people kept yelling, that was their power talking, each warrior a different noise. And lots of people were killed that day, lots of them wounded and trying to swim and drowning ...
>
> And very few of the [Lekwiltok] are left to go home, they killed nearly all of those [Lekwiltok]. (Elmendorf 1993, 148-50)

That battle marked the last time the Salish were bothered by the Lekwiltok. In Curtis' (1913, 34) account, the Coast Salish "allies lost not a single man." In a footnote, he mentions that Lekwiltok informants "refuse to discuss this disastrous affair, frankly admitting, when pressed, that they prefer to talk about their victories."

Conclusion

The intention of this chapter has not been to claim that the Coast Salish were nearly as warlike, as warlike, or more warlike than the northerners; rather, it is to counter claims that they were merely defensive or even pacifist. Such notions, buoyed by accounts of their "Continual Alarm," as recorded in *The Fort Langley Journals*, promote a sense of victimhood, as though the Salish were merely prey for northern raiders. These notions developed due to a late window into Coast Salish culture – a window that may well have resulted in representations of their culture that would not have been accurate even a few decades earlier. Such accounts ignore the important effect upon the Coast Salish of contact, which created a significant advantage for the Lekwiltok in terms of firearms and numbers of people affected by smallpox. In this chapter I bring together multiple sources of disciplinary evidence – archaeology, ethnohistory, ethnography, and oral traditions – in order to check this conception, which, I suggest, is a loosely and incorrectly applied generalization that ignores significant historical contingencies.

The archaeological evidence shows that the construction of defensive sites began many centuries ago. Moreover, these "defensive" sites are not representative of a passive people; rather, they indicate the active defence of territory, the rock-wall fortifications of the Fraser Valley and trench-embankment sites being unique to the Coast Salish region. Finally, the data pertaining to burials in the Late Period are limited, but it seems that, province-wide, interpersonal violence reaches its peak during this time. Ethnographically, there is evidence to indicate that there were unique styles of warfare, involving armour (or not), manner of attack, and spirit powers. The powers of warriors are even displayed in Coast Salish winter dancing ceremonials, and this reveals their connection to wider aspects of Coast Salish culture. The long duration of defensive practices (which is evident in archaeological finds) combined with the memories and practices of warfare (which are documented in ethnographies and oral traditions) are at odds with the sense of pacifism and victimhood presented in postcontact historical accounts. In fact, even historic evidence about firearms availability and the spread of disease counters this phantom, suggesting that it is a simplification and is devoid of context.

Sometimes, academic conceptions can be ideological. And, according to Slavoj Žižek (1994, 4), ideologies are typically of two forms, one of which involves "the eternalization of some historically limited condition."[3] This is precisely what has occurred in the historiography of Coast Salish warfare: the historic contingencies of a narrow window of time were universalized and applied to Coast Salish culture overall. Certainly, for a period, the Coast Salish were victims – a people subjected to northerners who suddenly outnumbered them due to epidemics and who had guns when they did not. Yet, despite such disparities, accounts of the battle of Maple Bay, among others, indicate that Coast Salish groups were successful in defeating northern marauders and even, apparently, put a stop to Lekwiltok raids.

Above, I mentioned that Bierwert (1999, 15-18) discusses the marginalization of the Coast Salish, particularly regarding art. This arose partly due to the culture-core concept, which identifies the north as core and the Salish areas as periphery (or hinterlands), as fading shadows of the core. Bierwert counters that Coast Salish traditions need to be studied on their own terms. A parallel argument may be applied to the archaeology of warfare: the purpose is not to present the Coast Salish as warlike or even more warlike than their northern neighbours but, rather, to show that Coast Salish culture must be assessed on its own terms and within its own dynamics. Priority should be given, first, to situating Coast Salish cultural practices, defensive or not, within their local terms, and, second, to placing these traditions within the wider traditions of the Northwest Coast as a whole. Perhaps then, by bringing together the multiple avenues of evidence at our disposal, we can steer between the polarities of "warlike" and "pacific" and achieve a more coherent conception of warfare in Coast Salish culture in both historic and prehistoric times.

Acknowledgments

This chapter benefited early on from conversations with David Schaepe, Stó:lō Nation archaeologist. As part of a session in honour of Charles Borden, a brief version of this chapter was presented at the Canadian Archaeological Association Conference, 38th Annual Meeting, Nanaimo, BC, 11-15 May 2005.

Notes

1 After attempting to demonstrate that firearms were of little consequence, Fisher (1976, 17-18) is compelled to wonder why the Natives wanted these guns: "If we accept the proposition that firearms were of limited utility as weapons, then we are left with the question: why did the coast Indians, or at least the Indian leaders, want to acquire large numbers of muskets?" Given that he has ruled out their use as weapons, Fisher is able to suggest only that these items were wanted for their symbolic value, simply to show that Natives were "partaking of the wealth of the white man." Or, he offered, perhaps these weapons had "emotional value," that the guns may have served as "phallic symbols."

2 Boyd (1996) challenges Harris' assertions, particularly his claim that the Kwakwaka'wakw "had never been affected by smallpox." Instead, Boyd argues that Simpson was merely noting that they had missed the epidemic of 1836-37. Boyd (1999, 27-28; 1996, 311-12) found only one account in Kwakwaka'wakw oral tradition concerning the deaths of the Hoyalas people of Quatsino Sound; however, he noted that other accounts state that they were decimated by warfare. Yet, even so, this concerns only one Kwakwaka'wakw group. In the end, he does acknowledge that "the relative lack of documentation for early smallpox among the Wakashan peoples is a problem that merits further investigation" (Boyd 1999, 38-39; 1996, 312).

3 The other type of ideology, according to Žižek (1994, 4), involves presenting significant historical changes as minor perturbations of no consequence.

References

Angelbeck, Bill. 2003. Stó:lō Forests: Traditional and Contemporary Values, Resources, and Uses of Forests. Report submitted to the Stó:lō Nation. Department of Anthropology and Sociology, University of British Columbia.

Barnett, Homer G. 1955. *The Coast Salish of British Columbia.* Eugene: University of Oregon Press.

Bierwert, Crisca. 1999. *Brushed by Cedar, Living by the River: Coast Salish Figures of Power.* Tucson: University of Arizona Press.

Blake, T. Michael. 1985. Canajaste: An Evolving Postclassic Maya State. PhD diss., University of Michigan.

Boas, Franz. 1889. Notes on the Snanaimuq. *American Anthropologist* 2 (4): 321-28.

Boyd, Robert. 1996. Commentary on Early Contact-Era Smallpox in the Pacific Northwest. *Ethnohistory* 43 (2): 307-28.

–. 1999. *The Coming of the Spirit of Pestilence: Introduced Infectious Diseases and Population Decline among Northwest Coast Indians, 1774-1874.* Seattle/Vancouver: University of Washington Press/UBC Press.

Bryan, Alan Lyle. 1963. *An Archaeological Survey of Northern Puget Sound.* Occasional Papers of the Idaho State University Museum No. 11. Pocatello, ID: Idaho State University.

Burley, David V. 1980. *Marpole: Anthropological Reconstructions of a Prehistoric Northwest Coast Culture Type.* Burnaby, BC: Archaeology Press.

Burley, David V., and Christopher Knüsel. 1989. Burial Patterns and Archaeological Interpretations: Problems in the Recognition of Ranked Society in the Coast Salish Region. Paper presented at the Circum-Pacific Prehistory Conference, 2-6 August, Seattle, Washington.

Buxton, Judith. 1969. Earthworks of Southwestern British Columbia. MA thesis, University of Calgary.

Cannon, Aubrey. 1992. Conflict and Salmon on the Interior Plateau of British Columbia. In *A Complex Culture of the British Columbia Plateau,* ed. Brian Hayden, 506-24. Vancouver: UBC Press.

Carlson, Keith Thor. 2001. Intercommunity Conflicts. In *A Stó:lō Coast Salish Historical Atlas,* ed. Keith Thor Carlson, 48-49. Vancouver: Douglas and McIntyre.

Chatters, James C. 1989. Pacifism and the Organization of Conflict on the Plateau of Northwestern America. In *Cultures in Conflict: Current Archaeological Perspectives,* ed. D. Tkaczuk and B. Vivian, 241-52. Calgary: University of Calgary Archaeological Association.

Codere, Helen. 1950. *Fighting with Property: A Study of Kwakiutl Potlatching and Warfare, 1792-1930.* Monographs of the American Ethnological Society, 18. New York: J.J. Augustin.

Cole, Douglas, and David Darling. 1990. History of the Early Period. In *Handbook of North American Indians.* Vol. 7, *Northwest Coast,* ed. W. Suttles, 119-34. Washington, DC: Smithsonian Institution.

Collins, June. 1950. Growth of Class Distinctions and Political Authority among the Skagit Indians during the Contact Period. *American Anthropologist* 52: 331-42.

–. 1974. *Valley of the Spirits: The Upper Skagit Indians of Western Washington.* Seattle: University of Washington Press.

Collison, William Henry, and Charles Lillard. 1981. *In the Wake of the War Canoe.* Victoria: Sono Nis Press.

Coupland, Gary. 1989. Warfare and Social Complexity on the Northwest Coast. In *Cultures in Conflict: Current Archaeological Perspectives,* ed. D. Tkaczuk and B. Vivian, 205-14. Calgary: University of Calgary Archaeological Association.

Curtis, Edward S. 1913. *The North American Indian*. Vol. 9, *Salishan Tribes of the Coast; The Chimakum and the Quilliute; the Willapa*. New York: Johnson Reprint.

Cybulski, Jerome S. 1990. Human Biology. In *Handbook of North American Indians*. Vol. 7, *Northwest Coast*, ed. W. Suttles, 52-59. Washington: Smithsonian Institution.

–. 1992. *The Greenville Burial Ground*. National Museum of Man, Mercury Series, Archaeological Survey of Canada No. 146. Ottawa: Canadian Museum of Civilization.

–. 1994. Culture Change, Demographic History, and Health and Disease on the Northwest Coast. In *In the Wake of Contact: Biological Responses to Conquest*, ed. C.S. Larsen and G.R. Milner, 75-85. New York: Wiley-Ness.

–. 1999. Trauma and Warfare at Prince Rupert Harbour. *Midden* 31 (2): 5-7.

de Laguna, Frederica. 1960. *Story of a Tlingit Community: A Problem in the Relationship between Archeological, Ethnological, and Historical Methods*. Bureau of American Ethnology Bulletin No. 172. Washington, DC: US Government Printing Office.

Elmendorf, William W. 1960. *The Structure of Twana Culture*. Research Studies Monographic Supplement No. 2. Pullman, WA: Washington State University Press.

–. 1993. *Twana Narratives: Native Historical Accounts of a Coast Salish Culture*. Seattle: University of Washington Press.

Ferguson, R. Brian. 1983. Warfare and Redistributive Exchange on the Northwest Coast. In *The Development of Political Organization in Native North America*, ed. Elisabeth Tooker, 133-47. Washington, DC: American Ethnological Society.

Ferguson, R. Brian, and Neil L. Whitehead. 1992. The Violent Edge of Empire. In *War in the Tribal Zone: Expanding States and Indigenous Warfare*, ed. R.B. Ferguson and N.L. Whitehead, 1-30. Santa Fe, NM: School of American Research Press.

Fisher, Robin. 1976. Arms and Men on the Northwest Coast, 1774-1825. *BC Studies* 29: 3-18.

–. 1977. *Contact and Conflict: Indian-European Relations in British Columbia, 1774-1890*. Vancouver: UBC Press.

Gunther, Erna. 1927. *Klallam Ethnography*. Seattle: University of Washington Press.

–. 1972. *Indian Life on the Northwest Coast of North America: As Seen by the Early Explorers and Fur Traders during the Last Decades of the Eighteenth Century*. Chicago: University of Chicago Press.

Harris, Cole. 1994. Voices of Disaster: Smallpox around the Strait of Georgia in 1782. *Ethnohistory* 41 (4): 591-626.

Jewitt, John Rodgers. [1803-05] 1987. *The Adventures and Sufferings of John R. Jewitt: Captive of Maquinna*, ed. Hilary Stewart. Vancouver: Douglas and McIntyre.

Keddie, Grant. 1984. Fortified Defensive Sites and Burial Cairns of the Songhees Indians. *Midden* 16 (4): 7-9.

–. 1996. Aboriginal Defensive Sites. *Discovery Magazine*. http://www.royalbcmuseum. bc.ca/Human_History/Archaeology.aspx?id-355.

Lambert, Patricia M. 2002. The Archaeology of War: A North American Perspective. *Journal of Archaeological Research* 10 (3): 207-41.

Lillard, Charles, ed. 1984. *Warriors of the North Pacific: Missionary Accounts of the Northwest Coast, the Skeena and Stikine Rivers and the Klondike, 1829-1900*. Victoria: Sono Nis Press.

MacDonald, George F. 1983. Prehistoric Art of the Northern Northwest Coast. In *Indian Art Traditions of the Northwest Coast*, ed. R.L. Carlson, 99-120. Burnaby, BC: Archaeology Press.

–. 1984. The Epic of Nekt: The Archaeology of Metaphor. In *The Tsimshian: Images of the Past; Views from the Present*, ed. Margaret Sequin, 65-81. Vancouver: UBC Press.

–. 1989. *Kitwanga Fort Report*. Hull, QC: Canadian Museum of Civilization.

MacDonald, George F., and Jerome S. Cybulski. 2001. Introduction: The Prince Rupert Harbour Project. In *Perspectives on Northern Northwest Coast Prehistory,* ed. J.S. Cybulski, 1-23. Hull, QC: Canadian Museum of Civilization.

Maclachlan, Morag, ed. 1998. *The Fort Langley Journals, 1827-30.* Vancouver: UBC Press.

Maschner, Herbert D.G. 1996. The Politics of Settlement Choice on the Prehistoric Northwest Coast: Cognition, GIS, and Coastal Landscapes. In *Anthropology, Space, and Geographic Information Systems,* ed. M. Aldenderfer and H. Maschner, 175-78. New York: Oxford University Press.

–. 1997. The Evolution of Northwest Coast Warfare. In *Troubled Times: Violence and Warfare in the Past,* ed. D. Martin and D. Frayer, 267-302. New York: Gordon and Breach.

Maschner, Herbert D.G., and Katherine L. Reedy-Maschner. 1998. Raid, Retreat, Defend (Repeat): The Archaeology and Ethnohistory of Warfare on the North Pacific Rim. *Journal of Anthropological Archaeology* 17 (1): 19-51.

McDonald, Archibald. 1998. Journal Kept by Archibald McDonald, 1829-30. In *The Fort Langley Journals, 1827-30,* ed. Morag Maclachlan, 98-141. Vancouver: UBC Press.

McMillan, Alan D. 1999. *Since the Time of the Transformers: The Ancient Heritage of the Nuu-chah-nulth, Ditidaht, and Makah.* Vancouver: UBC Press.

McMillan, James, and Archibald McDonald. 1998. Journal Kept by James McMillan and Archibald McDonald, 1828-29. In *The Fort Langley Journals, 1827-30,* ed. M. Maclachlan, 52-97. Vancouver: UBC Press.

Mitchell, Donald H. 1968. Excavations at Two Trench Embankments in the Gulf of Georgia Region. *Syesis* 1 (1-2): 29-46.

–. 1981a. Sebassa's Men. In *The World Is as Sharp as a Knife: An Anthology in Honour of Wilson Duff,* ed. Donald N. Abbott, 79-86. Victoria: British Columbia Provincial Museum.

–. 1981b. Test Excavations at Randomly Selected Sites in Eastern Queen Charlotte Strait. *BC Studies* 48: 103-23.

–. 1984. Predatory Warfare, Social Status, and the North Pacific Slave Trade. *Ethnology* 23 (1): 39-48.

–. 1990. Prehistory of the Coasts of Southern British Columbia and Northern Washington. In *Handbook of North American Indians.* Vol. 7, *Northwest Coast,* ed. W. Suttles, 340-58. Washington: Smithsonian Institution.

Moss, Madonna L., and Jon M. Erlandson. 1992. Forts, Refuge Rocks, and Defensive Sites: The Antiquity of Warfare along the North Pacific Coast of North America. *Arctic Anthropology* 29 (2): 73-90.

Ray, Verne F. 1933. *The Sanpoil and Nespelem.* University of Washington Publications in Anthropology 5. Seattle: University of Washington Press.

–. 1939. *Cultural Relations on the Plateau of Northwestern America.* Los Angeles: Publications of the Frederick Webb Hodge Anniversary Publication Fund, Southwest Museum.

Schaepe, David. 2000. Rock Wall Fortifications in the Lower Fraser Canyon. *Midden* 32 (4): 2-4.

–. 2001. Rock Wall Fortifications: Reconstructing a Fraser Canyon Defensive Network. In *A Stó:lō Coast Salish Historical Atlas,* ed. K.T. Carlson, 52-53. Vancouver: Douglas and McIntyre.

–. 2006. Rock Fortifications: Archaeological Insights into Precontact Warfare and Sociopolitical Organization among the Stó:lō of the Lower Fraser River Canyon, BC. *American Antiquity* 71 (4): 671-706.

Scouler, John. [1824] 1905. Dr. John Scouler's Journal of a Voyage to N.W. America, ed. F.G. Young. *Oregon Historical Quarterly* 6 (1): 54-75; (2): 159-205; (3): 276-87.

Smith, Harlan I. 1907. *Archaeology of the Gulf of Georgia and Puget Sound.* The Jesup North Pacific Expedition, ed. Franz Boas, vol. 2, part 6. New York: Memoir of the American Museum of Natural History.

–. 1934. Prehistoric Earthworks in Canada. Manuscripts on File, British Columbia Archives, Victoria.

Smith, Harlan I., and Gerard Fowke. 1901. *Cairns of British Columbia and Washington.* The Jesup North Pacific Expedition, ed. Franz Boas, vol. 2, part 2. New York: Memoir of the American Museum of Natural History.

Smith, Marian W. 1940. *The Puyallup-Nisqually.* New York: Columbia University Press.

Suttles, Wayne P. 1951. *Economic Life of the Coast Salish of Haro and Rosario Straits.* PhD diss., University of Washington. Reprinted in *Coast Salish and Western Washington Indians, I.* New York: Garland Publishing, 1974.

–. 1987. Plateau Pacifism Reconsidered – Ethnography, Ethnology, and Ethnohistory. In *Coast Salish Essays*, 282-86. Seattle: University of Washington Press.

–. 1989. They Recognize No Superior Chief: The Strait of Juan de Fuca in the 1790s. In *Culturas de la Costa Noroeste de America*, ed. J.L. Peset Reig, 251-64. Madrid: Turner.

–. 1998. The Ethnographic Significance of the Fort Langley Journals. In *The Fort Langley Journals, 1827-30*, ed. M. Maclachlan, 163-210. Vancouver: UBC Press.

Suttles, Wayne, and Barbara Lane. 1990. Southern Coast Salish. In *Handbook of North American Indians.* Vol. 7, *Northwest Coast,* ed. W. Suttles, 485-502. Washington: Smithsonian Institution.

Taylor, Herbert C. 1974. Anthropological Investigation of the Medicine Creek Tribes Relative to Tribal Identity and Aboriginal Possession of Lands. In *American Indian Ethnohistory: Indians of the Northwest.* Vol. 2, *Coast Salish and Western Washington Indians.* New York: Garland.

Taylor, Herbert C., and Wilson Duff. 1956. A Post-contact Southward Movement of the Kwakiutl. *Research Studies of the State College of Washington* 24 (1): 56-66.

Thom, Brian. 1995. The Dead and the Living: Burial Mounds and Cairns and the Development of Social Classes in the Gulf of Georgia Region. MA thesis, University of British Columbia.

Worcester, Donald E., and Thomas F. Schilz. 1984. The Spread of Firearms among the Indians on the Anglo-French Frontiers. *American Indian Quarterly* 8 (2): 103-15.

Žižek, Slavoj. 1994. The Spectre of Ideology. In *Mapping Ideology*, ed. S. Žižek, 1-33. New York: Verso Press.

10

Consuming the Recent for Constructing the Ancient: The Role of Ethnography in Coast Salish Archaeological Interpretation

Colin Grier

It has often been remarked in archaeological circles that the Northwest Coast of North America has a rich, fascinating, and even dramatic ethnographic record. This assessment results first and foremost from the richness of the cultural traditions of Northwest Coast peoples, but it also results from the way in which their unique and diverse social practices were captured and disseminated by a number of influential ethnographers, including Franz Boaz, Philip Drucker, and Wayne Suttles.

In creating a picture of Aboriginal Northwest Coast cultures, archaeology has, in many respects, stood a distant second to ethnography. While investigations into Coast Salish prehistory represent some of the earliest archaeological endeavours on the Northwest Coast, as a coherent discipline archaeology has a much more recent genesis than does ethnology. Also, compared to ethnographic field research, archaeological excavation proceeds slowly due to its labour-intensive nature. Moreover, the perishable nature of coastal material culture, particularly its plank and beam houses and wood-based artistic tradition, leaves the archaeological record appearing somewhat meagre relative to the ethnographic record.

While archaeology has nonetheless made substantive and unique contributions to Coast Salish studies, many anthropologists (here I include both ethnographers and archaeologists) have seen a relatively unproblematic relationship between the ethnographic and archaeological records. From this perspective, groups that existed following contact represent the most recent expression of those that have existed for millennia. In this view, the connection between prehistoric lifeways and ethnographically recorded practices is emphasized, with archaeology acting as a means to ascertain how far the ethnographic pattern extends into the prehistoric period (Sutherland 2001). Differences apparent between the past and the recent are downplayed or seen as logical, predictable, and gradual evolutionary changes. In this way, the significant social change evident in the prehistoric record is measured primarily with respect to the ethnographic picture. Given the problematic aspects inherent in the production of the ethnographic record in many areas of the Northwest Coast, this approach should be treated as itself problematic.

It is my contention that this uncritical view of the relationship between the archaeological and ethnographic records limits the contribution of archaeology to the understanding of Northwest Coast cultures. This is true for the coast as a whole, but it is particularly true for the Coast Salish peoples. Archaeologically, the Gulf of Georgia region – the Central Coast Salish world at contact – has been the most studied region of the Northwest Coast. While this does not necessarily mean that it is well understood from an archaeological perspective, it does mean that the issue of the relationship between ethnography and archaeology is particularly critical in the study of this region.

In this chapter I tackle three fundamental issues concerning that relationship: (1) How has the ethnographic record been consumed in the service of reconstructing ancient Coast Salish lifeways? (2) Has this practice been useful for interpreting the archaeological record? and (3) What potential approaches or strategies exist for employing ethnography in the service of reconstructing the past?

A major element in addressing these questions is the appreciation that both the archaeological and the ethnographic records are records of change – the archaeological in its inherently long-term view and the ethnographic in that it chronicles Coast Salish peoples at a time when radical change and devastating circumstances held sway. Thus, to achieve a working relationship between archaeological and ethnographic records, it is critical to contextualize these data within such change rather than to view them as an idealized pattern, practice, and image.

A four-fields anthropology approach tends to emphasize the commonalities of the many manifestations of anthropology, yet the archaeological and ethnographic records are fundamentally different. As a result, methodologically and, perhaps less obviously, theoretically, very different approaches are required for dealing with similarly construed problems. My main objective in this chapter is to identify how these two elements of the anthropological equation may productively articulate, and how this articulation may provide a sound basis for the future of the Coast Salish past.

How the Recent Plays into the Past

The most obvious place to start is with a basic question: Can the ethnographic record be used to model and describe societies that existed prior to European contact? Polling the scholarly literature reveals that archaeologists clearly believe that the answer is yes. Almost every archaeological report, chapter, or article presents a review of the archaeological problem from the point of view of what the ethnographic record tells us about the situation.

Indeed, much of what we "know" about the prehistory of the Coast Salish is rooted in the ethnographic record. For example, without some indication that social stratification existed in Coast Salish societies in historic times, there would be much more contention about whether prehistoric Coast Salish societies and even hunter-gatherer societies in general could develop social stratification. A similar situation exists with respect to slavery: if it were not so strongly represented in the discussions of ethnographers and ethnohistorians, archaeologists would be less motivated to consider such an institution as part of their reconstructions of the past. In general, both slavery and social stratification are extremely rare amongst societies with non-agricultural economies, and thus the Coast Salish ethnographic record vastly expands the variability hunter-gatherer archaeologists will entertain in the societies they study. This is particularly true when the long-term perspective of archaeology comes into play: What factors promoted such organizational approaches and how did they develop over time? The existence of such institutions in a rich ethnographic record promotes study of their development in the recent and ancient past, and it provides a central role for Coast Salish prehistory in the study of ourselves in the broader sense.

While greater perception of variability in small-scale societies can be construed as a net benefit of the extant ethnographic record, there are other effects that are not quite so productive. A legitimate and laudable objective of archaeological research is to piece together long-term history and trajectories of change. However, it is a different thing altogether to cast that long-term development as an inevitable progression toward the forms of indigenous societies that existed at European contact. Such a perspective has crept slowly and at times imperceptibly into Northwest Coast archaeology. One of the main academic syntheses of Northwest Coast prehistory, Matson and Coupland's *The Prehistory of the Northwest Coast* (1995), is organized around a single main theme – the "achievement" of cultural complexity. This gives the impression that, from their arrival in the New World, Northwest Coast cultures were committed to achieving such a state of economic and social organization over the long term.

The use of the ethnographic record as an endpoint to which all preceding archaeological data must be referenced is a recurring theme in archaeological reconstructions of Coast Salish and Northwest Coast prehistory. Roy Carlson (1996) provides a complex and speculative candelabra of connections to represent the evolutionary development of Northwest Coast societies out of their deep past, culminating in the "ethnographic pattern" (Figure 10.1). While interesting to ponder, there is very little archaeological data to support the specific relationships he posits; thus, the schematic does not seem to work as an explanation either for the Coast Salish past specifically or for Northwest Coast prehistory generally. Other perspectives, such as that offered by Croes and Hackenberger (1988), provide a somewhat more transparent rationale for the connections drawn between the past and present. They see population/resource imbalances as a "prime mover" that promoted successive economic shifts to more intensive storage economies over the last five thousand years. In their view, the particular economic organization recorded at contact came about as a result of a consistent effort to feed more mouths. Despite the somewhat deterministic flavour, the underlying theme is again a trajectory of development that logically shows how prehistoric social change was a steady and predictable progression toward the "ethnographic pattern."

These views hold in common explicit evolutionary links that have an element of teleology, whereby the outcome is preordained in the initial conditions. While I see no inherent problem in hypothesizing evolutionary links generally, there are other ways to model the situation. For example, positing an explicit evolutionary progression stands in contrast to the view that change toward increasing cultural "complexity" was an unintended consequence of social actors working within limited temporal and social contexts (e.g., Clark and Blake 1994, 17). While this distinction covers mostly theoretical territory, it does challenge us to identify how we see the broader trends of Coast Salish prehistory and to determine whether current positions are warranted. Unilinear evolutionary trajectories have been criticized for decades, and while the schemes presented by Northwest Coast archaeologists are not strictly the kind of positions that have drawn heavy fire, it is clear that evolutionary frameworks constrain the kinds of explanations that are considered relevant to reconstructing the past. Teleological positions structure what we perceive as data, and, within the data, what patterns we consider relevant to the problems we posit. Obviously, at some basic level there was a "real" Coast Salish history that unfolded. Explaining why it unfolded as it did is not particularly well served by the perspective that it could not have been otherwise.

But the advantage of an evolutionary perspective is that it clearly situates the problems of archaeological reconstruction of Coast Salish history within a local framework. Despite early statements to the contrary (e.g., Boas 1905, 96; Borden 1970, 109; Drucker 1955; Kroeber 1923), the Coast Salish archaeological record resists invoking wholesale migrations and population replacement as an explanation for social and economic

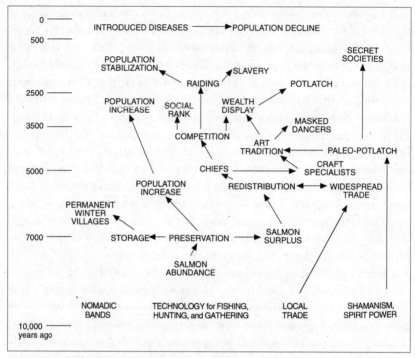

FIGURE 10.1 The evolutionary scheme presented by Roy Carlson (1996) to explain the development of Northwest Coast societies over the last ten millennia

change. This may be extended to the Northwest Coast in general, at least after the initial peopling of the region some ten millennia ago. Despite evidence for population expansions and movements in some areas of the coast (e.g., among the Wakashan [McMillan 2003]), the view taken by Ken Ames and Herbert Maschner (Ames and Maschner 1999, 85-86) seems quite reasonable: they see no compelling evidence for migrations as *the* driving central force in shaping the prehistory of coastal peoples. To echo Don Mitchell's anti-migrationist "Midden Manifesto" of thirty years earlier (Borden 1969, 255), this is tantamount to saying that, unless there is compelling evidence to the contrary, historic-period groups in the many areas of the Northwest Coast should be seen as the makers of their own prehistory. This is particularly true of the Coast Salish area. While migrations have in the past been used to explain their particular origin and character, and movements downriver from the Interior and upriver from the coast are still referenced in prehistoric reconstructions, these days the idea that the Coast Salish are a recent arrival in their traditional territory seems largely untenable (McMillan 2003).

But evolutionary developments, geographical origins, and theoretical positions aside, the real pressing questions are these: Were ancient Coast Salish societies like ethnographic ones, and, if so, in what sense? Did prehistoric societies have the same social institutions as did historic-period societies? And further, can the generalized models presented by ethnographers for historic-period Coast Salish societies be used appropriately and effectively to address archaeological problems?

The Wider Archaeological Debate

The relationship between ethnography and archaeology has been debated in the wider practice of archaeology for many years, and, indeed, such reflection was necessary for the coming of age of archaeology as a discipline. Ethnographies have had a strong allure for archaeologists, unquestionably, but fairly liberal use of ethnographic societies as ready-made explanations for past behaviour has been systematically challenged since the 1960s. While this debate has covered broad ground and has been at times highly epistemological (e.g., Wylie 1985), it is worth noting the cogent points made along the way as they can be applied directly to the use of Coast Salish ethnographic data as a vehicle for archaeological inference.

Early consideration of the use of ethnography focused on an appropriate methodology for the use of ethnographic data in the construction of interpretations of the archaeological record. These initial considerations were of a methodological nature, with programmatic overtones. Ascher (1961) and Binford (1967) presented cases that seemed quite careful in their application of observed behaviours to past activities, even in situations where the connection between present and past behaviours was seemingly obvious. In this sense, they represent "cautionary tales" that suggest we may be led astray in our reasoning when we fail to be discerning and judicious in the application of present situations to the archaeological past. But these studies were limited to considering what now mostly falls under the banner of "middle range research"; that is, building links between very specific observable behaviours and the material correlates produced in the archaeological record.

The 1980s gave rise to a much more theoretical debate (e.g., Hodder 1982; Gould and Watson 1982; Wylie 1985) centring on the epistemological justifications for using analogical reasoning in any past-meets-present or known-versus-unknown scenario. A key point in these discussions is that the use of ethnographic data for interpreting past cultures essentially functions as an analogy because it amounts to a comparison of what is reasonably well understood (can be observed) with what is less known (not observable). An ethnographic analogy is distinguished in that it posits an underlying rationale for the comparison, often a historical connection. Yet, in theory, the rationale could just as legitimately be an ecological or even organizational similarity at a fairly abstract level. The bottom line that was stressed in the 1980s was that, if a reasoned link supports the comparison between source and subject, then the strength of the analogy is improved. An interesting element of the debate in the 1980s was that it ruminated upon the more thorny areas in which analogies might be applied – the ideational realm. It is easy to see how hide smoking or fish drying could be very similar now and in the past since there is a basic mechanics to the processes that exists independent of time and space. But when we turn to symbol systems, ideologies, and art traditions, it is a trickier matter to posit that similarities between recent systems and past systems can be easily compared since the constraints that produce similarities over time and space are less clear.

Another manifestation of this discussion of the strength of ethnographic data as the source of analogy for the past came in the form of revisiting of the notion of a direct historical approach. On an intuitive level, the strongest rationale for comparing a modern society with an ancient society would seem to be a demonstrated historical connection. But can this alone justify using an ethnographic analogy as an explanation? An important consideration is that the direct historical approach assumes what should in fact first be demonstrated – that the history of an area or culture or group exhibits strong continuity. It is not my intention to argue against a direct historical approach here, as I think there is significant value in it, and it is much more reasonable to posit long-term continuity (even if that continuity exists only at the level of very general social structures and institutions) than a radical disjunction between the present and the past (unless major changes are suggested by the ethnographic or archaeological record itself). My point is to illuminate the notion that the direct historical approach is, in fact, an assumption about the relationship between past and present and not, in and of itself, an empirically justified or demonstrated connection. How this is specifically relevant to Coast Salish history I take up in a later section.

While, for many, the debate over the proper use of analogy has not been adequately resolved, a more pragmatic and pressing concern for present purposes is to distil the salient points of past debates that elicit general agreement and use these as a basis for entering into a discussion of the relationship between historic and prehistoric Coast Salish societies, between the archaeological and ethnographic records, and between archaeologists and their explanations. Three broad points are germane to this objective:

1 The use of an analogy is much stronger when specific "relational" connections can be demonstrated between source and subject, meaning
   that when an evolutionary, historical, or environmental similarity justi-
   fies the analogical comparison, its strength and relevance are greater.
2 Notwithstanding the above, the ethnographic record is best treated as a
   source for hypotheses about the material record of the past rather than
   a source for ready-made explanations, and ethnographic models should
   be evaluated against the archaeological data available.
3 If the ethnographic record is our main source of ideas about the past, a
   reliance on analogy may severely diminish our ability to see novel social
   forms that existed in the past but for which no recent example exists.

Ethnographic Explanation in Coast Salish Archaeology

A critical point to recognize at the outset of any discussion of the consumption of ethnography is that the ethnographic record itself is not
unproblematic. This applies both as a general statement and as it concerns
Coast Salish ethnography in particular. A recent discussion of the Coast
Salish ethnographic record by Miller (2004) effectively points out that many
ethnological truisms are quite capriciously derived and may not have been
generalized practice. These have become generalizations and accepted ethnological wisdom through their repetition and through the enduring nature of the ethnographies and ethnographers who offered them. While it is
not my intention to weigh in on the primarily ethnological issues at stake
here, it is worth noting that the ethnographic record is regularly presented
as unproblematic in archaeological contexts, and it is often cited and reca-
pitulated in abstracted and generalized ways in archaeological research.

Most archaeologists agree that the Marpole Period societies that existed
roughly 2,400 to 1,000 years ago in the Gulf of Georgia region incorporated the major social institutions, or organizational principles, that are
attributed to ethnographically recorded Coast Salish societies of the historic period. Archaeological data concerning burial practices (e.g., Burley
1988; Burley and Knusel 1989) indicate that some form of social stratification system had developed. The existence of large houses indicates that
intensive storage was practised (Ames 1996) and that plank houses similar
to the historically documented shed-roof style were the residence of choice
(Grier 2001; Lepofsky et al. 2000; Matson 2003).

While these observations allow us to connect historic-period Coast Salish
societies to the Marpole culture, we might also ask how Marpole societies
differed from their contact-period descendents. Answering such a question
is made more challenging by the realization that, if we seek answers in the

ethnographic record, it is difficult to envision the ways in which they might have differed. As Ames (2004) points out, the diversity of lifeways on the Northwest Coast (as with all of the Americas) was being significantly truncated in the protohistoric period. There may have been more variability in Coast Salish lifeways than we suppose. The rapid and widespread cultural loss associated with and even predating actual European contact presents serious problems for the archaeologist who uses the ethnographic record as the maximal range of possible social forms that characterized the Coast Salish throughout their prehistory. By the time George Vancouver sailed into Burrard Inlet in 1792, Coast Salish societies were not living in an "ethnographic present" but, rather, had already entered a period of rapid change (if not a state of crisis).

But should we not be able to work backward from consequence to cause to pre-existing condition – that is, to come to appreciate how contact affected the fundamental workings of "traditional" culture – in order to at least imagine Coast Salish societies as they were in precontact times? Perhaps. Posing this question requires determining the major impacts of the contact and colonization process on the fundamental workings of Coast Salish society, particularly as those workings are conceptualized and analyzed archaeologically. From this viewpoint, what were the factors involved and the responses pursued by the Coast Salish to cope with the immense pressures generated by contact forces, events, and consequences? Taking this tack is not to suggest that the responses were in any way homogeneous, yet these must be generalized to some degree to have utility for constructing archaeological characterizations of the past. In my assessment, major elements of the equation include (but are not limited to) the phenomena I discuss below.

Population Crash

Boyd's (1990) estimates for population loss due to European-introduced diseases are substantial, with a population drop on the Northwest Coast from near 200,000 people at around AD 1770 to 30,000 by AD 1870. While these numbers are generated with some assumptions, and the Coast Salish area may have fared better than most (Boyd 1990, 146), losses anywhere near this magnitude clearly would (and did) have a widespread disruptive effect, the implications of which could be anticipated as

1 Labour shortages: As pointed out by Ames (1996), the domestic mode of production of Northwest Coast groups was based on large households with complementary divisions of labour and specialist producers. Depopulation would have disrupted this basic productive engine of Coast

Salish society both through loss of labour contributions to the house-hold and the organization of suprahousehold collaborative mechanisms of resource acquisition, particularly in the mounting of labour task groups that acquired resources from distant regions of the Coast Salish world.

2 Territoriality: Patterns of territoriality and intergroup access rights to resource locations remain only loosely understood for precontact times. Yet defensive fortifications are an element of the late prehistoric archaeo-logical record and indicate the need and/or ability to defend territory against internal Salish encroachment or external raiding (Mitchell 1968; Moss and Erlandson 1992; Maschner 1997; Shaepe 2001). Defence of territory (not to mention the construction and maintenance of defen-sive fortifications) typically requires a significant level of population. The particulars of Coast Salish warfare in precontact times are only now be-coming a topic of systematic study, yet it is clear that a major drop in population would pose problems for the maintenance of territories that had evolved over time. The organization of defence itself (to the extent that defence existed in an organized sense) may have been undermined significantly. Defence of core territories and resources would become a key factor, particularly through summer months when, under normal circumstances, only a nominal population may have been left at winter village sites. In a depopulated situation, it may have been difficult to maintain a presence in all areas of one's territory year-round. Also, the opening up of previously defended space and protected resource loca-tions may have provided opportunities for new patterns of movement. This point may be of critical importance in considering ethnographically documented movements to and from as well as along the Fraser River.

3 Vacancies in leadership positions: Traditional leadership systems are based on succession, achievement of status within ranked hierarchies, and the availability of a suite of individuals of appropriate station to assume and achieve a leadership position. Loss of population can disrupt what were relatively stable power structures. As in times of heavy conflict any-where, the loss of a significant number of eligible leadership candidates makes power systems unpredictable and mechanisms for the appropri-ate control of the holdings of elite individual or families subject to ca-pricious shifts.

Introduction of European Goods

The introduction of European goods into the Northwest Coast economic sphere had profound effects on the indigenous system of economic value and, perhaps more important, provided access to new forms of wealth. These new forms of wealth were not necessarily acquired through traditional exchange mechanisms and social relations, and so circulated in new ways. Some specific developments related to this process may have been highly significant, including

1 New economic parameters of value: The introduction of foreign goods presented a situation in which new exotic goods of both prestige and functional utility could be acquired. This could have significantly disrupted traditional exchange networks and devalued traditional goods in economic or social status.

2 Circumvention of traditional means of prestige building: The flow of goods in a way that was not strictly controlled by traditional cultural mechanisms, coupled with access to wage labour opportunities, may have provided a means for those with aspirations for status to circumvent the constraints on social advancement that had existed within the traditional system. Wealth could come through fortuitous relations with Europeans rather than through a lifetime of achievement in traditional endeavours and relations. While, clearly, old constraints remained in place to various degrees, the flexibility of the system of access to wealth broadened.

3 New focal nodes of regional resource access: The establishment of Euro-Canadian forts within the Coast Salish world provided new focal nodes of resource access. This likely shifted seasonal-round pathways and levels of mobility. These new nodes of exchange appear to have precipitated seasonal aggregations of Central Coast Salish groups in specific locations that were not previously of regional significance, as at Fort Langley (Suttles 1998). Population level decreases may have been a factor here too, allowing aggregations in areas previously densely inhabited and perhaps defended.

The extent of the effect that accompanied the disruption of traditional value systems should not be underestimated. Codere's (1950, 1990) discussion of potlatching among Kwakwala speakers after 1849 provides some sense of the kinds of changes that can occur in systems that are subject to unusual pressures from new forms of economic capital. The potential for these changes to occur is not unique to the Coast Salish area or the Northwest Coast. Amongst Inupiat whalers of the late 1800s, similar circumvention and, ultimately, dismantling of traditional mechanisms of achieving the status of whaling captain *(umialik)* was brought about by young individuals with access to Euro-American whaling wage labour, trade goods, and mechanized whaling equipment (Burch 1975, 1981).

Seen in light of these points, the process of contact represents a form of disruption of preceding indigenous systems that had a particularly marked effect on the parameters of those systems in some of the specific ways that archaeologists typically set out to measure – mobility, exchange, seasonal rounds, and settlement distributions. In light of these points, there is obviously a large chasm over which we must leap to connect the ethnographic and archaeological records.

Archaeological Interpretation from Ethnographic Data: An Example

Where does this leave us in relation to using ethnographic information as a vehicle for archaeological interpretation? While it may appear as though I have implicitly been arguing that the changes associated with contact were too dramatic to make use of the record in any sensible fashion, that is neither my objective nor my intention. One must acknowledge that significant change has occurred, but this does not require one to reject the record as a source of useful – even critical – information. There is clearly a middle road to walk. To map out this direction, below I outline a specific example of how the ethnographic record has been used to interpret a single archaeological site, and I point out exactly where an uncritical use of ethnographic information to develop a broader interpretation leads us astray. My ultimate purpose, following this discussion, is to impart the notion that such situations do not represent simply an academic argument about methodology and interpretation but, rather, that the way in which archaeologists construct the Coast Salish past has a very real effect on the present and the future.

The site of False Narrows (Senewélets in Hul'qumi'num [Island Halkomelem]) was excavated under the direction of Donald Mitchell of the University of Victoria in 1966 and by John Sendey on behalf of the British Columbia Archaeological Sites Advisory Board in 1967. The site is situated on the southern shore of Gabriola Island, the most northerly of the southern Gulf Islands, ten kilometres from modern-day Nanaimo (Map 10.1). False Narrows was first recorded as a site in the early 1960s during a major archaeological survey of the Gulf Islands by John Sendey and Don Abbott. The site was identified as a major prehistoric village and, along with a number of other sites in the southern Gulf Islands, was considered worthy of immediate study. Around that time, the locality of False Narrows was being developed and subdivided for housing, and so the opportunity was there for archaeological investigations of the site to salvage archaeological information in advance of this development.

No comprehensive or detailed map of the existing surface archaeological features was completed prior to the major alterations of surface topography that accompanied development (though see Burley 1988, 14-15, for illustrations of the site locale). It remains unclear how many house depressions (platforms) in total existed at the site, but a number of individual depressions

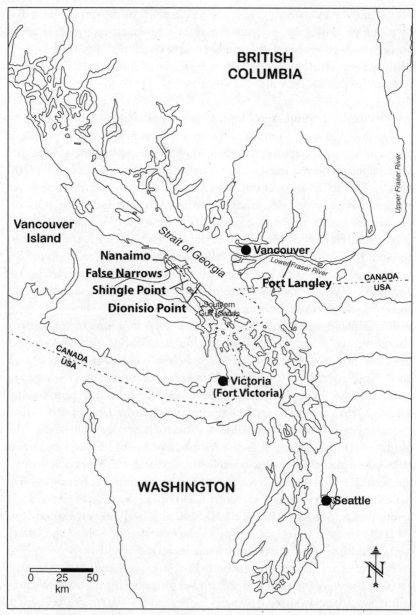

MAP 10.1 Archaeological sites, colonial-period forts, and modern urban centres in the Coast Salish region

were identified and noted during Don Mitchell's excavations. These depressions are similar in size and surface expression to those seen at other sites in the area that are now known to comprise the remains of plank house residences of the shed-roof type (e.g., at Dionisio Point on Galiano Island [Grier 2001] and Shingle Point on Valdes Island [Matson 2003]) (Figure 10.2). It is clear that the Senewélets locality was at one time home to a major village composed of numerous large plank houses. Archaeological excavations revealed an incredible array of material culture as well as a large number of human burials containing individuals of varying social status, wealth, and perhaps even ethnic origin (Gordon 1974; Burley 1988, 51; Curtin 2002). Also, the complex stratigraphy and hearth, house post, pit, and burial features are indicative of a long and multiperiod occupation that began during the Marpole Period, as many as 2,400 years ago.

David Burley (1988) of Simon Fraser University has produced the main published report for the False Narrows excavations. A decade after the initial excavations, he analyzed the recovered assemblages as part of his doctoral research. The ensuing published report did not appear until 1988, however, owing in part to the incredible amount of work involved in assembling data that the excavators had left in field record form. For undertaking this task, David Burley is owed many thanks since, without his efforts, this critical site and major excavation project would not form part of the published record of the history of Coast Salish peoples.

Burley offers broad interpretations of the site as well as the basic reporting and analysis of the results of the excavations. In a section entitled "False Narrows within Regional Settlement Pattern" (Burley 1988, 46-50), he uses the ethnographically recorded movements of the Snuneymuxw (Nanaimo Coast Salish) of Departure Bay to interpret the significance of the False Narrows site. The Snuneymuxw are described as having moved out of their winter villages in Nanaimo Harbour and Departure Bay to spring camps located in the Gulf Islands. This move was a temporary seasonal stop within their larger yearly movement to and from the Fraser River, where they acquired salmon and other resources. It is widely reported that salmon were obtained in large numbers by Hul'qumi'num groups fishing on the Fraser River, with the catch transported back to the islands (Mitchell and Donald 1988; Suttles 1998, 179-81) (see Map 10.2).

Major villages with large plank houses – those of the Nanaimo specifically and Central Coast Salish generally – were predominantly winter season residential sites (Coupland 1991; Ames 1996; Suttles 1991). These villages were sustained through the resource-poor winter months in large part through consumption of stored resources – primarily salmon. Putting up a vast amount of stores allowed (and indeed required) this high degree

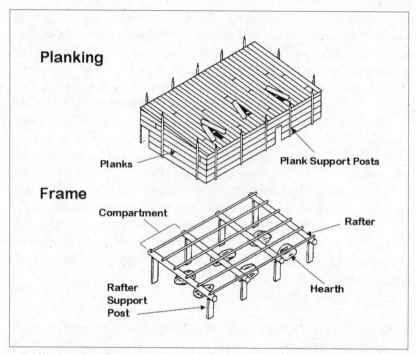

FIGURE 10.2 An idealized rendition of the shed-roof house constructed by Coast Salish peoples over the last few millennia

of winter residential sedentism. Ethnographic descriptions of seasonal patterns of occupation and movement (e.g., Barnett 1955; Duff 1952; Jenness n.d.) indicate that these villages were almost wholly abandoned (and houses "de-planked") in the spring so that the residents could disperse across the landscape to acquire blooming and returning resources that accompanied the onset of spring (Coupland 1991; Monks 1987).

Burley situates the False Narrows site within this defined seasonal round based on the descriptions of Jenness (n.d.) and Barnett (1955), who identify False Narrows specifically as a spring village constructed after the winter villages in Nanaimo Harbour were dismantled. Apparently, the specific draw of the Senewélets location was the major shellfish beds found in its vicinity. These shellfish, Burley (1988, 48) argues, could have been dried and taken across to the Fraser River and traded with mainlanders.

The overall picture presented, which is used to interpret patterns of movement and economics of the occupants of False Narrows over the last two millennia, is that the site reflects a spring resource collection locale. A broader implication that stems from extending the ethnographic picture back over two millennia is that the Gulf Islands have, over the long term,

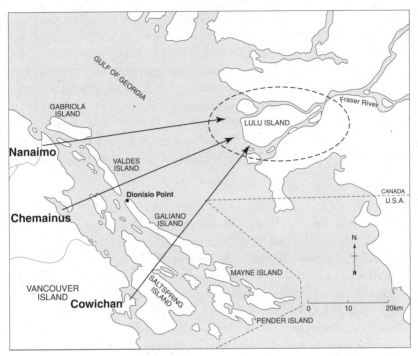

MAP 10.2 Movements of Vancouver Island–based Salish groups to the Fraser River as reconstructed for the historic period

been merely a seasonally occupied area visited and inhabited when resources were available. Thus, as the reasoning might go, the Gulf Islands have not been permanently inhabited; nor were they home to winter residential sites in the prehistoric past. Winter villages, in that they are indicative of stable, long-term occupation and are the locus of ceremonial season activities, form the core of the territory of Salish groups (Suttles 1991). Thus, the interpretation of the site has acute implications for charting the extent of prehistoric and historic-period territories.

Moreover, one might posit that the same interpretation could be extended to other Hul'qumi'num groups, such as the Cowichan, who also travelled to the Fraser River in the summer months. Interestingly, place names for some outer Gulf Islands locations are diminutive forms of those used for locations in "core" Cowichan territory on the east coast of Vancouver Island (Rozen 1985, 105-9), suggesting that some Gulf Islands locations were lesser, seasonal outposts of more permanent Cowichan habitations. Certainly, much more research could (and should) be undertaken to clarify historic-period Central Coast Salish seasonal rounds and land use. However, my quibble lies not with the accuracy of the ethnographic record as it pertains to historic period lifeways specifically; rather, the issues I have lie in the problems that arise when those ethnographically recorded patterns are applied in a straightforward fashion in reconstructions of the more distant past. I find the approach and interpretations presented by Burley for False Narrows quite problematic when reconciling the interpretation with the archaeological data obtained from the site and elsewhere in the Gulf Islands and, on the whole, feel that the case offers a particularly acute example of the pitfalls inherent in the application of an idealized ethnographic pattern to an archaeological problem. I make this contention for three main reasons:

1 It is difficult to envision the prehistoric component at False Narrows as a seasonally specific, limited resource acquisition location despite the indications to this effect in the ethnographic record. The archaeological assemblage is very diverse, probably too diverse to represent the remnants of a very limited range of activities conducted over the short term (even if the site was re-occupied over successive years). Almost the entire range of known Marpole artifact classes was recovered in a relatively small excavation area. These classes included tools for a variety of food acquisition tasks, such as harpoon gear, stone projectile points, and other complex technologies obviously not geared toward shellfish acquisition, as well as a broad suite of manufacturing items. Coupled with the archaeological documentation of major house platforms and the large cemetery identified at the location, all factors point to the site having been a major domestic habitation location. The faunal material recovered during the excavations has not been described in any detail; nor was the assemblage collected systematically (faunal materials typically were not systematically collected in major excavations in the Gulf Islands until recently). I suspect the faunal contingent would mimic the diversity of procured resources represented by the artifact assemblage from the site. Certainly the assemblages (both faunal and artifact) strike me as very similar to the winter village site I have excavated at Dionisio Point on nearby Galiano Island (Grier 2001).

2 Beyond the False Narrows site itself, major winter villages have been constructed and inhabited in the Gulf Islands since the Marpole Period. While few obvious house platforms or depressions exist today (a preservation and visibility issue, primarily), Marpole-age sites such as Dionisio Point on Galiano Island in the outer Gulf Islands indicate substantial occupation spanning centuries (Grier 2001). Moreover, the Dionisio Point site is located in an area that was/is not an ideal shellfish gathering location, suggesting that the "spring shellfish collecting

location" label assigned to False Narrows cannot be as easily applied to Dionisio Point. Other major village sites for which as much as two millennia of habitation have been documented (or can reasonably be inferred) include Montague Harbour, Penelakut Spit, Shingle Point, and Long Harbour, to name a mere few. It makes no sense, given the density of prehistoric archaeological sites and the nature of resource distributions, to view the Gulf Island archipelago as an interim habitation location for groups based on Vancouver Island rather than as a core area for groups based primarily in the islands. While the former may have been the case historically (though this remains debatable), we can posit many reasons why that pattern may be of recent genesis, as outlined earlier. The Lyackson (one of the Hul'qumi'num First Nations) clearly identify Valdes Island and not Vancouver Island as their ancestral territory, and they make no reference to Valdes Island village locations as peripheral to or seasonal extensions of permanent habitations elsewhere, even in the historic period. Archaeological research has largely borne this out. In conjunction with Eric McLay (Grier and McLay 2001), I have obtained radiocarbon dates that indicate five thousand years of habitation at Shingle Point on southwestern Valdes Island.

3 Perhaps the most critical point is embedded in much of the preceding discussion: the specific pattern of settlement and seasonal movement throughout the region recorded by ethnographers may have been heavily influenced and largely a product of factors related to contact, including population decimation, colonial encroachment, and the establishment of trading forts as new focal nodes on the regional exchange landscape. The ethnographic model of settlement pattern, with seasonal spring villages in the Gulf Islands, may be a very recent strategy for dealing with a very different economic and social situation than that which obtained prehistorically. This is not to say that permanent settlement in the Gulf Islands was abandoned solely due to contact, but aggregation into larger groups to combat population decline may have occurred, causing some long-standing locations of Gulf Island settlement to be abandoned. The southeastern shores of Vancouver Island saw early development in the history of colonial British Columbia, with settlers flooding in after the establishment of Fort Victoria in 1843 (Arnett 1999). The draw of wage labour and the lack of schools and other services contributed to the ultimate abandonment of the long-standing Lyackson village (Ta'aatka) at Shingle Point on Valdes Island. Moreover, the Penelakut village at Lamalchi on Kuper Island was shelled into ruin in 1863 by the British colonial navy, and the land upon which it stood was turned over to the church, providing another dramatic,

albeit not necessarily typical, example of how long-standing villages in the Gulf Islands were abandoned.

Beyond the Gulf Islands, the draw of Fort Langley on the lower reaches of the Fraser River may have accentuated the frequency and regularity of Fraser trips by groups throughout the Gulf of Georgia region. Established in the 1820s, Fort Langley preceded Fort Victoria by two decades and thus would have been the major initial draw for exchanges of indigenous commodities for European hard goods. The volume of trade and number of yearly visitors, as documented in *The Fort Langley Journals,* is quite astounding (Maclachlan 1998).

It is thus difficult to see the historic-period pattern Burley offers as unaffected by the major changes that were taking place in the region in the nineteenth and early twentieth centuries. But this assertion is not meant to imply that movements to the Fraser River prior to the establishment of European forts did not occur or were of no significance. Mitchell (1971) has argued that such movements and the position of groups relative to the Fraser River have defined their economic strategies for almost two millennia. The same point has been made by Suttles (1987), and I (Grier 2003) have also argued that widespread and regular interactions across the Gulf of Georgia have characterized at least the last two millennia. During this time the Fraser River has acted as a conduit that connects Coast Salish–speaking peoples economically, socially, and politically (see also Brown 1996). The critical point is that journeys by Hul'qumi'num peoples to the Fraser River area have been taking place for many millennia, but the context, frequency, and objectives of those movements have changed as a result of developing regional and local circumstances. We must understand the regional ebb and flow as a historically evolving system and work hard to situate our archaeological problems within this historical reality.

So it is clear that the ethnographic-based interpretation of False Narrows makes only a weak contribution to our understanding of the site itself and, moreover, can act to significantly skew the view of the regional situation. This situation obtains as a result of (1) the lack of a systematic attempt to test or evaluate whether the ethnographic model posited could be rejected as a reasonable explanation for the site; (2) a lack of consideration of possible alternative scenarios; and (3) only a limited appreciation for the historically embedded nature of the ethnographic data referenced.

The preceding argument might be dismissed as solely of academic or methodological concern or on the grounds that it presents a debate about the distant past that no longer has a direct bearing on current Coast Salish life. The role that archaeological interpretation plays in the current identity of Coast Salish peoples is complex, yet highly significant in both symbolic and pragmatic ways. In an era of treaty negotiations in the Province of British Columbia, it is incumbent upon First Nations to establish their traditional territory, resource use, and, thus, Aboriginal title in an empirical fashion. The ethnographic picture presents only a portion of the information that can be drawn upon for this purpose. Moreover, given the limited diversity in lifeways described in the ethnographic record, a distorted picture of long-term history can emerge. It is unfortunate and perhaps even detrimental if the historically recorded moment stands for the timeless past. Moreover, if one's view was based solely on the published interpretations for False Narrows, one might be persuaded to see the archaeology and ethnographic records in full accord on the issue of Coast Salish settlement patterns. The problem of constructing more complete versions of the Coast Salish past need not be seen as an issue of advocacy but, rather, of accuracy since how we as archaeologists go about our business has implications for those in the present.

The pursuit of a more carefully constructed Coast Salish prehistory is not simply a means to a modern legal end. While archaeology may be limited in its utility for redressing issues of the recent Coast Salish past within a modern legal framework, in a less direct, though perhaps more satisfying, way the accurate reconstruction of the past provides a measure of the challenges Coast Salish peoples have confronted and their resilience in constructing and implementing responses to a variety of novel and often unforeseen circumstances. Knowledge of the past provides Coast Salish peoples with a way to measure where they are in the present and a compass that may offer directions for facing the challenges of the future.

Conclusions

It is clear that the Old World–derived peoples who first entered the Americas at the end of the last Ice Age were very different from their descendants who lived on the continent when the Old and New Worlds met again some twelve millennia later. Prior to 5000 BP, much of the coast, including the Gulf of Georgia, appears to have had significantly different environmental circumstances, resources, sea levels, and cultures. This sets a practical limit of time over which a direct historical approach – extending into the past the use of ethnographic data in a historically justified way – can serve us. It is perhaps more reasonable to think of this limit as roughly two millennia, based on the inferred similarity in social institutions between Marpole and historic-period societies. But here I have argued that even within that time frame ethnographically recorded patterns cannot easily be said to reflect the specific organizational dynamics of prehistoric Coast Salish societies,

particularly if ethnographic analogy is used without thoughtful consideration as to how these data are in part an outcome of contact-period events
and processes.

We might take solace in the notion that the use of ethnographic data as
sources of hypotheses (rather than "off-the-shelf" explanations) about the
Coast Salish past would serve to alleviate the most serious problems inherent in the situation. However, my argument has been that this approach
has not been pursued rigorously, despite a fairly lengthy and useful discussion of exactly this necessity within the broader archaeological literature.
Perhaps this situation derives, at least in part, from the allure of the dramatic and compelling picture of Salish and Northwest Coast societies that
the classic ethnographic works provide.

Aptly added to these observations is the inescapable reality that the archaeological and ethnographic enterprises and records are, in important
respects, different in aim, scope, detail, and focus. Archaeological and
ethnographic research problems are often framed in incongruous ways. Moreover, the ethnographic record is, in many ways, strong where the archaeological record is weak and vice versa. As an archaeologist, I find that the
ethnographic record appears surprisingly mute on a great variety of key
problems of prehistory. For example, recent trends in Coast Salish archaeology have focused on household analysis (e.g., Grier 2003; Lepofsky et al.
2000). Yet, very few ethnographic narratives address in more than a cur-
sory or abstract fashion some very critical elements of household organization, including the day-to-day production and consumption patterns of
large households, the mobility of individual families in and out of specific
household corporate groups, or the status of individual families with respect to their chosen location of habitation within the house structure.
Clearly, information does exist on these topics (e.g., Barnett 1955; Smith
1947; Suttles 1991) but often not at the resolution that allows translation
of these statements into hypotheses testable with fine-grained archaeological data derived from prehistoric houses.

Another critical point is that archaeology substantively adds to the Coast
Salish past in sometimes obvious and at other times non-obvious ways.
The village at Dionisio Point (Grier 2001, 2003) – a major Marpole Period
village like False Narrows – is absent in both the ethnographic record and
the memory of the Penelakut Coast Salish. This is no surprise: radiocarbon
dates indicate that the village was abandoned some fifteen centuries ago.
But from this situation we receive a clear sense that the archaeological and
ethnographic records provide us with very different, though wonderfully
complementary, knowledge.

Moreover, it is increasingly evident that, in the future, the archaeological record will be the only source of new information available on historic-period and prior Coast Salish lifeways. Those who lived through the early contact period are gone, and those with direct experience and knowledge of many aspects of traditional lifeways are getting fewer. It is thus critical to develop an archaeology that works both in conjunction with and independently of the ethnographic record in a reflexive interplay. This notion extends beyond the various manifestations of anthropology. Since the Coast Salish past should and undoubtedly will be an integral part of any Coast Salish future, it is necessary to have a robust array of disciplines that work in concert and in their own particular directions but, ultimately, with the Coast Salish themselves to construct a comprehensive past upon which to build that future.

References

Ames, Kenneth M. 1996. Life in the Big House: Household Labor and Dwelling Size on the Northwest Coast. In *People Who Lived in Big Houses: Archaeological Perspectives on Large Domestic Structures*, ed. Gary Coupland and E.B. Banning, 131-50. Madison: Prehistory Press.

–. 2004. Supposing Hunter-Gatherer Variability. *American Antiquity* 69: 364-74.

Ames, Kenneth M., and Herbert D.G. Maschner. 1999. *Peoples of the Northwest Coast: Their Archaeology and Prehistory*. London: Thames and Hudson.

Arnett, Chris. 1999. *The Terror of the Coast*. Vancouver: Talonbooks.

Ascher, Robert. 1961. Analogy in Archaeological Interpretation. *Southwestern Journal of Anthropology* 17: 317-25.

Barnett, Homer G. 1955. *The Coast Salish of British Columbia*. Eugene: University of Oregon Press.

Binford, Lewis R. 1967. Smudge Pits and Hide Smoking: The Use of Analogy in Archaeological Reasoning. *American Antiquity* 32: 1-12.

Boas, Franz. 1905. The Jesup North Pacific Expedition. In *Proceedings of the International Congress of Americanists*, 13th Session, 91-100. Easton, PA: Eschenbach Printing.

Borden, Charles E. 1969. Discussion of Current Archaeological Research on the Northwest Coast. *Northwest Anthropological Research Notes* 3: 255-63.

–. 1970. Culture History of the Fraser Delta Region: An Outline. *BC Studies* 6-7: 95-112.

Boyd, Robert T. 1990. Demographic History, 1774-1874. In *Handbook of North American Indians*. Vol. 7, *Northwest Coast*, ed. Wayne Suttles, 135-48. Washington, DC: Smithsonian Institution.

Brown, Douglas R. 1996. Historic and Ancient Social Interaction in the Halkomelem Culture Region of the Central Northwest Coast. Paper presented at the 61st Annual Meeting of the Society for American Archaeology, New Orleans.

Burch, Ernest S. Jr. 1975. *Eskimo Kinsmen: Changing Family Relationships in Northwest Alaska*. New York: West Publishing.

–. 1981. *The Traditional Eskimo Hunters of Point Hope, Alaska: 1800-1875*. Barrow, AK: North Slope Borough.

Burley, David V. 1988. *Senewélets: Culture History of the Nanaimo Coast Salish and the False Narrows Midden.* Victoria: Royal British Columbia Museum.

Burley, David V., and Christopher Knusel. 1989. Burial Patterns and Archaeological Interpretation: Problems in the Recognition of Ranked Society in the Coast Salish Region. In *Development of Hunting-Fishing-Gathering Maritime Societies along the West Coast of North America,* ed. A. Blukis Onat, [unpaginated]. Pullman: Washington State University Press.

Carlson, Roy L. 1996. The Later Prehistory of British Columbia. In *Early Human Occupation in British Columbia,* ed. Roy L. Carlson and Luke Dalla Bonna, 215-26. Vancouver: UBC Press.

Clark, John E., and Michael Blake. 1994. The Power of Prestige: Competitive Generosity and the Emergence of Rank Societies in Lowland Mesoamerica. In *Factional Competition and Political Development in the New World,* ed. Elizabeth B. Brumfiel and John W. Fox, 17-30. Cambridge: Cambridge University Press.

Codere, Helen. 1950. *Fighting with Property: A Study of Kwakiutl Potlatching and Warfare, 1792-1930.* New York: J.J. Augustin.

–. 1990. Kwakiutl: Traditional Culture. In *Handbook of North American Indians.* Vol. 7, *Northwest Coast,* ed. Wayne Suttles, 359-77. Washington, DC: Smithsonian Institution.

Coupland, Gary. 1991. The Point Grey Site: A Marpole Spring Village Component. *Canadian Journal of Archaeology* 15: 73-96.

Croes, Dale R., and Steven Hackenberger. 1988. Hoko River Archaeological Complex: Modeling Prehistoric Northwest Coast Economic Evolution. In *Prehistoric Economies of the Pacific Northwest Coast,* ed. Barry L. Isaac, 19-85. Greenwich, CT: JAI Press.

Curtin, A. Joanne. 2002. *Prehistoric Mortuary Variability on Gabriola Island, British Columbia.* Burnaby, BC: University Archaeology Press.

Drucker, Philip. 1955. *Indians of the Northwest Coast.* New York: McGraw-Hill.

Duff, Wilson. 1952. *The Upper Stalo Indians of the Fraser River of BC.* Anthropology in British Columbia, Memoir No. 1. Victoria: British Columbia Provincial Museum.

Gordon, M. 1974. A Qualitative Analysis of Human Skeletal Remains from DgRw 4, Gabriola Island, BC. MA thesis, University of Calgary.

Gould, Richard A., and Patty Jo Watson. 1982. A Dialogue on the Meaning and Use of Analogy in Ethnoarchaeological Reasoning. *Journal of Anthropological Archaeology* 1: 355-81.

Grier, Colin. 2001. The Social Economy of a Prehistoric Northwest Coast Plankhouse. PhD diss., Arizona State University.

–. 2003. Dimensions of Regional Interaction in the Prehistoric Gulf of Georgia. In *Emerging from the Mist: Studies in Northwest Coast Culture History,* ed. R.G. Matson, Gary Coupland, and Quentin Mackie, 170-87. Vancouver: UBC Press.

Grier, Colin, and Eric B. McLay. 2001. No Project Is an Island: Reconstructing Hul'qumi'num Settlement History on Valdes Island. Paper presented at the BC Archaeology Forum, Burnaby, BC.

Hodder, Ian. 1982. *The Present Past: An Introduction to Anthropology for Archaeologists.* London: B.T. Batsford.

Jenness, Diamond. N.d. The Saanitch Indians of Vancouver Island. British Columbia Archives, Victoria, BC.

Lepofsky, Dana, Michael Blake, Douglas Brown, Sandra Morrison, Nicole Oakes, and Natasha Lyons. 2000. The Archaeology of the Scowlitz Site, SW British Columbia. *Journal of Field Archaeology* 27: 391-416.

Kroeber, Alfred L. 1923. American Culture and the Northwest Coast. *American Anthropologist* 25: 1-20.

Maclachlan, Morag, ed. 1998. *The Fort Langley Journals, 1827-30.* Vancouver: UBC Press.

Maschner, Herbert D.G. 1997. The Evolution of Northwest Coast Warfare. In *Troubled Times: Violence and Warfare in the Past,* ed. D. Martin and D. Frayer, 267-302. New York: Gordon and Breach.

Matson, R.G. 2003. The Coast Salish House: Lessons from Shingle Point, Valdes Island, British Columbia. In *Emerging from the Mist: Studies in Northwest Coast Culture History,* ed. R.G. Matson, Gary Coupland, and Quentin Mackie, 76-104. Vancouver: UBC Press.

Matson, R.G., and Gary Coupland. 1995. *The Prehistory of the Northwest Coast.* New York: Academic Press.

McMillan, Alan D. 2003. Reviewing the Wakashan Migration Hypothesis. In *Emerging from the Mist: Studies in Northwest Coast Culture History,* ed. R.G. Matson, Gary Coupland, and Quentin Mackie, 244-59. Vancouver: UBC Press.

Miller, Bruce Granville. 2004. Rereading the Ethnographic Record: The Problem of Justice in the Coast Salish World. In *Coming to Shore: Northwest Coast Ethnology, Traditions, and Visions,* ed. Marie Mauzé, Michael E. Harkin, and Sergei Kan, 305-22. Lincoln: University of Nebraska Press.

Mitchell, Donald H. 1968. Excavations at Two Trench Embankments in the Gulf of Georgia Region. *Syesis* 1: 29-46.

–. 1971. Archaeology of the Gulf of Georgia Area, a Natural Region and Its Culture Types. *Syesis* 4 (supplement 1): 1-228.

Mitchell, Donald H., and Leland Donald. 1988. Archaeology and the Study of Northwest Coast Economies. In *Prehistoric Economies of the Pacific Northwest Coast,* ed. Barry L. Isaac, 293-351. Greenwich, CT: JAI Press.

Monks, Gregory G. 1987. Prey as Bait: The Deep Bay Example. *Canadian Journal of Archaeology* 11: 119-42.

Moss, Madonna L., and Jon Erlandson. 1992. Forts, Refuge Rocks, and Defensive Sites: The Antiquity of Warfare along the North Pacific Coast of North America. *Arctic Anthropology* 29 (2): 73-90.

Rozen, David L. 1985. Place-Names of the Island Halkomelem Indian People. MA thesis, University of British Columbia.

Schaepe, David. 2001. Rock Wall Fortifications: Reconstructing a Fraser Canyon Defensive Network. In *A Stó:lō Coast Salish Historical Atlas,* ed. Keith Thor Carlson, 52-53. Vancouver: Douglas and McIntyre.

Smith, Marian. 1947. House Types of the Middle Fraser River. *American Antiquity* 4: 255-67.

Sutherland, Patricia D. 2001. Revisiting an Old Concept: The North Coast Interaction Sphere. In *Perspectives on Northern Northwest Coast Prehistory,* ed. Jerome S. Cybulski, 49-59. Hull, QC: Canadian Museum of Civilization.

Suttles, Wayne. 1987. Affinal Ties, Subsistence, and Prestige among the Coast Salish. In *Coast Salish Essays,* ed. Wayne Suttles, 15-25. Seattle: University of Washington Press.

–. 1991. The Shed-Roof House. In *A Time of Gathering: Native Heritage in Washington State,* ed. Robin K. Wright, 212-22. Seattle: University of Washington Press.

–. 1998. The Ethnographic Significance of the Fort Langley Journals. In *The Fort Langley Journals, 1827-30,* ed. Morag Maclachlan, 163-210. Vancouver: UBC Press.

Wylie, Alison. 1985. The Reaction against Analogy. *Advances in Archaeological Method and Theory* 8: 63-111.

Contributors

Bill Angelbeck is a PhD candidate in archaeology at the University of British Columbia; he acquired his master's degree in cultural anthropology at the University of Missouri. His research interests include the origins of social inequality, ideation and ideology, and warfare. He has conducted archaeological investigations in the Northwest Coast, the Central Plains, and the Southeastern Woodlands.

Crisca Bierwert is an anthropologist who has worked on cultural education and documentation projects with Coast Salish people for more than twenty years. Her scholarly publications situate community-centred studies within the context of political and scholarly issues. She has written articles and is the editor of *Lushootseed Texts: An Introduction to Puget Salish Narrative Aesthetics* (1996) and the author of *Brushed by Cedar, Living by the River: Coast Salish Figures of Power* (1999). She is currently the associate director at the Center for Research on Learning and Teaching at the University of Michigan, where she works to enhance university teaching and contributes to scholarship in the fields of faculty development and Aboriginal and ecological studies. She lives in Ann Arbor and maintains a home base for three grown sons.

Daniel L. Boxberger is professor of anthropology at Western Washington University in Bellingham, Washington. He has been working with the Coast Salish in various capacities since 1971. His primary interests are in natural resource use and control, which has landed him in the courtroom on numerous occasions as an expert witness. His most recent work focuses on First Nations legal proceedings and the role of the anthropologist in this process. He is the author of *To Fish in Common: The Ethnohistory of Lummi Indian Salmon Fishing* (1989) and *Native North Americans: An Ethnohistorical Approach* (1990) as well as numerous articles and government reports dealing with Coast Salish issues.

Keith Thor Carlson has been working with, among, and for the Stó:lō Coast Salish people since 1992. He is senior author and editor of *A Stó:lo Coast Salish Historical Atlas* (2001) and *You Are Asked to Witness: The Stó:lō in Canada's Pacific Coast*

History (1997). He currently teaches in the Department of History at the University of Saskatchewan and is working toward publishing two new Salish histories: a revised version of his PhD dissertation, "The Power of Place, the Problem of Time: A Study of History and Aboriginal Identity," and a re-examination of Native-newcomer relations derived from Salish historiography, tentatively titled "Orality, Literacy, and History: Memories of the 'Crown's Promise.'"

Brent Galloway (PhD, University of California, Berkeley, 1977) is currently a professor of linguistics in the Department of Indian Languages, Literatures, and Linguistics at First Nations University of Canada in Regina, Saskatchewan. He has conducted linguistic fieldwork with the Upriver Halkomelem since 1970, with the Nooksack since 1974, with the Samish between 1984 and 1988, with the Gullah between 1994 and 2000, and with the Assiniboine since 1996. He has written nine books and eighty other publications and papers on Halkomelem, Nooksack, Samish, Assiniboine, Gullah, cognitive semantics, phonology, morphology, applied linguistics, syntax, ethnolinguistics, and historical linguistics.

Colin Grier is a research director with Coast Research, an anthropological and archaeological research organization, as well as a research consultant for Indian Residential Schools Resolution Canada. He received his PhD from Arizona State University in 2001, and has pursued archaeological and ethnographic research focused on the development of precontact Hul'qumi'num Salish societies of the Gulf of Georgia region, with an emphasis on the formation of early villages and large households. He is lead editor of the recent volume *Beyond Affluent Foragers: Rethinking Hunter-Gatherer Complexity* (2006).

Alexandra Harmon, a 1972 graduate of the Yale Law School, advised and represented Indians in Washington State for approximately fifteen years, including a period as on-reservation staff attorney for the Skokomish Tribe and another period as on-reservation attorney for the Suquamish Tribe. In 1988, wishing to understand and teach about questions that arose in her legal work, she began graduate study in history at the University of Washington. Since earning a PhD in 1995, she has been on the University of Washington's American Indian Studies faculty and has published *Indians in the Making: Ethnic Relations and Indian Identities around Puget Sound* (1998).

Bruce Granville Miller is professor of anthropology at the University of British Columbia. Recent publications include *The Problem of Justice: Tradition and Law in the Coast Salish World* (2001) and *Invisible Indigenes: The Politics of Nonrecognition* (2003). He served as editor of *Culture*, the journal of the Canadian Anthropology Association, from 1994 to 1997. His research deals with indigenous-state relations, in particular prior justice practices and contemporary indigenous justice initiatives and the concept of indigeneity. He has recently co-edited *Extraordinary Anthropology: Transformations in the Field* (2007) with Jean-Guy Goulet.

Naxaxalhts'i, also known as **Albert (Sonny) McHalsie,** is currently the director/ cultural advisor of the Stó:lō Research and Resource Management Centre, working on behalf of the Stó:lō Nation and Stó:lō Tribal Council. He was a co-author of *I Am Stó:lō: Katherine Explores Her Heritage* (1997). He sat on the editorial board of and was a contributor to *A Stó:lō Coast Salish Historical Atlas* (2001). He has worked for the Stó:lō since 1985. He is a member of the Shxw'ōwhámél First Nation, is married, and is the proud father of two girls and six boys, and he has one grandson. He continues to fish at his ancestral fishing ground at Aseláw in the Fraser Canyon just north of Yale, British Columbia.

David M. Schaepe is senior archaeologist/manager for the Stó:lō Research and Resource Management Centre, associated with the Stó:lō Nation and Stó:lō Tribal Council. He has worked as an archaeologist/anthropologist for the Stó:lō since 1997. A PhD candidate in the Department of Anthropology at the University of British Columbia, he was awarded a SSHRC Graduate Fellowship in 2003. His academic background includes a BA in anthropology from New York University (1989) and an MA in archaeology from Simon Fraser University (1998). Dave has a number of publications in the field of archaeology and was an editorial board member and primary contributor to *A Stó:lō Coast Salish Historical Atlas* (2001).

Raymond (Rocky) Wilson is a commercial fisher and holds a BA in history and First Nations Studies from UBC. He is the elected chief of the Hwlitsum First Nation, located in the Canoe Pass–Delta area of British Columbia. He is a proud descendant of the Lamalchi/Hwlitsum people and sits on the Chiefs Council of the Union of BC Indian Chiefs. He worked for many years to gain federal recognition for his band under section 17(1) of the Canadian Indian Act.

Index

chum salmon (dogs), 58, 102-3, 131
Civil Rights Movement, 55-56
class: advice and, 3; identity and, 157-67;
knowledge of one's history and, 159,
163; longhouse accommodations and,
152; origins of, 163; study of, 157-58
CNR. *See* Canadian National Railway
(CNR)
Coast Salish, **xii**, **296**; cross-border
relations of, 37, 39; definition of, 31;
diversity of, 23, 30; division of, 6;
economy of, 294; European goods
introduced to, 293-94; groups within,
26n1; history of, 7, 30-49; interpersonal
relationships among, 147; language of,
26n1; leadership of, 293; marginalization of, 279; population of, 292-93;
precontact, 292; relations of, with other
tribes, 41; research/scholarship by, 10-
12, 14, 236-37, 245-54; scholarship
on, 1-26; self-governance of, 73-76;
settlements of, 152; territoriality of,
293; warfare of, 260-79. *See also* Coast
Salish culture; Coast Salish identity
Coast Salish culture: abandonment of,
82-83; discouraging of, by non-Indians,
47, 134; emergent forms of, 207-9;
Ewen's narratives about, 194-98;
landscape and, 239-41; revival of, 13,
229-30
Coast Salish Essays (Suttles), 1-2, 24, 31
Coast Salish identity: academic perspectives on, 30, 33, 139, 174; affiliation
processes and, 20-21, 38, 191; approaches to, 16-17, 30; archaeology
and, 302-3; class and, 157-67; complexity of, 17, 36, 44; contemporary, 49;
families and, 19-22; government as
source of, 18; history and, 30-49, 139,
174-75; individual perspective on, 33-
36; landscape and, 238-45; language
and, 30, 31; methods of forming, 139-
75; migrations and, 138, 174-75;
political/legal effects on, 38-46, 174;
postcontact, 139-75; pragmatic
character of, 17-18; social networks
and, 33-40, 48-49, 131-33, 191; tribal
identities and, 41-42, 45-48, 150;
unity/disunity of, 30, 55
Codere, Helen, 3, 262, 273, 294
coho (salmon), 58, 101, 103, 131

Cole, Douglas, 269
Collins, June, 3, 37-38, 66, 69, 270,
275, 276
Collison, William Henry, 261
colonialism: Aboriginal accounts of, 182-
84; anthropology and, 56-57, 77; Coast
Salish identity and, 139-75; ethno-
graphy and, 64; resources and, 58; in
Stó:lō area, 185; studies of, 182-83
Comanches, 269
Coming to Shore (Mauzé, Harkin, and
Kan), 5
common law, 55
community fission, 177n31
community self-representation, 23, 32,
256
conflict resolution, 244-46, 254
Constitution Act, 135
Constitution Express, 207
Cooper, Mrs., 146
Coqualeetza Education Training Centre,
214-17
Coquihalla River, 169
Coquihalla watershed, 89
Coquitlam, 159, 162-63, 165
Costello, J.A., 63
Coupland, Gary, 262, 286
Cowichan, 7, 272, 274, 277, 299
CPR. *See* Canadian Pacific Railroad (CPR)
cranberries, 100
Croes, Dale R., 287
Crosby, Thomas, 63
Cruikshank, Julie, 11, 33, 48, 183
Culamunthut (Charlie Wilson), 134
cultural landscape, 243, 251, 253-55
culture. *See* Coast Salish culture
culture ecological approach, 2, 239-40
culture historical approach, 239
culture of terror thesis, 139
culture-core concept, 279
Cultus Lake, 127, 145
Culuxtun (Jim Wilson), 133, 134
Curtis, Edward, 261, 270, 274, 277
Cybulski, Jerome S., 267-68

dancing. *See* longhouse dancers; winter
dance *(syuwel)*
Darling, David, 269
Darnell, Regna, 9
Davis, Henry, 220
defensive settlements, 263-67, **266**, 293

degeneration thesis, 139
Delgamuukw Test, 75
Delgamuukw v. British Columbia (1997),
   75
Department of Fisheries and Oceans, 97,
   136
Department of Indian Affairs (DIA), 134,
   135-36, 169
Devil's Mountain, 128
Dickinson, Nat, 217
Dionisio Point, 300, 304
dip nets, 98, 101-2
direct historical approach, 290
disease, 47, 134, 292. *See also* smallpox
Dixon, Gilbert, 101
doctors, Indian. *See shxwlá:m* (Indian
   doctors)
documentary evidence, 70-71
dog salmon. *See* chum salmon (dogs)
Douglas, Amelia, 84, 89, 90, 110-12
Drucker, Philip, 284
dry racks, for fishing, 98
Duff, Wilson, 3, 5, 66, 84, 87, 109-10,
   116, 128, 141, 142, 149, 152, 155,
   164, 167, 169, 173, 183, 186, 270

Easter Mass, 122
Eayem memorial, 91-92
economy: introduction of European
   goods to, 294; litigation concerning,
   12; Stó:lō, 187
Edwards, Ed, 5
Edwards, Harry, 152
Eells, Myron, 63
Efrat, Barbara, 213, 217, 221
elder, historical perspective of, 183-209
Eliza Expedition (1791), 274
Elmendorf, William, 2, 3, 4, 65, 69,
   239, 275
emergent cultural systems, 184, 207-9
Emory Creek, 169
English common law, 55
English language, 213
enrichment thesis, 139
Erlandson, Jon M., 263
Eskimo Administration (Jenness), 67
ethnicity, history and, 30
ethnography: Aboriginal reliance on, for
   cultural history, 47; analysis of personal
   reflections, 184-209; colonialism and,
   64; documentary evidence versus,

70-71; early, of Coast Salish, 63-65;
   flowering of, 65-68; problematic issues
   in, 291; warfare and, 261, 273-77.
   See also archaeology-ethnography
   relationship
ethnohistory: archaeology and, 261;
   discipline of, 8; land claims and, 69-71;
   warfare and, 261, 268-69
Ethnohistory (journal), 70
eulachon, 131
European contact. *See* colonialism
evolutionary approach, 287-88, **288**
Ewen, Fred, 183-209, 210n5
Ewen, Gilbert, 87
Ewen, Henry, 201-2
expert witnesses, 56, 62, 64, 70, 71-72

Faith of a Coast Salish Indian (Jenness),
   67
False Narrows, 295, 297-302
families: definition of, 19; fishing grounds
   ownership by, 96-100; functions of,
   19; genealogies of, 100; history of
   (sqwelqwel), 93, 101; interaction of,
   19-20; resources of, 21; size of, 21;
   stl'aleqem and, 128; study of, 19-22
Farrand, Livingston, 65
Ferguson, R. Brian, 263
Fernando, Vi, 4, **20**
Fetzer, Paul, 33, 213
Fidele, Esther, 213, 217
firearms, 269-72
First Nations. *See* Aboriginals
First Nations Summit, 254
First People, 161, 167
First Peoples' Language and Culture
   Committee of Washington State, 222-
   25, 229
First Salmon Ceremony, 73, 90-91
First Shoots Ceremony, 90
"fish in common," 55, 61, 72-73
Fisher, Robin, 270-71
Fisheries Act, 61, 97
fishing grounds: Fraser Canyon and,
   167; ownership of, 96-100. *See also*
   salmon; sturgeon
fishing industry, 60
fishing methods, 98-99, 101-2
fishing permits, 97
fission, 177n31
fissure points, 243-45, 251, 253-54

Moses, Jessie, 4, **20**
Moss, Madonna L., 263
mountain goats, 89
mourning process, 112-13
Musqueam, 16, 108, 117, 118, 133

Nanaimo, 159, 161-62, 274, 276, 297
Nanoose, 159
Narte, Phillip, 218, 225
Nash, Manning, 30
nation, as political entity, 235
National Indian Brotherhood, 235
Native Brotherhood, 135
Native peoples. *See* Aboriginals
natural resources. *See* resources
nature-culture relations, 238-45
Nault, Robert, 136
Nekt, 262
nets, fishing, 98-99
Newell, Dianne, 183
Nicomen, 212
Nisqually, 239, 275
Nlaka'pamux, 95, 108
No Child Shall Be Left Behind Act, 223
Nooksack, 35, 212, 213, 218, 223, 227-28
Nooksack language. *See* Lhéchelesem
Norris, Shirley, 216, 217
Northwest Coast scholarship, 24
Northwest Indian College, 56, 73, 226, 228
Northwestern Federation of American Indians, 35

Ohamil, 155-57, 171
Ohamil, Johnny, 99, 129
Okanagan, 102
Old Pierre, 67-68, 74, 158-59, 161
Old Snatlem, 276
oral histories: legal value of, 70, 75; of Stó:lō, 92-95
ownership of fishing grounds, 96-100
Oyewot, 105

Palmer, Andie, 11
Pat, Frank, 89, 111
Peace Arch memorial, 55
Peló:lhxw, 171
Pender Island, 264
Penelakut, 132, 134, 136, 137

Penelakut Spit, 301
People of the Twilight (Jenness), 66-67
personal narratives, ethnographic value of, 184-209
Pete, Rita, 92, 95-96
Peter, Susie Sampson, 11
Peters, Bertha, 104
Peters, Bobby, 128
Peters, Dennis S., 91, 92, 93, 96, 115
Peters, Herman. *See* Siya:mia (Herman Peters)
Peters, Jimmy, 87
Peters, Peter Dennis (Selthelmetheqw), 83, 95-97, 114-15, 118-21
Peters Reserve, 88, 192
Pettis, Henry, 98
Philips, Edward (Hicks), 102
Phillips, Elizabeth, 215-17, 219-20
Phillips, Nancy, 215
Pierre (Ewen's relative), 195
Pierre, Old. *See* Old Pierre
Pierre, Peter (Xa'xzultun'), 133
Pierre, Sarah, 133
Pilalt, 146, 148, 150, 155
pink salmon, 58, 102-3
Pitt Lake, 159
place names, 82-130; cultural analysis of, 238-39; heritage sites based on, 249; oral histories of, 92-95; ownership and, 95-103; relation to land and, 84-92, 108-12; *shxweli* and, 103-8; study of, 83-84; *sxwó:yxwey* and, 112-18
Point, Gwen, 110
Point, Mark, 216
Point, Roy, 216
Point, Steven, 216
pointing, 126
policy, scholarship and, 8, 63-68. *See also* litigation
polygamy, 147, 195
polygyny, 195
Popeleho:ys, 87
Popkum, 169, 171, 190
poststructuralism, 23
potlatch, 2, 24, 37, 39, 47, 134, 262, 294
Practical Phonetic System (PPS), 214
Prehistory of the Northwest Coast (Matson and Coupland), 286
Price, William, 40

Printed and bound in Canada by Friesens
Set in Galliard and Rotis Sans by Artegraphica Design Co. Ltd.
Copy editor: Joanne Richardson
Proofreader: Deborah Kerr
Indexer: David Luljak